ISBN 978-1-331-48095-2
PIBN 10196013

THEODORE WATTS-DUNTON

POET NOVELIST CRITIC

BY

JAMES DOUGLAS

WITH TWENTY-FOUR ILLUSTRATIONS

LONDON

HODDER AND STOUGHTON

27 PATERNOSTER ROW

1904

fu 1

HEODORE WATTS-DUNTON

POET NOVELIST CRITIC

BY
JAMES DOUGLAS

WITH TWENTY-FOUR ILLUSTRATIONS

LONDON
HODDER AND STOUGHTON
27 PATERNOSTER ROW
1904

SYNOPSIS

ILLUSTRATIONS

xi

NATURA BENIGNA

What power is this? what witchery wins my feet
To peaks so sheer they scorn the cloaking snow,
All silent as the emerald gulfs below,
Down whose ice-walls the wings of twilight beat?
What thrill of earth and heaven—most wild, most sweet—
What answering pulse that all the senses know,
Comes leaping from the ruddy eastern glow
Where, far away, the skies and mountains meet?
Mother, 'tis I reborn: I know thee well:
That throb I know and all it prophesies,
O Mother and Queen, beneath the olden spell
Of silence, gazing from thy hills and skies!
Dumb Mother, struggling with the years to tell
The secret at thy heart through helpless eyes.

REVERIE

Introduction

'It was necessary for Thomas Hood still to do one thing ere the wide circle and profound depth of his genius were to the full acknowledged : that one thing was—to die.'—DOUGLAS JERROLD.

ALTHOUGH in the inner circle of English letters this study of a living writer will need no apology, it may be well to explain for the general reader the reasons which moved me to undertake it.

Some time ago a distinguished scholar, the late S. Arthur Strong, Librarian of the House of Lords, was asked what had been the chief source of his education. He replied : " Cambridge, scholastically, and Watts-Dunton's articles in the ' Encyclopædia Britannica ' and the ' Athenæum ' from the purely literary point of view. I have been a reader of them for many years, and it would be difficult for me to say what I should have been without them." Mr. Richard Le Gallienne has said that he bought the ' Encyclopædia Britannica ' simply to possess one article—Mr. Watts-Dunton's article on Poetry. There are many other men of letters who would give similar testimony. With regard to his critical work, Mr. Swinburne in one of his essays, speaking of the treatise on Poetry, describes Mr. Watts-Dunton as ' the first critic of our time, perhaps the largest-minded and surest-sighted of any age,' [1] a judgment which, according to the article on Mr. Watts-Dunton in Chambers's ' Encyclopædia,' Rossetti endorsed. In this same article it is further said :—

" He came to exercise a most important influence on the art and culture of the day ; but although he has written enough to fill many volumes—in the ' Examiner,'

[1] ' Studies in Prose.'

W.-D.

Introduction

'It was necessary for Thomas Hood still to do one thing ere the wide circle and profound depth of his genius were to the full acknowledged : that one thing was—to die.'—DOUGLAS JERROLD.

ALTHOUGH in the inner circle of English letters this study of a living writer will need no apology, it may be well to explain for the general reader the reasons which moved me to undertake it.

Some time ago a distinguished scholar, the late S. Arthur Strong, Librarian of the House of Lords, was asked what had been the chief source of his education. He replied : " Cambridge, scholastically, and Watts-Dunton's articles in the ' Encyclopædia Britannica ' and the ' Athenæum ' from the purely literary point of view. I have been a reader of them for many years, and it would be difficult for me to say what I should have been without them." Mr. Richard Le Gallienne has said that he bought the ' Encyclopædia Britannica ' simply to possess one article—Mr. Watts-Dunton's article on Poetry. There are many other men of letters who would give similar testimony. With regard to his critical work, Mr. Swinburne in one of his essays, speaking of the treatise on Poetry, describes Mr. Watts-Dunton as ' the first critic of our time, perhaps the largest-minded and surest-sighted of any age,' [1] a judgment which, according to the article on Mr. Watts-Dunton in Chambers's ' Encyclopædia,' Rossetti endorsed. In this same article it is further said ·—

" He came to exercise a most important influence on the art and culture of the day ; but although he has written enough to fill many volumes—in the ' Examiner,'

[1] ' Studies in Prose.'

W.-D.

the 'Athenæum' (since 1876), the 'Nineteenth Century,' the 'Fortnightly Review,' etc.—he has let year
after year go by without his collecting his essays, which,
always dealing with first principles, have ceased to be
really anonymous, and are quoted by the press both in
England and in Germany as his. But, having wrapped
up his talents in a weekly review, he is only ephemerally
known to the general public, except for the sonnets
and other poems that, from the 'Athenæum,' etc., have
found their way into anthologies, and for the articles on
poetic subjects that he has contributed to the 'Encyclopædia Britannica,' 'Chambers's Encyclopædia,' etc.
The chief note of his poetry—much of it written in
youth—is its individuality, the source of its inspiration
Nature and himself. For he who of all men has most
influenced his brother poets has himself remained least
influenced by them. So, too, his prose writings—literary mainly, but ranging also over folk-lore, ethnology,
and science generally—are marked as much by their independence and originality as by their suggestiveness,
harmony, incisive vigour, and depth and breadth of insight. They have made him a force in literature to
which only Sainte-Beuve, not Jeffrey, is a parallel."[1]

These citations from students of Mr. Watts-Dunton's
work, written before his theory of the 'Renascence of
Wonder' was exemplified in 'Aylwin' and 'The
Coming of Love,' show, I think, that this book would
have had a right to exist even if his critical writings
had been collected into volumes; but as this collection
has never been made, and I believe never will be made
by the author, I feel that to do what I am now doing is
to render the reading public a real service. For many

[1] 'Chambers's Encyclopædia,' vol. x., p. 581.

years he has been urged by his friends to collect his critical articles, but although several men of letters have offered to relieve him of that task, he has remained obdurate.

Speaking for myself, I scarcely remember the time when I was not an eager student of Mr. Watts-Dunton's writings. Like most boys born with the itch for writing, I began to spill ink on paper in my third lustre. The fermentation of the soul which drove me to write a dreadful elegy, modelled upon 'Lycidas,' on the death of an indulgent aunt, also drove me to welter in drowsy critical journals. By some humour of chance I stumbled upon the 'Athenæum,' and there I found week by week writing that made me tingle with the rapture of discovery. The personal magic of some unknown wizard led me into realms of gold and kingdoms of romance. I used to count the days till the 'Athenæum' appeared in my Irish home, and I spent my scanty pocket money in binding the piled numbers into ponderous tomes. Well I remember the advent of the old, white-bearded Ulster book-binder, bearing my precious volumes : even now I can smell the pungent odour of the damp paste and glue. In those days I was a solitary bookworm, living far from London, and I vainly tried to discover the name of the magician who was carrying me into so 'many goodly states and kingdoms.' With boyish audacity I wrote to the editor of the 'Athenæum,' begging him to disclose the secret ; and I am sure my naïve appeal provoked a smile in Took's Court. But although the editor was dumb, I exulted in the meagre apparition of my initials, ' J. D.,' under the solemn rubric, ' To Correspondents.'

It was by collating certain signed sonnets and signed articles with the unsigned critical essays that I at last discovered the name of my hero, Theodore Watts. Of course, the sonnets set me sonneteering, and when my execrable imitation of 'Australia's Mother' was printed in the 'Belfast News-Letter' I felt like Byron when he woke up and found himself famous. Afterwards, when I had plunged into the surf of literary London, I learnt that the writer who had turned my boyhood into a romantic paradise was well known in cultivated circles, but quite unknown outside them.

There was, indeed, no account of him in print. It was not till 1887 that I found a brief but masterly memoir in 'Celebrities of the Century.' The article concluded with the statement that in the 'Athenæum' and in the Ninth Edition of the 'Encyclopædia Britannica' Mr. Watts-Dunton had 'founded a school of criticism which discarded conventional authority, and sought to test all literary effects by the light of first principles merely.' These words encouraged me, for they told me that as a boy I had not been wrong in thinking that I had discovered a master and a guide in literature. Then came the memoir of Philip Bourke Marston by the American poetess, Louise Chandler Moulton, in which she described Mr. Watts-Dunton as 'a poet whose noble work won for him the intimate friendship of Rossetti and Browning and Lord Tennyson, and was the first link in that chain of more than brotherly love which binds him to Swinburne, his housemate at present and for many years past.' I also came across Clarence Stedman's remarks upon the opening of 'The Coming of Love,' 'Mother Carey's Chicken,' first printed in the 'Athenæum.' He was enthusiastic about the poet's perception of 'Nature's grander aspects,' and spoke of his poetry as being 'quite independent of any bias derived from the eminent poets with whom his life has been closely associated.'

' When afterwards I made his acquaintance, our intercourse led to the formation of a friendship which has deepened my gratitude for the spiritual and intellectual guidance I have found in his writings for nearly twenty years. Owing to the popularity of 'The Coming of Love' and of 'Aylwin'—which the late Lord Acton, in 'The Annals of Politics and Culture,' placed at the head of the three most important books published in 1898—Mr. Watts-Dunton's name is now familiar to every fairly educated person. About few men living is there so much literary curiosity; and this again is a reason for writing a book about him.

The idea of making an elaborate study of his work, however, did not come to me until I received an invitation from Dr. Patrick, the editor of Chambers's 'Cyclopædia of English Literature,' to write for that publication an article on Mr. Watts-Dunton—an article which had been allotted to Professor Strong, but which he had been obliged through indisposition to abandon at the last moment. I undertook to do this. But within the limited space at my command I was able only very briefly to discuss his work as a poet. Soon afterwards I was invited by my friend, Dr. Robertson Nicoll, to write a monograph upon Mr. Watts-Dunton for Messrs. Hodder & Stoughton, and, if I should see my way to do so, to sound him on the subject. My only difficulty was in approaching Mr. Watts-Dunton, for I knew how constantly he had been urged by the press to collect his essays, and how persistently he had declined to do so. Nevertheless, I wrote to him, telling him how gladly I should undertake the task, and how sure I was that the book was called for. His answer was so characteristic that I must give it here :—

"My dear Mr. Douglas,—It must now be something like fifteen years since Mr. John Lane, who was
then compiling a bibliography of George Meredith,
asked me to consent to his compiling a bibliography of
my articles in the 'Athenæum' and elsewhere, and
although I emphatically declined to sanction such a
bibliography, he on several occasions did me the honour
to renew his request. I told him, as I have told one or
two other generous friends, that although I had put into
these articles the best criticism and the best thought at
my command, I considered them too formless to have
other than an ephemeral life. I must especially mention the name of Mr. Alfred Nutt, who for years has
been urging me to let him publish a selection from my
critical essays. I am really proud to record this, because
Mr. Nutt is not only an eminent publisher but an admirable scholar and a man of astonishing accomplishments. I had for years, let me confess, cherished the
idea that some day I might be able to take my various
expressions of opinion upon literature, especially upon
poetry, and mould them into a coherent and, perhaps,
into a harmonious whole. This alone would have satisfied me. But year by year the body of critical writing
from my pen has grown, and I felt and feel more and more
unequal to the task of grappling with such a mass. To
the last writer of eminence who gratified me by suggest-
ing a collection of these essays—Dr. Robertson Nicoll—I
wrote, and wrote it with entire candour, that in my opinion the view generally taken of the value of them is too
generous. Still, they are the result of a good deal of
reflection and not a little research, especially those in
the 'Encyclopædia Britannica,' and I am not so entirely without literary aspiration as not to regret that,
years ago, when the mass of material was more manage-

able, I neglected to collect them and edit them myself. But the impulse to do this is now gone. Owing to the quite unexpected popularity of 'The Coming of Love' and of 'Aylwin,' my mind has been diverted from criticism, and plunged into those much more fascinating waters of poetry and fiction in which I used to revel long before. If you really think that a selection of passages from the articles, and a critical examination and estimate of the imaginative work would be of interest to any considerable body of readers, I do not know why I should withhold my consent. But I confess, judging from such work of your own as I have seen, I find it difficult to believe that it is worth your while to enter upon any such task.

I agree with you that it is difficult to see how you are to present and expound the principles of criticism advanced in the 'Encyclopædia Britannica,' the 'Athenæum,' etc., without discussing those two imaginative works the writing of which inspired the canons and generalizations in the critical work—'Aylwin' and 'The Coming of Love.' As regards 'Aylwin,' however, I cannot help wincing under the thought that in these days when so much genius is at work in prose fiction, your discussion will seem to give quite an undue prominence to a writer who has published but one novel. This I confess does disturb me somewhat, and I wish you to bear well in mind this aspect of the matter before you seriously undertake the book. As to the prose fiction of the present moment, I constantly stand amazed at its wealth. If, however, you do touch upon 'Aylwin,' I hope you will modify those generous— too generous—expressions of yours which, I remember, you printed in a review of the book when it first appeared."

After getting this sanction I set to work, and soon
found that my chief obstacle was the superabundance of
material, which would fill several folio volumes. But although it is undoubtedly ' a mighty maze, it is ' not
without a plan.' In a certain sense the vast number
of Mr. Watts-Dunton's generalizations upon literature,
art, philosophy, and what Emerson calls ' the conduct
of life,' revolve round certain fixed principles which
have guided me in the selection I have made. I also
found that to understand these principles of romantic art,
it was necessary to make a thorough critical study of
the romance, ' Aylwin,' and of the book of poems, ' The
Coming of Love.' I think I have made that study, and
that I have connected the critical system with the
imaginative work more thoroughly than has been done
by any other writer, although the work of Mr. Watts-
Dunton, both creative and critical, has been acutely
discussed, not only in England but also in France and in
Italy.

The creative originality of his criticism is as absolute
as that of his poetry and fiction. He poured into his
criticism the intellectual and imaginative force which
other men pour into purely artistic channels, for he
made criticism a vehicle for his humour, his philosophy,
and his irony. His criticisms are the reflections of
a lifetime. Their vitality is not impaired by the im-
permanence of their texts. No critic has surpassed his
universality of range. Out of a full intellectual and
imaginative life he has evolved speculations which cut
deep not only into the fibre of modern thought but into
the future of human development. Great teachers have
their day and their disciples. Mr. Watts-Dunton's day
and disciples belong to the young future whose dawn
some of us already descry. For, as Mr. Justin McCarthy

wrote of 'Aylwin,' ' it is inspired by the very spirit of
youth,' and this is why so many of the younger writers
are beginning to accept him as their guide. Mr. Watts-
Dunton has built up a new optimistic philosophy of life
which, I think, is sure to arrest the devastating march of
the pessimists across the history of the soul of man. That
is the aspect of his work which calls for the comprehen-
sion of the new generation. The old cosmogonies are
dead ; here is the new cosmogony, the cosmogony in
which the impulse of wonder reasserts its sovereignty,
proclaiming anew the nobler religion of the spiritual
imagination, with a faith in Natura Benigna which no
assaults of science can shake.

But, although the main object of this book is to focus,
as it were, the many scattered utterances of Mr. Watts-
Dunton in prose and poetry upon the great subject of
the Renascence of Wonder, I have interspersed here and
there essays which do not touch upon this theme, and
also excerpts from those obituary notices of his friends
which formed so fascinating a part of his contributions
to the 'Athenæum.' For, of course, it was necessary
to give the charm of variety to the book. Rossetti used
to say, I believe, that there is one quality necessary in a
poem which very many poets are apt to ignore—the
quality of being amusing. I have always thought
that there is great truth in this, and I have also thought
that the remark is applicable to prose no less than to
poetry. This is why I have occasionally enlivened these
pages with extracts from his picturesque monographs;
indeed, I have done more than this. Not having known
Mr. Watts-Dunton's great contemporaries myself, I have
looked about me for the aid of certain others who did
know them. I have not hesitated to collect from various
sources such facts and details connected with Mr. Watts-

Dunton and his friends as are necessarily beyond the scope of my own experience and knowledge. Among these I must prominently mention one to whom I have been specially indebted for reminiscences of Mr. Watts-Dunton and his circle. This is Mr. Thomas St. E. Hake, eldest son of the 'parable poet,' a gentleman of much too modest and retiring a disposition, who, from Mr. Watts-Dunton's first appearance in London right onwards, was brought into intimate relations with himself, his relatives, Rossetti, William Morris, Westland Marston, Philip Bourke Marston, Madox Brown, George Borrow, Stevenson, Minto, and many others. I have not only made free use of his articles, but I have had the greatest aid from him in many other respects, and it is my bare duty to express my gratitude to him for his services. I have also to thank the editor of the 'Athenæum' for cordially granting me permission to quote so freely from its columns; and I take this opportunity of acknowledging my debt to the many other publications from which I have drawn materials for this book.

Chapter I

THE RENASCENCE OF WONDER

"'The renascence of wonder,' to employ Mr. Watts-Dunton's appellation for what he justly considers the most striking and significant feature in the great romantic revival which has transformed literature, is proclaimed by this very appellation not to be the achievement of any one innovator, but a general reawakening of mankind to a perception that there were more things in heaven and earth than were dreamt of in Horatio's philosophy."—DR. R. GARNETT: Monograph on Coleridge.

UNDOUBTEDLY the greatest philosophical generalization of our time is expressed in the four words, 'The Renascence of Wonder.' They suggest that great spiritual theory of the universe which, according to Mr. Watts-Dunton, is bound to follow the wave of materialism that set in after the publication of Darwin's great book. This phrase, which I first became familiar with in his 'Encyclopædia Britannica' article on Rossetti, seems really to have been used first in 'Aylwin.' The story seems originally to have been called 'The Renascence of Wonder,' but the title was abandoned because the writer believed that an unsuggestive name, such as that of the autobiographer, was better from the practical point of view. For the knowledge of this I am indebted to Mr. Hake, who says :—

"During the time that Mr. Swinburne was living in Great James Street, several of his friends had chambers in the same street, and among them were my late father, Dr. Gordon Hake—Rossetti's friend and physician—Mr. Watts-Dunton and myself. Mr. Watts-Dunton, as is well known, was a brilliant raconteur long before he became famous as a writer. I have heard him tell scores of stories full of plot and character that have never appeared in print. On a certain occasion he was suffering from one of his periodical eye troubles that had used occasionally to embarrass him. He had just been telling Mr. Swinburne the plot of a suggested story, the motive of which was the 'renascence of wonder in art and poetry' depicting certain well-known characters.

I offered to act as his amanuensis in writing the story, and did so, with the occasional aid of my father and brothers. The story was sent to the late F. W. Robinson, the novelist, then at the zenith of his vogue, who declared that he 'saw a fortune in it,' and it was he who advised the author to send it to Messrs. Hurst & Blackett. As far as I remember, the time occupied by the work was between five and six months. When a large portion of it was in type it was read by many friends, —among others by the late Madox Brown, who thought some of the portraits too close, as the characters were then all living, except one, the character who figures as Cyril. Although unpublished, it was so well known that an article upon it appeared in the 'Liverpool Mercury.' This was more than twenty years ago."

The important matter before us, however, is not when he first used this phrase, which has now become a sort of literary shorthand to express a wide and sweeping idea, but what it actually imports. Fortunately Mr. Watts-

Dunton has quite lately given us a luminous exposition of what the words do precisely mean. Last year he wrote for that invaluable work, Chambers's 'Cyclopædia of English Literature,' the Introduction to volume iii., and no one can any longer say that there is any ambiguity in this now famous phrase :—

"As the storm-wind is the cause and not the effect of the mighty billows at sea, so the movement in question was the cause and not the effect of the French Revolution. It was nothing less than a great revived movement of the soul of man, after a long period of prosaic acceptance in all things, including literature and art. To this revival the present writer, in the introduction to an imaginative work dealing with this movement, has already, for convenience' sake, and in default of a better one, given the name of the Renascence of Wonder. As was said on that occasion, 'The phrase, the Renascence of Wonder, merely indicates that there are two great impulses governing man, and probably not man only, but the entire world of conscious life : the impulse of acceptance—the impulse to take unchallenged and for granted all the phenomena of the outer world as they are—and the impulse to confront these phenomena with eyes of inquiry and wonder.' It would seem that something works as inevitably and as logically as a physical law in the yearning which societies in a certain stage of development show to get away, as far away as possible, from the condition of the natural man ; to get away from that despised condition not only in material affairs, such as dress, domestic arrangements and economies, but also in the fine arts and in intellectual methods, till, having passed that inevitable stage, each society is liable to suffer (even if it does not in some cases actually suffer) a reaction, when nature and art are likely again to take the place of convention and artifice. Anthropologists have often asked, what was that lever-power lying enfolded in the dark womb of some remote semi-human brain, which, by first stirring, lifting, and vitalizing other potential and latent faculties, gave birth to man ? Would it be rash to assume that this lever-power was a vigorous movement of the faculty of wonder ? But certainly it is not rash, as regards the races of man, to affirm that the more intelligent the race the less it is governed by the instinct of acceptance, and the more it is governed by the instinct of wonder, that instinct which leads to the movement of challenge. The alternate action of the two great warring instincts is specially seen just now in the Japanese. Here the instinct of challenge which results in progress became active up to a certain point, and then suddenly became arrested, leaving the instinct of acceptance to have full play, and then everything became crystallized. Ages upon ages of an immense activity of the instinct of challenge were required before the Mongolian savage was developed into the Japanese of the period before the nature-worship of 'Shinto' had been assaulted by dogmatic Buddhism. But by that time the instinct of challenge had resulted in such a high state of civilization that acceptance set [in and there was an end, for the time being, of progress. There is no room here to say even a few words upon other great revivals in past times, such, for instance, as the Jewish-Arabian renascence of the ninth and tenth centuries, when the interest in philosophical speculation, which had previously been arrested, was revived ; when the old sciences were revived ; and when some modern sciences were born. There are, of course, different kinds of wonder."

This passage has a peculiar interest for me, because I instinctively compare it with the author's speech delivered at the St. Ives old Union Book Club dinner when he was a boy. It shows the same wide vision, the same sweep, and the same rush of eloquence. It is in view of this great generalization that I have determined to quote that speech later.

The essay then goes on in a swift way to point out the different kinds of wonder ·—

"Primitive poetry is full of wonder—the naïve and eager wonder of the healthy child. It is this kind of wonder which makes the 'Iliad' and the 'Odyssey' so delightful. The wonder of primitive poetry passes as the primitive conditions of civilization pass; and then for the most part it can only be succeeded by a very different kind of wonder—the wonder aroused by a recognition of the mystery of man's life and the mystery of nature's theatre on which the human drama is played—the wonder, in short, of Æschylus and Sophocles. And among the Romans, Virgil, though living under the same kind of Augustan acceptance in which Horace, the typical poet of acceptance, lived, is full of this latter kind of wonder. Among the English poets who preceded the great Elizabethan epoch there is no room, and indeed there is no need, to allude to any poet besides Chaucer; and even he can only be slightly touched upon. He stands at the head of those who are organized to see more clearly than we can ourselves see the wonder of the 'world at hand.' Of the poets whose wonder is of the simply terrene kind, those whose eyes are occupied by the beauty of the earth and the romance of human life, he is the English king. But it is not the wonder of Chaucer that is to be specially discussed in the following sentences. It is the spiritual wonder which in our literature came afterwards. It is that kind of wonder which filled the souls of Spenser, of Marlowe, of Shakespeare, of Webster, of Ford, of Cyril Tourneur, and of the old ballads : it is that poetical attitude which the human mind assumes when confronting those unseen powers of the universe who, if they did not weave the web in which man finds himself entangled, dominate it. That this high temper should have passed and given place to a temper of prosaic acceptance is quite inexplicable, save by the theory of the action and reaction of the two great warring impulses advanced in the foregoing extract from the Introduction to 'Aylwin.' Perhaps the difference between the temper of the Elizabethan period and the temper of the Chaucerian on the one hand, and Augustanism on the other, will be better understood by a brief reference to the humour of the respective periods."

Then come luminous remarks upon his theory of absolute and relative humour, which I shall deal with in relation to that type of absolute humour, his own Mrs. Gudgeon in 'Aylwin.'

I will now quote a passage from an article in the 'Quarterly Review' on William Morris by one of Morris's intimate friends ·—

"The decorative renascence in England is but an expression of the spirit of the pre-Raphaelite movement —a movement which has been defined by the most eminent of living critics as the renascence of the ' spirit of wonder ' in poetry and art. So defined, it falls into proper relationship with the continuous development of English literature, and of the romantic movement, during the last century and a half, and is no longer to be

considered an isolated phenomenon called into being by
an erratic genius.   The English Romantic school, from
its first inception with Chatterton, Macpherson, and the
publication of the Percy ballads, does not, as Mr. Watts-
Dunton has finely pointed out, aim merely at the revival
of natural language ; it seeks rather to reach through art
and the forgotten world of old romance, that world of
wonder and mystery and spiritual beauty of which poets
gain glimpses through

> magic casements, opening on the foam
> Of perilous seas, in faery lands forlorn.''

In an essay on Rossetti, Mr. Watts-Dunton says : —

" It was by inevitable instinct that Rossetti turned to
that mysterious side of nature and man's life which to
other painters of his time had been a mere fancy-land,
to be visited, if at all, on the wings of sport.   It is not
only in such masterpieces of his maturity as Dante's
Dream, La Pia, etc., but in such early designs as How
they Met Themselves, La Belle Dame sans Merci,
Cassandra, etc., that Rossetti shows how important a
figure he is in the history of modern art, if modern art
claims to be anything more than a mechanical imitation
of the facts of nature.

For if there is any permanent vitality in the Renascence of Wonder in modern Europe, if it is not a mere
passing mood, if it is really the inevitable expression of
the soul of man in a certain stage of civilization (when
the sanctions which have made and moulded society are
found to be not absolute and eternal, but relative, mundane, ephemeral, and subject to the higher sanctions
of unseen powers that work behind ' the shows of

things '), then perhaps one of the first questions to ask
in regard to any imaginative painter of the nineteenth
century is, In what relation does he stand to the newly-
awakened spirit of romance ?   Had he a genuine and
independent sympathy with that temper of wonder and
mystery which all over Europe had preceded and now
followed the temper of imitation, prosaic acceptance,
pseudo-classicism, and domestic materialism ?   Or was his
apparent sympathy with the temper of wonder, reverence
and awe the result of artistic environment dictated to him
by other and more powerful and original souls around him?
I do not say that the mere fact of a painter's or poet's
showing but an imperfect sympathy with the Renas
cence of Wonder is sufficient to place him below a poet
in whom that sympathy is more nearly complete, because we should then be driven to place some of the disciples of Rossetti above our great realistic painters, and
we should be driven to place a poet like the author of
' The Excursion ' and ' The Prelude ' beneath a poet
like the author of ' The Queen's Wake ' ; but we do say
that, other things being equal or anything like equal, a
painter or poet of our time is to be judged very much by
his sympathy with that great movement which we call
the Renascence of Wonder—call it so because the word
romanticism never did express it even before it had been
vulgarized by French poets, dramatists, doctrinaires, and
literary harlequins.

To struggle against the prim traditions of the eighteenth century, the unities of Aristotle, the delineation of
types instead of character, as Chateaubriand, Madame
de Staël, Balzac, and Hugo struggled, was well.   But in
studying Rossetti's works we reach the very key of those
' high palaces of romance ' which the English mind had
never, even in the eighteenth century, wholly forgotten,

but whose mystic gates no Frenchman ever yet unlocked. Not all the romantic feeling to be found in all the French romanticists (with their theory that not earnestness but the grotesque is the life-blood of romance) could equal the romantic spirit expressed in a single picture or drawing of Rossetti's, such, for instance, as Beata Beatrix or Pandora.

For while the French romanticists—inspired by the theories (drawn from English exemplars) of Novalis, Tieck, and Herder—cleverly simulated the old romantic feeling, the 'beautifully devotional feeling' which Holman Hunt speaks of, Rossetti was steeped in it : he was so full of the old frank childlike wonder and awe which preceded the great renascence of materialism that he might have lived and worked amidst the old masters. Hence, in point of design, so original is he that to match such ideas as are expressed in Lilith, Hesterna Rosa, Michael Scott's Wooing, the Sea Spell, etc., we have to turn to the sister art of poetry, where only we can find an equally powerful artistic representation of the idea at the core of the old romanticism—the idea of the evil forces of nature assailing man through his sense of beauty. We must turn, we say, not to art—not even to the old masters themselves—but to the most perfect efflorescence of the poetry of wonder and mystery—to such ballads as 'The Demon Lover,' to Coleridge's 'Christabel' and 'Kubla Khan,' to Keats's 'La Belle Dame sans Merci,' for parallels to Rossetti's most characteristic designs."

These words about Coleridge recall to the students of Mr. Watts-Dunton's work a splendid illustration of the true wonder of the great poetic temper which he gives in the before-mentioned essay on The Renascence of

Wonder in Chambers's ' Cyclopædia of English Literature ' :—

" Coleridge's ' Christabel,' ' The Ancient Mariner,'
and ' Kubla Khan ' are, as regards the romantic spirit,
above—and far above—any work of any other English
poet.   Instances innumerable might be adduced showing how his very nature was steeped in the fountain from
which the old balladists themselves drew, but in this
brief and rapid survey there is room to give only one.
In the ' Conclusion ' of the first part of ' Christabel '
he recapitulates and summarizes, in lines that are at once
matchless as poetry and matchless in succinctness of
statement, the entire story of the bewitched maiden
and her terrible foe which had gone before ·—

> A star hath set, a star hath risen,
> O Geraldine ! since arms of thine
> Have been the lovely lady's prison.
> O Geraldine ! one hour was thine—
> Thou'st had thy will ! By tairn and rill,
> The night-birds all that hour were still.
> But now they are jubilant anew,
> From cliff and tower, tu-whoo ! tu-whoo !
> Tu-whoo ! tu-whoo ! from wood and fell !

Here we get that feeling of the inextricable web in
which the human drama and external nature are woven
which is the very soul of poetic wonder.   So great is the
maleficent power of the beautiful witch that a spell is
thrown over all Nature.   For an hour the very woods and
fells remain in a shuddering state of sympathetic consciousness of her—

> The night-birds all that hour were still.

When the spell is passed Nature awakes as from a hideous
nightmare, and ' the night-birds ' are jubilant anew.

This is the very highest reach òf poetic wonder—finer, if that be possible, than the night-storm during the murder of Duncan."

And now let us turn again to the essay upon Rossetti from which I have already quoted :—

" Although the idea at the heart of the highest romantic poetry (allied perhaps to that apprehension of the warring of man's soul with the appetites of the flesh which is the basis of the Christian idea), may not belong exclusively to what we call the romantic temper (the Greeks, and also most Asiatic peoples, were more or less familiar with it, as we see in the ' Salámán ' and ' Absál ' of Jámi), yet it became a peculiarly romantic note, as is seen from the fact that in the old masters it resulted in that asceticism which is its logical expression and which was once an inseparable incident of all romantic art. But, in order to express this stupendous idea as fully as the poets have expressed it, how is it possible to adopt the asceticism of the old masters ?   This is the question that Rossetti asked himself, and answered by his own progress in art."

In the same article, Mr. Watts-Dunton discusses the crowning specimen of Rossetti's romanticism before it had, as it were, gone to seed and passed into pure mysticism, the grand design, ' Pandora,' of which he possesses by far the noblest version :—

" In it is seen at its highest Rossetti's unique faculty of treating classical legend in the true romantic spirit. The grand and sombre beauty of Pandora's face, the mysterious haunting sadness in her deep blue-grey eyes as she tries in vain to re-close the fatal box from which are still escaping the smoke and flames that shape themselves as they curl over her head into shadowy spirit faces, grey with agony, between tortured wings of sullen fire, are in the highest romantic mood."

It is my privilege to be allowed to give here a reproduction of this masterpiece, for which I and my publishers cannot be too grateful. The influence of Mr. Watts-Dunton's teachings is seen in the fact that the idea of the Renascence of Wonder has become expanded by theological writers and divines in order to include within its scope subjects connected with religion. Among others Dr. Robertson Nicoll has widened its ambit in a remarkable way in an essay upon Dr. Alexander White's 'Appreciation' of Bishop Butler. He quotes one of the Logia discovered by the explorers of the Egypt Fund :—'Let not him that seeketh cease from his search until he find, and when he finds he shall wonder : wondering he shall reach the kingdom, and when he reaches the kingdom he shall have rest.' He then points out that Bishop Butler was 'one of the first to share in the Renascence of Wonder, which was the Renascence of religion.'

And now I must quote a passage alluding to the generalization upon absolute and relative humour which I shall give later when discussing the humour of Mrs. Gudgeon. I shall not be able in these remarks to dwell upon Mr. Watts-Dunton as a humourist, but the extracts will speak for themselves. Writing of the great social Pyramid of the Augustan age, Mr. Watts-Dunton says :—

" This Augustan pyramid of ours had all the symmetry which Blackstone so much admired in the English constitution and its laws ; and when, afterwards, the American colonies came to revolt and set up a pyramid of their own, it was on the Blackstonian model. At the base—patient as the tortoise beneath the elephant in the Indian cosmogony—was the people, born to be the base and born for nothing else. Resting on this foundation were the middle classes in their various strata, each stratum sharply marked off from the others. Then above these was the strictly genteel class, the patriciate, picturesque and elegant in dress if in nothing else, whose privileges were theirs as a matter of right. Above the patriciate was the earthly source of gentility, the monarch, who would, no doubt, have been the very apex of the sacred structure save that a little—a very little— above him sat God, the suzerain to whom the prayers even of the monarch himself were addressed. The leaders of the Rebellion had certainly done a daring thing, and an original thing, by striking off the apex of this pyramid, and it might reasonably have been expected that the building itself would collapse and crumble away. But it did nothing of the kind. It was simply a pyramid with the apex cut off—a structure to serve afterwards as a model of the American and French pyramids, both of which, though aspiring to be original structures, are really built on exactly the same scheme of hereditary honour and dishonour as that upon which the pyramids of Nineveh and Babylon were no doubt built. Then came the Restoration : the apex was restored : the structure was again complete ; it was, indeed, more solid than ever, stronger than ever.

With regard to what we have called the realistic side of the romantic movement as distinguished from its purely poetical and supernatural side, Nature was for the Augustan temper much too ungenteel to be described realistically. Yet we must not suppose that in the eighteenth century Nature turned out men without imaginations, without the natural gift of emotional speech, and without the faculty of gazing honestly in her face. She does not work in that way. In the time of the mammoth and the cave-bear she will give birth to a great artist whose materials may be a flint and a tusk. In the period before Greece was Greece, among a handful of Achaians she will give birth to the greatest poet, or, perhaps we should say, the greatest group of poets, the world has ever yet seen. In the time of Elizabeth she will give birth, among the illiterate yeomen of a diminutive country town, to a dramatist with such inconceivable insight and intellectual breadth that his generalizations cover not only the intellectual limbs of his own time, but the intellectual limbs of so complex an epoch as the twentieth century."

Rossetti had the theory, I believe, that important as humour is in prose fiction and also in worldly verse, it cannot be got into romantic poetry, as he himself understood romantic poetry ; for he did not class ballads like Kinmont Willie, where there are such superb touches of humour, among the romantic ballads. And, as Mr. Watts-Dunton has somewhere remarked, his poems, like Morris's, are entirely devoid of humour, although both the poets were humourists. But the readers of Rhona's Letters in 'The Coming of Love' will admit that a delicious humour can be imported into the highest romantic poetry.

With one more quotation from the essay in Chambers's 'Cyclopædia of English Literature,' I must conclude my remarks upon the keynote of all Mr. Watts-Dunton's work, whether imaginative or critical ·—

" The period of wonder in English poetry may perhaps be said to have ended with Milton. For Milton, although born only twenty-three years before the first of the great poets of acceptance, Dryden, belongs properly to the period of romantic poetry. He has no relation whatever to the poetry of Augustanism which followed Dryden, and which Dryden received partly from France and partly from certain contemporaries of the great romantic dramatists themselves, headed by Ben Jonson. From the moment when Augustanism really began— in the latter decades of the seventeenth century—the periwig poetry of Dryden and Pope crushed out all the natural singing of the true poets. All the periwig poets became too 'polite' to be natural. As acceptance is, of course, the parent of Augustanism or gentility, the most genteel character in the world is a Chinese mandarin, to whom everything is vulgar that contradicts the symmetry of the pyramid of Cathay."

One of the things I purpose to show in this book is that the most powerful expression of the Renascence of Wonder is not in Rossetti's poems, nor yet in his pictures, nor is it in 'Aylwin,' but in 'The Coming of Love.' But in order fully to understand Mr. Watts-Dunton's work it is necessary to know something of his life-history, and thanks to the aid I have received from certain of his friends, and also to a little topographical work, the 'History of St. Ives,' by Mr. Herbert E. Norris, F.E.S., I shall be able to give glimpses of his early life long before he was known in London.

Chapter II

COWSLIP COUNTRY

SOME time ago I was dipping into the 'official pictorial guides' of those three great trunk railways, the Midland, the Great Northern, and the Great Eastern, being curious to see what they had to say about St. Ives—not the famous town in Cornwall, but the little town in Huntingdonshire where, according to Carlyle, Oliver Cromwell spent those five years of meditation upon which his after life was nourished. In the Great Northern Guide I stumbled upon these words : ' At Slepe Hall dwelt the future Lord Protector, Oliver Cromwell, but by many this little Huntingdonshire town will be even better known as the birthplace of Mr. Theodore Watts-Dunton, whose exquisite examples of the English sonnet and judicious criticisms in the kindred realms of poetry and art are familiar to lovers of our national literature.' ' Well,' I thought, when I found similar remarks in the other two guides, ' here at least is one case in which a prophet has honour in his own country.' This set me musing over a subject which had often tantalized me during my early Irish days, the whimsical workings of the Spirit of Place. To a poet, what are the advantages and what are the disadvantages of being born in a microcosm like St. Ives ? If the fame of Mr. Watts-Dunton as a poet were as great as that of his living friend, Mr. Swinburne, or as that of his dead friend, Rossetti, I should not have been surprised to find the place of his birth thus

associated with his name. But whether or not Rossetti
was right in saying that Mr. Watts-Dunton ' had sought
obscurity as other poets seek fame,' it is certain that
until quite lately he neglected to claim his proper place
among his peers. Doubtless, as the ' Journal des Débats ' has pointed out, the very originality of his work,
both in subject and in style, has retarded the popular
recognition of its unique quality ; but although the names
of Rossetti and Swinburne echo through the world, there
is one respect in which they were less lucky than their
friend. They were born in the macrocosm of London,
where the Spirit of Place has so much to attend to that
his memory can find but a small corner even for the
author of ' The Blessed Damozel,' or for the author of
' Atalanta in Calydon.'

Mr. Watts-Dunton was born in the microcosm which
was in those corn law repeal days a little metropolis in
Cowslip Country—Buttercup Land, as the Ouse lanes
are sometimes called, and therefore he was born to
good luck. Cowslip Country will be as closely associated
with him and with Rhona Boswell as Wessex is associated
with Thomas Hardy and with Tess of the D'Urbervilles.
For the poet born in a microcosm becomes identified with
it in the public eye, whereas the poet born in a macrocosm is seldom associated with his birthplace.

To the novelist, if not to the poet, there is a still greater
advantage in being born in a microcosm. He sees the
drama of life from a point of view entirely different from
that of the novelist born in the macrocosm. The human
microbe, or, as Mr. John Morley might prefer to say, the
human cheese-mite in the macrocosm sees every other
microbe or every other cheese-mite on the flat, but in
the microcosm he sees every other microbe or every
other cheese-mite in the round.

Mr. Watts-Dunton's work is saturated with memories of the Ouse. Cowper had already described the Ouse, but it was Mr. Watts-Dunton who first flung the rainbow of romance over the river and over the sweet meadows of Cowslip Land, through which it flows. In these lines he has described a sunset on the Ouse ·—

> More mellow falls the light and still more mellow
> Around the boat, as we two glide along
> 'Tween grassy banks she loves where, tall and strong,
> The buttercups stand gleaming, smiling, yellow.
> She knows the nightingales of 'Portobello';
> Love makes her know each bird! In all that throng
> No voice seems like another: soul is song,
> And never nightingale was like its fellow;
> For, whether born in breast of Love's own bird,
> Singing its passion in those islet bowers
> Whose sunset-coloured maze of leaves and flowers
> The rosy river's glowing arms engird,
> Or born in human souls—twin souls like ours—
> Song leaps from deeps unplumbed by spoken word.

Now, will it be believed that this lovely river—so famous too among English anglers for its roach, perch, pike, dace, chub, and gudgeon—has been libelled? Yes, it has been libelled, and libelled by no less a person than Thomas Carlyle. Mr. Norris, vindicating with righteous wrath the reputation of his beloved Ouse, says :—

" There is, as far as I know, nothing like the Ouse elsewhere in England. I do not mean that our river surpasses or even equals in picturesqueness such rivers as the Wye, the Severn, the Thames, but that its beauty is unique. There is not to be seen anywhere else so wide and stately a stream moving so slowly and yet so clearly. Consequently there is no other river which reflects with

THE OUSE AT HOUGHTON MILL, HUNTS

(From a Water Colour by Fraser)

such beauty th

This, I think, it

which is both

of the Ouse dr:

ing of floating

ceptive faculti

made a good d

visit to St. Ive

time exploring

Cromwell, he

hour there be

the objects at

covered from

enormous flee

seen at that ti

of this fleet of

Carlyle, in hi

contempt for

bottom. An

this descripti

followed by :

is what make

Hemingford

instead of see

broad mirror

by the reflec

and white w:

If the beau

it so eloque

pictorial fac:

a friend 'W

The 1

And :

such beauty the scenery of the clouds floating overhead. This, I think, is owing to the stream moving over a bottom which is both flat and gravelly. When Carlyle spoke of the Ouse dragging m a half-stagnant way under a coating of floating oils, he showed ' how vivid were his perceptive faculties and also how untrustworthy.' I have made a good deal of enquiry into the matter of Carlyle's visit to St. Ives, and have learnt that, having spent some time exploring Ely Cathedral in search of mementoes of Cromwell, he rode on to St. Ives, and spent about an hour there before proceeding on his journey. Among the objects at which he gave a hasty glance was the river, covered from the bridge to the Holmes by one of those enormous fleets of barges which were frequently to be seen at that time, and it was from the newly tarred keels of this fleet of barges that came the oily exudation which Carlyle, in his ignorance of the physical sciences and his contempt for them, believed to arise from a greasy riverbottom. And to this mistake the world is indebted for this description of the Ouse, which has been slavishly followed by all subsequent writers on Cromwell. This is what makes strangers, walking along the tow-path of Hemingford meadow, express so much surprise when, instead of seeing the oily scum they expected, they see a broad mirror as clear as glass, whose iridescence is caused by the reflection of the clouds overhead and by the gold and white water lilies on the surface of the stream."

If the beauty of the Ouse inspired Mr. Norris to praise it so eloquently in prose, we need not wonder at the pictorial fascination of what Rossetti styled in a letter to a friend ' Watts's magnificent star sonnet ' :—

The mirrored stars lit all the bulrush spears,
And all the flags and broad-leaved lily-isles ;

The ripples shook the stars to golden smiles,
Then smoothed them back to happy golden spheres.
We rowed—we sang ; her voice seemed in mine ears
An angel's, yet with woman's dearer wiles ;
But shadows fell from gathering cloudy piles
And ripples shook the stars to fiery tears.

What shaped those shadows like another boat
Where Rhona sat and he Love made a liar ?
There, where the Scollard sank, I saw it float,
While ripples shook the stars to symbols dire ;
We wept—we kissed—while starry fingers wrote,
And ripples shook the stars to a snake of fire.

According to Mr. Sharp, Rossetti pronounced this sonnet to be the finest of all the versions of the Döppelganger idea, and for many years he seriously purposed to render it in art. It is easy to understand why Rossetti never carried out his intention, for the pictorial magic of the sonnet is so powerful that even the greatest of all romantic painters could hardly have rendered it on canvas. Poetry can suggest to the imagination deeper mysteries than the subtlest romantic painting.

No sonnet has been more frequently localized—erroneously localized than this. It is often supposed to depict the Thames above Kew, but Mr. Norris says that 'every one familiar with Hemingford Meadow will see that it describes the Ouse backwater near Porto Bello, where the author as a young man was constantly seen on summer evenings listening from a canoe to the blackcaps and nightingales of the Thicket.'

That excellent critic, Mr. Earl Hodgson, the editor of Dr. Gordon Hake's 'New Day,' seems to think that the 'lily-isles' are on the Thames at Kelmscott, while other writers have frequently localized these 'lily-isles'

on the Avon at Stratford. But, no doubt, Mr. Norris
is right in placing them on the Ouse.

This, however, gives me a good opportunity of saying
a few words about Mr. Watts-Dunton's love of the
Avon. The sacred old town of Stratford-on-Avon has
always been a favourite haunt of Mr. Watts-Dunton's.
No poet of our time has shown a greater love of our
English rivers, but he seems to love the Avon even more
passionately than the Ouse. He cannot describe the soft
sands of Petit Bot Bay in Guernsey without bringing in
an allusion to ' Avon's sacred silt.' It was at Stratford-
on-Avon that he wrote several of his poems, notably the
two sonnets which appeared first in the ' Athenæum,'
and afterwards in the little volume, ' Jubilee Greetings
at Spithead to the Men of Greater Britain.' They are
entitled ' The Breath of Avon : To English-speaking
Pilgrims on Shakspeare's Birthday ' :—

Whate'er of woe the Dark may hide in womb
For England, mother of kings of battle and song—
Rapine, or racial hate's mysterious wrong,
Blizzard of Chance, or fiery dart of Doom—
Let breath of Avon, rich of meadow-bloom,
Bind her to that great daughter sever'd long—
To near and far-off children young and strong—
With fetters woven of Avon's flower perfume.
Welcome, ye English-speaking pilgrims, ye
Whose hands around the world are join'd by him,
Who make his speech the language of the sea,
Till winds of Ocean waft from rim to rim
The Breath of Avon : let this great day be
A Feast of Race no power shall ever dim.

From where the steeds of Earth's twin oceans toss
Their manes along Columbia's chariot-way ;
From where Australia's long blue billows play ;

From where the morn, quenching the Southern Cross,
Startling the frigate-bird and albatross
Asleep in air, breaks over Table Bay—
Come hither, pilgrims, where these rushes sway
'Tween grassy banks of Avon soft as moss!
For, if ye found the breath of Ocean sweet,
Sweeter is Avon's earthy, flowery smell,
Distill'd from roots that feel the coming spell
Of May, who bids all flowers that lov'd him meet
In meadows that, remembering Shakspeare's feet,
Hold still a dream of music where they fell.

It was during a visit to Stratford-on-Avon in 1880 that Mr. Watts-Dunton wrote the cantata, 'Christmas at the Mermaid,' a poem in which breathes the very atmosphere of Shakespeare's town. There are no poetical descriptions of the Avon that can stand for a moment beside the descriptions in this poem, which I shall discuss later.

A typical meadow of Cowslip Country, or, as it is sometimes called, 'The Green Country,' is Hemingford Meadow, adjoining St. Ives. It is a level tract of land on the banks of the Ouse, consisting of deposits of alluvium from the overflowings of the river. In summer it is clothed with gay flowers, and in winter, during floods and frosts, it is used as a skating-ground, for St. Ives, being on the border of the Fens, is a famous skating centre. On the opposite side of the meadow is The Thicket, of which I am able to give a lovely picture. This, no doubt, is the scene described in one of Mr. Watts-Dunton's birthday addresses to Tennyson :—

Another birthday breaks : he is with us still.
There through the branches of the glittering trees
The birthday sun gilds grass and flower : the breeze
Sends forth methinks a thrill—a conscious thrill

'THE THICKET,' ST. IVES

(From a Water Colour by Fraser)

That tells yon meadows by the steaming rill—
Where, o'er the clover waiting for the bees,
The mist shines round the cattle to their knees
'Another birthday breaks: he is with us still!'

The meadow leads to what the 'oldest rustic inhabitant' calls the 'First Hemingford,' or 'Hemingford Grey.' The imagination of this same 'oldest inhabitant' used to go even beyond the First Hemingford to the Second Hemingford, and then of course came Ultima Thule! The meadow has quite a wide fame among those students of nature who love English grasses in their endless varieties. Owing to the richness of the soil, the luxuriant growth of these beautiful grasses is said to be unparalleled in England. For years the two Hemingfords have been the favourite haunt of a group of landscape painters the chief of whom are the brothers Fraser, two of whose water-colours are reproduced in this book.

Nowhere can the bustling activity of haymaking be seen to more advantage than in Cowslip Country, which extends right through Huntingdonshire into East Anglia. It was not, however, near St. Ives, but in another somewhat distant part of Cowslip Country that the gypsies depicted in 'The Coming of Love' took an active part in haymaking. But alas! in these times of mechanical haymaking the lover of local customs can no longer hope to see such a picture as that painted in the now famous gypsy haymaking song which Mr. Watts-Dunton puts into the mouth of Rhona Boswell. Moreover, the prosperous gryengroes depicted by Borrow and by the author of 'The Coming of Love' have now entirely vanished from the scene. The present generation knows them not. But it is impossible for the student of Mr. Watts-Dunton's poetry to ramble along any part

of Cowslip Country, with the fragrance of newly-made
hay in his nostrils, without recalling this chant, which
I have the kind permission of the editor of the 'Saturday Review' (April 19, 1902) to quote :—

hay sun	Make the kas while the kem says, ' Make it !'
	Shinin' there on meadow an' grove,
gypsy girls	Sayin, ' You Romany chies, you take it,
	Toss it, tumble it, cock it, rake it,
song	Singin' the ghyllie the while you shake it
summer	To lennor and love ! '
	Hark, the sharpenin' scythes that tingle !
farmers	See they come, the farmin' ryes !
	' Leave the dell,' they say, ' an' pingle !
Gentile woman	Never a gorgie, married or single,
hay	Can toss the kas in dell or dingle
gypsy girls	Like Romany chies.'
hay	Make the kas while the kem says ' Make it !'
grass	Bees are a-buzzin' in chaw an' clover
	Stealin' the honey from sperrits o' morn,
hares field	Shoshus leap in puv an' cover,
	Doves are a-cooin' like lover to lover,
	Larks are awake an' a-warblin' over
homes	Their kairs in the corn.
hay sun	Make the kas while the kem says ' Make it !'
hay wind	Smell the kas on the baval blowin' !
Gentiles	What is that the gorgies say ?
	Never a garden rose a-glowin',
	Never a meadow flower a-growin',
	Can match the smell from a Rington mowin'
	Of new made hay.
	All along the river reaches
	' Cheep, cheep, chee !'—from osier an' sedge ;
	' Cuckoo, cuckoo !' rings from the beeches ;
birds	Every chirikel's song beseeches
summer	Ryes to larn what lennor teaches
	From copse an' hedge.
hay sun	Make the kas while the kem says ' Make it !'

Lennor sets 'em singin' an' pairin',	summer
Chirikels all in tree an' grass,	birds
Farmers say, ' Them gals are darin',	girls
Sometimes dukkerin', sometimes snarin';	fortune-telling
But see their forks at a quick kas-kairin','	haymaking
Toss the kas !	hay

Make the kas while the kem says, ' Make it !'	hay sun
Shinin' there on meadow an' grove,	
Sayin', ' You Romany chies, you take it,	gypsy girls
Toss it, tumble it, cock it, rake it,	
Singin' the ghyllie the while you shake it	song
To lennor and love !'	summer

Mr. Norris tells us that the old Saxon name of St. Ives
was Slepe, and that Oliver Cromwell is said to have resided as a farmer for five years in Slepe Hall, which
was pulled down in the late forties.   When Mr. Watts-
Dunton's friend, Madox Brown, went down to St. Ives
to paint the scenery for his famous picture, 'Oliver
Cromwell at St. Ives,' he could present only an imaginary farm.

Perhaps my theory about the advantage of a story-
teller being born in a microcosm accounts for that faculty
of improvizing stories full of local colour and character which, according to friends of D. G. Rossetti,
would keep the poet-painter up half the night, and which
was dwelt upon by Mr. Hake in his account of the
origin of ' Aylwin ' which I have already given.   I may
give here an anecdote connected with Slepe Hall which
I have heard Mr. Watts-Dunton tell, and which would
certainly make a good nucleus for a short story.   It is
connected with Slepe Hall, of which Mr. Clement
Shorter, in some reminiscences of his published some
time ago, writes : " My mother was born at St. Ives, in
Huntingdonshire, and still owns by inheritance some

freehold cottages built on land once occupied by Slepe Hall, where Oliver Cromwell is supposed to have farmed. At Slepe Hall, a picturesque building, she went to school in girlhood. She remembers Mr. Watts-Dunton, the author of 'Aylwin,' who was also born at St. Ives, as a pretty little boy then unknown to fame."

When the owners of Slepe Hall, the White family, pulled it down, they sold the materials of the building and also the site and grounds in building lots. It was then discovered that the house in which Cromwell was said to have lived was built upon the foundations of a much older house whose cellars remained intact. This was, of course, a tremendous event in the microcosm, and the place became a rendezvous of the schoolboys of the neighbourhood, whose delight from morning to eve was to watch the workmen in their task of demolition. In the early stages of this work, when the upper stories were being demolished, curiosity was centred on the great question as to what secret chamber would be found, whence Oliver Cromwell's ghost, before he was driven into hiding by his terror of the school girls, used to issue, to take his moonlit walks about the grounds, and fish for roach in the old fish ponds. But no such secret chamber could be found. When at length the work had proceeded so far as the foundations, the centre of curiosity was shifted : a treasure was supposed to be hidden there ; for, although, as a matter of fact, Cromwell was born at Huntingdon and lived at St. Ives only five years, it was not at Huntingdon, but at the little Nonconformist town of St. Ives, that he was the idol : it was indeed the old story of every hero of the world—

Imposteur à la Mecque et prophète à Mèdine.

Although in all probability Cromwell never lived

SLEPE HALL ; CROMWELL'S SUPPOSED RESIDENCE AT ST. IVES
(From an Oil Painting)

Photo. Poole, Putney

at Slepe Hall, [but at the Green End Farm at the other end of the town, there was a legend that, before the Ironsides started on a famous expedition, Noll went back to St. Ives and concealed his own plate, and the plate of all his rebel friends, in Slepe Hall cellars. No treasure turned up, but what was found was a collection of old bottles of wine which was at once christened 'Cromwell's wine' by the local humourist of the town, who was also one of its most prosperous inhabitants, and who felt as much interest as the boys in the exploration. The workmen, of course, at once began knocking off the bottles' necks and drinking the wine, and were soon in what may be called a mellow condition; the humourist, being a teetotaler, would not drink, but he insisted on the boys being allowed to take away their share of it in order that they might say in after days that they had drunk Oliver Cromwell's wine and perhaps imbibed some of the Cromwellian spirit and pluck. Consequently the young urchins carried off a few bottles and sat down in a ring under a tree called 'Oliver's Tree,' and knocked off the tops of the bottles and began to drink. The wine turned out to be extremely sweet, thick and sticky, and appears to have been a wine for which Cowslip Land has always been famous—elder wine. Abstemious by temperament and by rearing as Mr. Watts-Dunton was, he could not resist the temptation to drink freely of Cromwell's elder-wine; so freely, in fact, that he has said, ' I was never even excited by drink except once, and that was when I came near to being drunk on Oliver Cromwell's elder-wine.' The wine was probably about a century old.

I should have stated that Mr. Watts-Dunton at the age of eleven or twelve was sent to a school at Cambridge, where he remained for a longer time than is usual. He received there and afterwards at home a somewhat elaborate education, comprising the physical sciences, particularly biology, and also art and music. As has been said in the notice of him in 'Poets and Poetry of the Century,' he is one of the few contemporary poets with a scientific knowledge of music. Owing to his father's passion for science, he was specially educated as a naturalist, and this accounts for the innumerable allusions to natural science in his writings, and for his many expressions of a passionate interest in the lower animals.

Upon the subject of " the great human fallacy expressed in the phrase, 'the dumb animals,' " Mr. Watts Dunton has written much, and he has often been eloquent about 'those who have seen through the fallacy, such as St. Francis of Assisi, Cowper, Burns, Coleridge, and Bisset, the wonderful animal-trainer of Perth of the last century, who, if we are to believe the accounts of him, taught a turtle in six months to fetch and carry like a dog ; and having chalked the floor and blackened its claws, could direct it to trace out any given name in the company.'

" Of course," he says, " the 'lower animals ' are no more dumb than we are. With them, as with us, there is the same yearning to escape from isolation—to get as close as may be to some other conscious thing—which is a great factor of progress. With them, as with us, each individual tries to warm itself by communication with the others around it by arbitrary signs ; with them, as with us, countless accidents through countless years have contributed to determine what these signs and sounds shall be. Those among us who have gone at all underneath conventional thought and conventional expression—those who have penetrated underneath conventional feeling—know that neither thought nor emotion can really be expressed at all. The voice cannot do it, as we see by comparing one language with another. Wordsworth calls language the incarnation of thought. But the mere fact of there being such a Babel of different tongues disproves this. If there were but one universal language, such as speculators dream of, the idea might, at least, be not superficially absurd. Soul cannot communicate with soul save by signs made by the body; and when you can once establish a Lingua Franca between yourself and a 'lower animal,' interchange of feeling and even of thought is as easy with them as it is with men. Nay, with some temperaments and in some moods, the communication is far, far closer. 'When I am assailed with heavy tribulation,' said Luther, 'I rush out among my pigs rather than remain alone by myself.' And there is no creature that does not at some points sympathize with man. People have laughed at Erskine because every evening after dinner he used to have placed upon the table a vessel full of his pet leeches, upon which he used to lavish his endearments. Neither I nor my companion had a pet passion for leeches. Erskine probably knew leeches better than we, for, as the Arabian proverb says, mankind hate only the thing of which they know nothing. Like most dog lovers, we had no special love for cats, but that was clearly from lack of knowledge. 'I wish women would purr when they are pleased,' said Horne Tooke to Rogers once."

Chapter III

THE CRITIC IN THE BUD

ONE of my special weaknesses is my delight in forgotten records of the nooks of old England and 'ould Ireland'; I have a propensity for 'dawdling and dandering' among them whenever the occasion arises, and I am yielding to it here.

Besides the interesting history of St. Ives from which I have been compelled to quote so liberally Mr. Norris has written a series of brochures upon the surrounding villages. One of these, called 'St. Ives and the Printing Press,' has greatly interested me, for it reveals the wealth of the material for topographical literature which in the rural districts lies ready for the picking up. I am tempted to quote from this, for it shows how strong since Cromwell's time the temper which produced Cromwell has remained. During the time when at Cambridge George Dyer and his associates, William Frend, Fellow of Jesus, and John Hammond of Fenstanton, Fellow of Queen's, revolted against the discipline and the doctrine of the Church of England, St. Ives was the very place where the Cambridge revolutionists had their books printed. The house whence issued these fulminations was the 'Old House' in Crown Street, now pulled down, which for a time belonged to Mr. Watts-Dunton's father, having remained during all this time a printing office. Mr.

Norris gives a very picturesque description of this old printing office at the top of the house, with its pointed roof, ' king posts' and panelling, reminding one of the pictures of the ancient German printing offices. Mr. Norris also tells us that it was at the house adjoining this, the 'Crown Inn,' that William Penn died in 1718, having ridden thither from Huntingdon to hear the lawsuit between himself and the St. Ives churchwardens. According to Mr. Norris, the fountain-head of the Cambridge revolt was the John Hammond above alluded to, who was a friend of Mr. Watts-Dunton's father when the latter was quite a young man under articles for a solicitor. A curious character must have been this long-forgotten rebel, to whom Dyer addressed an ode, with an enormous tail of learned notes showing the eccentric pedantry which was such an infinite source of amusement to Lamb, and inspired some of Elia's most delightful touches of humour. This poem of Dyer's opens thus ·—

> Though much I love th' Æolian lyre,
>   Whose varying sounds beguil'd my youthful day,
>   And still, as fancy guides, I love to stray
> In fabled groves, among th' Aonian choir :
> Yet more on native fields, thro' milder skies,
>   Nature's mysterious harmonies delight :
> There rests my heart ; for let the sun but rise,
>   What is the moon's pale orb that cheer'd the
>   lonesome night ?
> I cannot leave thee, classic ground,
>   Nor bid your labyrinths of song adieu ;
>   Yet scenes to me more dear arise to view :
> And my ear drinks in notes of clearer sound.
> No purple Venus round my Hammond's bow'r,
>   No blue-ey'd graces, wanton mirth diffuse,
> The king of gods here rains no golden show'r,
>   Nor have these lips e'er sipt Castilian dews.

At the 'Old House' in Crown Street there used to be held in Dyer's time, if not earlier, the meetings of the St. Ives old Union Book Club, and at this very Book Club, Walter Theodore Watts first delivered himself of his boyish ideas about science, literature, and things in general. Filled with juvenile emphasis as it is, I mean to give here nearly in full that boyish utterance. It interests me much, because I seem to to see in it adumbrations of many interesting extracts from his works with which I hope to enrich these pages. I cannot let slip the opportunity of taking advantage of a lucky accident—the accident that a member of Mr. Watts-Dunton's family was able to furnish me with an old yellow-brown newspaper cutting in which the speech is reported. In 1854, 'W. Theodore Watts,' as he is described in the cutting, although too young to be himself a member—if he was not still at school at Cambridge, he had just left it—on account of his father's great local reputation as a man of learning, was invited to the dinner, and called upon to respond to the toast, 'Science.' In the 'Cambridge Chronicle' of that date the proceedings of the dinner were reported, and great prominence was given to the speech of the precocious boy, a speech delivered, as is evident by the allusions to persons present, without a single note, and largely improvized. The subject which he discussed was 'The Influence of Science upon Modern Civilization ' ·—

" It is one of the many beautiful remarks of the great philosophical lawyer, Lord Bacon, that knowledge resembles a tree, which runs straight for some time, and then parts itself into branches. Now, of all the branches of the tree of knowledge, in my opinion, the most hopeful one for humanity is physical science—that branch of the tree which, before the time of the great lawyer, had scarcely begun to bud, and which he, above all men, helped to bring to its present wondrous state of development. I am aware that the assertion that Lord Bacon is the Father of Physical Science will be considered by many of you as rather heterodox, and fitting to come from a person young and inexperienced as myself. It is heterodox ; it clashes, for instance, with the venerable superstition of ' the wisdom of the ancients '—a superstition, by the bye, as old in our literature as my friend Mr. Wright's old friend Chaucer, whom we have this moment been talking about, and who, I remember, has this sarcastic verse to the point :—

> For out of the olde fieldes, as men saith,
> Cometh all this new corn from yeare to yeare,
> And out of olde bookes ; in good faith,
> Cometh all this new science that men lere.

But, gentlemen, if by the wisdom of the ancients we mean their wisdom in matters of Physical Science (as some do), I contend that we simply abuse terms ; and that the phrase, whether applied to the ancients more properly, or to our own English ancestors, is a fallacy. It is the error of applying qualities to communities of men which belong only to individuals. There can be no doubt that, of contemporary individuals, the oldest of them has had the greatest experience, and is therefore, or ought therefore, to be the wisest ; but with generations of men, surely the reverse of this must be the fact. As Sydney Smith says in his own inimitably droll way, ' Those who came first (our ancestors), are the young people, and have the least experience. Our ancestors up to the Conquest were children in arms—chubby boys in the time of Edward the First ; striplings under Eliza-

beth ; men in the reign of Queen Anne ; and we only are
the white-bearded, silver-headed ancients who have
treasured up, and are prepared to profit by, all the
experience which human life can supply.

And, gentlemen, I think the wit was right, both as
regards our own English ancestors, and the nations of
antiquity.   What, for instance, was the much-vaunted
Astronomy of the ancient Chaldeans—what but the
wildest Astrology ?   What schoolboy has not chuckled
over the ingenious old Herodotus's description of the
sun being blown out of the heavens ?   Or again, at
old Plutarch's veracious story of the hedgehogs and
the grapes ? Nay, there are absurdities enough in
such great philosophers as Pliny, Plato, and Aristotle,
to convince us that the ancients were profoundly
ignorant in most matters appertaining to the Physical
Sciences.

Gentlemen, I would be the last one in the room to
disparage the ancients : my admiration of them amounts
simply to reverence.   But theirs was essentially the day
of poetry and imagination ; our day—though there are
still poets among us, as Alexander Smith has been
proving to us lately—is, as essentially, the day of Science.
I might, if I had time, dwell upon another point here—
the constitution of the Greek mind (for it is upon Greece
I am now especially looking as the soul of antiquity).
Was that scientific ?   Surely not.

The predominant intuition of the Greek mind, as
you well know, was beauty, sensuous beauty.   This pre-
vailing passion for the beautiful exhibits itself in everything they did, and in everything they said : it breathes
in their poetry, in their oratory, in their drama, in their
architecture, and above all in their marvellous sculpture.
The productions of the Greek intellect are pure temples

of the beautiful, and, as such, will never fade and decay, for

A thing of beauty is a joy for ever.

Nevertheless, I may as well confess at once that I believe that Science could never have found a home in the Europe of antiquity. Athens was too imaginative and poetical. Sparta was too warlike and barbarous. Rome was too sensual and gross. It had to wait for the steady Teutonic mind—the plodding brains of modern England and modern Germany. That Homer is the father of poetry—that Æschylus is a wonder of sublimity—that Sophocles and Euripides are profound masters of human passion and human pathos—that Aristophanes is an exhaustless fountain of sparkling wit and richest humour—no one in this room, or out of it, is more willing to admit than I am. But is that to blind us to the fact, gentlemen, that Humboldt and Murchison and Lyell are greater natural philosophers than Lucretius or Aristotle ?

The Athenian philosopher, Socrates, believed that he was accompanied through life by a spiritual good genius and evil genius. Every right action he did, and every right thought that entered his mind, he attributed to the influence of his good Genius ; while every bad thought and action he attributed to his evil Genius. And this was not the mere poetic figment of a poetic brain : it was a living and breathing faith with him. He believed it in his childhood, in his youth, in his manhood, and he believed it on his death-bed, when the deadly hemlock was winding its fold, like the fatal serpent of Laocoon, around his giant brain. Well, gentlemen, don't let us laugh at this idea of the grand old Athenian ; for it is, after all, a beautiful one, and typical of many great truths. And I have often thought that the idea might be applied to a greater man than Socrates. I mean the great man—mankind. He, too, has his good genius and his evil genius. The former we will designate science, the latter we will call superstition. For ages upon ages, superstition has had the sway over him—that evil genius, who blotted out the lamp of truth that God had implanted within his breast, and substituted all manner of blinding errors—errors which have made him play

Such fantastic tricks before high heaven
As make the angels weep.

This evil genius it was who made him look upon the fair face of creation, not as a book in which God may be read, as St. Paul tells us, but as a book full of frightful and horrid mysteries. In a word, the great Man who ought to have been only a little lower than the angels, has been made, by superstition, only a little above the fiends.

But, at last, God has permitted man's long, long experience to be followed by wisdom ; and we have thrown off the yoke of this ancient enemy, and clasped the hands of Science—Science, that good genius who makes matter the obedient slave of mind ; who imprisons the ethereal lightning and makes it the messenger of commerce ; who reigns king of the raging sea and winds ; who compresses the life of Methusaleh into seventy years ; who unlocks the casket of the human frame, and ranges through its most secret chambers, until at last nothing, save the mysterious germ of life itself, shall be hidden ; who maps out all the nations of the earth ; showing how the sable Ethiopian, the dusky Polynesian, the besotted Mongolian, the intellectual European, are but differently developed exemplars of the same type of manhood, and warning man that he is still his ' brother's keeper ' now as in the primeval days of Cain and Abel.

The good genius, Science, it is who bears us on his dædal wings up into the starry night, there where ' God's name is writ in worlds,' and discourses to us of the laws which bind the planets revolving around their planetary suns, and those suns again circling for ever around the great central sun—' The Great White Throne of God ! '

The good genius, Science, it is who takes us back through the long vista of years, and shows us this world of ours, this beautiful world which the wisest and the best of us are so unwilling to leave, first, as a vast drop of liquid lava-fire, starting on that mysterious course which is to end only with time itself ; then, as a dark humid mass, ' without form and void,' where earth, sea, and sky, are mingled in unutterable confusion ; then, after countless, countless ages, having grown to something like the thing of beauty the Creator had intended, bringing forth the first embryonic germs of vegetable life, to be succeeded, in due time, by gigantic trees and towering ferns, compared with which the forest monarchs of our day are veritable dwarfs ; then, slowly, gradually, developing the still greater wonder of animal life, from the primitive, half-vegetable, half-conscious forms, till such mighty creatures as the Megatherium, the Saurian, the Mammoth, the Iguanodon, roam about the luxuriant forests, and bellow in chaotic caves, and wallow in the teeming seas, and circle in the humid atmosphere, making the earth rock and tremble beneath their monstrous movements ; then, last of all, the wonder of wonders, the climax towards which the whole had been tending, the noblest and the basest work of God— the creation of the thinking, reasoning, sinning animal, Man.

And thus, gentlemen, will this good genius still go on, instructing and improving, and purifying the human mind, and aiding in the grand work of developing the divinity within it.   I know, indeed, that it is a favourite argument of some people that modern civilization will decline and vanish, ' like the civilizations of old.' But I venture to deny it in toto.   From a human point of view, it is utterly impossible.   And without going into the question (for I see the time is running on) as to whether ancient civilization really has passed away, or whether the old germ did not rather spring into new life after the dark ages, and is now bearing fruit, ten thousand times more glorious than it ever did of old ; without arguing this point, I contend that all comparisons between ancient civilization and modern must of necessity be futile and fallacious.   And for this reason, that independently of the civilizing effects of Christianity, Science has knit the modern nations into one : whereas each nation of antiquity had to work out its own problems of social and political life, and come to its own conclusions.   So isolated, indeed, was one nation from another, that nations were in some instances ignorant of each other's existence. A new idea, or invention, born at Nineveh, was for Assyria alone ; at Athens, for Greece alone ; at Rome, for Italy alone.   There was no science then to ' put a girdle round about the earth ' (as Puck says) ' in forty minutes.' But now, a new idea brought to light in modern London, or Paris, or New York, is for the whole world ; it is wafted on the wings of science around the whole habitable globe—from Ireland to New Zealand, from India to Peru.   I am not going to say, gentlemen, that Britannia must always be the ruler of the waves.   The day may come that will see her sink to a second-rate, a third-rate, or a fourth-rate power in Europe.   In spite of all we have been saying this evening, the day may come that will see Russia the dominant power in Europe.   The day may come that will see Sydney and Melbourne the fountain heads of refinement and learning. It may have been ordained in Heaven at the first that each race upon the globe shall be in its turn the dominant race—that the negro race shall one day lord it over the Caucasian, as the Caucasian race is now lording it over the negro. Why not ? It would be only equity. But I am not talking of races ; I am not talking of nationalities. I speak again of the great man, Mankind—the one indivisible man that Science is making him. He will never retrograde, because ' matter and mind comprise the universe,' and matter must entirely sink beneath the weight of mind—because good must one day conquer ill, or why was the world made ? Henceforth his road is onward— onward. Science has helped to give him such a start that nothing shall hold him back—nothing can hold him back— save a fiat, a direct fiat from the throne of Almighty God."

But I am wandering from the subject of the ' Old House ' in Crown Street and its connection with printing. The last important book that was ever printed there was a very remarkable one. It was the famous essay on Pantheism by Mr. Watts-Dunton's friend, the Rev. John Hunt, D.D., at that time a curate of the St. Ives Church—a book that was the result of an enormous amount of learning, research, and original thought, a book, moreover, which has had a great effect upon modern thought. It has passed through several editions since it was printed at St. Ives in 1866.

Chapter IV

CHARACTERS IN THE MICROCOSM

MRS. CRAIGIE has recently protested against the metropolitan fable that London enjoys a monopoly of culture, and has reminded us that in the provinces may be found a great part of the intellectual energy of the nation. It would be hard to find a more intellectual environment than that in which Theodore Watts grew up. Indeed, his early life may be compared to that of John Stuart Mill, although he escaped the hardening and narrowing influences which marred the austere educational system of the Mill family. Mr. Watts-Dunton's father was in many respects a very remarkable man. 'He was,' says the famous gypsologist, F. H. Groome, in Chambers's 'Encyclopædia, a naturalist intimately connected with Murchison, Lyell, and other geologists, a pre-Darwinian evolutionist of considerable mark in the scientific world of London, and the Gilbert White of the Ouse valley.' There is, as the ' Times ' said in its review of ' Aylwin,' so much of manifest Wahrheit mingled with the Dichtung of the story, that it is not surprising that attempts have often been made to identify all the characters. Many of these guesses have been wrong ; and indeed, the only writer who has spoken with authority seems to be Mr. Hake, who, in two papers in ' Notes and Queries ' identified many of the characters.

Until he wrote on the subject, it was generally assumed that the spiritual protagonist from whom springs the entire action of the story, Philip Aylwin, was Mr. Watts-Dunton's father. Mr. Hake, however, tells us that this is not so. Philip Aylwin is a portrait of the author's uncle, an extraordinary man of whom I shall have something to say later. I feel myself fortunate in having discovered an admirable account of Mr. Watts-Dunton's father in Mr. Norris's 'History of St. Ives ' ·—

" For many years one of the most interesting of St. Ivian figures was the late Mr. J. K. Watts, who was born at St. Ives in 1808, though his family on both sides came from Hemingford Grey and Hemingford Abbots. According to the following extracts from 'The Cambridge Chronicle and University Journal' of August 15, 1884, Mr. Watts died quite suddenly on August 7 of that year: 'We record with much regret the sudden death at Over of our townsman, Mr. J. K. Watts, who died after an hour's illness of heart disease at Berry House, whither he had been taken after the seizure. Dr. J. Ellis, of Swavesey, was called in, but without avail. At the inquest the post-mortem examination disclosed that the cause of death was a long-standing fatty degeneration of the heart, which had, on several occasions, resulted in syncope. Deceased had been driven to Willingham and back to Over upon a matter of business with Mr. Hawkes, and the extreme heat of the weather seems to have acted as the proximate cause of death.

Mr. Watts had practised in St. Ives from 1840, and was one of the oldest solicitors in the county. He had also devoted much time and study to scientific subjects, and was, in his earlier life, a well-known figure in the

scientific circles of London.   He was for years connected
with Section E of the British Association for the Ad-
vancement of Science, and elected on the Committee.
He read papers on geology and cognate subjects before
that Association and other Societies during the time
that Murchison and Lyell were the apostles of geology.
Afterwards he made a special study of luminous meteors,
nnd in the Association's reports upon this subject some
of the most interesting observations of luminous meteors
are those recorded by Mr. Watts.   He was one of the
earliest Fellows of the Geographical Society, and one of
the Founders of the Anthropological Society.'

Mr. Watts never collected his papers and essays, but
up to the last moment of his life he gave attention to
those subjects to which he had devoted himself, as may
be seen by referring to the ' Antiquary ' for 1883 and
1884, where will be found two articles on Cambridge-
shire Antiquities, one of which did not get into type till
several months after his death.   It was, however, not
by Archæology, but by his geological and geographical
writings that he made his reputation.   And it was these
which brought him into contact with Murchison, Liv-
ingstone, Lyell, Whewell, and Darwin, and also with the
geographers, some of whom, such as Du Chaillu, Findlay,
Dr. Norton Shaw, visited him at the Red House on
the Market Hill, now occupied by Mr. Matton.   In the
sketches of the life of Dr. Latham it is mentioned that
the famous ethnologist was a frequent visitor to Mr.
Watts at St. Ives.   Since his death there have been frequent references to him as a man of ' encyclopædic
general knowledge.'

He was of an exceedingly retiring disposition, and
few men in St. Ives have been more liked or more generally respected.   His great delight seemed to be roaming

about in meadows and lanes observing the changes of the vegetation and the bird and insect life in which our neighbourhood is as rich as Selborne itself. On such occasions the present writer has often met him and had many interesting conversations with him upon subjects connected with natural science."

With regard to the family of Mr. Watts-Dunton's mother, the Duntons, although in the seventeenth century a branch of the family lived in Huntingdonshire, some of them being clergymen there for several generations, they are entirely East Anglian; and some very romantic chapters in the history of the family have been touched upon by Dr. Jessopp in his charming essay, ' Ups and Downs of an Old Nunnery.' This essay was based upon a paper, communicated by Miss Mary Bateson to the Norfolk and Norwich Archæological Society, and treating of the Register of Crab House Nunnery. In 1896 Walter Theodore Watts added his mother's to his father's name, by a deed in Chancery.

I could not give a more pregnant instance of the difference in temperament between a father and a son than by repeating a story about Mr. Watts-Dunton which Rossetti (who was rich in anecdotes of his friend) used to tell. When the future poet and critic was a boy in jackets pursuing his studies at the Cambridge school, he found in the school library a copy of Wells's ' Stories after Nature,' and read them with great avidity. Shortly afterwards, when he had left school and was reading all sorts of things, and also cultivating on the sly a small family of Gryengroes encamped in the neighbourhood, he was amazed to find, in a number of the ' Illuminated Magazine,' a periodical which his father, on account of Douglas Jerrold, had taken in from the first, one of the 'Stories after Nature' reprinted with an illustration by the designer and engraver Linton. He said to his father, 'Why, I have read this story before!' 'That is quite impossible,' said his father, 'quite impossible that you should have before read a new story in a new number of a magazine.' 'I have read it before; I know all about it,' said the boy. 'As I do not think you untruthful,' said the father, 'I think I can explain your hallucination about this matter.' 'Do, father,' said the son. 'Well,' said the father, 'I do not know whether or not you are a poet. But I do know that you are a dreamer of dreams. You have told me before extraordinary stories to the effect that when you see a landscape that is new to you, it seems to you that you have seen it before.' 'Yes, father, that often occurs.' 'Well, the reason for that is this, as you will understand when you come to know a little more about physiology. The brain is divided into two hemispheres, exactly answering to each other, and they act so simultaneously that they work like one brain; but it often happens that when dreamers like you see things or read things, one of the hemispheres has lapsed into a kind of drowsiness, and the other one sees the object for itself; but in a second or two the lazy hemisphere wakes up and thinks it has seen the picture before.' The explanation seemed convincing, and yet it could not convince the boy.

The very next month the magazine gave another of the stories, and the father said, 'Well, Walter, have you read this before?' 'Yes,' said the boy falteringly, 'unless, of course, it is all done by the double brain, father.' And so it went on from month to month. When the boy had grown into a man and came to meet Rossetti, one of the very first of the literary subjects discussed between them was that of Charles Wells's 'Joseph and His Brethren' and 'Stories after Nature.' Rossetti was agreeably surprised that although his new friend knew nothing of 'Joseph and His Brethren,' he was very familiar with the 'Stories after Nature.' 'Well,' said Mr. Watts-Dunton, 'they appeared in the "Illuminated Magazine."' 'Who should have thought,' said Rossetti, 'that the "Illuminated Magazine" in its moribund days, when Linton took it up, should have got down to St. Ives. Its circulation, I think, was only a few hundreds. Among Linton's manœuvres for keeping the magazine alive was to reprint and illustrate Charles Wells's "Stories after Nature" without telling the public that they had previously appeared in book form.' 'They did then appear in book form first ?' said Mr. Watts-Dunton. 'Yes, but there can't have been over a hundred or two sold,' said Rossetti. 'I discovered it at the British Museum.' 'I read it at Cambridge in my school library,' said Mr. Watts-Dunton. It was the startled look on Rossetti's face which caused Mr. Watts-Dunton to tell him the story about his father and the 'Illuminated Magazine.'

It was a necessity that a boy so reared should feel the impulse to express himself in literature rather early. But it will be new to many, and especially to the editor of the 'Athenæum,' that as a mere child he contributed to its pages. When he was a boy he read the 'Athenæum,' which his father took in regularly. One day he caught a correspondent of the 'Athenæum'—no less a person than John P. Collier—tripping on a point of Shakespearean scholarship, being able to do so by chance. He had stumbled on the matter in question while reading one of his father's books. He wrote to the editor in his childish round hand, stigmatizing the blun-

der with youthful scorn. In due time the correction
was noted in the Literary Gossip of the journal. Soon
after, his father had occasion to consult the book, and
finding a pencil mark opposite the passage, he said,
'Walter, have you been marking this book?' 'Yes,
father.' 'But you know I object?' 'Yes, father,
but I was interested in the point.' 'Why,' said his
father, 'somebody has been writing about this very passage
to the "Athenæum."' 'Yes, father,' replied the boy,
red and ungrammatical with proud confusion, 'it was
me.' 'You!' cried his astonished father, 'you!' And
thus the matter was explained. Mr. Watts-Dunton
confesses that he was never tired of thumbing that,
his first contribution to the 'Athenæum.'

Whatever may have been the influence of his father
upon Mr. Watts-Dunton, it was not, I think, nearly so
great as that of his uncle, James Orlando Watts. His
father may have made him scientific : his uncle seems to
have made him philosophical with a dash of mysticism.
As I have already pointed out, Mr. Hake has identified this
uncle as the prototype of Philip Aylwin, the father of
the hero. The importance of this character in 'Aylwin'
is shown by the fact that, if we analyze the story, we find
that the character of Philip is its motive power. After
his death, everything that occurs is brought about by
his doctrines and his dreams, his fantasies and his whims.
This effect of making a man dominate from his grave the
entire course of the life of his descendants seems to
be unique in imaginative literature ; and yet, although
the fingers of some critics (notably Mr. Coulson Kernahan) burn close to the subject, there they leave it. What
Mr. Watts-Dunton calls 'the tragic mischief' of the
drama is not brought about by any villain, but by the

vagaries and mystical speculations of a dead man, the author of 'The Veiled Queen.' There were few things in which James Orlando Watts did not take an interest. He was a deep student of the drama, Greek, English, Spanish, and German. And it is a singular fact that this dreamy man was a lover of the acted drama. One of his stories in connection with acting is this. A party of strolling players who went to St. Ives got permission to act for a period in a vast stone-built barn, called Priory Barn, and sometimes Cromwell's Barn. Mr. J. O. Watts went to see them, and on returning home after the performance said, ' I have seen a little actor who is a real genius. He reminds me of what I have read about Edmund Kean's acting. I shall go and see him every night. And he went. The actor's name was Robson. When, afterwards, Mr. Watts went to reside in London, he learnt that an actor named Robson was acting in one of the second-rate theatres called the Grecian Saloon. He went to the theatre and found, as he expected, that it was the same actor who had so impressed him down at St. Ives. From that time he followed Robson to whatsoever theatre in London he went, and afterward became a well-known figure among the playgoers of the Olympic. He always contended that Robson was the only histrionic genius of his time. Mr. Hake seems to have known James Orlando Watts only after he had left St. Ives to live in London :—

" He was," says Mr. Hake, " a man of extraordinary learning in the academic sense of the word, and he possessed still more extraordinary general knowledge. He lived for many years the strangest kind of hermit life, surrounded by his books and old manuscripts. His two great passions were philology and

occultism, but he also took great interest in rub-
bings from brass monuments. He knew more, I
think, of those strange writers discussed in Vaughan's
' Hours with the Mystics ' than any other person—including perhaps, Vaughan himself ; but he managed to
combine with his love of mysticism a deep passion for the
physical sciences, especially astronomy. He seemed to
be learning languages up to almost the last year of his
life. His method of learning languages was the opposite
of that of George Borrow—that is to say, he made great
use of grammars ; and when he died, it is said that from
four to five hundred treatises on grammar were found
among his books. He used to express great contempt for
Borrow's method of learning languages from dictionaries
only. I do not think that any one connected with literature—with the sole exception of Mr. Swinburne, my
father, and Dr. R. G. Latham—knew so much of him as I
did. His personal appearance was exactly like that of
Philip Aylwin, as described in the novel. Although he
never wrote poetry, he translated, I believe, a good deal
from the Spanish and Portuguese poets. I remember
that he was an extraordinary admirer of Shelley. His
knowledge of Shakespeare and the Elizabethan dramatists was a link between him and Mr. Swinburne.

At a time when I was a busy reader at the British
Museum reading room, I used frequently to see him,
and he never seemed to know anyone among the readers
except myself, and whenever he spoke to me it was always in a hushed whisper, lest he should disturb the other
readers, which in his eyes would have been a heinous
offence. For very many years he had been extremely
well known to the second-hand booksellers, for he was
a constant purchaser of their wares. He was a great
pedestrian, and, being very much attached to the north

of London, would take long, slow tramps ten miles out in the direction of Highgate, Wood Green, etc. I have a very distinct recollection of calling upon him in Myddelton Square at the time when I was living close to him in Percy Circus. Books were piled up from floor to ceiling, apparently in great confusion; but he seemed to remember where to find every book and what there was in it. It is a singular fact that the only person outside those I have mentioned who seems to have known him was that brilliant but eccentric journalist, Thomas Purnell, who had an immense opinion of him and used to call him 'the scholar.' How Purnell managed to break through the icy wall that surrounded the recluse always puzzled me; but I suppose they must have come across one another at one of those pleasant inns in the north of London where 'the scholar' was taking his chop and bottle of Beaune. He was a man that never made new friends, and as one after another of his old friends died he was left so entirely alone that, I think, he saw no one except Mr. Swinburne, the author of 'Aylwin,' and myself. But at Christmas he always spent a week at The Pines, when and where my father and I used to meet him. His memory was so powerful that he seemed to be able to recall, not only all that he had read, but the very conversations in which he had taken a part. He died, I think, at a little over eighty, and his faculties up to the last were exactly like those of a man in the prime of life. He always reminded me of Charles Lamb's description of George Dyer.

Such is my outside picture of this extraordinary man; and it is only of externals that I am free to speak here, even if I were competent to touch upon his inner life. He was a still greater recluse than the 'Philip Aylwin' of the novel. I think I am right in saying that he took up one or two Oriental tongues when he was seventy years of age. Another of his passions was numismatics, and it was in these studies that he sympathized with the author of ' Aylwin's ' friend, the late Lord de Tabley. I remember one story of his peculiarities which will give an idea of the kind of man he was. He had a brother, Mr. William K. Watts, who was the exact opposite of him in every way—strikingly good-looking, with great charm of manner and savoir faire, but with an ordinary intellect and a very superficial knowledge of literature, or, indeed, anything else, except records of British military and naval exploits—where he was really learned. Being full of admiration of his student brother, and having a parrot-like instinct for mimicry, he used to talk with great volubility upon all kinds of subjects wherever he went, and repeat in the same words what he had been listening to from his brother, until at last he got to be called the ' walking encyclopædia.' The result was that he got the reputation of being a great reader and an original thinker, while the true student and book-lover was frequently complimented on the way in which he took after his learned brother. This did not in the least annoy the real student, it simply amused him, and he would give with a dry humour most amusing stories as to what people had said to him on this subject." [1]

Balzac might have made this singular anecdote the nucleus of one of his stories. I may add that the editor of ' Notes and Queries,' Mr. Joseph Knight, knew James Orlando Watts, and he has stated that he ' can testify to the truth ' of Mr. Hake's ' portraiture.'

[1] ' Notes and Queries,' August 2, 1902.

Chapter V

EARLY GLIMPSES OF THE GYPSIES

ALTHOUGH an East Midlander by birth it seems to have been to East Anglia that Mr. Watts-Dunton's sympathies were most strongly drawn. It was there that he first made acquaintance with the sea, and it was to East Anglia that his gypsy friends belonged.

On the East Anglian side of St. Ives, opposite to the Hemingford side already described, the country, though not so lovely as the western side, is at first fairly attractive; but it becomes less and less so as it nears the Fens. The Fens, however, would seem to have a charm of their own, and Mr. Watts-Dunton himself has described them with a vividness that could hardly be surpassed. It was here as a boy that he made friends with the Gryengroes — that superior variety of the Romanies which Borrow had known years before. These gypsies used to bring their Welsh ponies to England and sell them at the fairs. I must now go back for some years in order to enrich my pages with Mr. Watts-Dunton's graphic description of his first meeting with the gypsies in the Fen country, which appeared in ' Great Thoughts ' in 1903.

" I shall never forget my earliest recollections of them. My father used sometimes to drive in a dogcart to see friends of his through about twelve miles of Fen country,

and he used to take me with him.   Let me say that the Fen
country is much more striking than is generally supposed.
Instead of leafy quick hedgerows, as in the midlands, or
walls, as in the north country, the fields are divided by
dykes ; not a tree is to be seen in some parts for miles and
miles.   This gives an importance to the skies such as is
observed nowhere else except on the open sea.   The flashing opalescent radiance of the sea is apt to challenge the
riches of the sky, and in a certain degree tends to neutralize
it ; but in the Fen country the level, monotonous greenery
of the crops in summer, and, in autumn and winter, the
vast expanse of black earth, make the dome of the sky,
by contrast, so bright and glorious that in cloudless
weather it gleams and suggests a roof of rainbows ; and
in cloudy weather it seems almost the only living sight
in the universe, and becomes thus more magical still.
And as to sunsets, I do not know of any, either by land
or sea, to be compared with the sunsets to be seen in the
Fen country.   The humidity of the atmosphere has, no
doubt, a good deal to do with it.   The sun frequently
sets in a pageantry of gauzy vapour of every colour, quite
indescribable.

The first evening that I took one of these drives,
while I was watching the wreaths of blue curling smoke
from countless heaps of twitch-grass, set burning by the
farm-labourers, which stretched right up to the sky-line,
my father pulled up the dogcart and pointed to a ruddy
fire glowing, flickering, and smoking in an angle where
a green grassy drove-way met the dark-looking high-road
some yards ahead.   And then I saw some tents, and then
a number of dusky figures, some squatting near the fire,
some moving about. ' The gypsies ! ' I said, in the
greatest state of exultation, which soon fled, however,
when I heard a shrill whistle and saw a lot of these dusky

people running and leaping like wild things towards the dog-cart. ' Will they kill us, father ? ' I said. ' Kill us ? No,' he said, laughing ; ' they are friends of mine. They've only come to lead the mare past the fire and keep her from shying at it.' They came flocking up. So far from the mare starting, as she would have done at such an invasion by English people, she seemed to know and welcome the gypsies by instinct, and seemed to enjoy their stroking her nose with their tawny but well-shaped fingers, and caressing her neck. Among them was one of the prettiest little gypsy girls I ever saw. When the gypsies conducted us past their camp I was fascinated by the charm of the picture. Outside the tents in front of the fire, over which a kettle was suspended from an upright iron bar, which I afterwards knew as the kettle-prop, was spread a large dazzling white table-cloth, covered with white crockery, among which glittered a goodly number of silver spoons. I afterwards learnt that to possess good linen, good crockery, and real silver spoons, was as ' passionate a desire in the Romany chi as in the most ambitious farmer's wife in the Fen country.' It was from this little incident that my intimacy with the gypsies dated. I associated much with them in after life, and I have had more experiences among them than I have yet had an opportunity of recording in print."

This pretty gypsy girl was the prototype, I believe, of the famous Rhona Boswell herself.

It must of course have been after the meeting with Rhona in the East Midlands—supposing always that we are allowed to identify the novelist with the hero, a bold supposition—that Mr. Watts-Dunton again came across her—this time in East Anglia. Whether this is so or not, I must give this picture of her from ' Aylwin ' :—

" It was at this time that I made the acquaintance of
Winnie's friend, Rhona Boswell, a charming little Gypsy
girl.   Graylingham Wood and Rington Wood, like the
entire neighbourhood, were favourite haunts of a superior
kind of Gypsies called Gryengroes, that is to say, horse-
dealers.   Their business was to buy ponies in Wales and
sell them in the Eastern Counties and the East Midlands.
Thus it was that Winnie had known many of the East
Midland Gypsies in Wales.   Compared with Rhona
Boswell, who was more like a fairy than a child, Winnie
seemed quite a grave little person.   Rhona's limbs were
always on the move, and the movement sprang always
from her emotions.   Her laugh seemed to ring through
the woods like silver bells, a sound that it was impossible
to mistake for any other.   The laughter of most Gypsy
girls is full of music and of charm, and yet Rhona's
laughter was a sound by itself, and it was no doubt this
which afterwards, when she grew up, attracted my kins-
man, Percy Aylwin, towards her.   It seemed to emanate,
not from her throat merely, but from her entire frame.
If one could imagine a strain of merriment and fun blending with the ecstatic notes of a skylark soaring and singing,
one might form some idea of the laugh of Rhona Boswell.
Ah, what days they were !   Rhona would come from
Gypsy Dell, a romantic place in Rington Manor, some
miles off, especially to show us some newly devised coronet
of flowers that she had been weaving for herself.   This
induced Winnie to weave for herself a coronet of seaweeds, and an entire morning was passed in grave discussion as to which coronet excelled the other."

Chapter VI

SPORT AND WORK

IT was at this period that, like so many young Englishmen who were his contemporaries, he gave attention to field sports, and took interest in that athleticism which, to judge from Wilkie Collins's scathing pictures, was quite as rampant and absurd then as it is in our own time. It was then too that he acquired that familiarity with the figures prominent in the ring which startles one in his reminiscences of George Borrow. But it will scarcely interest the readers of this book to dwell long upon this subject. Nor have I time to repeat the humorous stories I have heard him tell about the queer characters who could then be met at St. Ives Fair (said to have been the largest cattle fair in England), and at another favourite resort of his, Stourbridge Fair, near Cambridge. Stourbridge Fair still exists, but its glory was departing when Mr. Watts-Dunton was familiar with it ; and now, possibly, it has departed for ever. Of Cambridge and the entire county he tells many anecdotes. Here is a specimen :—

Once in the early sixties he and his brother and some friends were greatly exercised by the news that Deerfoot, the famous American Indian runner in whom Borrow took such an interest, was to run at Cambridge against the English champion. When the day came, they drove to Cambridge in a dog-cart from St. Ives, about a

dozen miles. The race took place in a field called
Fenner's Ground, much used by cricketers. This is how,
as far as I can recall the words, he tells the anecdote : —

"The place was crammed with all sorts of young
men—'varsity men and others. There were not many
young farmers or squires or yeomen within a radius of
a good many miles that did not put in an appearance
on that occasion. The Indian won easily, and at the
conclusion of the race there was a frantic rush to get
near him and shake his hand. The rush was so wild and
so insensate that it irritated me more than I should at
the present moment consider it possible to be irritated.
But I ought to say that at that time of my life I had
developed into a strangely imperious little chap. I had
been over-indulged—not at home, but at the Cambridge
school to which I had been sent—and spoilt. This
seems odd, but it's true. It was the boys who spoilt me
in a curious way—a way which will not be understood
by those who went to public schools like Eton, where the
fagging principle would have stood in the way of the
development of the curious relation between me and
my fellow-pupils which I am alluding to. There is an
inscrutable form of the monarchic instinct in the genus
homo which causes boys, without in the least knowing
why, to select one boy as a kind of leader, or rather emperor, and spoil him, almost unfit him indeed for that
sense of equality which is so valuable in the social struggle
for life that follows school-days. This kind of emperor
I had been at that school. It indicated no sort of real
superiority on my part ; for I learnt that immediately
after I had left the vacant post it was filled by another
boy—filled for an equally inscrutable reason. The result
of it was that I became (as I often think when I recall

those days) the most masterful young urchin that ever lived. If I had not been so, I could not have got into a fury at being jostled by a good-humoured crowd. My brother, who had not been so spoilt at school, was very different, and kept urging me to keep my temper. 'It's capital fun,' he said ; 'look at this blue-eyed young chap jostling and being jostled close to us. He's fond of a hustle, and no mistake. That's the kind of chap I should like to know'; and he indicated a young 'varsity man of whose elbow at that moment I was unpleasantly conscious, and who seemed to be in a state of delight at other elbows being pushed into his ribs. I soon perceived that certain men whom he was with seemed angry, not on their own account, but on account of this youth of the laughing lips and blue eyes. As they were trying to make a ring round him, 'Hanged if it isn't the Prince!' said my brother. 'And look how he takes it! Surely you can stand what he stands!' It was, in fact, the Prince of Wales, who had come to see the American runner. I needed only two or three years of buffeting with the great life outside the schoolroom to lose all my imperiousness and learn the essential lesson of give-and-take."

For a time Mr. Watts-Dunton wavered about being articled to his father as a solicitor. His love of the woods and fields was too great at that time for him to find life in a solicitor's office at all tolerable. Moreover, it would seem that he who had been so precocious a student, and who had lived in books, felt a temporary revulsion from them, and an irresistible impulse to study Nature apart from books, to study her face to face. And it was at this time that, as the 'Encyclopædia Britannica' remarks, he 'moved much among the East Anglian gypsies, of whose superstitions and folklore he

made a careful study.'   But of this period of his life I
have but little knowledge.   Judging from Groome's remarks upon ' Aylwin ' in the ' Bookman,' he alone had
Mr. Watts-Dunton's full confidence in the matter.   So
great was his desire to pore over the book of nature,
there appears to have been some likelihood, perhaps I
ought to say some danger, of his feeling the impulse
which had taken George Borrow away from civilization.
He seems, besides, to have shared with the Greeks
and with Montaigne a belief in the value of leisure.
It was at this period, to judge from his writings, that
he exclaimed with Montaigne, ' Have you known how
to regulate your conduct, you have done a great deal
more than he who has composed books.   Have you known
how to take repose, you have done more than he who
has taken empires and cities.'   I suppose, however, that
this was the time when he composed that unpublished
' Dictionary for Nature-worshippers,' from   which   he
often used to quote in the ' Athenæum.'   There is nothing in his writings so characteristic as those definitions.
Work and Sport are thus defined : ' Work : that activity
of mind or body which exhausts the vital forces without
yielding pleasure or health to the individual.   Sport :
that activity of mind or body which, in exhausting the
vital forces, yields pleasure and health to the individual.
The activity, however severe, of a born artist at his easel,
of a born poet at his rhymings, of a born carpenter at
his plane, is sport.   The activity, however slight, of the
born artist or poet at the merchant's desk, is work.   Hence,
to work is not to pray   We have called the heresy of
Work modern because it is the characteristic one of our
time ; but, alas ! like all heresies, it is old.   It was preached
by Zoroaster in almost Mr. Carlyle's words when Con-
cord itself was in the woods and ere Chelsea was.'

'Evening Dreams with the Poets'
(From an Oil Painting at 'The Pines')

In one of his books Mr. Watts-Dunton writes with
great eloquence upon this subject :—

"How hateful is the word 'experience' in the mouth
of the littérateur.   They all seem to think that this
universe exists to educate them, and that they should
write books about it.   They never look on a sunrise
without thinking what an experience it is ; how it is
educating them for bookmaking.   It is this that so often
turns the true Nature-worshipper away from books altogether, that makes him bless with what at times seems
such malicious fervour those two great benefactors of the
human race, Caliph Omar and Warburton's cook.

In Thoreau there was an almost perpetual warring
of the Nature instinct with the Humanity instinct.
And, to say the truth, the number is smaller than even
Nature - worshippers themselves are aware — those in
whom there is not that warring of these two great primal
instincts.   For six or eight months at a time there are
many, perhaps, who could revel in 'utter solitude,' as
companionship with Nature is called ; with no minster
clock to tell them the time of day, but, instead, the bleating of sheep and the lowing of cattle in the morning, the
shifting of the shadows at noon, and the cawing of rooks
going home at sunset.   But then to these, there comes
suddenly, and without the smallest warning, a half-
recognized but secretly sweet pleasure in looking at the
smooth high-road, and thinking that it leads to the city
—a beating of the heart at the sound of the distant
railway-whistle, as the train winds its way, like a vast
gliding snake, to the whirlpool they have left.

In order to realize the folly of the modern Carlylean
heresy of work, it is necessary to realize fully how infinitely rich is Nature, and how generous, and couse-

quently what a sacred duty as well as wise resolve it is that, before he 'returns unto the ground,' man should drink deeply while he may at the fountain of Life. Let it be enough for the Nature-worshipper to know that he, at least, has been blessed. Suppose he were to preach in London or Paris or New York against this bastard civilization, and expatiate on Nature's largess, of which it robs us ? Suppose he were to say to people to whom opinion is the breath of life, 'What is it that this civilization of yours can give you by way of compensation for that of which it robs you ? Is it your art ? Is it your literature ? Is it your music ? Is it your science ? ' Suppose, for instance, he were to say to the collector of Claudes, or Turners, or David Coxes : ' Your possessions are precious undoubtedly, but what are even they when set against the tamest and quietest sunrise, in the tamest and quietest district of Cambridge or Lincoln, in this tame and quiet month, when, over the treeless flat you may see, and for nothing, purple bar after purple bar trembling along the grey, as the cows lift up their heads from the sheet of silver mist in which they are lying ? How can you really enjoy your Turners, you who have never seen a sunrise in your lives ? ' Or suppose he were to say to the opera-goer : ' Those notes of your favourite soprano were superb indeed ; and superb they ought to be to keep you in the opera-house on a June night, when all over the south of England a thousand thickets, warm with the perfumed breath of the summer night, are musical with the gurgle of the nightingales.' Thoreau preached after this fashion, and was deservedly laughed at for his pains.

Yet it is not a little singular that this heresy of the sacredness of work should be most flourishing at the very time when the sophism on which it was originally built is exploded ; the sophism, we mean, that Nature herself is the result of Work, whereas she is the result of growth. One would have thought that this was the very time for recognizing what the sophism had blinded us to, that Nature's permanent temper—whatever may be said of this or that mood of hers—is the temper of Sport, that her pet abhorrence, which is said to be a vacuum, is really Work.   We see this clearly enough in what are called the lower animals—whether it be a tiger or a gazelle, a ferret or a coney, a bat or a butterfly—the final cause of the existence of every conscious thing is that it should sport. It has no other use than that.   For this end it was that ' the great Vishnu yearned to create a world.'   Yet over the toiling and moiling world sits Moloch Work ; while those whose hearts are withering up with hatred of him are told by certain writers to fall down before him and pretend to love.

The worker of the mischief is, of course, civilization in excess, or rather, civilization in wrong directions.   For this word, too, has to be newly defined in the Dictionary before mentioned, where you will find it thus given :— Civilization : a widening and enriching of human life. Bastard or Modern Western Civilization : the art of inventing fictitious wants and working to supply them. In bastard civilization life becomes poorer and poorer, paltrier and paltrier, till at last life goes out of fashion altogether, and is supplanted by work.   True freedom is more remote from us than ever.   For modern Freedom is thus defined : the exchange of the slavery of feudality for the slavery of opinion.   Thoreau realized this, and tried to preach men back to common-sense and Nature. Here was his mistake—in trying to preach.   No man ever yet had the Nature-instinct preached into him."

Chapter VII

EAST ANGLIA

WHATEVER may have been those experiences with the gryengroes which made Groome, when speaking of the gypsies of 'Aylwin,' say 'the author writes only of what he knows,' it seems to have been after his intercourse with the gypsies that he and a younger brother, Alfred Eugene Watts (elsewhere described), were articled as solicitors to their father. His bent, however, was always towards literature, especially poetry, of which he had now written a great deal —indeed, the major part of the volume which was destined to lie unpublished for so many years. But be fore I deal with the most important period of Mr. Watts-Dunton's life—his life in London—it seems necessary to say a word or two about his visits to East Anglia, and especially to the Norfolk coast. There are some admirable remarks upon the East Coast in Mr. William Sharp's chapter on 'Aylwinland' in 'Literary Geography,' and he notes the way in which Rhona Boswell links it with Cowslip Land; but he does not give examples of the poems which thus link it, such as the double roundel called 'The Golden Hand.'

72

THE GOLDEN HAND [1]

PERCY

Do you forget that day on Rington strand
When, near the crumbling ruin's parapet,
I saw you stand beside the long-shore net
The gorgios spread to dry on sunlit sand ?

RHONA

Do I forget ?

PERCY

You wove the wood-flowers in a dewy band
Around your hair which shone as black as jet :
No fairy's crown of bloom was ever set
Round brows so sweet as those the wood-flowers spanned.

I see that picture now ; hair dewy-wet :
Dark eyes that pictures in the sky expand :
Love-lips (with one tattoo ' for dukkerin ') tanned   good-luck
By sunny winds that kiss them as you stand.

RHONA

Do I forget ?
The Golden Hand shone there : it's you forget,
Or p'raps us Romanies ondly understand
The way the Lover's Dukkeripen is planned
Which shone that second time when us two met.

PERCY

Blest ' Golden Hand ' !

RHONA

The wind, that mixed the smell o' violet
Wi' chirp o' bird, a-blowin' from the land

[1] Among the gypsies of all countries the happiest possible ' Dukkeri-
'pen ' (i.e. prophetic symbol of Natura Mystica) is a hand-shaped golden
cloud floating in the sky.   It is singular that the same idea is found
among races entirely disconnected with them—the Finns, for instance,
with whom Ukko, the ' sky god,' or ' angel of the sunrise,' was called
the ' golden king ' and ' leader of the clouds,' and his Golden Hand
was more powerful than all the army of Death.   The ' Golden Hand '
is sometimes called the Lover's Dukkeripen.

Where my dear Mammy lies, said as it fanned
My heart-like, ' Them 'ere tears makes Mammy fret.'
She loves to see her chavi lookin' grand,
So I made what you call'd a coronet,
And in the front I put her amulet :
She sent the Hand to show she sees me yet.

child

PERCY
Blest ' Golden Hand ' !

In the same way that the velvety green of Hunts is
seen in the verses I have already quoted, so the softer side
of the inland scenery of East Anglia is described in the
following lines, where also we find an exquisite use of the
East Anglian fancy about the fairies and the foxglove
bells.

At a waltz during certain Venetian revels after the lib-
eration from the Austrian yoke, a forsaken lover stands
and watches a lady whose child-love he had won in
England :—

Has she forgotten for such halls as these
    The domes the angels built in holy times,
    When wings were ours in childhood's flowery climes
To dance with butterflies and golden bees ?—
Forgotten how the sunny-fingered breeze
    Shook out those English harebells' magic chimes
    On that child-wedding morn, 'neath English limes,
'Mid wild-flowers tall enough to kiss her knees ?

The love that childhood cradled—girlhood nursed—
    Has she forgotten it for this dull play,
    Where far-off pigmies seem to waltz and sway
Like dancers in a telescope reversed ?
    Or does not pallid Conscience come and say,
' Who sells her glory of beauty stands accursed ' ?

But was it this that bought her—this poor splendour
    That won her from her troth and wild-flower wreath
    Who ' cracked the foxglove bells ' on Grayland Heath,

Or played with playful winds that tried to bend her,
Or, tripping through the deer-park, tall and slender,
  Answered the larks above, the crakes beneath,
Or mocked, with glitter of laughing lips and teeth,
When Love grew grave—to hide her soul's surrender ?

Mr. Sharp has dwelt upon the striking way in which
the scenery and atmosphere are rendered in ' Aylwin,'
but this, as I think, is even more clearly seen in the
poems. And in none of these is it seen so vividly as in
that exhilarating poem, ' Gypsy Heather,' published
in the ' Athenæum,' and not yet garnered in a volume.
This poem also shows his lyrical power, which never
seems to be at its very best unless he is depicting Romany life and Romany passion. The metre of this
poem is as original as that of ' The Gypsy Haymaking
Song,' quoted in an earlier chapter. It has a swing like
that of no other poem :—

GYPSY HEATHER

' If you breathe on a heather-spray and send it to your man it'll show
him the selfsame heather where it wur born.'—SINFI LOVELL.

[Percy Aylwin, standing on the deck of the ' Petrel,' takes from his
pocket a letter which, before he had set sail to return to the south seas,
the Melbourne post had brought him—a letter from Rhona, staying
then with the Boswells on a patch of heath much favoured by the Boswells, called ' Gypsy Heather.' He takes from the envelope a withered
heather-spray, encircled by a little scroll of paper on which Rhona has
written the words, ' Remember Gypsy Heather.']

I

Remember Gypsy Heather ?
Remember Jasper's camping-place
  Where heath-bells meet the grassy dingle,
And scents of meadow, wood and chase,
  Wild thyme and whin-flower seem to mingle ?
Remember where, in Rington Furze,
  I kissed her and she asked me whether

I ' thought my lips of teazel-burrs,
That pricked her jis like whin-bush spurs,
pretty mouth   Felt nice on a rinkenny moey like hers ? '—
      Gypsy Heather !

II

     Remember Gypsy Heather ?
Remember her whom nought could tame
     But love of me, the poacher-maiden
Who showed me once my father's game
     With which her plump round arms were laden
Who, when my glances spoke reproach,
     Said, " Things o' fur an' fin an' feather
Like coneys, pheasants, perch an' loach,
An' even the famous ' Rington roach,'
Wur born for Romany chies to poach ! "—
      Gypsy Heather !

III

     Remember Gypsy Heather ?
Atolls and reefs, you change, you change
     To dells of England dewy and tender ;
You palm-trees in yon coral range
     Seem ' Rington Birches ' sweet and slender
Shading the ocean's fiery glare :
     We two are in the Dell together—
My body is here, my soul is there
With lords of trap and net and snare,
The Children of the Open Air,—
      Gypsy Heather !

IV

     Remember Gypsy Heather ?
Its pungent breath is on the wind,
     Killing the scent of tropic water ;
I see her suitors swarthy skinned,
     Who pine in vain for Jasper's daughter.
The ' Scollard,' with his features tanned
     By sun and wind as brown as leather—

His forehead scarred with Passion's brand—
Scowling at Sinfi tall and grand,
Who sits with Pharaoh by her hand,
    Gypsy Heather!

V

    Remember Gypsy Heather?
Now Rhona sits beneath the tree
    That shades our tent, alone and weeping;
And him, the 'Scollard,' him I see:
    From bush to bush I see him creeping—
I see her mock him, see her run
    And free his pony from the tether,
Who lays his ears in love and fun,
And gallops with her in the sun
Through lace the gossamers have spun,—
    Gypsy Heather!

VI

    Remember Gypsy Heather?
She reaches 'Rington Birches'; now,
    Dismounting from the 'Scollard's' pony,
She sits alone with heavy brow,
    Thinking, but not of hare or coney.
The hot sea holds each sight, each sound
    Of England's golden autumn weather:
The Romanies now are sitting round
The tea-cloth spread on grassy ground;
Now Rhona dances heather-crowned,—
    Gypsy Heather!

VII

    Remember Gypsy Heather?
She's thinking of this withered spray
    Through all the dance; her eyes are gleaming
Darker than night, yet bright as day,
    While round her a gypsy shawl is streaming;
I see the lips—the upper curled,
    A saucy rose-leaf, from the nether,

Whence—while the floating shawl is twirled,
As if a ruddy cloud were swirled—
Her scornful laugh at him is hurled,
    Gypsy Heather!

VIII

    Remember Gypsy Heather?
In storm or calm, in sun or rain,
   There's magic, Rhona, in the writing
Wound round these flowers whose purple stain
   Dims the dear scrawl of Love's inditing:
Dear girl, this spray between the leaves
   (Now fading like a draggled feather
With which the nesting song-bird weaves)
Makes every wave the vessel cleaves
Seem purple of heather as it heaves,
    Gypsy Heather!

IX

    Remember Gypsy Heather?
Oh, Rhona! sights and sounds of home
   Are everywhere; the skylark winging
Through amber cloud-films till the dome
   Seems filled with love, our love, a-singing.
The sea-wind seems an English breeze
   Bearing the bleat of ewe and wether
Over the heath from Rington Leas,
Where, to the hymn of birds and bees,
You taught me Romany 'neath the trees,—
    Gypsy Heather!

Another reason that makes it necessary for me to touch upon the inland part of East Anglia is that I have certain remarks to make upon what are called 'the Omarian poems of Mr. Watts-Dunton.' Although, as I have before hinted, St. Ives, being in Hunts, belongs topographically to the East Midlands, its sympathies are East Anglian. This perhaps is partly because it is the extreme east of Hunts, and partly because the mouth of the Ouse is at Lynn : to those whom Mr. Norris affectionately calls St. Ivians and Hemingfordians, the seaside means Yarmouth, Lowestoft, Cromer, Hunstanton, and the towns on the Suffolk coast. The splendour of Norfolk ale may also partly account for it. This perhaps also explains why the famous East Anglian translator of Omar Khay-yàm would seem to have been known to a few Omarians on the banks of the Ouse and Cam as soon as the great discoverer of good things, Rossetti, pounced upon it in the penny box of a second-hand bookseller. Readers of Mr. Watts-Dunton's obituary notice of F. H. Groome in the ' Athenæum ' will recall these words :—

"It was not merely upon Romany subjects that Groome found points of sympathy at ' The Pines ' during that first luncheon ; there was that other subject before mentioned, Edward FitzGerald and Omar Khay-yàm. We, a handful of Omarians of those antediluvian days, were perhaps all the more intense in our cult be-cause we believed it to be esoteric. And here was a guest who had been brought into actual personal con-tact with the wonderful old ' Fitz.' As a child of eight he had seen him, talked with him, been patted on the head by him. Groome's father, the Archdeacon of Suffolk, was one of FitzGerald's most intimate friends. This was at once a delightful and a powerful link between Frank Groome and those at the luncheon table ; and when he heard, as he soon did, the toast to ' Omar Khay-yàm,' none drank that toast with more gusto than he. The fact is, as the Romanies say, true friendship, like true love, is apt to begin at first sight."

This is the poem alluded to : it is entitled, ' Toast to Omar Khayyàm : An East Anglian echo-chorus in-

scribed to old Omarian Friends in memory of happy days
by Ouse and Cam ' :—

CHORUS

In this red wine, where memory's eyes seem glowing,
  And days when wines were bright by Ouse and Cam,
And Norfolk's foaming nectar glittered, showing
What beard of gold John Barleycorn was growing,
We drink to thee, right heir of Nature's knowing,
    Omar Khayyàm!

I

Star-gazer, who canst read, when Night is strowing
  Her scriptured orbs on Time's wide oriflamme,
  Nature's proud blazon : ' Who shall bless or damn ?
Life, Death, and Doom are all of my bestowing ! '
    CHORUS : Omar Khayyàm!

II

Poet, whose stream of balm and music, flowing
  Through Persian gardens, widened till it swam
  A fragrant tide no bank of Time shall dam—
Through Suffolk meads, where gorse and may were blowing,—
    CHORUS : Omar Khayyàm!

III

Who blent thy song with sound of cattle lowing,
  And caw of rooks that perch on ewe and ram,
  And hymn of lark, and bleat of orphan lamb,
And swish of scythe in Bredfield's dewy mowing ?
    CHORUS : Omar Khayyàm!

IV

'Twas Fitz, ' Old Fitz,' whose knowledge, farther going
  Than lore of Omar, ' Wisdom's starry Cham,'
  Made richer still thine opulent epigram :
Sowed seed from seed of thine immortal sowing.—
    CHORUS : Omar Khayyàm!

V

In this red wine, where Memory's eyes seem glowing,
  And days when wines were bright by Ouse and Cam,

And Norfolk's foaming nectar glittered, showing
What beard of gold John Barleycorn was growing,
We drink to thee till, hark! the cock is crowing!
    Omar Khayyàm!

It was many years after this—it was as a member of
another Omar Khayyàm Club of much greater celebrity
than the little brotherhood of Ouse and Cam—not large
enough to be called a club—that Mr. Watts-Dunton
wrote the following well-known sonnet ·—

PRAYER TO THE WINDS

On planting at the head of FitzGerald's grave two rose-trees
whose ancestors had scattered their petals over the tomb of Omar
Khayyàm.

"My tomb shall be on a spot where the north wind may strow
roses upon it."
                    OMAR KHAYYÀM TO KWÁJAH NIZAMI.

Hear us, ye winds! From where the north-wind strows
    Blossoms that crown ' the King of Wisdom's ' tomb,
    The trees here planted bring remembered bloom,
Dreaming in seed of Love's ancestral rose,
To meadows where a braver north-wind blows
    O'er greener grass, o'er hedge-rose, may, and broom,
    And all that make East England's field-perfume
Dearer than any fragrance Persia knows.

Hear us, ye winds, North, East, and West, and South !
This granite covers him whose golden mouth
    Made wiser ev'n the Word of Wisdom's King:
Blow softly over Omar's Western herald
    Till roses rich of Omar's dust shall spring
From richer dust of Suffolk's rare FitzGerald.

I must now quote another of Mr. Watts-Dunton's
East Anglian poems, partly because it depicts the weird
charm of the Norfolk coast, and partly because it illustrates that sympathy between the poet and the lower

animals which I have already noted. I have another
reason : not long ago, that good East Anglian, Mr. Rider
Haggard interested us all by telling how telepathy
seemed to have the power of operating between a dog
and its beloved master in certain rare and extraordinary
cases. When the poem appeared in the 'Saturday
Review' (December 20, 1902), it was described as 'part
of a forthcoming romance.' It records a case of telepathy between man and dog quite as wonderful as that
narrated by Mr. Rider Haggard :—

CAUGHT IN THE EBBING TIDE

The mightiest Titan's stroke could not withstand
   An ebbing tide like this. These swirls denote
   How wind and tide conspire. I can but float
To the open sea and strike no more for land.
Farewell, brown cliffs, farewell, beloved sand
   Her feet have pressed—farewell, dear little boat
   Where Gelert,[1] calmly sitting on my coat,
Unconscious of my peril, gazes bland !

All dangers grip me save the deadliest, fear :
   Yet these air-pictures of the past that glide—
   These death-mirages o'er the heaving tide—
Showing two lovers in an alcove clear,
   Will break my heart. I see them and I hear
As there they sit at morning, side by side.

THE FIRST VISION

With Raxton elms behind—in front the sea,
   Sitting in rosy light in that alcove,
   They hear the first lark rise o'er Raxton Grove ;
'What should I do with fame, dear heart?' says he.
'You talk of fame, poetic fame, to me
   Whose crown is not of laurel but of love—
   To me who would not give this little glove
On this dear hand for Shakspeare's dower in fee.

[1] A famous swimming dog belonging to the writer.

While, rising red and kindling every billow,
  The sun's shield shines 'neath many a golden spear,
To lean with you against this leafy pillow,
  To murmur words of love in this loved ear—
To feel you bending like a bending willow,
  This is to be a poet—this, my dear!'

O God, to die and leave her—die and leave
  The heaven so lately won !—And then, to know
What misery will be hers—what lonely woe !—
To see the bright eyes weep, to see her grieve
Will make me a coward as I sink, and cleave
  To life though Destiny has bid me go.
  How shall I bear the pictures that will glow
Above the glowing billows as they heave ?

One picture fades, and now above the spray
  Another shines : ah, do I know the bowers
  Where that sweet woman stands—the woodland flowers,
In that bright wreath of grass and new-mown hay—
  That birthday wreath I wove when earthly hours
Wore angel-wings,—till portents brought dismay ?

THE SECOND VISION

Proud of her wreath as laureate of his laurel,
  She smiles on him—on him, the prouder giver,
  As there they stand beside the sunlit river
Where petals flush with rose the grass and sorrel:
The chirping reed-birds, in their play or quarrel,
  Make musical the stream where lilies quiver—
  Ah! suddenly he feels her slim waist shiver.
She speaks : her lips grow grey—her lips of coral!

'From out my wreath two heart-shaped seeds are swaying,
  The seeds of which that gypsy girl has spoken—
  'Tis fairy grass, alas! the lover's token.'
She lifts her fingers to her forehead, saying,
  'Touch the twin hearts.' Says he, ''Tis idle playing':
He touches them ; they fall—fall bruised and broken.

Shall I turn coward here who sailed with Death
  Through many a tempest on mine own North Sea,
  And quail like him of old who bowed the knee—
Faithless—to billows of Genesereth ?
Did I turn coward when my very breath
  Froze on my lips that Alpine night when he
  Stood glimmering there, the Skeleton, with me,
While avalanches rolled from peaks beneath ?

Each billow bears me nearer to the verge
  Of realms where she is not—where love must wait.—
If Gelert, there, could hear, no need to urge
  That friend, so faithful, true, affectionate,
  To come and help me, or to share my fate.
Ah ! surely I see him springing through the surge.

<blockquote>
[The dog, plunging into the tide and striking
   towards him with immense strength, reaches
   him and swims round him.]
</blockquote>

Oh, Gelert, strong of wind and strong of paw
  Here gazing like your namesake, ' Snowdon's Hound,'
  When great Llewelyn's child could not be found,
And all the warriors stood in speechless awe—
Mute as your namesake when his master saw
  The cradle tossed—the rushes red around—
  With never a word, but only a whimpering sound
To tell what meant the blood on lip and jaw.

In such a strait, to aid this gaze so fond,
  Should I, brave friend, have needed other speech
Than this dear whimper ? Is there not a bond
  Stronger than words that binds us each to each ?
But Death has caught us both. 'Tis far beyond
  The strength of man or dog to win the beach.

Through tangle-weed—through coils of slippery kelp
  Decking your shaggy forehead, those brave eyes
  Shine true—shine deep of love's divine surmise
As hers who gave you—then a Titan whelp !
I think you know my danger and would help !
  See how I point to yonder smack that lies

At anchor—Go! His countenance replies.
Hope's music rings in Gelett's eager yelp!

[The dog swims swiftly away down the tide.

Now, life and love and death swim out with him!
  If he should reach the smack, the men will guess
  The dog has left his master in distress.
You taught him in these very waves to swim—
  'The prince of pups,' you said, 'for wind and limb'
  And now those lessons, darling, come to bless.

Envoy

(The day after the rescue : Gelert and I walking along the sand.)

'Twas in no glittering tourney's mimic strife,—
  'Twas in that bloody fight in Raxton Grove,
  While hungry ravens croaked from boughs above,
And frightened blackbirds shrilled the warning fife—
'Twas there, in days when Friendship still was rife,
  Mine ancestor who threw the challenge-glove
  Conquered and found his foe a soul to love,
Found friendship—Life's great second crown of life.

So I this morning love our North Sea more
  Because he fought me well, because these waves
Now weaving sunbows for us by the shore
  Strove with me, tossed me in those emerald caves
  That yawned above my head like conscious graves—
I love him as I never loved before.

In these days when so much is written about the intelligence of the lower animals, when ' Hans,' the ' thinking horse,' is ' interviewed ' by eminent scientists, the exploit of the Second Gelert is not without interest. I may, perhaps, mention a strange experience of my own. The late Betts Bey, a well-known figure in St. Peter's Port, Guernsey, had a fine black retriever, named Caro. During a long summer holiday which we spent in Guernsey, Caro became greatly attached to a friend, and Betts Bey presented him to her. He was a magnificent fellow, valiant as a lion, and a splendid diver and swimmer. He often plunged off the parapet of the bridge which spans the Serpentine. Indeed, he would have dived from any height. His intelligence was surprising. If we wished to make him understand that he was not to accompany us, we had only to say, ' Caro, we are going to church ! ' As soon as he heard the word ' church ' his barks would cease, his tail would drop, and he would look mournfully resigned. One evening, as I was writing in my room, Caro began to scratch outside the door, uttering those strange ' woof-woofs ' which were his canine language. I let him in, but he would not rest. He stood gazing at me with an intense expression, and, turning towards the door, waited impatiently. For some time I took no notice of his dumb appeal, but his excitement increased, and suddenly a vague sense of ill seemed to pass from him into my mind. Drawn half-consciously I rose, and at once with a strange half-human whine Caro dashed upstairs. I followed him. He ran into a bedroom, and there in the dark I found my friend lying unconscious. It is well-nigh certain that Caro thus saved my friend's life.

Chapter VIII

LONDON

BETWEEN Mr. Watts-Dunton and the brother who came next to him, before mentioned, there was a very great affection, although the difference between them, mentally and physically, was quite noticeable. They were articled to their father on the same day and admitted solicitors on the same day, a very unusual thing with solicitors and their sons. Mr. Watts-Dunton afterwards passed a short term in one of the great conveyancing offices in London in order to become proficient in conveyancing. His brother did the same in another office in Bedford Row; but he afterwards practised for himself. Mr. A. E. Watts soon had a considerable practice as family solicitor and conveyancer. Mr. Hake identifies him with Cyril Aylwin, but before I quote Mr. Hake's interesting account of him, I will give the vivid description of Cyril in ' Aylwin ' :—

" Juvenile curls clustered thick and short beneath his wideawake. He had at first struck me as being not much more than a lad, till, as he gave me that rapid, searching glance in passing, I perceived the little crow's feet round his eyes, and he then struck me immediately as being probably on the verge of thirty-five. His figure was slim and thin, his waist almost girlish in its fall. I should have considered him small, had not the unusually deep, loud, manly, and sonorous voice with which he had accosted Sinfi conveyed an impression of size and weight such as even big men do not often produce. This deep voice, coupled with that gaunt kind of cheek which we associate with the most demure people, produced an effect of sedateness   but in the one glance I had got from those watchful, sagacious, twinkling eyes, there was an expression quite peculiar to them, quite inscrutable, quite indescribable."

Cyril Aylwin was at first thought to be a portrait of Whistler, which is not quite so outrageously absurd as the wild conjecture that William Morris was the original of Wilderspin. Mr. Hake says :—

" I am especially able to speak of this character, who has been inquired about more than any other in the book. I knew him, I think, even before I knew Rossetti and Morris, or any of that group. He was a brother of Mr. Watts-Dunton's—Mr. Alfred Eugene Watts. He lived at Sydenham, and died suddenly, either in 1870 or 1871, very shortly after I had met him at a wedding party. Among the set in which I moved at that time he had a great reputation as a wit and humorist. His style of humour always struck me as being more American than English. While bringing out humorous things that would set a dinner table in a roar, he would himself maintain a perfectly unmoved countenance. And it was said of him, as 'Wilderspin' says of 'Cyril Aylwin,' that he was never known to laugh."[1]

After a time Mr. Watts-Dunton joined his brother, and the two practised together in London. They also lived together at Sydenham. Some time after this, how-

[1] 'Notes and Queries,' June 7, 1902.

ever, Mr. Watts-Dunton determined to abandon the law
for literature. The brothers migrated to Sydenham, because at that time Mr. Watts-Dunton pursued music
with an avidity and interest which threatened for
a time to interfere with those literary energies which it
was now his intention to exercise. At that time the
orchestral concerts at the Crystal Palace under Manns,
given every morning and every afternoon, were a great
attraction to music lovers, and Mr. Watts-Dunton,
who lived close by, rarely missed either the morning
or the afternoon concert. It was in this way that
he became steeped in German music; and afterwards, when he became intimate with Dr. F. Hueffer,
the musical critic of the 'Times,' and the exponent of
Wagner in Great Britain, he became a thorough Wag-
nerian.

It was during this time, and through the extraordinary
social attractions of his brother, that Mr. Watts-Dunton
began to move very much in London life, and saw a great
deal of what is called London society. After his brother's death he took chambers in Great James Street,
close to Mr. Swinburne, with whom he had already
become intimate. And according to Mr. Hake, in his
paper in 'T. P.'s Weekly' above quoted from, it was
here that he wrote 'Aylwin.' I have already alluded
to his record of this most interesting event :—

"I have just read," he says, "with the greatest interest the article in your number of Sept. 18, 1903, called
'How Authors Work Best.' But the following sentence
in it set me reflecting : 'Flaubert took ten years to write
and repolish "Madame Bovary," Watts-Dunton twenty
years to write, recast, and conclude "Aylwin."'" The
statement about 'Aylwin' has often been made, and in

these days of hasty production it may well be taken by the
author as a compliment ; but it is as entirely apocryphal
as that about Scott's brother having written the Waverley Novels, and as that about Bramwell Brontë having
written ' Wuthering Heights.'   As to ' Aylwin,' I happen
to be in a peculiarly authoritative position to speak upon
the genesis of this very popular book.   If any one were
to peruse the original manuscript of the story he would
find it in four different handwritings—my late father's,
and two of my brothers', but principally in mine.

Yet I can aver that it was not written by us, and also
that its composition did not take twenty years to achieve.
It was dictated to us."

Dr. Gordon Hake is mainly known as the 'parable poet,'
but as a fact he was a physician of extraordinary talent,
who had practised first at Bury St. Edmunds and afterwards at Spring Gardens, until he partly retired to be
private physician to the late Lady Ripon.   After her death
he left practice altogether in order to devote himself to
literature, for which he had very great equipments.   As
' Aylwin ' touched upon certain subtle nervous phases
it must have been a great advantage to the author to
dictate these portions of the story to so skilled and experienced a friend.   The rare kind of cerebral exaltation
into which Henry Aylwin passed after his appalling experience in the Cove, in which the entire nervous system
was disturbed, was not what is known as brain fever.   The
record of it in ' Aylwin ' is, I understand, a literal account
of a rare and wonderful case brought under the professional notice of Dr. Hake.

As physician to Rossetti, a few years after the death of
his beloved wife, Dr. Hake's services must have been
priceless to the poet-painter ; for, as is only too well

known, Rossetti's grief for the death of his wife had for some time a devastating effect upon his mind. It was one of the causes of that terrible insomnia to relieve himself from which he resorted to chloral, though later on the attacks upon him by certain foes intensified the distressing ailment. The insomnia produced fits of melancholia, an ailment, according to the skilled opinion of Dr. Hake, more difficult than all others to deal with; for when the nervous system has sunk to a certain state of depression, the mind roams over the universe, as it were, in quest of imaginary causes for the depression. This accounts for the ' cock and bull ' stories that were somewhat rife immediately after Rossetti's death about his having expressed remorse on account of his ill-treatment of his wife. No one of his intimates took the least notice of these wild and whirling words. For he would express remorse on account of the most fantastic things when the fits of melancholia were upon him; and when these fits were past he would smile at the foolish things he had said. I get this knowledge from a very high authority, Dr. Hake's son—Mr. Thomas St. E. Hake, before mentioned —who knew Rossetti intimately from 1871 until his death, having lived under the same roof with him at Cheyne Walk, Bognor and Kelmscott. After Rossetti's most serious attack of melancholia, his relations and friends persuaded him to stay with Dr. Hake at Roehampton, and it was there that the terrible crisis of his illness was passed.

It is interesting to know that in the original form of ' Aylwin ' the important part taken in the development of the story by D'Arcy was taken by Dr. Hake, under the name of Gordon, and that afterwards, when all sorts of ungenerous things were written about Rossetti, D'Arcy was substituted for Gordon in order to give the author

an opportunity of bringing out and showing the world
the absolute nobility and charm of Rossetti's character.

Among the many varieties of life which Mr. Watts-
Dunton saw at this time was life in the slums; and this
was long before the once fashionable pastime of ' slum-
ming ' was invented. The following lines in Dr. Hake's
' New Day ' allude to the deep interest that Mr. Watts-
Dunton has always shown in the poor—shown years
before the writers who now deal with the slums had
written a line. Artistically, they are not fair specimens
of Dr. Gordon Hake's verses, but nevertheless it is
interesting to quote them here :—

> Know you a widow's home ? an orphanage ?
>   A place of shelter for the crippled poor ?
> Did ever limbless men your care engage
>   Whom you assisted of your larger store ?
> Know you the young who are to early die—
>   At their frail form sinks not your heart within ?
> Know you the old who paralytic lie
>   While you the freshness of your life begin ?
> Know you the great pain-bearers who long carry
>   The bullet in the breast that does not kill ?
> And those who in the house of madness tarry,
>   Beyond the blest relief of human skill ?
> These have you visited, all these assisted,
> In the high ranks of charity enlisted.

That Mr. Watts-Dunton has retained his interest in
the poor is shown by the sonnet, ' Father Christmas
in Famine Street,' which was originally printed as ' an
appeal ' on Christmas Eve in the ' Athenæum ' :—

> When Father Christmas went down Famine Street
>   He saw two little sisters : one was trying
>   To lift the other, pallid, wasted, dying,
> Within an arch, beyond the slush and sleet.

A Corner in 'The Pines,' showing the Painted and Carved Cabinet

Pho   Poole, Putney

From out the glazing eyes a glimmer sweet
   Leapt, as in answer to the other's sighing,
   While came a murmur, 'Don't 'ee keep on crying—
I wants to die: you'll get my share to eat.'
Her knell was tolled by joy-bells of the city
Hymning the birth of Jesus, Lord of Pity,
   Lover of children, Shepherd of Compassion.
Said Father Christmas, while his eyes grew dim,
   'They do His bidding—if in thrifty fashion:
They let the little children go to Him.'

With this sonnet should be placed that entitled, 'Dickens Returns on Christmas Day':—

A ragged girl in Drury Lane was heard to exclaim: 'Dickens dead? Then will Father Christmas die too?'—June 9, 1870.

'Dickens is dead!' Beneath that grievous cry
   London seemed shivering in the summer heat;
   Strangers took up the tale like friends that meet:
'Dickens is dead!' said they, and hurried by;
Street children stopped their games—they knew not why,
   But some new night seemed darkening down the street.
   A girl in rags, staying her wayworn feet,
Cried, 'Dickens dead? Will Father Christmas die?'

City he loved, take courage on thy way!
   He loves thee still, in all thy joys and fears.
Though he whose smile made bright thine eyes of grey
   Though he whose voice, uttering thy burthened years,
   Made laughters bubble through thy sea of tears—
Is gone, Dickens returns on Christmas Day!

Let me say here, parenthetically, that 'The Pines' is so far out of date that for twenty-five years it has been famous for its sympathy with the Christmas sentiment which now seems to be fading, as this sonnet shows:—

THE CHRISTMAS TREE AT ' THE PINES.'

Life still hath one romance that naught can bury—
   Not Time himself, who coffins Life's romances—
  For still will Christmas gild the year's mischances,
If Childhood comes, as here, to make him merry—
To kiss with lips more ruddy than the cherry—
   To smile with eyes outshining by their glances
  The Christmas tree—to dance with fairy dances
And crown his hoary brow with leaf and berry.

And as to us, dear friend, the carols sung
   Are fresh as ever. Bright is yonder bough
Of mistletoe as that which shone and swung
   When you and I and Friendship made a vow
  That Childhood's Christmas still should seal each brow
Friendship's, and yours, and mine—and keep us young.

I may also quote from ' Prophetic Pictures at Venice '
this romantic description of the Rosicrucian Christmas :—

(The morning light falls on the Rosicrucian panel - picture
called ' The Rosy Scar,' depicting Christian galley - slaves on
board an Algerine galley, watching, on Christmas Eve, for the
promised appearance of Rosenkreutz, as a ' rosy phantom.' The
Lover reads aloud the descriptive verses on the frame.)

While Night's dark horses waited for the wind,
   He stood—he shone—where Sunset's fiery glaives
Flickered behind the clouds ; then, o'er the waves,
He came to them, Faith's remnant sorrow-thinned.
The Paynim sailors clustering, tawny-skinned,
   Cried, ' Who is he that comes to Christian slaves ?
  Nor water-sprite nor jinni of sunset caves,
The rosy phantom stands nor winged nor finned.'

All night he stood till shone the Christmas star ;
   Slowly the Rosy Cross, streak after streak,
Flushed the grey sky—flushed sea and sail and spar,
   Flushed, blessing every slave's woe-wasted cheek.
  Then did great Rosenkreutz, the Dew-King speak :
' Sufferers, take heart ! Christ lends the Rosy Scar.'

Chapter IX

GEORGE BORROW

IT was not until 1872 that Mr. Watts-Dunton was introduced to Borrow by Dr. Gordon Hake, Borrow's most intimate friend.

The way in which this meeting came about has been familiar to the readers of an autobiographical romance (not even yet published!) wherein Borrow appears under the name of Dereham, and Hake under the name of Gordon. But as some of these passages in a modified form have appeared in print in an introduction by Mr. Watts-Dunton to the edition of Borrow's 'Lavengro,' published by Messrs. Ward, Lock & Co., in 1893, there will be nothing incongruous in my quoting them here :—

" Great as was the difference in age between Gordon and me, there soon grew up an intimacy between us. It has been my experience to learn that an enormous deal of nonsense has been written about difference of age between friends of either sex. At that time I do not think I had one intimate friend of my own age except Rosamond, while I was on terms of something like intimacy with two or three distinguished men, each one of whom was certainly old enough to be my father. Basevi was one of these : so was Lineham. I daresay it was owing to some idiosyncrasy of mine, but the intimacy between me and the young fellows with whom I was brought into

contact was mainly confined to matters connected with
field-sports. I found it far easier to be brought into
relations of close intimacy with women of my own age
than with men. But as Basevi told me that it was
the same with himself, I suppose that this was not an
eccentricity after all. When Gordon and I were together it never occurred to me that there was any difference in our ages at all, and he told me that it was the same
with himself.

One day when I was sitting with him in his delightful
house near Roehampton, whose windows at the back
looked over Richmond Park, and in front over the wildest
part of Wimbledon Common, one of his sons came in
and said that he had seen Dereham striding across the
common, evidently bound for the house.

'Dereham !' I said. 'Is there a man in the world
I should so like to see as Dereham ? '

And then I told Gordon how I had seen him years
before swimming in the sea off Yarmouth, but had
never spoken to him.

'Why do you want so much to see him ? ' asked
Gordon.

'Well, among other things I want to see if he is a
true Child of the Open Air.'

Gordon laughed, perfectly understanding what I
meant. But it is necessary here to explain what that
meaning was.

We both agreed that, with all the recent cultivation
of the picturesque by means of watercolour landscape,
descriptive novels, 'Cook's excursions,' etc., the real
passion for Nature is as rare as ever it was—perhaps rarer.
It was, we believed, quite an affair of individual temperament : it cannot be learned ; it cannot be lost.
That no writer has ever tried to explain it shows how

little it is known. Often it has but little to do with
poetry, little with science. The poet, indeed, rarely has
it at its very highest; the man of science as rarely. I
wish I could define it. In human souls—in one, perhaps, as much as in another—there is always that instinct
for contact which is a great factor of progress; there
is always an irresistible yearning to escape from isolation,
to get as close as may be to some other conscious thing.
In most individuals this yearning is simply for contact
with other human souls; in some few it is not. There
are some in every country of whom it is the blessing, not
the bane that, owing to some exceptional power, or to
some exceptional infirmity, they can get closer to 'Natura Benigna' herself, closer to her whom we now call
'Inanimate Nature,' than to brother, sister, wife, or
friend. Darwin among English savants, and Emily
Brontë among English poets, and Sinfi Lovell among
English gypsies, showed a good deal of the characteristics of the 'Children of the Open Air.'   But in regard
to Darwin, besides the strength of his family ties, the
pedantic inquisitiveness, the methodizing pedantry of
the man of science; in Emily Brontë, the sensitivity to
human contact; and in Sinfi Lovell, subjection to the
love passion—disturbed, and indeed partially stifled, the
native instinct with which they were undoubtedly endowed. I was perfectly conscious that I belonged to
the third case of Nature-worshippers—that is, I was one
of those who, howsoever strongly drawn to Nature and
to a free and unconventional life, felt the strength of
the love passion to such a degree that it prevented my
claiming to be a genuine Child of the Open Air.
     Between the true 'Children of the Open Air' and
their fellows there are barriers of idiosyncrasy, barriers
of convention, or other barriers quite indefinable, which

they find most difficult to overpass, and, even when they succeed in overpassing them, the attempt is not found to be worth the making. For, what this kind of Nature-worshipper finds in intercourse with his fellow-men is, not the unegoistic frankness of Nature, his first love, inviting him to touch her close, soul to soul—but another ego enisled like his own—sensitive, shrinking, like his own—a soul which, love him as it may, is, nevertheless, and for all its love, the central ego of the universe to itself, the very Alcyone round whom all other Nature-worshippers revolve like the rest of the human constellations. But between these and Nature there is no such barrier, and upon Nature they lavish their love, ' a most equal love ' that varies no more with her change of mood than does the love of a man for a beautiful woman, whether she smiles, or weeps, or frowns. To them a Highland glen is most beautiful ; so is a green meadow ; so is a mountain gorge or a barren peak ; so is a South American savannah. A balmy summer is beautiful, but not more beautiful than a winter's sleet beating about the face, and stinging every nerve into delicious life.

To the ' Child of the Open Air ' life has but few ills ; poverty cannot touch him. Let the Stock Exchange rob him of his bonds, and he will go and tend sheep in Sacramento Valley, perfectly content to see a dozen faces in a year ; so far from being lonely, he has got the sky, the wind, the brown grass, and the sheep. And as life goes on, love of Nature grows, both as a cultus and a passion, and in time Nature seems ' to know him and love him ' in her turn.

Dereham entered, and, suddenly coming upon me, there was no retreating, and we were introduced.

He tried to be as civil as possible, but evidently he was much annoyed. Yet there was something in the

very tone of his voice that drew my heart to him, for to
me he was the hero of my boyhood still. My own shyness was being rapidly fingered off by the rough handling
of the world, but his retained all the bloom of youth, and
a terrible barrier it was; yet I attacked it manfully. I
knew from his books that Dereham had read but little
except in his own out-of-the-way directions; but then,
unfortunately, like all specialists, he considered that in
these his own special directions lay all the knowledge that
was of any value. Accordingly, what appeared to Dere
ham as the most striking characteristic of the present age
was its ignorance. Unfortunately, too, I knew that for
strangers to talk of his own published books, or of gypsies,
appeared to him to be ' prying,' though there I should
have been quite at home. I knew, however, from his
books that in the obscure English pamphlet literature
of the last century, recording the sayings and doings of
eccentric people and strange adventures, Dereham was
very learned, and I too chanced to be far from ignorant
in that direction. I touched on Bamfylde Moore
Carew, but without effect. Dereham evidently con
sidered that every properly educated man was familiar
with the story of Bamfylde Moore Carew in its every
detail. Then I touched upon beer, the British bruiser,
' gentility nonsense,' and other ' nonsense '; then upon
etymology—traced hoity-toityism to ' toit,' a roof—but
only to have my shallow philology dismissed with a
withering smile. I tried other subjects in the same
direction, but with small success, till in a lucky moment
I bethought myself of Ambrose Gwinett. There is a
very scarce eighteenth century pamphlet narrating the
story of Ambrose Gwinett, the man who, after having
been hanged and gibbeted for murdering a traveller with
whom he had shared a double-bedded room at a seaside

inn, revived in the night, escaped from the gibbet-irons, went to sea as a common sailor, and afterwards met on a British man-of-war the very man he had been hanged for murdering. The truth was that Gwinett's supposed victim, having been seized on the night in question with a violent bleeding at the nose, had risen and left the house for a few minutes' walk in the sea-breeze, when the press-gang captured him and bore him off to sea, where he had been in service ever since. I introduced the subject of Ambrose Gwinett, and Douglas Jerrold's play upon it, and at once the ice between us thawed and we became friends.

We all went out of the house and looked over the common. It chanced that at that very moment there were a few gypsies encamped on the sunken road opposite to Gordon's house. These same gypsies, by the by, form the subject of a charming sketch by Herkomer which appeared in the 'Graphic.' Borrow took the trouble to assure us that they were not of the better class of gypsies, the gryengroes, but basket-makers. After passing this group we went on the common. We did not at first talk much, but it delighted me to see the mighty figure, strengthened by the years rather than stricken by them, striding along between the whin bushes or through the quags, now stooping over the water to pluck the wild mint he loved, whose lilac-coloured blossoms perfumed the air as he crushed them, now stopping to watch the water wagtails by the ponds.

After the stroll we turned back and went, at Dereham's suggestion, for a ramble through Richmond Park, calling on the way at the 'Bald-Faced Stag' in Kingston Vale, in order that Dereham should introduce me to Jerry Abershaw's sword, which was one of the special

glories of that once famous hostelry.   A divine summer
day it was I remember—a day whose heat would have
been oppressive had it not been tempered every now and
then by a playful silvery shower falling from an occasional wandering cloud, whose slate-coloured body
thinned at the edges to a fringe of lace brighter than any
silver.

These showers, however, seemed, as Dereham remarked, merely to give a rich colour to the sunshine, and
to make the wild flowers in the meadows on the left
breathe more freely.   In a word, it was one of those uncertain summer days whose peculiarly English charm
was Dereham's special delight.   He liked rain, but he
liked it falling on the green umbrella (enormous, shaggy,
like a gypsy-tent after a summer storm) he generally
carried.   As we entered the Robin Hood Gate we were
confronted by a sudden weird yellow radiance, magical
and mysterious, which showed clearly enough that in the
sky behind us there was gleaming over the fields and
over Wimbledon Common a rainbow of exceptional
brilliance, while the raindrops sparkling on the ferns
seemed answering every hue in the magic arch far away.
Dereham told us some interesting stories of Romany
superstition in connection with the rainbow—how, by
making a ' trus'hul ' (cross) of two sticks, the Romany chi
who ' pens the dukkerin can wipe the rainbow out of the
sky,' etc.   Whereupon Gordon, quite as original a man
as Dereham, and a humourist of a rarer temper, launched
out into a strain of wit and whim, which it is not my
business here to record, upon the subject of the ' Spirit
of the Rainbow ' which I, as a child, went out to find.

Dereham loved Richmond Park, and he seemed to
know every tree.   I found also that he was extremely
learned in deer, and seemed familiar with every dappled

coat which, washed and burnished by the showers, seemed to shine in the sun like metal. Of course, I observed him closely, and I began to wonder whether I had encountered, in the silvery-haired giant striding by my side, with a vast umbrella under his arm, a true 'Child of the Open Air.'

'Did a true Child of the Open Air ever carry a gigantic green umbrella that would have satisfied Sarah Gamp herself?' I murmured to Gordon, while Dereham lingered under a tree and, looking round the Park, said in a dreamy way, 'Old England! Old England!?'

It was the umbrella, green, manifold and bulging, under Dereham's arm, that made me ask Gordon, as Dereham walked along beneath the trees, 'Is he a genuine Child of the Open Air?' And then, calling to mind the books he had written, I said: 'He went into the Dingle, and lived alone—went there, not as an experiment in self-education, as Thoreau went and lived by Walden Pond. He could enjoy living alone, for the 'horrors' to which he was occasionally subject did not spring from solitary living. He was never disturbed by passion as was the Nature-worshipper who once played such selfish tricks with Sinfi Lovell, and as Emily Brontë would certainly have been had she been placed in such circumstances as Charlotte Brontë placed Shirley.'

'But the most damning thing of all,' said Gordon, 'is that umbrella, gigantic and green: a painful thought that has often occurred to me.'

'Passion has certainly never disturbed his nature-worship,' said I. 'So devoid of passion is he that to depict a tragic situation is quite beyond his powers. Picturesque he always is, powerful never. No one reading an account of the privations of the hero of this story finds himself able to realize from Dereham's description the misery of a young man tenderly reared, and with all the pride of an East Anglian gentleman, living on bread and water in a garret, with starvation staring him in the face. It is not passion,' I said to Gordon, ' that prevents Dereham from enjoying the peace of the Nature-worshipper. It is Ambition ! His books show that he could never cleanse his stuffed bosom of the perilous stuff of ambition. To become renowned, judging from many a peroration in his books, was as great an incentive to Dereham to learn languages as to Alexander Smith's poet-hero it was an incentive to write poetry.'

' Ambition and the green gamp,' said Gordon· ' But look, the rainbow is fading from the sky without the intervention of gypsy sorceries; and see how the ferns are changing colour with the change in the light.'

But I soon found that if Dereham was not a perfect Child of the Open Air, he was something better : a man of that deep sympathy with human kind which the ' Child of the Open Air ' must needs lack.

Knowing Dereham's extraordinary shyness and his great dislike of meeting strangers, Gordon, while Dereham was trying to get as close to the deer as they would allow, expressed to me his surprise at the terms of cordial friendship that sprang up between us during that walk. But I was not surprised : there were several reasons why Dereham should at once take to me—reasons that had nothing whatever to do with any inherent attractiveness of my own.

By recalling what occurred I can throw a more brilliant light upon Dereham's character than by any kind of analytical disquisition.

Two herons rose from the Ponds and flew away to where they probably had their nests. By the expression on Dereham's face as he stood and gazed at them, I knew that, like myself, he had a passion for herons.

'Were there many herons around Whittlesea Mere before it was drained ? ' I said.

'I should think so,' said he dreamily, 'and every kind of water bird.'

Then, suddenly turning round upon me with a start, he said, 'But how do you know that I knew Whittlesea Mere ? '

'You say in one of your books that you played among the reeds of Whittlesea Mere when you were a child.'

'I don't mention Whittlesea Mere in any of my books,' he said.

'No,' said I, 'but you speak of a lake near the old State prison at Norman Cross, and that was Whittlesea Mere.'

'Then you know Whittlesea Mere ? ' said Dereham, much interested.

'I know the place that was Whittlesea Mere before it was drained,' I said, 'and I know the vipers around Norman Cross, and I think I know the lane where you first met that gypsy you have immortalized. He was a generation before my time. Indeed, I never was thrown much across the Petulengroes in the Eastern Counties, but I knew some of the Hernes and the Lees and the Lovells.'

I then told him what I knew about Romanies and vipers, and also gave him Marcianus's story about the Moors being invulnerable to the viper's bite, and about their putting the true breed of a suspected child to the test by setting it to grasp a viper—as he, Dereham, when a child, grasped one of the vipers of Norman Cross.

'The gypsies,' said Dereham, 'always believed me

to be a Romany. But surely you are not a Romany Rye ? '

' No,' I said, ' but I am a student of folk-lore ; and besides, as it has been my fortune to see every kind of life in England, high and low, I could not entirely neglect the Romanies, could I ? '

' I should think not,' said Dereham indignantly. ' But I hope you don't know the literary class among the rest.'

' Gordon is my only link to that dark world,' I said, ' and even you don't object to Gordon. I am purer than he, purer than you, from the taint of printers' ink.'

He laughed. ' Who are you ? '

' The very question I have been asking myself ever since I was a child in short frocks,' I said, ' and have never yet found an answer. But Gordon agrees with me that no well-bred soul should embarrass itself with any such troublesome query.'

This gave a chance to Gordon, who in such local reminiscences as these had been able to take no part. The humorous mystery of Man's personality had often been a subject of joke between him and me in many a ramble in the Park and elsewhere. At once he threw himself into a strain of whimsical philosophy which partly amused and partly vexed Dereham, who stood waiting to return to the subject of the gypsies and East Anglia.

' ' You are an Englishman ? ' said Dereham.

' Not only an Englishman, but an East Englishman,' I said, using a phrase of his own in one of his books—' if not a thorough East Anglian, an East Midlander ; who, you will admit, is nearly as good.'

' Nearly,' said Dereham.

And when I went on to tell him that I once used to drive a genuine ' Shales mare,' a descendant of that same famous Norfolk trotter who could trot fabulous miles an hour, to whom he with the Norfolk farmers raised his hat in reverence at the Norwich horse fair ; and when I promised to show him a portrait of this same East Anglian mare with myself behind her in a dogcart—an East Anglian dogcart ; when I praised the stinging salt-ness of the sea water off Yarmouth, Lowestoft, and Cromer, the quality which makes it the best, the most buoyant, the most delightful of all sea-water to swim in ; when I told him that the only English river in which you could see reflected the rainbow he loved was ' the glassy Ouse ' of East Anglia, and the only place in England where you could see it reflected in the wet sand was the Norfolk coast ; and when I told him a good many things showing that I was in very truth, not only an Englishman, but an East Englishman, my conquest of Dereham was complete, and from that moment we became friends.

Gordon meanwhile stood listening to the rooks in the distance. He turned and asked Dereham whether he had never noticed a similarity between the kind of muffled rattling roar made by the sea waves upon a distant pebbly beach and the sound of a large rookery in the distance.

' It is on sand alone,' said Dereham, ' that the sea strikes its true music—Norfolk sand ; a rattle is not music.'

' The best of the sea's lutes,' I said, ' is made by the sands of Cromer.' "

These famous walks with Borrow (or Dereham, as he is called in the above quotation) in Richmond Park and

the neighbourhood, have been thus described by the
'Gordon' of the story in one of the sonnets in
'The New Day' :—

> And he the walking lord of gipsy lore !
>   How often 'mid the deer that grazed the park,
> Or in the fields and heath and windy moor,
>   Made musical with many a soaring lark,
> Have we not held brisk commune with him there,
>   While Lavengro, there towering by your side,
> With rose complexion and bright silvery hair,
>   Would stop amid his swift and lounging stride
> To tell the legends of the fading race—
>   As at the summons of his piercing glance,
> Its story peopling his brown eyes and face,
>   While you called up that pendant of romance
> To Petulengro with his boxing glory,
> Your Amazonian Sinfi's noble story !

In the ' Encyclopædia Britannica ' and in Chambers'
' Cyclopædia of English Literature,' and scattered
through scores of articles in the ' Athenæum,' I find
descriptions of Borrow and allusions to him without
number. They afford absolutely the only portrait of
that wonderful man that exists or is ever likely to exist.
But, of course, it is quite impossible for me to fill my
pages with Borrow when there are so many more important figures waiting to be introduced. Still, I must
find room for the most brilliant little Borrow scene of all,
for it will flush these pages with a colour which I feel
they need. Mr. Watts-Dunton has been described as the
most picturesque of all living writers, whether in verse
or in prose, and it is not for me to gainsay that judgment ;
but never, I think, is he so picturesque as when he is writing about Borrow.

I am not quite clear as to where the following picture of

gypsy life is to be localized ; but the scenery seems to be that of the part of England where East Anglia and the Midlands join.   It adds interest to the incident to know that the beautiful gypsy girl was the prototype of Rhona Boswell, and that Dereham is George Borrow.   This also is a chapter from the unpublished story before mentioned, which was afterwards modified to be used in an introductory essay to another of Borrow's books :—

" It was in the late summer, just before the trees were clothed with what Dereham called ' gypsy gold,' and the bright green of the foliage showed scarcely a touch of bronze—at that very moment, indeed, when the spirits of all the wild flowers that have left the commons and the hedgerows seem to come back for an hour and mingle their half-forgotten perfumes with the new breath of calamint, ground ivy, and pimpernel.   Dereham gave me as hearty a greeting as so shy a man could give.   He told me that he was bound for a certain camp of gryengroes, old friends of his in his wandering days.   In conversation I reminded him of our previous talk, and I told him I chanced at that very moment to have in my pocket a copy of the volume of Matthew Arnold in which appears ' The Scholar-Gypsy.'   Dereham said he well remembered my directing his attention to ' The Scholar-Gypsy.' After listening attentively to it, Dereham declared that there was scarcely any latter-day poetry worth reading, and also that, whatever the merits of Matthew Arnold's poem might be, from any supposed artistic point of view, it showed that Arnold had no conception of the Romany temper, and that no gypsy could sympathise with it, or even understand its motive in the least degree.   I challenged this, contending that howsoever Arnold's classic language might soar above a gypsy's intelligence, the motive was so clearly developed that the most illiterate person could grasp it.

'I wish,' said Dereham, 'you would come with me to the camp and try the poem upon the first intelligent gypsy woman we meet at the camp. As to gypsy men,' said he, 'they are too prosaic to furnish a fair test.'

We agreed, and as we were walking across the country Dereham became very communicative, and talked very volubly upon gentility-nonsense, and many other pet subjects of his. I already knew that he was no lover of the aristocracy of England, or, as he called them, the 'trumpery great,' although in other regards he was such a John Bull. By this time we had proceeded a good way on our little expedition. As we were walking along, Dereham's eyes, which were as long-sighted as a gypsy's, perceived a white speck in a twisted old hawthorn-bush some distance off. He stopped and said : 'At first I thought that white speck in the bush was a piece of paper, but it's a magpie,'—next to the water-wagtail, the gypsies' most famous bird. On going up to the bush we discovered a magpie couched among the leaves. As it did not stir at our approach, I said to him : 'It is wounded—or else dying—or is it a tamed bird escaped from a cage ?' 'Hawk !' said Dereham laconically, and turned up his face and gazed into the sky. 'The magpie is waiting till the hawk has caught his quarry and made his meal. I fancied he has himself been 'chivvied' by the hawk, as the gypsies would say.'

And there, sure enough, beneath one of the silver clouds that speckled the dazzling blue, a hawk—one of the kind which takes its prey in the open rather than in the thick woodlands—was wheeling up and up, trying its best to get above a poor little lark in order to swoop at

and devour it. That the magpie had seen the hawk and
had been a witness of the opening of the tragedy of the
lark was evident, for in its dread of the common foe of all
well-intentioned and honest birds, it had forgotten its
fear of all creatures except the hawk. Man, in such a
crisis as this, it looked upon as a protecting friend.

As we were gazing at the bird a woman's voice at our
elbows said,—

'It's lucky to chivvy the hawk what chivvies a magpie. I shall stop here till the hawk's flew away.'

We turned round, and there stood a fine young
gypsy woman, carrying, gypsy fashion, a weakly child
that in spite of its sallow and wasted cheek proclaimed
itself to be hers. By her side stood a young gypsy girl.
She was beautiful—quite remarkably so—but her beauty
was not of the typical Romany kind. It was, as I afterwards learned, more like the beauty of a Capri girl.

She was bareheaded — there was not even a gypsy
handkerchief on her head—her hair was not plaited, and
was not smooth and glossy like a gypsy girl's hair, but
flowed thick and heavy and rippling down the back of
her neck and upon her shoulders. In the tumbled tresses
glittered certain objects, which at first sight seemed to
be jewels. They were small dead dragonflies, of the
crimson kind called 'sylphs.'

To Dereham these gypsies were evidently well known.
The woman with the child was one of the Boswells ; I
dare not say what was her connection, if any, with ' Boswell the Great '—I mean Sylvester Boswell, the gram-
marian and ' well-known and popalated gypsy of Cod-
ling Gap,' who, on a memorable occasion, wrote so eloquently about the superiority of the gypsy mode of life
to all others, 'on the accont of health, sweetness of air,
and for enjoying the pleasure of Nature's life.'

Dereham told me in a whisper that her name was
Perpinia, and that the other gypsy, the girl of the dragonflies, was the famous beauty of the neighbourhood—
Rhona Boswell, of whom many stories had reached him
with regard to Percy Aylwin, a relative of Rosamond's
father.

After greeting the two, Dereham looked at the
weakling child with the deepest interest, and said to the
mother : ' This chavo ought not to look like that—with
such a mother as you, Perpinia ' ' And with such a
daddy, too,' said she. ' Mike's stronger for a man nor
even I am for a woman '—a glow of wifely pride passing
over her face ; ' and as to good looks, it's him as has got
the good looks, not me. But none on us can't make it
out about the chavo. He's so weak and sick he don't
look as if he belonged to Boswell's breed at all.'

' How many pipes of tobacco do you smoke in a
day ? ' said I, looking at the great black cutty pipe pro-
truding from Perpinia's finely cut lips, and seeming
strangely out of place there.

' Can't say,' said she, laughing.

' About as many as she can afford to buy,' inter-
rupted ' the beauty of the Ouse,' as Rhona Boswell was
called. ' That's all. Mike don't like her a-smokin'
He says it makes her look like a old Londra Irish woman
in Common Garding Market.'

' You must not smoke another pipe,' said I to the
mother—' not another pipe till the child leaves the breast.'

' What ? ' said Perpinia defiantly. ' As if I could live
without my pipe ! '

' Fancy Pep a-living without her baccy ! ' laughed
Rhona.

' Your child can't live with it,' said I to Perpinia.
' That pipe of yours is full of a poison called nicotine.'

'Nick what ?' said Rhona, laughing. 'That's a new kind of nick. Why, you smoke yourself!'

'Nicotine,' said I. 'And the first part of Pep's body that the poison gets into is her breast, and——'

'Gets into my burk,'[1] said Perpinia. 'Get along wi' ye.'

'Yes.'

'Do it pison Pep's milk ?' said Rhona.

'Yes.'

'That ain't true,' said Perpinia—'can't be true.'

'It is true,' said I. 'If you don't give up that pipe for a time, the child will die, or else be a ricketty thing all his life. If you do give it up, it will grow up to be as fine a gypsy as ever your husband can be.'

'Chavo agin pipe, Pep!' said Rhona.

'Lend me your pipe, Perpinia,' said Dereham, in that hail-fellow-well-met tone of his, which he reserved for the Romanies—a tone which no Romany could ever resist. And he took it gently from the woman's lips. 'Don't smoke any more till I come to the camp and see the chavo again.'

'He be's a good friend to the Romanies,' said Rhona, in an appeasing tone.

'That's true,' said the woman; 'but he's no business to take my pipe out o' my mouth for all that.'

She soon began to smile again, however, and let Dereham retain the pipe. Dereham and I then moved away towards the dusty high-road leading to the camp, and were joined by Rhona. Perpinia remained, keeping guard over the magpie that was to bring luck to the sinking child.

It was determined now that Rhona was the very

---

[1] Bosom.

person to be used as the test-critic of the Romany mind upon Arnold's poem, for she was exceptionally intelligent. So instead of going to the camp, the oddly assorted little party of three struck across the ferns, gorse, and heather towards ' Kingfisher brook,' and when we reached it we sat down on a fallen tree.

Nothing, as afterwards I came to know, delights a gypsy girl so much, in whatever country she may be born, as to listen to a story either told or read to her, and when I pulled my book from my pocket the gypsy girl began to clap her hands. Her anticipation of enjoyment sent over her face a warm glow.

Her complexion, though darker than an English girl's, was rather lighter than an ordinary gypsy's. Her eyes were of an indescribable hue; but an artist who has since then painted her portrait for me, described it as a mingling of pansy purple and dark tawny. The pupils were so large that, being set in the somewhat almond-shaped and long-eyelashed lids of her race, they were partly curtained both above and below, and this had the peculiar effect of making the eyes seem always a little contracted and just about to smile. The great size and deep richness of the eyes made the straight little nose seem smaller than it really was ; they also lessened the apparent size of the mouth, which, red as a rosebud, looked quite small until she laughed, when the white teeth made quite a wide glitter.

Before three lines of the poem had been read she jumped up and cried, ' Look at the Devil's needles ! They're come to sew my eyes up for killing their brothers.'

And surely enough a gigantic dragon-fly, whose body-armour of sky blue and jet black, and great lace-woven wings, shining like a rainbow gauze, caught the sun as he

swept dazzling by, did really seem to be attracted either
by the wings of his dead brothers or by the lights shed
from the girl's eyes.

'I dussn't set here,' said she. 'Us Romanies call this
'Dragon-fly Brook.' And that's the king o' the dragonflies : he lives here.'

As she rose she seemed to be surrounded by dragonflies of about a dozen different species of all sizes, some
crimson, some bronze, some green and gold, whirling and
dancing round her as if they meant to justify their Romany name and sew up the girl's eyes.

'The Romanies call them the Devil's needles,' said
Dereham ; 'their business is to sew up pretty girls'
eyes.

In a second, however, they all vanished, and the girl
after a while sat down again to listen to the 'lil,' as she
called the story.

Glanville's prose story, upon which Arnold's poem
is based, was read first. In this Rhona was much interested. But when I went on to read to her Arnold's
poem, though her eyes flashed now and then at the lovely
bits of description—for the country about Oxford is
quite remarkably like the country in which she was born
—she looked sadly bewildered, and then asked to have it
all read again. After a second reading she said in a medi-
tative way : 'Can't make out what the lil's all about—
seems all about nothink ! Seems to me that the pretty
sights what makes a Romany fit to jump out o' her skin
for joy makes this 'ere gorgio want to cry. What a rum
lot gorgios is surely ! '

And then she sprang up and ran off towards the
camp with the agility of a greyhound, turning round
every few moments, pirouetting and laughing aloud.

A LETTER BOX ON THE BROADS
(From an Oil Painting at 'The Pines')

' Let's go to the camp ! ' said Dereham ' That was all true about the nicotine—was it not ? '

' Partly, I think,' said I, ' but not being a medical man I must not be too emphatic. If it is true it ought to be a criminal offence for any woman to smoke in excess while she is suckling a child.'

' Say it ought to be a criminal offence for a woman to smoke at all,' growled Dereham. ' Fancy kissing a woman's mouth that smelt of stale tobacco—pheugh ! ' ' "

After giving these two delightful descriptions of Bor row and his environment, I will now quote Mr. Watts-Dunton's description of their last meeting :—

' The last time I ever saw Borrow was shortly before he left London to live in the country. It was, I remember well, on Waterloo Bridge, where I had stopped to gaze at a sunset of singular and striking splendour, whose gorgeous clouds and ruddy mists were reeling and boiling over the West End. Borrow came up and stood leaning over the parapet, entranced by the sight, as well he might be. Like most people born in flat districts, he had a passion for sunsets. Turner could not have painted that one, I think, and certainly my pen could not describe it ; for the London smoke was flushed by the sinking sun and had lost its dunness, and, reddening every moment as it rose above the roofs, steeples, and towers, it went curling round the sinking sun in a rosy vapour, leaving, however, just a segment of a golden rim, which gleamed as dazzlingly as in the thinnest and clearest air—a peculiar effect which struck Borrow deeply. I never saw such a sunset before or since, not even on Waterloo Bridge ; and from its association with ' the last of Borrow ' I shall never forget it.'

A TALK ON WATERLOO BRIDGE

THE LAST SIGHT OF GEORGE BORROW

We talked of 'Children of the Open Air,'
  Who once on hill and valley lived aloof,
  Loving the sun, the wind, the sweet reproof
Of storms, and all that makes the fair earth fair,
Till, on a day, across the mystic bar
  Of moonrise, came the 'Children of the Roof,'
  Who find no balm 'neath evening's rosiest woof,
Nor dews of peace beneath the Morning Star.

We looked o'er London where men wither and choke,
  Roofed in, poor souls, renouncing stars and skies,
  And lore of woods and wild wind-prophecies—
Yea, every voice that to their fathers spoke :
And sweet it seemed to die ere bricks and smoke
  Leave never a meadow outside Paradise.

While the noble music of this double valediction in poetry and prose is sounding in our ears, my readers and I, 'with wandering steps and slow,' may also fitly take our reluctant leave of George Borrow.

Chapter X

THE ACTED DRAMA

IT was during the famous evenings in Dr. Marston's house at Chalk Farm that Mr. Watts-Dunton was for the first time brought into contact with the theatrical world. I do not know that he was ever closely connected with that world, but in the set in which he specially moved at this time he seems to have been almost the only one who was a regular playgoer and first-nighter, for Rossetti's playgoing days were nearly over, and Mr. Swinburne never was a playgoer. Mr. Watts-Dunton still takes, as may be seen in his sonnet to Ellen Terry, which I shall quote, a deep interest in the acted drama and in the acting profession, although of late years he has not been much seen at the theatres. When, after a while, he and Minto were at work on the 'Examiner' Mr. Watts-Dunton occasionally, although I think rarely, wrote a theatrical critique for that paper. The only one I have had an opportunity of reading is upon Miss Neilson—not the Miss Julia Neilson who is so much admired in our day ; but the powerful, dark-eyed creole-looking beauty, Lilian Adelaide Neilson, who, after being a mill-hand and a barmaid, became a famous tragedian, and made a great impression in Juliet, and in impassioned poetical parts of that kind. The play in which she appeared on that occasion was a play by Tom Taylor, called ' Anne

Boleyn,' in which Miss Neilson took the part of the heroine. It was given at the Haymarket in February 1876. I do not remember reading any criticism in which so much admirable writing—acute, brilliant, and learned—was thrown away upon so mediocre a play. Mr. Watts-Dunton's remarks upon Miss Neilson's acting were, however, not thrown away, for the subject seems to have been fully worthy of them ; and I, who love the acted drama myself, regret that the actress's early death in 1880, robbed me of the pleasure of seeing her. She was one of the actresses whom Mr. Watts-Dunton used to meet on Sunday evenings at Marston's, and I have heard him say that her genius was as apparent in her conversation as in her acting. Miss Corkran has recently sketched one of these meetings, and has given us a graphic picture of Mr. Watts-Dunton there, contrasting his personal appearance with that of Mr. Swinburne. They must indeed have been delightful gatherings to a lover of the theatre, for there Miss Neilson, Miss Glyn, Miss Ada Cavendish, and others were to be met—met in the company of Irving, Sothern, Hermann Vezin, and many another famous actor.

That Mr. Watts-Dunton had a peculiar insight into histrionic art was shown by what occurred on his very first appearance at the Marston evenings, whither he was taken by his friend, Dr. Gordon Hake, who used to tell the following story with great humour ; and Rossetti also used to repeat it with still greater gusto. I am here again indebted to his son, Mr. Hake—who was also a friend of Dr. Marston, Ada Cavendish, and others— for interesting reminiscences of these Marston evenings which have never been published. Mr. Watts-Dunton at that time was, of course, quite unknown, except in a very small circle of literary men and artists.

Three or four dramatic critics, several poets, and two actresses, one of whom was Ada Cavendish, were talking about Irving in 'The Bells,' which was a dramatization by a writer named Leopold Lewis of the 'Juif Polonais' of Erckmann-Chatrian. They were all enthusiastically extolling Irving's acting; and this is not surprising, as all will say who have seen him in the part. But while some were praising the play, others were running it down. "What I say," said one of the admirers, "is that the motif of 'The Bells,' the use of the idea of a sort of embodied conscience to tell the audience the story and bring about the catastrophe, is the newest that has appeared in drama or fiction—it is entirely original."

"Not entirely, I think," said a voice which, until that evening, was new in the circle. They turned round to listen to what the dark-eyed young stranger, tanned by the sun to a kind of gypsy colour, who looked like William Black, quietly smoking his cigarette, had to say.

"Not entirely new?" said one. "Who was the originator, then, of the idea?"

"I can't tell you that," said the interrupting voice, "for it occurs in a very old Persian story, and it was evidently old even then. But Erckmann-Chatrian took it from a much later story-teller. They adapted it from Chamisso."

"Is that the author of 'Peter Schlemihl'?" said one.

"Yes," replied Mr. Watts-Dunton, "but Chamisso was a poet before he was a prose writer, and he wrote a rhymed story in which the witness of a murder was the sunrise, and at dawn the criminal was affected in the same way that Matthias is affected by the sledge bells. The idea that the sensorium, in an otherwise perfectly sane brain, can translate sights and sound into accusations of a crime is, of course, perfectly true, and in the play it is wonderfully given by Irving."

"Well," said Dr. Marston, "that is the best account I have yet heard of the origin of 'The Bells.'"

Then the voice of one of the disparagers of the play said: "There you are! The very core of Erckmann-Chatrian's story and Lewis's play has been stolen and spoilt from another writer. The acting, as I say, is superb—the play is rot."

"Well, I do not think so," said Mr. Watts-Dunton. "I think it a new and a striking play."

"Will you give your reasons, sir?" said Dr. Marston, in that old-fashioned courtly way which was one of his many charms.

"Certainly," said Mr. Watts-Dunton, "if it will be of any interest. You recollect Coleridge's remarks upon expectation and surprise in drama. I think it a striking play because I cannot recall any play in which the entire source of interest is that of pure expectation unadulterated by surprise. From the opening dialogue, before ever the burgomaster appears, the audience knows that a murder has been committed, and that the murderer must be the burgomaster, and yet the audience is kept in breathless suspense through pure expectation as to whether or not the crime will be brought home to him, and if brought home to him, how."

"Well," said the voice of one of the admirers of the play, "that is the best criticism of 'The Bells' I have yet heard." After this the conversation turned upon Jefferson's acting of Rip Van Winkle, and many admirable remarks fell from a dozen lips. When there was a pause in these criticisms, Dr. Marston turned to Mr. Watts-Dunton and said, "Have you seen Jefferson in 'Rip van Winkle,' sir?"

" Yes, indeed," was the reply, " many times; and I hope to see it many more times. It is wonderful. I think it lucky that I have been able to see the great exemplar of what may be called the Garrick type of actor, and the great exemplar of what may be called the Edmund Kean type of actor."

On being asked what he meant by this classification, Mr. Watts-Dunton launched out into one of those wide-sweeping but symmetrical monologues of criticism in which beginning, middle, and end, were as perfectly marked as though the improvization had been a well-considered essay—the subject being the style of acting typified by Garrick and the style of acting typified by Robson. As this same idea runs through Mr. Watts-Dunton's criticism of Got in ' Le Roi s'Amuse ' (which I shall quote later), there is no need to dwell upon it here.

" As an instance," he said, " of Jefferson's supreme power in this line of acting, one might refer to Act II. of the play, where Rip mounts the Catskill Mountains in the company of the goblins. Rip talks with the goblins one after the other, and there seems to be a dramatic dialogue going on. It is not till the curtain falls that the audience realizes that every word spoken during that act came from the lips of Rip, so entirely have Jefferson's facial expression and intonation dramatized each goblin."

Between Mr. Watts-Dunton and our great Shakespearean actress, Ellen Terry, there has been an affectionate friendship running over nearly a quarter of a century. This is not at all surprising to one who knows Miss Terry's high artistic taste and appreciation of poetry. Among the poems expressing that friendship, none is more pleasing than the sonnet that appeared in the 'Magazine of Art' to which Mr. Bernard Partridge contributed his superb drawing of Miss Terry in the part of Queen Katherine.   It is entitled, 'Queen Katherine: on seeing Miss Ellen Terry as Katherine in King Henry VIII':—

> Seeking a tongue for tongueless shadow-land,
>   Has Katherine's soul come back with power to quell
>   A sister-soul incarnate, and compel
> Its bodily voice to speak by Grief's command ?
> Or is it Katherine's self returns to stand
>   As erst she stood defying Wolsey's spell—
>   Returns with those vile wrongs she fain would tell
> Which memory bore to Eden's amaranth strand ?
>
> Or is it thou, dear friend—this Queen, whose face
>   The salt of many tears hath scarred and stung ?—
>   Can it be thou, whose genius, ever young,
> Lighting the body with the spirit's grace,
> Is loved by England—loved by all the race
>   Round all the world enlinked by Shakespeare's tongue !

With one exception I do not find any dramatic criticisms by Mr. Watts-Dunton in the 'Athenæum.'   In deed, I should not expect to find him trenching upon the domain of the greatest dramatic critic of our time, Mr. Joseph Knight.   No one speaks with greater admiration of Mr. Knight than his friend of thirty years' standing, Mr. Watts-Dunton himself; and when an essay on 'King John' was required for the series of Shakespeare essays to accompany Mr. Edwin Abbey's famous illustrations in 'Harper's Magazine,' it was Mr. Knight whom Mr. Watts-Dunton invited to discuss this important play.   The exception I allude to is the criticism of Victor Hugo's 'Le Roi s'Amuse,' which appeared in the 'Athenæum' of December 2, 1882.

The way in which it came about that Mr. Watts-

Dunton undertook for the ' Athenæum ' so important a piece of dramatic criticism is interesting. In 1882 M. Vacquerie, the editor of ' Le Rappel,' a relative of Hugo's, and a great friend of Mr. Swinburne and Mr. Watts-Dunton, together with other important members of the Hugo cenacle, determined to get up a representation of ' Le Roi s'Amuse ' on the jubilee of its first representation, since when it had never been acted. Vacquerie sent two fauteuils, one for Mr. Swinburne and one for Mr. Watts-Dunton ; and the two poets were present at that memorable representation. Long before the appointed day there was on the Continent, from Paris to St. Petersburg, an unprecedented demand for seats ; for it was felt that this was the most interesting dramatic event that had occurred for fifty years.

Consequently the editor of the ' Athenæum ' for once invited his chief literary contributor to fill the post which the dramatic editor of the paper, Mr. Joseph Knight, generously yielded to him for the occasion, and the following article appeared :—

"Paris, November 23, 1882.

"I felt that the revival, at the Theatre Français, of ' Le Roi s'Amuse,' on the fiftieth anniversary of its original production, must be one of the most interesting literary events of our time, and so I found it to be. Victor Hugo was there, sitting with his arms folded across his breast, calm but happy, in a stage box. He expressed himself satisfied and even delighted with the acting. The poet's appearance was fuller of vitality and more Olympian than ever. Between the acts he left the theatre and walked about in the square, leaning on the arm of his illustrious poet friend and family connection, Auguste

Vacquerie, to whose kindness I was indebted for a seat in the fauteuils d'orchestre, which otherwise I should have found to be quite unattainable, so unprecedented was the demand for places. It is said that a thousand francs were given for a seat. Never before was seen, even in a French theatre, an audience so brilliant and so illustrious. I did not, however, see any English face I knew save that of Mr. Swinburne, who at the end of the third act might have been seen talking to Hugo in his box. Among the most appreciative and enthusiastic of those who assisted at the representation was the French poet, who perhaps in the nineteenth century stands next to Hugo for intellectual massiveness, M. Leconte de Lisle. And I should say that every French poet and indeed every man of eminence was there.

Considering the extraordinary nature of the piece, the cast was perhaps as satisfactory as could have been hoped for. Fond as is M. Hugo of spectacular effects, and even of coups de théâtre, no other dramatist gives so little attention as he to the idiosyncrasies of actors. It is easy to imagine that Shakespeare in writing his lines was not always unmindful of an actor like Burbage. But in depicting Triboulet, Hugo must have thought as little about the specialities of Ligier, who took the part on the first night in 1832, as of the future Got, who was to take it on the second night in 1882. And the same may be said of Blanche in relation to the two actresses who successively took that part. This is, I think, exactly the way in which a dramatist should work. The contrary method is not more ruinous to drama as a literary form than to the actor's art. To write up to an actor's style destroys all true character-drawing; also it ends by writing up to the actor's mere manner, who from that moment is, as an artist, doomed. On the whole, the

performance wanted more glow and animal spirits.   The
François I of M. Mounet-Sully was full of verve, but this
actor's voice is so exceedingly rich and emotional that
the king seemed more poetic, and hence more sympathetic to the audience, than was consistent with a character who in a sense is held up as the villain of the piece.
The true villain, here, however, as in 'Torquemada,'
'Notre Dame de Paris,' 'Les Misérables,' and, indeed,
in all Hugo's characteristic works, is not an individual at
all, but Circumstance.   Circumstance placed Francis, a
young and pleasure-loving king, over a licentious court.
Circumstance gave him a court jester with a temper
which, to say the least of it, was peculiar for such times
as those.   Circumstance, acting through the agency of
certain dissolute courtiers, thrust into the king's very
bedroom the girl whom he loved and who belonged to a
class from whom he had been taught to expect subser-
vience of every kind.   The tragic mischief of the rape
follows almost as a necessary consequence.   Add to this
the fact that Circumstance contrives that the girl
Maguelonne, instead of aiding her more conscientious
brother in killing the disguised king at the bidding of
'the client who pays,' falls unexpectedly in love with
him ; while Circumstance also contrives that Blanche
shall be there ready at the very spot at the very moment
where and when she is imperatively wanted as a substituted victim ;—and you get the entire motif of 'Le Roi
s'Amuse '—man enmeshed in a web of circumstance, the
motif of 'Notre Dame de Paris,' the motif of 'Torquemada,' and, in a certain deep sense, perhaps the proper
motif in romantic drama.   For when the vis matrix of
classic drama, the supernatural interference of conscious
Destiny, was no longer available to the artist, something
akin to it—something nobler and more powerful than

the stage villain—was found to be necessary to save tragedy from sinking into melodrama. And this explains so many of the complexities of Shakespeare.

In the dramas of Victor Hugo, however, the romantic temper has advanced quite as far as it ought to advance not only in the use of Circumstance as the final cause of the tragic mischief, but in the use of the grotesque in alliance with the terrible. The greatest masters of the terrible-grotesque till we get to the German romanticists were the English dramatists of the sixteenth and the early portion of the seventeenth century, and of course by far the greatest among these was Shakespeare. For the production of the effect in question there is nothing comparable to the scenes in ' Lear ' between the king and the fool—scenes which seem very early in his life to have struck Hugo more than anything else in literature. Outside the Elizabethan dramatists, however, there can be no doubt that (leaving out of the discussion the great German masters in this line) Hugo is the greatest worker in the terrible-grotesque that has appeared since Burns. I need only point to Quasimodo and Triboulet and compare them not merely with such attempts in this line as those of writers like Beddoes, but even with the magnificent work of Mr. Browning, who though far more subtle than Hugo is without his sublimity and amazing power over chiaroscuro. Now, the most remarkable feature of the revival of ' Le Roi s'Amuse,' and that which made me above all other reasons desirous to see it, was that the character of Triboulet was to be rendered by an actor of rare and splendid genius, but who, educated in the genteel comedy of modern France and also in the social subtleties of Molière, seemed the last man in Paris to give that peculiar expression of the romantic temper which I have called the terrible-grotesque.

That M. Got's success in a part so absolutely un-
suited to him should have been as great as it was is, in
my judgment, the crowning success of his life. It is as
though Thackeray, after completing 'Philip,' had set
himself to write a romance in the style of 'Notre Dame
de Paris,' and succeeded in the attempt. Yet the success
of M. Got was relative only, I think. The Triboulet
was not the Triboulet of the reader's own imaginings,
but an admirable Triboulet of the Comédie Française.
Perhaps, however, the truth is that there is not an actor
in Europe who could adequately render such a character
as Triboulet.

This is what I mean : all great actors are divisible into
two groups, which are by temperament and endowment
the exact opposites of each other. There are those who,
like Garrick, producing their effects by means of a self-
dominance and a conservation of energy akin to that of
Goethe in poetry, are able to render a character, coldly
indeed, but with matchless verisimilitude in its every
nuance. And there are those who, like Edmund Kean
and Robson, 'live' in the character so entirely that self-
dominance and conservation of energy are not possible,
and who, whensoever the situation becomes very intense,
work miracles of representation by sheer imaginative
abandon, but do so at the expense of that delicacy of light
and shade in the entire conception which is the great
quest of the actor as an artist. And if it should be found
that in order to render Triboulet there is requisite for
the more intense crises of the piece the abandon of
Kean and Robson, and at the same time, for the carrying
on of the play, the calm, self-conscious staying power of
Garrick, the conclusion will be obvious that Triboulet
is essentially an unactable character. I will illustrate
this by an instance. The reader will remember that in

the third act of ' Le Roi s'Amuse,' Triboulet's daughter
Blanche, after having been violated by the king at the
Louvre, rushes into the antechamber, where stands her
father surrounded by the group of sneering courtiers who,
unknown both to the king and to Triboulet, have ab-
ducted her during the night and set her in the king's way.
When the girl tells her father of the terrible wrong that
has been done to her, he passes at once from the mood
of sardonic defiance which was natural to him into a
state of passion so terrible that a sudden and magical
effect is produced : the conventional walls between him,
the poor despised court jester, and the courtiers, are suddenly overthrown by the unexpected operation of one of
those great human instincts which make the whole world
kin ·—

> TRIBOULET (faisant trois pas, et balayant du geste tous les seigneurs interdits).
>   Allez-vous-en d'ici !
>
>   Et, si le roi François par malheur se hasarde
>   A passer près d'ici, (à Monsieur de Vermandois) vous êtes de sa garde,
>   Dites-lui de ne pas entrer,—que je suis là.
> M. DE PIENNE.   On n'a jamais rien vu de fou comme cela.
> M. DE GORDES (lui faisant signe de se retirer).   Aux fous comme aux enfants
>   on cède quelque chose.
>   Veillons pourtant, de peur d'accident.   [Ils sortent.
> TRIBOULET (s'asseyant sur le fauteuil du roi et relevant sa fille.) Allons, cause.
>   Dis-moi tout. (Il se retourne, et, apercevant Monsieur de Cossé, qui est
>   resté, il se lève à demi en lui montrant la porte). M'avez-vous en
>   tendu, monseigneur ?
> M. DE COSSÉ (tout en se retirant comme subjugué par l'ascendant du bouffon).
>   Ces fous, cela se croit tout permis, en honneur !
>   [Il sort.

Now in reading ' Le Roi s'Amuse,' startling as is the
situation, it does not seem exaggerated, for Victor Hugo's
lines are adequate in simple passion to effect the dramatic
work, and the reader feels that Triboulet was wrought
up to the state of exaltation to which the lines give ex-

pression, that nothing could resist him, and that the proud courtiers must in truth have cowered before him in the manner here indicated by the dramatist.   In literature the artist does not actualize ; he suggests, and leaves the reader's imagination free.   But an actor has to actualize this state of exaltation—he has to bring the physical condition answering to the emotional condition before the eyes of the spectator ; and if he fails to display as much of the ' fine frenzy ' of passion as is requisite to cow and overawe a group of cynical worldlings, the situation becomes forced and unnatural, inasmuch as they are overawed without a sufficient cause.   That an actor like Robson could and would have risen to such an occasion no one will doubt who ever saw him (for he was the very incarnation of the romantic temper), but then the exhaustion would have been so great that it would have been impossible for him to go on bearing the entire weight of this long play as M. Got does.   The actor requires, as I say, the abandon characteristic of one kind of histrionic art together with the staying power characteristic of another.   Now, admirable as is M. Got in this and in all scenes of ' Le Roi s'Amuse,' he does not pass into such a condition of exalted passion as makes the retirement of the courtiers seem probable.   For artistic perfection there was nothing in the entire representation that surpassed the scenes between Saltabadil and Maguelonne in the hovel on the banks of the Seine.   It would be difficult, indeed, to decide which was the more admirable, the Saltabadil of M. Febvre or the Maguelonne of Jeanne Samary.

AT THE THÉÂTRE FRANÇAIS

NOVEMBER 22, 1882

Poet of pity and scourge of sceptred crime
Titan of light, with scarce the gods for peers—

What thoughts come to thee through the mist of years
There sitting calm, master of Fate and Time ?
Homage from every tongue, from every clime,
    In place of gibes, fills now thy satiate ears.
    Mine own heart swells, mine eyelids prick with tears
In very pride of thee, old man sublime !

And thou, the mother who bore him, beauteous France,
    Round whose fair limbs what web of sorrow is spun !—
I see thee lift thy tear-stained countenance—
    Victress by many a victory he hath won ;
I hear thy voice o'er winds of Fate and Chance
    Say to the conquered world : ' Behold my son ! '

I may mention here that Mr. Watts-Dunton has always shown the greatest admiration of the actor's art and the greatest interest in actors and actresses. He has affirmed that ' the one great art in which women are as essential as men—the one great art in which their place can never be supplied by men—is in the acted drama, which the Greeks held in such high esteem that Æschylus and Sophocles acted as stage managers and showmasters, although the stage mask dispensed with much of the necessity of calling in the aid of women.'

' Great as is the importance of female poets,' says Mr. Watts-Dunton, ' men are so rich in endowment, that literature would be a worthy expression of the human mind if there had been no Sappho and no Emily Brontë —no Mrs. Browning—no Christina Rossetti. Great as is the importance of female novelists, men again are so rich in endowment that literature would be a worthy expression of the human mind if there had been no Georges Sand, no Jane Austen, no Charlotte Brontë, no George Eliot, no Mrs. Gaskell, no Mrs. Craigie. As to painting and music, up to now women have not been notable workers in either of these departments, notwithstanding Rosa Bonheur and one or two others. But, to say nothing of France, what in England would have been the acted drama, whether in prose or verse, without Mrs. Siddons, Mrs. Hermann Vezin, Adelaide Neilson, Miss Glyn, in tragedy; without Mrs. Bracegirdle, Kitty Clive, Julia Neilson, Ellen Terry, Irene Vanbrugh and Ada Rehan in comedy?'

People who run down actresses should say at once that the acted drama is not one of the fine arts at all. Mr. Watts-Dunton has often expressed the opinion that there is in England a great waste of histrionic endowment among women, owing to the ignorant prejudice against the stage which even now is prevalent in England. 'An enormous waste of force,' says he, 'there is, of course, in other departments of intellectual activity, but nothing like the waste of latent histrionic powers among Englishwomen.' And he supplies many examples of this which have come under his own observation, among which I can mention only one.

'Some years ago,' he said to me, 'I was invited to go to see the performance of a French play given by the pupils of a fashionable school in the West End of London. Apart from the admirable French accent of the girls I was struck by the acting of two or three performers who showed some latent dramatic talent. I have always taken an interest in amateur dramatic performances, for a reason that Lady Archibald Campbell in one of her writings has well discussed, namely, that what the amateur actor or actress may lack in knowledge of stage traditions he or she will sometimes more than make up for by the sweet flexibility and abandon of nature. The amateur will often achieve that rarest of all artistic excellencies, whether in poetry, painting, sculpture, music, or histrionics—

naïveté : a quality which in poetry is seen in its perfection in the finest of the writings of Coleridge ; in acting, it is perhaps seen in its perfection in Duse. Now, on the occasion to which I refer, one of these schoolgirl actresses achieved, as I thought, and as others thought with me, this rare and perfect flower of histrionics ; and when I came to know her I found that she joined wide culture and an immense knowledge of Shakespeare, Corneille, Racine, and Molière with an innate gift for rendering them. In any other society than that of England she would have gone on the stage as a matter of course, but the fatal prejudice about social position prevented her from following the vocation that Nature intended for her. Since then I have seen two or three such cases, not so striking as this one, but striking enough to make me angry with Philistinism.'

With this sympathy for histrionic art, it is not at all surprising that Mr. Watts-Dunton took the greatest interest in the open-air plays organized by Lady Archibald Campbell at Coombe. I have seen a brilliant description of these plays by him which ought to have been presented to the public years ago. It forms, I believe, a long chapter of an unpublished novel. Turning over the pages of Davenport Adams's ' Dictionary of the Drama,' which every lover of the theatre must regret he did not live to complete, I come accidentally upon these words : " One of the most recently printed epilogues is that which Theodore Watts-Dunton wrote for an amateur performance of Banville's ' Le Baiser ' at Coombe, Surrey, in August, 1889." And this reminds me that I ought to quote this famous epilogue here ; for Professor Strong in his review of ' The Coming of Love ' in ' Literature ' speaks of the amazing command over metre and colour and story displayed in the poem. It is, I believe, the only poem in the English language in which an elaborate story is fully told by poetic suggestion instead of direct statement.

A REMINISCENCE OF THE OPEN-AIR PLAYS.

Epilogue for the open-air performance of Banville's 'Le Baiser, in which Lady Archibald Campbell took the part of ' Pierrot ' and Miss Annie Schletter the part of the ' Fairy.'—Coombe, August 9, 1889.

To Pierrot in Love
The Clown whose kisses turned a Crone to a Fairy-queen

What dost thou here in Love's enchanted wood,
 Pierrot, who once wert safe as clown and thief—
Held safe by love of fun and wine and food—
 From her who follows love of Woman, Grief—
Her who of old stalked over Eden-grass
 Behind Love's baby-feet—whose shadow threw
On every brook, as on a magic glass,
Prophetic shapes of what should come to pass
 When tears got mixt with Paradisal dew ?

Kisses are loved but for the lips that kiss
 Thine have restored a princess to her throne,
Breaking the spell which barred from fairy bliss
 A fay, and shrank her to a wrinkled crone ;
But, if thou dream'st that thou from Pantomime
 Shalt clasp an angel of the mystic moon,
Clasp her on banks of Love's own rose and thyme,
While woodland warblers ring the nuptial-chime—
 Bottom to thee were but a week buffoon.

When yonder fairy, long ago, was told
 The spell which caught her in malign eclipse,
Turning her radiant body foul and old,
 Would yield to some knight-errant's virgin lips,
And when, through many a weary day and night,
 She, wondering who the paladin would be
Whose kiss should charm her from her grievous plight,
Pictured a-many princely heroes bright,
 Dost thou suppose she ever pictured thee ?

'Tis true the mischief of the foeman's charm
    Yielded to thee—to that first kiss of thine.
We saw her tremble—lift a rose-wreath arm,
    Which late, all veined and shrivelled, made her pine ;
We saw her fingers rise and touch her cheek,
    As if the morning breeze across the wood,
Which lately seemed to strike so chill and bleak
Through all the wasted body, bent and weak,
    Were light and music now within her blood.

'Tis true thy kiss made all her form expand—
    Made all the skin grow smooth and pure as pearl,
Till there she stood, tender, yet tall and grand,
    A queen of Faery, yet a lovesome girl,
Within whose eyes—whose wide, new-litten eyes—
    New-litten by thy kiss's re-creation—
Expectant joy that yet was wild surprise
Made all her flesh like light of summer skies
    When dawn lies dreaming of the morn's carnation.

But when thou saw'st the breaking of the spell
    Within whose grip of might her soul had pined,
Like some sweet butterfly that breaks the cell
    In which its purple pinions slept confined,
And when thou heard'st the strains of elfin song
    Her sisters sang from rainbow cars above her—
Didst thou suppose that she, though prisoned long,
And freed at last by thee from all the wrong,
    Must for that kiss take Harlequin for lover ?

Hearken, sweet fool ! Though Banville carried thee
    To lawns where love and song still share the sward
Beyond the golden river few can see,
    And fewer still, in these grey days, can ford ;
And though he bade the wings of Passion fan
    Thy face, till every line grows bright and human,
Feathered thy spirit's wing for wider span,
And fired thee with the fire that comes to man
    When first he plucks the rose of Nature, Woman ;

And though our actress gives thee that sweet gaze
   Where spirit and matter mingle in liquid blue—
That face, where pity through the frolic plays—
   That form, whose lines of light Love's pencil drew—
That voice whose music seems a new caress
   Whenever passion makes a new transition
From key to key of joy or quaint distress—
   That sigh, when, now, thy fairy's loveliness
Leaves thee alone to mourn Love's vanished vision :

Still art thou Pierrot—naught but Pierrot ever ;
   For is not this the very word of Fate ·
' No mortal, clown or king, shall e'er dissever
   His present glory from his past estate ' ?
Yet be thou wise and dry those foolish tears ;
   The clown's first kiss was needed, not the clown,
By her, who, fired by hopes and chilled by fears,
Sought but a kiss like thine for years on years :
   Be wise, I say, and wander back to town.

Recurring to the Marston gatherings, I reproduce here, from the same unpublished story to which I have already alluded, the following interesting account of them and of other social reunions of the like kind.

" Many of those who have reached life's meridian, or passed it, will remember the sudden rise, a quarter of a cen‧ tury ago, of Rossetti, Swinburne, and William Morris— poets who seemed for a time to threaten the ascendency of Tennyson himself. Between this galaxy and the latest generation of poets there rose, culminated, and apparently set, another—the group which it was the foolish fashion to call ' the pre-Raphaelite poets,' some of whom yielded, or professed to yield, to the influence of Rossetti, some to that of William Morris, and some to that of Swinburne. Round them all, however, there was the aura of Baude- laire or else of Gautier. These—though, as in all such

cases, nature had really made them very unlike each other
—formed themselves into a set, or rather a sect, and tried
apparently to become as much like each other as possible,
by studying French models, selecting subjects more or
less in harmony with the French temper, getting up their
books after the fashion that was as much approved then
as contemporary fashions in books are approved now, and
by various other means. They had certain places of
meeting, where they held high converse with themselves.
One of these was the hospitable house, in Fitzroy Square,
of the beloved and venerable painter, Mr. Madox
Brown, whose face, as he sat smiling upon his Eisteddfod,
radiating benevolence and encouragement to the un-
fledged bards he loved, was a picture which must be
cherished in many a grateful memory now. Another
was the equally hospitable house, in the neighbourhood
of Chalk Farm, where reigned the dramatist, Westland
Marston, and where his blind poet-boy Philip lived.
Here O'Shaughnessy would come with a glow of triumph
on his face, which indicated clearly enough what he was
carrying in his pocket—something connecting him with
the divine Théophile—a letter from the Gallic Olympus
perhaps, or a presentation copy sent from the very top
of the Gallic Parnassus. It was on one of these occasions that Rossetti satirically advised one of the cenacle
to quit so poor a language as that of Shakespeare and
write entirely in French, which language Morris immediately defined as ' nosey Latin.' It is a pity that
some literary veteran does not give his reminiscences of
those Marston nights, or rather Marston mornings, for
the symposium began at about twelve and went on till
nearly six—those famous gatherings of poets, actors, and
painters, enlinking the days of Macready, Phelps, Miss
Glyn, Robert Browning, Dante Rossetti, and R. H.

Horne, with the days of poets, actors, and painters like Mr. Swinburne, Morris, and Mr. Irving. Yet these pre-Raphaelite bards had another joy surpassing even that of the Chalk Farm symposium, that of assisting at those literary and artistic feasts which Rossetti used occasionally to give at Cheyne Walk. Generosity and geniality incarnate was the mysterious poet-painter to those he loved; and if the budding bard yearned for sympathy, as he mostly does, he could get quite as much as he deserved, and more, at 16 Cheyne Walk. To say that any artist could take a deeper interest in the work of a friend than in his own seems bold, yet it could be said of Rossetti. The mean rivalries of the literary character that so often make men experienced in the world shrink away from it, found no place in that great heart. To hear him recite in his musical voice the sonnet or lyric of some unknown bard or bardling—recite it in such a way as to lend the lines the light and music of his own marvellous genius, while the bard or bardling listened with head bowed low, so that the flush on his cheek and the moisture in his eye should not be seen— this was an experience that did indeed make the bardic life ' worth living.' "

Chapter XI

DANTE GABRIEL ROSSETTI

Thou knowest that island, far away and lone,
  Whose shores are as a harp, where billows break
  In spray of music and the breezes shake
O'er spicy seas a woof of colour and tone,
While that sweet music echoes like a moan
  In the island's heart, and sighs around the lake,
  Where, watching fearfully a watchful snake,
A damsel weeps upon her emerald throne.

Life's ocean, breaking round thy senses' shore,
  Struck golden song, as from the strand of Day ·
  For us the joy, for thee the fell foe lay—
Pain's blinking snake around the fair isle's core,
  Turning to sighs the enchanted sounds that play
Around thy lovely island evermore.

I AM now brought to a portion of my study which may well give me pause—the relations between Mr. Watts-Dunton and Rossetti. The latest remarks upon them are, I think, the best ; they are by Mr. A. C. Benson in his monograph on Rossetti in the ' English Men of Letters ' ·—

" It would be impossible to exaggerate the value of his friendship for Rossetti. Mr. Watts-Dunton understood him, sympathized with him, and with self-denying and unobtrusive delicacy shielded him, so far as any one can be shielded, from the rough contact of the world.

It was for a long time hoped that Mr. Watts-Dunton would give the memoir of his great friend to the world, but there is such a thing as knowing a man too well to be his biographer. It is, however, an open secret that a vivid sketch of Rossetti's personality has been given to the world in Mr. Watts-Dunton's well-known romance 'Aylwin,' where the artist D'Arcy is drawn from Rossetti   Though singularly independent in judgment, it is clear that, at all events in the later years of his life, Rossetti's taste was, unconsciously, considerably affected by the critical preferences of Mr. Watts-Dunton. I have heard it said by one[1] who knew them both well that it was often enough for Mr. Watts-Dunton to express a strong opinion for Rossetti to adopt it as his own, even though he might have combated it for the moment.

At the end of each part [of 'Rose Mary'] comes a curious lyrical outburst called the Beryl-songs, the chant of the imprisoned spirits, which are intended to weld the poem together and to supply connections. It is said that Mr. Watts-Dunton, when he first read the poem in proof, said to Rossetti that the drift was too intricate for an ordinary reader. Rossetti took this to heart, and wrote the Beryl-songs to bridge the gaps ; Mr. Watts-Dunton, on being shown them, very rightly disapproved, and said humorously that they turned a fine ballad into a bastard opera. Rossetti, who was ill at the time, was so much disconcerted and upset at the criticism, that Mr. Watts-Dunton modified his judgment, and the interludes were printed. But at a later day Rossetti himself

[1] I think I am not far wrong in saying that he whom Mr. Benson heard make this remark was a more illustrious poet than even D. G. Rossetti, the greatest poet indeed of the latter half of the nineteenth century, the author of ' Erechtheus ' and ' Atalanta in Calydon.'

came round to the opinion that they were inappropriate. They are curiously wrought, rhapsodical, irregular songs, with fantastic rhymes, and were better away. . . .

Then he began to settle down into the production of the single-figure pictures, of which Mr. Watts-Dunton wrote that 'apart from any question of technical short-comings, one of Rossetti's strongest claims to the attention of posterity was that of having invented, in the three-quarter length pictures painted from one face, a type of female beauty which was akin to none other, which was entirely new, in short—and which, for wealth of sublime and mysterious suggestion, unaided by complex dramatic design, was unique in the art of the world."

It is well known that Rossetti wished his life—if written at all—to be written by Mr. Watts-Dunton, unless his brother should undertake it. It is also well known that the brother himself wished it, but pressure of other matters prevented Mr. Watts-Dunton from undertaking it. I expected difficulties in approaching with regard to the delicate subject of his relations with Rossetti, but I was not prepared to find them so great as they have proved to be. When I wrote to him and asked him whether the portrait of D'Arcy in 'Aylwin' was to be accepted as a portrait of Rossetti, and when I asked him to furnish me with some materials and facts to form the basis of this chapter, I received from him the following letter ·—

"MY DEAR MR. DOUGLAS,—I have never myself affirmed that D'Arcy was to be taken as an actual portrait of Rossetti. Even if I thought that a portrait of him could be given in any form of imaginative literature,

PANDORA.

I have views of my own as to the propriety of giving actual portraits of men with whom a novelist or poet has been brought into contact. It is quite impossible for an imaginative writer to avoid the imperious suggestions of his memory when he is conceiving a character. Thousands of times in a year does one come across critical remarks upon the prototypes of the characters of such great novelists as Scott, Dickens, Thackeray, the Brontës, George Eliot, George Meredith, Thomas Hardy, and the rest. And I believe that every one of these writers would confess that his prominent characters were suggested to him by living individuals or by individuals who figure in history—but suggested only. And as to the ethics of so dealing with friends and acquaintances I have also views of my own. These are easily stated. The closer the imaginative writer gets to the portrait of a friend, or even of an acquaintance, the more careful must he be to set his subject in a genial and even a generous light. It would be a terrible thing if every man who has been a notable figure in life were to be represented as this or that at the sweet will of everybody who has known him. Generous treatment, I say, is demanded of every writer who makes use of the facets of character that have struck him in his intercourse with friend or acquaintance. I will give you an instance of this. When I drew De Castro in ' Aylwin ' I made use of my knowledge of a certain individual. Now this individual, although a man of quite extraordinary talents, brilliance, and personal charm, bore not a very good name, because he was driven to live upon his wits. He had endowments so great and so various that I cannot conceive any line of life in which he was not fitted to excel—but it was his irreparable misfortune to have been trained to no business and no profession, and to have been

thrown upon the world without means, and without
useful family connections. Such a man must either
sink beneath the oceanic waves of London life, or he
must make a struggle to live upon his wits. This individual made that struggle—he struck out with a vigour
that, as far as I know, was without example in London
society. He got to know, and to know intimately, men
like Ruskin, G. F. Watts, D. G. Rossetti, Mr. W. M.
Rossetti, William Morris, Mr. Swinburne, Sir Edward
Burne Jones, Cruikshank, and I know not what important
people besides. When he was first brought into touch
with the painters, he knew nothing whatever of art ; in
two or three years, as I have heard Rossetti say, he was a
splendid ' connoisseur.' If he had been brought up as
a lawyer he must have risen to the top of the profession.
If he had been brought up as an actor he must, as I have
heard a dramatist say, have risen to the top. But from
his very first appearance in London he was driven to live
upon his wits. And here let me say that this man, who
was a bitter unfriend of my own, because I was compelled to stand in the way of certain dealings of his, but
whom I really could have liked if he had not been obliged
to live upon his wits at the expense of certain friends of
mine, formed the acquaintance of the great men I have
enumerated, not so much from worldly motives, as I
believe, as from real admiration. But being driven to
live upon his wits, he had not sufficient moral strength
to afford a conscience, and the queerest stories were told
—some of them true enough—of his dealings with those
great men. Whistler's anecdotes of him at one period
set many a table in a roar ; and yet so winsome was the
man that after a time he became as intimate with Whistler as ever. If he had possessed a private income, and if
that income had been carefully settled upon him, I be-

lieve he would have been one of the most honest of men ;
I know he would have been one of the most generous.
His conduct to the late Treffry Dunn, from whom he
could not have expected the least return except that of
gratitude, was proof enough of his generosity. Of course
to make use of so strange a character as this was a great
temptation to me when I wrote ' Aylwin.' But in what
has been called my ' thumb-nail portrait of him,' I
treated the peccadilloes attributed to him in a playful
and jocose way. It would have been quite wrong to
have painted otherwise than in playful colours a character
like this. Like every other man and woman in this
world, he left behind him people who believed in
him and loved him. It would have been cruel to wound
these, and unfair to the man ; and yet because I
gave only a slight suggestion of his sublime quackery
and supreme blarney, a writer who also knew something
about him, but of course not a thousandth part of what
I knew, said that I had tried my hand at depicting him
in ' Aylwin,' but with no great success. As a matter of
fact, I did not attempt to give a portrait of him : I
simply used certain facets of his character to work out
my story, and then dismissed him. On the other hand,
where the character of a friend or acquaintance is noble,
the imagination can work more freely—as in the case of
Philip Aylwin, Cyril Aylwin, Wilderspin, Rhona Boswell, Winifred Wynne, Sinfi Lovell. And as to Rossetti, whom I have been charged by certain critics
with having idealized in my picture of D'Arcy, all I have
to say on that point is this—that if the noble and fascinating qualities which Rossetti showed had been leavened
with mean ones I should not, in introducing his character
into a story, have considered it right or fair or generous
to dwell upon those mean ones. But as a matter of

fact, during my whole intercourse with him he displayed
no such qualities.   The D'Arcy that I have painted is
not one whit nobler, more magnanimous, wide-minded,
and generous, than was D. G. Rossetti.   As I have said
on several occasions, he could and did take as deep an interest in a friend's work as in his own.   And to benefit
a friend was the greatest pleasure he had in life.   I loved
the man so deeply that I should never have introduced
D'Arcy into the novel had it not been in the hope of
silencing the misrepresentations of him that began as
soon as ever Rossetti was laid in the grave at Birchington, by depicting his character in colours as true as
they were sympathetic.   It has been the grievous fate
of Rossetti to be the victim of an amount of detraction which is simply amazing and inscrutable.   I cannot
in the least understand why this is so.   It is the great
sorrow of my life.   There is a fatality of detraction about
his name which in its unreasonableness would be gro
tesque were it not heartrending.   It would turn my
natural optimism about mankind into pessimism were it
not that another dear friend of mine—a man of equal
nobility of character, and almost of equal genius, has
escaped calumny altogether—William Morris.   This
matter is a painful puzzle to me.   The only great man
of my time who seems to have shared something of
Rossetti's fate, is Lord Tennyson.   There seems to be a
general desire to belittle him, to exaggerate such angu-
larities as were his, and to speak of that almost childlike
simplicity of character which was an ineffable charm in
him as springing from boorishness and almost from lout-
ishness.   On the other hand, another great genius, Browning, for whom I had and have the greatest admiration,
seems to be as fortunate as Morris in escaping the de-
tractor.   But I am wandering from Rossetti.   I do not

feel any impulse to write reminiscences of him. Too much has been written about him already—of late a great deal too much. The only thing written about him that has given me comfort—I may say joy, is this—it has been written by a man who knew him before I did, who knew him at the time he lost his wife. Mr. Val Prinsep, R.A., has declared that in Rossetti's relations with his wife there was nothing whatever upon which his conscience might reasonably trouble him. I do not remember the exact words, but this was the substance of them. Mr. Val Prinsep is a man of the highest standing, and he knew Rossetti intimately, and he has declared in print that Rossetti could have had no qualms of conscience in regard to his relations with his wife. This, I say, is a source of great comfort to me and to all who loved Rossetti. That he was whimsical, fanciful, and at times most troublesome to his friends, no one knows better than I do.

No one, I say, is more competent to speak of the whims and the fancies and the troublesomeness of Rossetti than I am ; and yet I say that he was one of the noblest-hearted men of his time, and lovable—most lovable."

It would be worse than idle to enter at this time of day upon the painful subject of the "Buchanan affair." Indeed, I have often thought it is a great pity that it is not allowed to die out. The only reason why it is still kept alive seems to be that, without discussing it, it is impossible fully to understand Rossetti's nervous illness, about which so much has been said. I remember seeing in Mr. Watts-Dunton's essay on Congreve in 'Chambers's Encyclopædia' a definition of envy as the 'literary leprosy.' This phrase has often been quoted in reference

to the case of Buchanan, and also in reference to a recent
and much more ghastly case between two intimate friends.
Now, with all deference to Mr. Watts-Dunton, I cannot
accept it as a right and fair definition. It is a fact no
doubt that the struggle in the world of art—whether
poetry, music, painting, sculpture, or the drama—is unlike that of the mere strivers after wealth and position,
inasmuch as to praise one man's artistic work is in a certain way to set it up against the work of another. Still,
one can realize, without referring to Disraeli's 'Curi-
osities of Literature," that envy is much too vigorous
in the artistic life. Now, whatever may have been
the good qualities of Buchanan—and I know he had
many good qualities—it seems unfortunately to be true
that he was afflicted with this terrible disease of envy.
There can be no question that what incited him to
write the notorious article in the 'Contemporary
Review' entitled 'The Fleshly School of Poetry,' was
simply envy—envy and nothing else. It was during the
time that Rossetti was suffering most dreadfully from the
mental disturbance which seems really to have originated
in this attack and the cognate attacks which appeared in
certain other magazines, that the intimacy between Mr.
Watts-Dunton and Rossetti was formed and cemented.
And it is to this period that Mr. William Rossetti alludes
in the following words : " ' Watts is a hero of friendship ' was, according to Mr. Caine, one of my brother's
last utterances, easy enough to be credited."
    That he deserved these words I think none will deny ;
and that the friendship sprang from the depths of the
nature of a man to whom the word ' friendship ' meant
not what it generally means now, a languid sentiment,
but what it meant in Shakespeare's time, a deep passion,
is shown by what some deem the finest lines Mr. Watts-

Dunton ever wrote—I mean those lines which he puts
into the mouth of Shakespeare's Friend in 'Christmas at the Mermaid,' lines part of which have been
admirably turned into Latin by Mr. E. D. Stone,[1] and
published by him in the second volume of that felicitous
series of Latin translations, 'Florilegium Latinum '·—

'MR. W. H.'

To sing the nation's song or do the deed
That crowns with richer light the motherland,
Or lend her strength of arm in hour of need
When fangs of foes shine fierce on every hand,
Is joy to him whose joy is working well—
Is goal and guerdon too, though never fame.

[1] As Mr. Swinburne has pronounced Mr. Stone's translation to
be in itself so fine as to be almost a work of genius, I will quote
it here :—

Θεῖος ἀοιδός

Felix, qui potuit gentem illustrare canendo,
quique decus patriae claris virtutibus addit
succurritque laboranti, tutamque periclis
eruit, hostilesque minas avertit acerbo
dente lacessitae ; bene, quicquid fecerit audax,
explevisse iuvat : metam tenet ille quadrigis,
praemia victor habet, quamvis tuba vivida famae
ignoret titulos, vel si flammante sagitta
oppugnet Livor quam mens sibi muniit arcem.
quod si fata mihi virtutis gaudia tantae
invideant, nec fas Anglorum extendere fines
latins, et nitidae primordia libertatis,
Anglia cui praecepit iter, cantare poetae ;
si numeris laudare meam vel marte Parentem
non mihi contingat, nec Divom adsumere vires
atque inconcessos sibi vindicet alter honores,
dignior ille mihi frater, quem iure saluto—
illum divino praestantem numine amabo.

Should find a thrill of music in his name;
Yea, goal and guerdon too, though Scorn should aim
Her arrows at his soul's high citadel

But if the fates withhold the joy from me
To do the deed that widens England's day,
Or join that song of Freedom's jubilee
Begun when England started on her way—
Withhold from me the hero's glorious power
To strike with song or sword for her, the mother,
And give that sacred guerdon to another,
Him will I hail as my more noble brother
Him will I love for his diviner dower.

Enough for me who have our Shakspeare's love
To see a poet win the poet's goal,
For Will is he; enough and far above
All other prizes to make rich my soul.
Ben names my numbers golden. Since they tell
A tale of him who in his peerless prime
Fled us ere yet one shadowy film of time
Could dim the lustre of that brow sublime,
Golden my numbers are: Ben praiseth well.

It seems to me to be needful to bear in mind these
lines, and the extremely close intimacy between these
two poet-friends in order to be able to forgive entirely
the unexampled scourging of Buchanan in the following
sonnet if, as some writers think, Buchanan was meant :—

THE OCTOPUS OF THE GOLDEN ISLES
'WHAT! WILL THEY EVEN STRIKE AT ME?'

Round many an Isle of Song, in seas serene,
  With many a swimmer strove the poet-boy,
  Yet strove in love: their strength, I say, was joy
To him, my friend—dear friend of godlike mien!
But soon he felt beneath the billowy green
  A monster moving—moving to destroy:
  Limb after limb became the tortured toy
Of coils that clung and lips that stung unseen.

"And canst thou strike ev'n me?" the swimmer said,
  As rose above the waves the deadly eyes,
  Arms flecked with mouths that kissed in hellish wise,
Quivering in hate around a hateful head.—
  I saw him fight old Envy's sorceries:
I saw him sink: the man I loved is dead!

Here we get something quite new in satire—something in which poetry, fancy, hatred, and contempt, are mingled. The sonnet appeared first in the 'Athenæum,' and afterwards in 'The Coming of Love.' If Buchanan or any special individual was meant, I doubt whether any man has a moral right to speak about another man in such terms as these.

All the friends of Rossetti have remarked upon the extraordinary influence exercised upon him by Mr. Watts-Dunton. Lady Mount Temple, a great friend of the painter-poet, used to tell how when she was in his studio and found him in a state of great dejection, as was so frequently the case, she would notice that Rossetti's face would suddenly brighten up on hearing a light footfall in the hall—the footfall of his friend, who had entered with his latch-key—and how from that moment Rossetti would be another man. Rossetti's own relatives have recorded the same influence. I have often thought that the most touching thing in Mr. W. M. Rossetti's beautiful monograph of his brother is the following extract from his aged mother's diary at Birchington-on-Sea, when the poet is dying :—

'March 28, Tuesday. Mr. Watts came down; Gabriel rallied marvellously.

This is the last cheerful item which it is allowed me to record concerning my brother; I am glad that it stands associated with the name of Theodore Watts.'

Here is another excerpt from the brother's diary ·—

'Gabriel had, just before Shields entered the draw-ing-room for me, given two violent cries, and had a con-vulsive fit, very sharp and distorting the face, followed by collapse. All this passed without my personal cog-nizance. He died 9.31 p.m.; the others—Watts, mother, Christina, and nurse, in room; Caine and Shields in and out; Watts at Gabriel's right side, partly supporting him.'

That Mr. Watts-Dunton's influence over Rossetti extended even to his art as a poet is shown by Mr. Benson's words already quoted. I must also quote the testimony of Mr. Hall Caine, who says, in his 'Recol-lections' ·—

"Rossetti, throughout the period of my acquaintance with him, seemed to me always peculiarly and, if I may be permitted to say so without offence, strangely liable to Mr. Watts' influence in his critical estimates; and the case instanced was perhaps the only one in which I knew him to resist Mr. Watts's opinion upon a matter of poetical criticism, which he considered to be almost final, as his letters to me, printed in Chapter VIII of this volume, will show. I had a striking instance of this, and of the real modesty of the man whom I had heard and still hear spoken of as the most arrogant man of genius of his day, on one of the first occasions of my seeing him. He read out to me an additional stanza to the beautiful poem 'Cloud Confines.' As he read it, I thought it very fine, and he evidently was very fond of it himself. But he surprised me by saying that he should not print it. On my asking him why, he said :

'Watts, though he admits its beauty, thinks the poem would be better without it.'

'Well, but you like it yourself,' said I.

'Yes,' he replied, 'but in a question of gain or loss to a poem I feel that Watts must be right.'

And the poem appeared in 'Ballads and Sonnets' without the stanza in question."

Here is another beautiful passage from Mr. Hall Caine's 'Recollections'—a passage which speaks as much for the writer as for the object of his enthusiasm :—

"As to Mr. Theodore Watts, whose brotherly devotion to him and beneficial influence over him from that time forward are so well known, this must be considered by those who witnessed it to be almost without precedent or parallel even in the beautiful story of literary friendships, and it does as much honour to the one as to the other. No light matter it must have been to lay aside one's own long-cherished life-work and literary ambitions to be Rossetti's closest friend and brother, at a moment like the present, when he imagined the world to be conspiring aginst him ; but through these evil days, and long after them, down to his death, the friend that clung closer than a brother was with him, as he himself said, to protect, to soothe, to comfort, to divert, to interest and inspire him—asking, meantime, no better reward than the knowledge that a noble mind and nature was by such sacrifice lifted out of sorrow. Among the world's great men the greatest are sometimes those whose names are least on our lips, and this is because selfish aims have been so subordinate in their lives to the welfare of others as to leave no time for the personal achievements that win personal distinction ; but when the world

comes to the knowledge of the price that has been paid
for the devotion that enables others to enjoy their re-
nown, shall it not reward with a double meed of grati
tude the fine spirits to whom ambition has been as nothing against fidelity of friendship.   Among the latest
words I heard from Rossetti was this · 'Watts is a hero
of friendship'; and indeed, he has displayed his capacity
for participation in the noblest part of comradeship, that
part, namely, which is far above the mere traffic that too
often goes by the name, and wherein self-love always
counts upon being the gainer.   If in the end it should
appear that he has in his own person done less than
might have been hoped for from one possessed of his
splendid gifts, let it not be overlooked that he has influenced in a quite incalculable degree, and influenced for
good, several of the foremost among those who in their
turn have influenced the age.   As Rossetti's faithful
friend and gifted medical adviser, Mr. John Marshall,
has often declared, there were periods when Rossetti's
very life may be said to have hung upon Mr. Watts'
power to cheer and soothe."

This anecdote is also told by Mr. Caine :—

" Immediately upon the publication of his first volume, and incited thereto by the early success of it, he
had written the poem ' Rose Mary,' as well as two lyrics
published at the time in ' The Fortnightly Review';
but he suffered so seriously from the subsequent assaults
of criticism, that he seemed definitely to lay aside all hope
of producing further poetry, and, indeed, to become
possessed of the delusion that he had for ever lost all
power of doing so.   It is an interesting fact, well known
in his own literary circle, that his taking up poetry afresh
was the result of a fortuitous occurrence.   After one of

his most serious illnesses, and in the hope of drawing off
his attention from himself, and from the gloomy forebodings which in an invalid's mind usually gather about
his own too absorbing personality, a friend prevailed upon
him, with infinite solicitation, to try his hand afresh at
a sonnet. The outcome was an effort so feeble as to be
all but unrecognizable as the work of the author of the
sonnets of 'The House of Life,' but, with more shrewd
ness and friendliness (on this occasion) than frankness,
the critic lavished measureless praise upon it and urged
the poet to renewed exertion. One by one, at longer or
shorter intervals, sonnets were written, and this exercise
did more towards his recovery than any other medicine,
with the result besides that Rossetti eventually regained
all his old dexterity and mastery of hand. The artifice
had succeeded beyond every expectation formed of it,
serving, indeed, the twofold end of improving the invalid's health by preventing his brooding over unhealthy
matters, and increasing the number of his accomplished works. Encouraged by such results, the friend
went on to induce Rossetti to write a ballad, and this
purpose he finally achieved by challenging the poet's
ability to compose in the simple, direct, and emphatic
style, which is the style of the ballad proper, as distin
guished from the elaborate, ornate, and condensed diction which he had hitherto worked in. Put upon his
mettle, the outcome of this second artifice practised
upon him was that he wrote 'The White Ship' and
afterwards 'The King's Tragedy.'

Thus was Rossetti already immersed in this revived
occupation of poetic composition, and had recovered a
healthy tone of body, before he became conscious of
what was being done with him. It is a further amusing
fact that one day he requested to be shown the first

sonnet which, in view of the praise lavished upon it by the friend on whose judgment he reposed, had encouraged him to renewed effort. The sonnet was bad : the critic knew it was bad, and had from the first hour of its production kept it carefully out of sight, and was now more than ever unwilling to show it. Eventually, however, by reason of ceaseless importunity, he returned it to its author, who, upon reading it, cried : ' You fraud ! You said this sonnet was good, and it's the worst I ever wrote ! ' ' The worst ever written would perhaps be a truer criticism,' was the reply, as the studio resounded with a hearty laugh, and the poem was committed to the flames. It would appear that to this occurrence we probably owe a large portion of the contents of the volume of 1881."

Mr. William Rossetti is ever eager to testify to the beneficent effect of Mr. Watts-Dunton's intimacy upon his brother ; and quite lately Madox Brown's grandson, Mr. Ford Madox Hueffer, who, from his connection with the Rossetti family, speaks with great authority, wrote : ' In 1873 came Mr. Theodore Watts, without whose practical friendship and advice, and without whose literary aids and sustenance, life would have been from thenceforth an impracticable affair for Rossetti.' Mr. Hueffer speaks of the great change that came over Rossetti's work when he wrote ' The King's Tragedy ' and ' The White Ship ' :—

" It should be pointed out that ' The White Ship ' was one of Rossetti's last works, and that in it he was aiming at simplicity of narration, under the advice of Mr. Theodore Watts. In this he was undoubtedly on the right track, and the ' rhymed chronicles ' might have disappeared had Rossetti lived long enough to revise the poem as sedulously as he did his earlier work, and to revise it with the knowledge of narrative-technique that the greater part of the poem shows was coming to be his."

It was impossible for a man of genius to live so secluded a life as Rossetti lived at Cheyne Walk and at Kelmscott for several years, without wild, unauthenticated stories getting about concerning him. Among other things Rossetti, whose courtesy and charm of manner were, I believe, proverbial, was now charged with a rudeness, or rather boorishness like that which with equal injustice, apparently, is now being attributed to Tennyson. Stories got into print about his rude bearing towards people, sometimes towards ladies of the most exalted position. And these apocryphal and disparaging legends would no doubt have been still more numerous and still more offensive, had it not been for the influence of his watchful and powerful friend. Here is an interesting letter which Rossetti addressed to the 'World,' and which shows the close relations between him and Mr. Watts-Dunton :—

" 16 CHEYNE WALK, CHELSEA, S.W.
December 28, 1878.
My attention has been directed to the following paragraph which has appeared in the newspapers : ' A very disagreeable story is told about a neighbour of Mr. Whistler's, whose works are not exhibited to the vulgar herd ; the Princess Louise in her zeal therefore, graciously sought them at the artist's studio, but was rebuffed by a ' Not at home ' and an intimation that he was not at the beck and call of princesses. I trust it is not true,' continues the writer of the paragraph, ' that so medievally minded a gentleman is really a stranger

to that generous loyalty to rank and sex, that dignified obedience,' etc.

The story is certainly disagreeable enough; but if I am pointed out as the 'near neighbour of Mr. Whistler's' who rebuffed, in this rude fashion, the Princess Louise, I can only say that it is a canard devoid of the smallest nucleus of truth. Her Royal Highness has never called upon me, and I know of only two occasions when she has expressed a wish to do so. Some years ago Mr. Theodore Martin spoke to me upon the subject, but I was at that time engaged upon an important work, and the delays thence arising caused the matter to slip through. And I heard no more upon the subject till last summer, when Mr. Theodore Watts told me that the Princess, in conversation, had mentioned my name to him, and that he had then assured her that I should feel 'honoured and charmed to see her,' and suggested her making an appointment. Her Royal Highness knew that Mr. Watts, as one of my most intimate friends, would not have thus expressed himself without feeling fully warranted in so doing; and had she called she would not, I trust, have found me wanting in that 'generous loyalty' which is due, not more to her exalted position, than to her well-known charm of character and artistic gifts. It is true that I do not run after great people on account of their mere social position, but I am, I hope, never rude to them; and the man who could rebuff the Princess Louise must be a curmudgeon indeed.

                                D. G. ROSSETTI."

At the very juncture in question Lord Lorne was suddenly and unexpectedly appointed Governor-General of Canada, and, leaving England, Her Royal Highness did not return until Rossetti's health had somewhat suddenly broken down, and it was impossible for him to see any but his most intimate friends.

My account of the friendship between Mr. Watts-Dunton and Rossetti would not be complete without the poem entitled, 'A Grave by the Sea,' which I think may be placed beside Milton's 'Lycidas,' Shelley's 'Adonais,' Matthew Arnold's 'Thyrsis,' and Swinburne's 'Ave Atque Vale,' as one of the noblest elegies in our literature ·—

A GRAVE BY THE SEA

I

Yon sightless poet [1] whom thou leav'st behind,
  Sightless and trembling like a storm-struck tree,
  Above the grave he feels but cannot see,
Save with the vision Sorrow lends the mind,
Is he indeed the loneliest of mankind?
    Ah no!—For all his sobs, he seems to me
    Less lonely standing there, and nearer thee,
Than I—less lonely, nearer—standing blind!

Free from the day, and piercing Life's disguise
  That needs must partly enveil true heart from heart,
  His inner eyes may see thee as thou art
In Memory's land—see thee beneath the skies
Lit by thy brow—by those beloved eyes,
  While I stand by him in a world apart.

II

I stand like her who on the glittering Rhine
  Saw that strange swan which drew a faëry boat
  Where shone a knight whose radiant forehead smote
Her soul with light and made her blue eyes shine

[1] Philip Bourke Marston.

For many a day with sights that seemed divine,
  Till that false swan returned and arched his throat
  In pride, and called him, and she saw him float
Adown the stream : I stand like her and pine.

I stand like her, for she, and only she,
Might know my loneliness for want of thee.
  Light swam into her soul, she asked not whence,
Filled it with joy no clouds of life could smother,
  And then, departing like a vision thence,
Left her more lonely than the blind, my brother.

III

Last night Death whispered : ' Death is but the name
  Man gives the Power which lends him life and light,
  And then, returning past the coast of night,
Takes what it lent to shores from whence it came.
What balm in knowing the dark doth but reclaim
  The sun it lent, if day hath taken flight ?
  Art thou not vanished—vanished from my sight—
Though somewhere shining, vanished all the same ?

With Nature dumb, save for the billows' moan,
  Engirt by men I love, yet desolate—
Standing with brothers here, yet dazed and lone,
  King'd by my sorrow, made by grief so great
That man's voice murmurs like an insect's drone—
  What balm, I ask, in knowing that Death is Fate ?

IV

Last night Death whispered : ' Life's purblind procession,
  Flickering with blazon of the human story—
  Time's fen-flame over Death's dark territory—
Will leave no trail, no sign of Life's aggression.
Yon moon that strikes the pane, the stars in session,
  Are weak as Man they mock with fleeting glory.
  Since Life is only Death's frail feudatory,
How shall love hold of Fate in true possession ? '

I answered thus : 'If Friendship's isle of palm
  Is but a vision, every loveliest leaf,
Can Knowledge of its mockery soothe and calm
  This soul of mine in this most fiery grief ?
  If Love but holds of Life through Death in fief,
What balm in knowing that Love is Death's—what balm ? '

V

Yea, thus I boldly answered Death—even I
  Who have for boon—who have for deathless dower—
  Thy love, dear friend, which broods, a magic power,
Filling with music earth and sea and sky :
'O Death,' I said, 'not Love, but thou shalt die ;
  For, this I know, though thine is now the hour,
  And thine these angry clouds of doom that lour,
Death striking Love but strikes to deify.'

Yet while I spoke I sighed in loneliness,
For strange seemed Man, and Life seemed comfortless,
  And night, whom we two loved, seemed strange and dumb ;
And, waiting till the dawn the promised sign,
  I watched—I listened for that voice of thine,
  Though Reason said : 'Nor voice nor face can come.'

BIRCHINGTON,
      EASTERTIDE, 1882.

Mr. Watts-Dunton has written many magnificent
sonnets, but the sonnet in this sequence beginning—

Last night Death whispered : 'Life's purblind procession,'

is, I think, the finest of them all. The imaginative conception packed into these fourteen lines is cosmic in its sweep.
In the metrical scheme the feminine rhymes of the octave
play a very important part. They suggest pathetic suspense, mystery, yearning, hope, fear ; they ask, they wonder,
they falter. But in the sestet the words of destiny are
calmly and coldly pronounced, and every rhyme clinches

the voice of doom, until the uttermost deep of despair
is sounded in the iterated cry of the last line. The crafts-
manship throughout is masterly. There is, indeed, one
line which is not unworthy of being ranked with the
great lines of English poetry :

> Yon moon that strikes the pane, the stars in session.

Here by a bold use of the simple verb ' strikes ' a whole
poem is hammered into six words. As to the interesting
question of feminine rhymes, while I admit that they
should never be used without an emotional mandate, I
think that here it is overwhelming.

I have tried to show the beauty of the friendship between these two rare spirits by means of other testimony than my own, for although I have been granted the
honour of knowing Rossetti's ' friend of friends,' I
missed the equal honour of knowing Rossetti, save through
that ' friend of friends.' But to know Mr. Watts-Dunton
seems almost like knowing Rossetti, for when at The Pines
he begins to recall those golden hours when the poets
used to hold converse, the soul of Rossetti seems to come
back from the land of shadows, as his friend depicts his
winsome ways, his nobility of heart, his generous interest in
the work of others, that lovableness of nature and charm
of personality which, if we are to believe Mr. Ford Madox
Hueffer, worked, in some degree, ill for the poet. Mr.
Hueffer, who, as a family connection, may be supposed
to represent the family tradition about ' Gabriel,' has
some striking and pregnant words upon the injurious
effect of Rossetti's being brought so much into contact
with admirers from the time when Mr. Meredith and
Mr. Swinburne were his housemates at Cheyne Walk.
" Then came the ' Pre-Raphaelite ' poets like Philip

Marston, O'Shaughnessy, and 'B. V.'   Afterwards there came a whole host of young men like Mr. William Sharp, who were serious admirers, and to-day are in their places or are dead or forgotten ; and others again who came for the ' pickings.'   They were all more or less enthusiasts."

Mr. Hake, in ' Notes and Queries' (June 7, 1902), says :

"With regard to the green room in which Winifred took her first breakfast at ' Hurstcote,' I am a little in confusion.   It seems to me more like the green dining-room in Cheyne Walk, decorated with antique mirrors, which was painted by Dunn, showing Rossetti reading his poems aloud.   This is the only portrait of Rossetti that really calls up the man before me.   As Mr. Watts-Dunton is the owner of Dunn's drawing, and as so many people want to see what Rossetti's famous Chelsea house was like inside, it is a pity he does not give it as a frontispiece to some future edition of ' Aylwin.'   Unfortunately, Mr. G. F. Watts's picture, now in the National Portrait Gallery, was never finished, and I never saw upon Rossetti's face the dull, heavy expression which that portrait wears.   I think the poet told me that he had given the painter only one or two sittings.   As to the photographs, none of them is really satisfactory."

I am fortunate in being able to reproduce here the picture of the famous ' Green Dining Room ' at 16 Cheyne Walk, to which Mr. Hake refers.   Mr. Hake also writes in the same article : "With regard to the two circular mirrors surrounded by painted designs telling the story of the Holy Grail, ' in old black oak frames carved with knights at tilt,' I do not remember seeing these there.   But they are evidently the mirrors decorated with copies by Dunn of the lost Holy Grail frescoes once existing on the walls of the Union Reading-Room at Oxford. These beautiful decorations I have seen at 'The Pines,' but not elsewhere." I am sure that my readers will be interested in the photograph of one of these famous mirrors, which Mr. Watts-Dunton has generously permitted to be specially taken for this book.

And here again I must draw upon Dr. Gordon Hake's fascinating book of poetry, 'The New Day,' which must live, if only for its reminiscences of the life poetic lived at Chelsea, Kelmscott, and Bognor :—

THE NEW DAY

I

In the unbroken silence of the mind
　　Thoughts creep about us, seeming not to move,
And life is back among the days behind—
　　The spectral days of that lamented love—
Days whose romance can never be repeated.
　　The sun of Kelmscott through the foliage gleaming,
We see him, life-like, at his easel seated,
　　His voice, his brush, with rival wonders teeming.
These vanished hours, where are they stored away ?
　　Hear we the voice, or but its lingering tone ?
Its utterances are swallowed up in day ;
　　The gabled house, the mighty master gone.
Yet are they ours : the stranger at the hall—
What dreams he of the days we there recall ?

II

O, happy days with him who once so loved us !
　　We loved as brothers, with a single heart,
The man whose iris-woven pictures moved us
　　From Nature to her blazoned shadow—Art.
How often did we trace the nestling Thames
　　From humblest waters on his course of might,

ONE OF THE CARVED MIRRORS AT 'THE PINES,' DECORATED WITH DUNN'S
COPY OF THE LOST ROSSETTI FRESCOES AT THE OXFORD UNION

Down where the weir the bursting current stems—
  There sat till evening grew to balmy night,
Veiling the weir whose roar recalled the strand
  Where we had listened to the wave-lipped sea,
That seemed to utter plaudits while we planned
  Triumphal labours of the day to be.
The words were his : ' Such love can never die ; '
The grief was ours when he no more was nigh.

III

Like some sweet water-bell, the tinkling rill
  Still calls the flowers upon its misty bank
To stoop into the stream and drink their fill.
  And still the shapeless rushes, green and rank,
Seem lounging in their pride round those retreats,
  Watching slim willows dip their thirsty spray.
Slowly a loosened weed another meets ;
  They stop, like strangers, neither giving way.
We are here surely if the world, forgot,
  Glides from our sight into the charm, unbidden ;
We are here surely at this witching spot,—
  Though Nature in the reverie is hidden.
A spell so holds our captive eyes in thrall,
It is as if a play pervaded all.

IV

Sitting with him, his tones as Petrarch's tender,
  With many a speaking vision on the wall,
The fire, a-blaze, flashing the studio fender,
  Closed in from London shouts and ceaseless brawl
'Twas you brought Nature to the visiting,
  Till she herself seemed breathing in the room,
And Art grew fragrant in the glow of spring
  With homely scents of gorse and heather bloom.
Or sunbeams shone by many an Alpine fountain,
  Fed by the waters of the forest stream ;
Or glacier-glories in the rock-girt mountain,
  Where they so often fed the poet's dream ;
Or else was mingled the rough billow's glee
With cries of petrels on a sullen sea.

V

Remember how we roamed the Channel's shore,
    And read aloud our verses, each in turn,
While rhythmic waves to us their music bore,
    And foam-flakes leapt from out the rocky churn.
Then oft with glowing eyes you strove to capture
    The potent word that makes a thought abiding,
And wings it upward to its place of rapture,
    While we discoursed to Nature, she presiding.
Then would the poet-painter gaze in wonder
    That art knew not the mighty reverie
That moves earth's spirit and her orb asunder,
    While ocean's depths, even, seem a shallow sea.
Yet with rare genius could his hand impart
His own far-searching poesy to art.

The fourth of these exquisite sonnets delights me most
of all.   It makes me see the recluse in his studio, sitting
snugly with his feet in the fender, when suddenly the door
opens and the poet of Nature brings with him a new
atmosphere — the   salt   atmosphere   which   envelops
'Mother Carey's Chicken,' and the attenuated mountain air of Natura Benigna. And yet perhaps the
description of

    'The sun of Kelmscott through the foliage gleaming'

is equally fascinating.
    Mr. Watts-Dunton himself, with a stronger hand and
more vigorous brush, has in his sonnet 'The Shadow
on the Window Blind,' made Kelmscott Manor and the
poetic life lived there still more memorable ·—

    Within this thicket's every leafy lair
        A song-bird sleeps : the very rooks are dumb,
        Though red behind their nests the moon has swum—
    But still I see that shadow writing there !—
    Poet, behind yon casement's ruddy square,

Whose shadow tells me why you do not come—
Rhyming and chiming of thine insect-hum,
Flying and singing through thine inch of air—

Come thither, where on grass and flower and leaf
  Gleams Nature's scripture, putting Man's to shame:
'Thy day,' she says, 'is all too rich and brief
  Thy game of life too wonderful a game—
To give to Art entirely or in chief
  Drink of these dews—sweeter than wine of Fame.'

'Aylwin,' too, is full of vivid pictures of Rossetti at Chelsea and Kelmscott.

The following description of the famous house and garden, 16 Cheyne Walk, has been declared by one of Rossetti's most intimate friends to be marvellously graphic and true ·—

" On sending in my card I was shown at once into the studio, and after threading my way between some pieces of massive furniture and pictures upon easels, I found D'Arcy lolling lazily upon a huge sofa. Seeing that he was not alone, I was about to withdraw, for I was in no mood to meet strangers. However, he sprang up and introduced me to his guest, whom he called Symonds, an elegant-looking man in a peculiar kind of evening dress, who, as I afterwards learnt, was one of Mr. D'Arcy's chief buyers. This gentleman bowed stiffly to me.

He did not stay long; indeed, it was evident that the appearance of a stranger somewhat disconcerted him.

After he was gone D'Arcy said: 'A good fellow! One of my most important buyers. I should like you to know him, for you and I are going to be friends, I hope.'

'He seems very fond of pictures,' I said.

'A man of great taste, with a real love of art and music.'

A little while after this gentleman's departure, in came De Castro, who had driven up in a hansom. I certainly saw a flash of anger in his eyes as he recognized me, but it vanished like lightning, and his manner became cordiality itself. Late as it was (it was nearly twelve), he pulled out his cigarette case, and evidently intended to begin the evening. As soon as he was told that Mr. Symonds had been there, he began to talk about him in a disparaging manner. Evidently his métier was, as I had surmised, that of a professional talker. Talk was his stock-in-trade.

The night wore on and De Castro, in the intervals of his talk, kept pulling out his watch. It was evident that he wanted to be going, but was reluctant to leave me there. For my part, I frequently rose to go, but on getting a sign from D'Arcy that he wished me to stay I sat down again. At last D'Arcy said :

'You had better go now, De Castro—you have kept that hansom outside for more than an hour and a half ; and besides, if you stay still daylight our friend here will stay longer, for I want to talk with him alone.'

De Castro got up with a laugh that seemed genuine enough, and left us.

D'Arcy, who was still on the sofa, then lapsed into a silence that became after a while rather awkward. He lay there, gazing abstractedly at the fireplace.

'Some of my friends call me, as you heard De Castro say the other night, Haroun-al-Raschid, and I suppose I am like him in some things. I am a bad sleeper, and to be amused by De Castro when I can't sleep is the chief of blessings. De Castro, however, is not so bad as he seems. A man may be a scandal-monger without being really malignant. I have known him go out of his way to do a struggling man a service.'

Next morning, after I had finished my solitary breakfast, I asked the servant if Mr. D'Arcy had yet risen. On being told that he had not, I went downstairs into the studio, where I had spent the previous evening. After examining the pictures on the walls and the easels, I walked to the window and looked out at the garden. It was large, and so neglected and untrimmed as to be a veritable wilderness. While I was marvelling why it should have been left in this state, I saw the eyes of some animal staring at me from a distance, and was soon astonished to see that they belonged to a little Indian bull. My curiosity induced me to go into the garden and look at the creature. He seemed rather threatening at first, but after a while allowed me to go up to him and stroke him. Then I left the Indian bull and explored this extraordinary domain. It was full of unkempt trees, including two fine mulberries, and surrounded by a very high wall. Soon I came across an object which, at first, seemed a little mass of black and white oats moving along, but I presently discovered it to be a hedgehog. It was so tame that it did not curl up as I approached it, but allowed me, though with some show of nervousness, to stroke its pretty little black snout. As I walked about the garden, I found it was populated with several kinds of animals such as are never seen except in menageries or in the Zoological Gardens. Wombats, kangaroos, and the like, formed a kind of happy family.

My love of animals led me to linger in the garden. When I returned to the house I found that D'Arcy had already breakfasted, and was at work in the studio.

After greeting me with the greatest cordiality, he said :

' No doubt you are surprised at my menagerie.

Every man has one side of his character where the child
remains. I have a love of animals which, I suppose, I
may call a passion. The kind of amusement they can
afford me is like none other. It is the self-consciousness
of men and women that makes them, in a general way,
intensely unamusing. I turn from them to the unconscious brutes, and often get a world of enjoyment. To
watch a kitten or a puppy play, or the funny antics of a
parrot or a cockatoo, or the wise movements of a wombat,
will keep me for hours from being bored.'

'And children,' I said—'do you like children ? '

'Yes, so long as they remain like the young animals
—until they become self-conscious, I mean, and that is
very soon. Then their charm goes. Has it ever occurred
to you how fascinating a beautiful young girl would be
if she were as unconscious as a young animal ? What
makes you sigh ? '

My thoughts had flown to Winifred breakfasting
with her ' Prince of the Mist ' on Snowdon. And I said
to myself, ' How he would have been fascinated by a
sight like that ! '

My experience of men at that time was so slight that
the opinion I then formed of D'Arcy as a talker was not
of much account. But since then I have seen very much
of men, and I find that I was right in the view I then took
of his conversational powers. When his spirits were at
their highest he was without an equal as a wit, without
an equal as a humourist. He had more than even Cyril
Aylwin's quickness of repartee, and it was of an incom-
parably rarer quality. To define it would be, of course,
impossible, but I might perhaps call it poetic fancy
suddenly stimulated at moments by animal spirits into
rapid movements—so rapid, indeed, that what in slower
movement would be merely fancy, in him became wit.

Beneath the coruscations of this wit a rare and deep intellect was always perceptible.

His humour was also so fanciful that it seemed poetry
at play, but here was the remarkable thing : although he
was not unconscious of his other gifts, he did not seem
to be in the least aware that he was a humourist of the
first order ; every ' jeu d'esprit ' seemed to leap from
him involuntarily, like the spray from a fountain.   A
dull man like myself must not attempt to reproduce
these qualities here.

While he was talking he kept on painting."

Chapter XII

WILLIAM MORRIS

IT is natural after writing about Rossetti to think of William Morris. In my opinion the masterpiece among all Mr. Watts-Dunton's 'Athenæum' monographs is the one upon him. Between these two there was an intimacy of the closest kind—from 1873 to the day of the poet's death. This, no doubt, apart from Mr. Watts-Dunton's graphic power, accounts for the extraordinary vividness of the portrait of his friend. I have heard more than one eminent friend of William Morris say that from a few paragraphs of this monograph a reader gains a far more vivid picture of this fascinating man than is to be gained from reading and re-reading anything else that has been published about him. It is a grievous loss to literature that the man so fully equipped for writing a biography of Morris is scarcely likely to write one. Morris, when he was busy in Queen's Square, used to be one of the most frequent visitors at the gatherings at Danes Inn with Mr. Swinburne, Dr. Westland Marston, Madox Brown, and others, on Wednesday evenings; and he and Mr. Watts-Dunton were frequently together at Kelmscott during the time of the joint occupancy of the old Manor house, and also after Rossetti's death.

When Mr. Watts-Dunton wrote 'Aylwin' he did not contemplate that the Hurstcote of the story would immediately be identified with Kelmscott Manor. The

KELMSCOTT MANOR
From a Water Colour by Miss May Morris

Pbo . Poole, Putney

pictures of localities and the descriptions of the characters were so vivid that Hurstcote was at once identified with Kelmscott, and D'Arcy was at once identified with Rossetti. Morris's passion for angling is slightly introduced in the later chapters of the book, and this is not surprising, for some of the happiest moments of Mr. Watts-Dunton's life were spent at Kelmscott. Treffry Dunn's portrait of him, sitting on a fallen tree beside the back-water, was painted at Kelmscott, and the scenery and the house are admirably rendered in the picture.

Mr. Hake, in 'Notes and Queries' (June 7, 1902) mentions some interesting facts with regard to 'Hurstcote Manor' and Morris ·—

" Morris, whom I had the privilege of knowing very well, and with whom I have stayed at Kelmscott during the Rossetti period, is alluded to in 'Aylwin' (chap. lx. book xv.) as the 'enthusiastic angler' who used to go down to 'Hurstcote' to fish. At that time this fine old seventeenth century manor house was in the joint occupancy of Rossetti and Morris. Afterwards it was in the joint occupancy of Morris and (a beloved friend of the two) the late F. S. Ellis, who, with Mr. Cockerell, was executor under Morris's will. The series of 'large attics in which was a number of enormous oak beams' supporting the antique roof, was a favourite resort of my own ; but all the ghostly noise that I there heard was the snoring of young owls—a peculiar sound that had a special fascination for Rossetti ; and after dinner Rossetti, my brother, and I, or Mr. Watts-Dunton and I, would go to the attics to listen to them.

With regard to 'Hurstcote' I well knew 'the large bedroom, with low-panelled walls and the vast antique bedstead made of black carved oak ' upon which Winifred Wynne slept.   In fact, the only thing in the description of this room that I do not remember is the beautiful ' Madonna and Child,' upon the frame of which was written ' Chiaro dell' Erma ' (readers of ' Hand and Soul ' will remember that name).   I wonder whether it is a Madonna by Parmigiano, belonging to Mr. Watts-Dunton, which was much admired by Leighton and others, and which has been exhibited.   This quaint and picturesque bedroom leads by two or three steps to the tapestried room ' covered with old faded tapestry—so faded, indeed, that its general effect was that of a dull grey texture '—depicting the story of Samson.   Rossetti used the tapestry room as a studio, and I have seen in it the very same pictures that so attracted the attention of Winifred Wynne : the ' grand brunette ' (painted from Mrs. Morris) ' holding a pomegranate in her hand '; the ' other brunette, whose beautiful eyes are glistening and laughing over the fruit she is holding up ' (painted from the same famous Irish beauty, named Smith, who appears in ' The Beloved '), and the blonde ' under the apple blossoms ' (painted from a still more beautiful woman—Mrs. Stillman).   These pictures were not permanently placed there, but, as it chanced, they were there (for retouching) on a certain occasion when I was visiting at Kelmscott."

Among the remarkable men that Mr. Watts-Dunton used to meet at Kelmscott, was Morris's friend, Dr. John Henry Middleton, Slade Professor of Fine Art in the University of Cambridge and Art Director of the South Kensington Museum—a man of extraordinary gifts, who promised to be one of the foremost of the scholarly writers of our time, but who died prematurely.

Some of Mr. Watts-Dunton's anecdotes of the causeries at Kelmscott between Morris, Middleton, and himself, are so interesting that it is a pity they have never been recorded in print.   Middleton was one of Mr. Watts-Dunton's collaborators in the ninth edition of the 'Encyclopædia Britannica,' to which he contributed the article on 'Rome,' one of the finest essays in that work.

Morris was notoriously indifferent to critical expressions about his work; and he used to declare that the only reviews of his works which he ever took the trouble to read were the reviews by Mr. Watts-Dunton in the 'Athenæum.'   And the poet might well say this, for those who have studied, as I have, those elaborate and brilliant essays upon 'Sigurd,' 'The House of the Wolfings,' 'The Roots of the Mountains,' 'The Glittering Plain,' 'The Well at the World's End,' 'The Tale of Beowulf,' 'News from Nowhere,' 'Poems by the Way,' will be inclined to put them at the top of all Mr. Watts-Dunton's purely critical work.   The 'Quarterly Review,' in the article upon Morris, makes allusion to the relations between Mr. Watts-Dunton and Morris; so does the writer of the admirable article upon Morris in the new edition of Chambers's 'Cyclopædia of English Literature.'   I record these facts, not in order to depreciate the work of other men, but as a justification for the extracts I am going to make from Mr. Watts-Dunton's monograph in the 'Athenæum.'

The article contains these beautiful meditations on Pain and Death :—

" Each time that I saw him he declared, in answer to my inquiries, that he suffered no pain whatever.   And a comforting thought this is to us all—that Morris suffered no pain.   To Death himself we may easily be reconciled

—nay, we might even look upon him as Nature's final beneficence to all her children, if it were not for the cruel means he so often employs in fulfilling his inevitable mission.   The thought that Morris's life had ended in the tragedy of pain—the thought that he to whom work was sport, and generosity the highest form of enjoyment, suffered what some men suffer in shuffling off the mortal coil—would have been intolerable almost.   For among the thousand and one charms of the man, this, perhaps, was the chief, that Nature had endowed him with an enormous capacity of enjoyment, and that Circumstance, conspiring with Nature, said to him, ' Enjoy.'   Born in easy circumstances, though not to the degrading trouble of wealth—cherishing as his sweetest possessions a devoted wife and two daughters, each of them endowed with intelligence so rare as to understand a genius such as his— surrounded by friends, some of whom were among the first men of our time, and most of whom were of the very salt of the earth—it may be said of him that Misfortune, if she touched him at all, never struck home. If it is true, as Mèrimée affirms, that men are hastened to maturity by misfortune, who wanted Morris to be mature ?   Who wanted him to be other than the radiant boy of genius that he remained till the years had silvered his hair and carved wrinkles on his brow, but left his blue-grey eyes as bright as when they first opened on the world ?   Enough for us to think that the man must, indeed, be specially beloved by the gods who in his sixty-third year dies young.   Old age Morris could not have borne with patience.   Pain would not have developed him into a hero.   This beloved man, who must have died some day, died when his marvellous powers were at their best—and died without pain.   The scheme of life and death does not seem so much awry, after all.

At the last interview but one that ever I had with him—it was in the little carpetless room from which so much of his best work was turned out—he himself surprised me by leading the conversation upon a subject he rarely chose to talk about—the mystery of life and death. The conversation ended with these words of his : ' I have enjoyed my life—few men more so—and death in any case is sure.' "

It is in this same vivid word-picture that occur Mr. Watts-Dunton's reflections upon the wear and tear of genius :—

" It is difficult not to think that the cause of causes of his death was excessive exercise of all his forces, especially of the imaginative faculty. When I talked to him, as I often did, of the peril of such a life of tension as his, he pooh-poohed the idea. ' Look at Gladstone,' he would say, ' look at those wise owls your chancellors and your judges. Don't they live all the longer for work ? It is rust that kills men, not work.' No doubt he was right in contending that in intellectual efforts such as those he alluded to, where the only faculty drawn upon is the ' dry light of intelligence,' a prodigious amount of work may be achieved without any sapping of the sources of life. But is this so where that fusion of all the faculties which we call genius is greatly taxed ? I doubt it. In all true imaginative production there is, as De Quincey pointed out many years ago, a movement, not of ' the thinking machine ' only, but of the whole man—the whole ' genial ' nature of the worker—his imagination, his judgment, moving in an evolution of lightning velocity from the whole of the work to the part, from the part to the whole, together with every emotion of the soul. Hence when, as in the case of Walter Scott, of

Charles Dickens, and presumably of Shakespeare too, the
emotional nature of Man is overtaxed, every part of the
frame suffers, and cries out in vain for its share of that
nervous fluid which is the true vis vitæ.

We have only to consider the sort of work Morris
produced, and its amount, to realize that no human powers
could continue to withstand such a strain.   Many are of
opinion that ' The Lovers of Gudrun ' is his finest poem ;
he worked at it from four o'clock in the morning till four
in the afternoon, and when he rose from the table he had
produced 750 lines !   Think of the forces at work in
producing a poem like ' Sigurd.'   Think of the mingling
of the drudgery of the Dryasdust with the movements of
an imaginative vision unsurpassed in our time ; think, I
say, of the collating of the ' Volsunga Saga ' with the
' Nibelungenlied,' the choosing of this point from the
Saga-man, and of that point from the later poem of the
Germans, and then fusing the whole by imaginative
heat into the greatest epic of the nineteenth century.
Was there not work enough here for a considerable portion of a poet's life ?   And yet so great is the entire mass
of his work that ' Sigurd ' is positively overlooked in
many of the notices of his writings which have appeared
in the last few days in the press, while in the others it is
alluded to in three words ; and this simply because the
mass of other matter to be dealt with fills up all the available space of a newspaper."

Mr. Watts-Dunton's critical acumen is nowhere more
strikingly seen than in his remarks upon Morris's translation of the Odyssey :—

" Some competent critics are dissatisfied with Morris's
translation ; yet in a certain sense it is a triumph.   The
two specially Homeric qualities—those, indeed, which

set Homer apart from all other poets—are eagerness and dignity. Never again can they be fully combined, for never again will poetry be written in the Greek hexameters and by a Homer. That Tennyson could have given us the Homeric dignity his magnificent rendering of a famous fragment of the Iliad shows. Chapman's translations show that the eagerness also can be caught. Morris, of course, could not have given the dignity of Homer, but then, while Tennyson has left us only a few lines speaking with the dignity of the Iliad, Morris gave us a translation of the entire Odyssey, which, though it missed the Homeric dignity, secured the eagerness as completely as Chapman's free-and-easy paraphrase, and in a rendering as literal as Buckley's prose crib, which lay frankly by Morris's side as he wrote   Morris's translation of the Odyssey and his translation of Virgil, where he gives us an almost word-for-word translation and yet throws over the poem a glamour of romance which brings Virgil into the sympathy of the modern reader, would have occupied years with almost any other poet. But these two efforts of his genius are swamped by the purely original poems, such as 'The Defence of Guenevere,' 'Jason,' 'The Earthly Paradise,' 'Love is Enough,' 'Poems by the Way,' etc. And then come his translations from the Icelandic. Mere translation is, of course, easy enough, but not such translation as that in the 'Saga Library.' Allowing for all the aid he got from Mr. Magnusson, what a work this is! Think of the imaginative exercise required to turn the language of these Saga-men into a diction so picturesque and so concrete as to make each Saga an English poem—for poem each one is, if Aristotle is right in thinking that imaginative substance and not metre is the first requisite of a poem."

In connection with William Morris, readers of ' The Coming of Love ' will reca'l the touching words in the ' Prefatory Note ' :—

" Had it not been for the intervention of matters of a peculiarly absorbing kind—matters which caused me to delay the task of collecting these verses—I should have been the most favoured man who ever brought out a volume of poems, for they would have been printed by William Morris, at the Kelmscott Press. As that projected edition of his was largely subscribed for, a word of explanation to the subscribers is, I am told, required from me. Among the friends who saw much of that great poet and beloved man during the last year of his life, there was one who would not and could not believe that he would die—myself. To me he seemed human vitality concentrated to a point of quenchless light ; and when the appalling truth that he must die did at last strike through me, I had no heart and no patience to think about anything in connection with him but the loss that was to come upon us. And, now, whatsoever pleasure I may feel at seeing my verses in one of Mr. Lane's inviting little volumes will be dimmed and marred by the thought that Morris's name also might have been, and is not, on the imprint."

As a matter of fact this incident in the publication of ' The Coming of Love ' is an instance of that artistic conscientiousness which up to a certain point is of inestimable value to the poet, but after that point is reached, baffles him. The poem had been read in fragments and deeply admired by that galaxy of poets among whom Mr. Watts-Dunton moved. Certain fragments of it had appeared in the ' Athenæum ' and other journals, but the publication of the entire poem had been delayed owing to the fact that certain portions of it had been lent and lost. Morris not only offered to bring out at the Kelmscott Press an édition de luxe of the book, but he actually took the trouble to get a full list of subscribers, and insisted upon allowing the author a magnificent royalty. Nothing, however, would persuade Mr. Watts-Dunton to bring out the book until these lost portions could be found, and notwithstanding the generous urgings of Morris, the matter stood still; and then, when the book was ready, Morris was seized by that illness which robbed us of one of the greatest writers of the nineteenth century. And even after Morris's death the poet's executors and friends, the late Mr. F. S. Ellis and the well-known bibliographer, Mr. Sydney C. Cockerell, were willing and even desirous that the Kelmscott edition of the poems should be brought out. Subsequently, when a large portion of the lost poems was found, the volume was published by Mr. John Lane. This anecdote alone explains why Mr. Watts-Dunton is never tired of dwelling upon the nobility of Morris's nature, and upon his generosity in small things as well as in large.

Another favourite story of his in connection with this subject is the following. When Morris published his first volume in the Kelmscott Press, he sent Mr. Watts-Dunton a presentation copy of the book. He also sent him a presentation copy of the second and third. But knowing how small was the profit at this time from the books issued by the Kelmscott Press, Mr. Watts-Dunton felt a little delicacy in taking these presentation copies, and told Mrs. Morris that she should gently protest against such extravagance. Mrs. Morris assured him that it would be perfectly useless to do so.

But when the edition of Keats was coming out, Mr. Watts-Dunton determined to grapple with the matter, and one Sunday afternoon when he was at Kelmscott House, he said to Morris:

'Morris, I wish you to put my name down as a subscriber to the Keats, and I give my commission for it in the presence of witnesses. I am a paying subscriber to the Keats.'

'All right, old chap, you're a subscriber.'

In spite of this there came the usual presentation copy of the Keats; and when Mr. Watts-Dunton was at Kelmscott House on the following Sunday afternoon, he told Morris that a mistake had been made. Morris laughed.

'All right, there's no mistake—that is my presentation copy of Keats.'

But when at last the magnum opus of the Kelmscott Press was being discussed—the marvellous Chaucer with Burne-Jones's illustrations—Mr. Watts-Dunton knew that here a great deal of money was to be risked, and probably sunk, and he said to Morris:

'Now, Morris, I'm going to talk to you seriously about the Chaucer. I know that it's going to be a dead loss to you, and I do really and seriously hope that you do not contemplate anything so wild as to send me a presentation copy of that book. You know my affection for you, and you know I speak the truth, when I tell you that it would give me pain to accept it.'

'Well, old chap, very likely this time I shall have to stay my hand, for, between ourselves, I expect I shall drop some money over it; but the Chaucer will be at The Pines, because Ned Jones and I are going to join in the presentation of a copy to Algernon Swinburne.'

After this Mr. Watts-Dunton's mind was set at rest, as he told Mrs. Morris. But when Mr. Swinburne's copy reached 'The Pines' it was accompanied by another one—'Theodore Watts-Dunton from William Morris.'

Another anecdote, illustrative of his generosity, Mr. Watts-Dunton also tells. Mr. Swinburne, wishing to possess a copy of 'The Golden Legend,' bought the Kelmscott edition, and one day Mr. Watts-Dunton told Morris this. Morris gave a start as though a sudden pain had struck him.

'What! Algernon pay ten pounds for a book of mine! Why I thought he did not care for black letter reproductions, or I would have sent him a copy of every book I brought out.'

And when he did bring out another book, two copies were sent to 'The Pines,' one for Mr. Watts-Dunton and one for Mr. Swinburne.

Mr. Watts-Dunton, speaking about 'The Water of the Wondrous Isles,' tells this amusing story :—

"Once, many years ago, Morris was inveigled into seeing and hearing the great poet-singer Stead, whose rhythms have had such a great effect upon the 'art poetic,' the author of 'The Perfect Cure,' and 'It's Daddy this and Daddy that,' and other brilliant lyrics. A friend with whom Morris had been spending the evening, and who had been talking about poetic energy and poetic art in relation to the chilly reception accorded to 'Sigurd,' persuaded him—much against his will—to turn in for a few seconds to see Mr. Stead, whose performance consisted of singing a song, the burden of which was 'I'm a perfect cure!' while he leaped up into the air without bending his legs and twirled round like a dervish. 'What made you bring me to see this damned tomfoolery ? ' Morris grumbled ; and on being told that it was to give him an example of poetic energy at its tensest, without poetic art, he grumbled still more and shouldered his way out. If Morris were now alive— and all England will sigh, ' Ah, would he were ! '—he would confess, with his customary emphasis, that the poet had nothing of the slightest importance to learn, even from the rhythms of Mr. Stead, marked as they were by terpsichorean pauses that were beyond the powers of the ' Great Vance.' "

Chapter XIII

THE 'EXAMINER'

LONG before Mr. Watts-Dunton printed a line, he was a prominent figure in the literary and artistic sets in London ; but, as Mr. Hake has said, it was merely as a conversationalist that he was known. His conversation was described by Rossetti as being like that of no other person moving in literary circles, because he was always enunciating new views in phrasings so polished that, to use Rossetti's words, his improvized locutions were as perfect as 'fitted jewels.' Those who have been privileged to listen to his table-talk will attest the felicity of the image. Seldom has so great a critic had so fine an audience. Rossetti often lamented that Theodore Watts' spoken criticism had never been taken down in short-hand. For a long time various editors who had met him at Rossetti's, at Madox Brown's, at Westland Marston's, at Whistler's breakfasts, and at the late Lord Houghton's, endeavoured to persuade him to make practical use in criticism of the ideas that flowed in a continuous stream from his lips. But, as Rossetti used to affirm, he was the one man of his time who, with immense literary equipment, was without literary ambition. This peculiarity of his was eloquently described by the late Dr. Gordon Hake in his 'New Day' :—

> You say you care not for the people's praise,
>   That poetry is its own recompense ;
> You care not for the wreath, the dusty bays,
>   Given to the whirling wind and hurried hence

The first editor who secured Theodore Watts, after repeated efforts to do so, was the late Professor Minto, and this only came about because during his editorship of the 'Examiner' both he and Watts resided in Danes Inn, and were constantly seeing each other.

It was Minto who afterwards declared that "the articles in the 'Examiner' and the 'Athenæum' are gold-mines, in which we others are apt to dig unconsciously without remembering that the nuggets are Theodore Watts's, who is too lazy to peg out his claim." The first article by him that appeared in Minto's paper attracted great attention and roused great curiosity. This indeed is not surprising, for, as I found when I read it, it was as remarkable for pregnancy of thought and of style as the latest and ripest of his essays. A friend of his, belonging to the set in which he moved, who remembers the appearance of this article, has been kind enough to tell me the following anecdote in connection with it. The contributors to the paper at that time consisted of Minto, Dr Garnett, Swinburne, Edmund Gosse, 'Scholar' Williams, Comyns Carr, Walter Pollock, Duffield (the translator of 'Don Quixote'), Professor Sully, Dr. Marston, William Bell Scott, William Black, and many other able writers. On the evening of the day when Theodore Watts's first article appeared, there was a party at the house of William Bell Scott in Chelsea, and every one was asking who this new contributor was. It was one of the conditions under which the article was written that its authorship was to be kept a secret. Bell Scott, who took a great interest in the 'Examiner,' was especially inquisitive about the new writer. After having in vain tried to get from Minto the name of the writer, he went up to Watts, and said: "I would give almost anything to know who the writer

is who appears in the 'Examiner' for the first time to-
day." "What makes you inquire about it?" said Watts.
"What is the interest attaching to the writer of such
fantastic stuff as that? Surely it is the most mannered
writing that has appeared in the 'Examiner' for a long
time!" Then, turning to Minto, he said: "I can't
think, Minto, what made you print it at all." Scott,
who had a most exalted opinion of Watts as a critic, was
considerably abashed at this, and began to endeavour to
withdraw some of his enthusiastic remarks. This set
Minto laughing aloud, and thus the secret got out.

From that hour Watts became the most noticeable
writer among a group of critics who were all noticeable.
Week after week there appeared in this historic paper
criticism as fine as had ever appeared in it in the time of
Leigh Hunt, and as brilliant as had appeared in it in the
time of Fonblanque. At this time Minto used to entertain his contributors on Monday evening in the room
over the publisher's office in the Strand, and I have
been told by one who was frequently there that these
smoking symposia were among the most brilliant in London. One can well imagine this when one remembers
the names of those who used to attend the meetings.

It was through the 'Examiner' that Watts formed
that friendship with William Black which his biographer,
Sir Wemyss Reid, alludes to. Between these two there
was one subject on which they were especially in sympathy
—their knowledge and love of nature. At that time
Black was immensely popular. In personal appearance
there was, I am told, a superficial resemblance between
the two, and they were constantly being mistaken for each
other; and yet, when they were side by side, it was evident that the large, dark moustache and the black eyes were
almost the only points of resemblance between them.

It was at the then famous house in Gower Street of
Mr. Justin McCarthy that Black and Mr. Watts-Dunton
first met.   Speaking as an Irishman of a younger
but not, I fear, of so genial a generation, I hear tantalizing accounts of the popular gatherings at the
home of the most charming and the most distinguished
Irishman of letters in the London of that time,
where so many young men of my own country were
welcomed as warmly as though they had not yet to
win their spurs.   No one speaks more enthusiastically
of the McCarthy family than Mr. Watts-Dunton, who
seems to have been on terms of friendship with them
almost as soon as he settled in London.   Mr. Watts-
Dunton was always a lover of McCarthy's novels,
but on his first visit to Gower Street Mr. McCarthy
was, as usual, full of the subject not of his own novels,
but of another man's.   He urged his new friend to read
' Under the Greenwood Tree,' almost forcing him to
take the book away with him, which he did : this was
the way in which Mr. Watts-Dunton became for the
first time acquainted with a story which he always avers
is the only book that has ever revived the rich rustic
humour of Shakespeare's early comedies.   A perfect household of loving natures, warm Irish hearts, bright Irish
intellects, cultivated and rare, according to Mr. Watts-
Dunton's testimony, was that little family in Gower
Street.   I think he will pardon me for repeating one
quaint little story about himself and Black in connection
with this first visit to the McCarthys.   On entering the
room Mr. Watts-Dunton was much struck with what appeared to be real musical genius in a bright-eyed little lady
who was delighting the party with her music.   This was
at the period in his own life which Mr. Watts-Dunton
calls his ' music-mad period.'   And after a time he got

talking with the lady. He was a little surprised that he was at once invited by the musical lady to go to a gathering at her house. But he was as much pleased as surprised to be so welcomed, and incontinently accepted the invitation. It never entered his mind that he had been mistaken for another man, until the other man entered the room and came up to the lady. She, on her part, began to look in an embarrassed way from one to the other of the two swarthy, black-moustached gentlemen. She had mistaken Mr. Watts-Dunton for William Black, with whom her acquaintance was but slight. The contretemps caused much amusement when the husband of the lady, an eminent novelist, who knew Mr. Watts-Dunton well, introduced him to his wife. I do not know what was the end of the comedy, but no doubt it was a satisfactory one. It could not be otherwise among such people as Justin McCarthy would be likely to gather round him.

At that time, to quote the words of the same friend of Mr. Watts-Dunton, Watts used frequently to meet at Bell Scott's and Rossetti's Professor Appleton, the editor of the 'Academy.' The points upon which these two touched were as unlike the points upon which Watts and William Black touched as could possibly be. They were both students of Hegel; and when they met, Appleton, who had Hegel on the brain, invariably drew Watts aside for a long private talk. People used to leave them alone, on account of the remoteness of the subject that attracted the two. Watts had now made up his mind that he would devote himself to literature, and, indeed, his articles in the 'Examiner' showed that he had only to do so to achieve a great success. Appleton rarely left Watts without saying, " I do wish you would write for the 'Academy.' I want you to let me send you all the books on the transcendentalists that come to the 'Academy,' and let me have articles giving the pith of them at short intervals." This invitation to furnish the 'Academy' with a couple of columns condensing the spirit of many books about subjects upon which only a handful of people in England were competent to write, seemed to Watts a grotesque request, seeing that he was at this very time the leading writer on the 'Examiner,' and was being constantly approached by other editors. It was consequently the subject of many a joke between Minto, William Black, Watts, and the others present at the famous 'Examiner' gatherings. After a while Mr. Norman MacColl, who was then the editor of the 'Athenæum,' invited Watts to take an important part in the reviewing for the 'Athenæum.' At first he told the editor that there were two obstacles to his accepting the invitation—one was that the work that he was invited to do was largely done by his friend Marston, and that, although he would like to join him, he scarcely saw his way, on account of the 'Examiner,' which was ready to take all the work he could produce. On opening the matter to Dr Marston, that admirably endowed writer would not hear of Watts's considering him in the matter. The 'Athenæum' was then, as now, the leading literary organ in Europe, and the editor's offer was, of course, a very tempting one, and Watts was determined to tell Minto about it. And this he did.

"Now, Minto," he said, "it rests entirely with you whether I shall write in the 'Athenæum' or not." Minto, between whom and Watts there was a deep affection, made the following reply:

"My dear Theodore, I need not say that it will not be a good day for the 'Examiner' when you join the

'Athenæum.' The 'Examiner' is a struggling paper which could not live without being subsidized by Peter Taylor, and it is not four months ago since Leicester Warren said to me that he and all the other readers of the 'Examiner' looked eagerly for the 'T. W.' at the foot of a literary article. The 'Athenæum' is both a powerful and a wealthy paper. In short, it will injure the 'Examiner' when your name is associated with the 'Athenæum.' But to be the leading voice of such a paper as that is just what you ought to be, and I cannot help advising you to entertain MacColl's proposal."

In consequence of this Mr. Watts-Dunton closed with Mr. MacColl's offer, and his first article in the 'Athenæum' appeared on July 8, 1876.

Chapter XIV

THE 'ATHENÆUM'

AS the first review which Mr. Watts-Dunton contributed to the 'Athenæum' has been so often discussed, and as it is as characteristic as any other of his
style, I have determined to reprint it entire. It has the
additional interest, I believe, of being the most rapidly
executed piece of literary work which Mr. Watts-Dunton
ever achieved. Mr. MacColl, having secured the new
writer, tried to find a book for him, and failed, until
Mr. Watts-Dunton asked him whether he intended to
give an article upon Skelton's ' Comedy of the Noctes
Ambrosianæ.' The editor said that he had not thought
of giving the book a considerable article, but that, if
Mr. Watts-Dunton liked to take it, it should be sent to
him. As the article was wanted on the following day, it
was dictated as fast as the amanuensis—not a shorthand
writer—could take it down.

It has no relation to the Renascence of Wonder, nor is
it one of his great essays, such as the one on the Psalms, or
his essays on Victor Hugo, but in style it is as characteristic as any :—

' Is it really that the great squeezing of books has at
last begun ? Here, at least, is the ' Noctes Ambrosi
anæ ' squeezed into one volume.

Long ago we came upon an anecdote in Castellan,
the subject of which, as far as we remember, is this.

The library of the Indian kings was composed of so many volumes that a thousand camels were necessary to remove it. But once on a time a certain prince who loved reading much and other pleasures more, called a Brahmin to him, and said: 'Books are good, O Brahmin, even as women are good, yet surely, of both these goods a prince may have too many; and then, O Brahmin, which of these two vexations is sorest to princely flesh it were hard to say; but as to the books, O Brahmin, squeeze 'em!' The Brahmin, understanding well what the order to 'squeeze 'em' meant (for he was a bookman himself, and knew that, as there goes much water and little flavour to the making of a very big pumpkin, so there go much words and few thoughts to the making of a very big book), set to work, aided by many scribes—striking out all the idle words from every book in the library; and when the essence of them had been extracted it was found that ten camels could carry that library without ruffling a hair. And therefore the Brahmin was appointed 'Grand Squeezer' of the realm. Ages after this, another prince, who loved reading much and other pleasures a good deal more, called the Grand Squeezer of his time and said: 'Thy duties are neglected, O Grand Squeezer! Thy life depends upon the measure of thy squeezing.' Thereupon the Grand Squeezer, in fear and trembling, set to work and squeezed and squeezed till the whole library became at last a load that a foal would have laughed at, for it consisted but of one book, a tiny volume, containing four maxims. Yet the wisdom in the last library was the wisdom in the first.

The appearance of Mr. Skelton's condensation of the 'Noctes Ambrosianæ' reminds us of this story, and of a certain solemn warning we always find it our

duty to administer to those who show a propensity
towards the baneful coxcombry of authorship—the warning that the literature of our country is already in a
fair way of dying for the want of a Grand Squeezer, and
that unless such a functionary be appointed within
the next ten years, it will be smothered by itself. Yet
our Government will keep granting pension after pension to those whom the Duke of Wellington used to
call 'the writing fellows,' for adding to the camel's burden, instead of distributing the same amount among an
army of diligent and well-selected squeezers. We say
an army of squeezers, for it is not merely that almost
every man, woman, and child among us who can
write, prints, while nobody reads, and, to judge from
the 'spelling bees,' nobody even spells, but that the
fecundity of man as a 'writing animal' is on the in-
crease, and each one requires a squeezer to himself.
This is the alarming thing. Where are we to find so
many squeezers ? Nay, in many cases there needs a
separate sub-squeezer for the writer's every book.
Take, for instance, the case of the Carlyle squeezer—
what more could be expected from him in a lifetime
than that he should squeeze 'Frederick the Great'—
that enormous, rank and pungent 'haggis' from which,
properly squeezed, such an ocean would flow of 'oniony
liquid' that compared with it the famous 'haggis-
deluge' of the 'Noctes' which nearly drowned in gravy
'Christopher,' 'the Shepherd,' and 'Tickler' in Ambrose's parlour, would be, both for quantity and flavour,
but 'a beaker full of the sweet South' ? Yet what
would be the squeezing of Mr. Carlyle ; what would be
the squeezing of De Quincey, or of Landor, or of Southey,
to the squeezing of the tremendous Professor Wilson—the
mighty Christopher, who for about thirty years literally

talked in type upon every matter of which he had any knowledge, and upon every matter of which he had none; whose 'words, words, words' are, indeed, as Hallam, with unconscious irony, says, 'as the rush of mighty waters'?

What would be left after the squeezing of him it would be hard to guess; for, says the Chinese proverb, 'if what is said be not to the purpose, a single word is already too much.'

Mr. Skelton should have borne this maxim in mind in his manipulations upon the 'Noctes Ambrosianæ.' He loves the memory of the fine old Scotsman, and has squeezed this enormous pumpkin with fingers that are too timid of grip. In squeezing Professor Wilson you cannot overdo it. There are certain parts we should have especially liked squeezed away; and among these—will Mr. Skelton pardon us?—are the 'amazingly humourous' ones, such as the 'opening of the haggis,' which, Mr. Skelton tells us, 'manifests the humour of conception as well as the humour of character, in a measure that has seldom been surpassed by the greatest masters'; 'the amazing humour' of which consists in the Shepherd's sticking his supper knife into a 'haggis' (a sheep's paunch filled with the 'pluck' minced, with suet, onions, salt, and pepper), and thereby setting free such a flood of gravy that the whole party have to jump upon the chairs and tables to save themselves from being drowned in it! In truth, Mr. Skelton should have reversed his method of selection; and if, in operating upon the Professor's twelve remaining volumes, he will, instead of retaining, omit everything 'amazingly humourous,' he will be the best Wilson-squeezer imaginable.

Yet, his intentions here were as good as could be. The 'Noctes' are dying of dropsy, so Mr. Skelton, to save them, squeezes away all the political events—so important once, so unimportant now—all the foolish laudation, and more foolish abuse of those who took part in them. He eliminates all the critiques upon all those 'greatest poems' and those 'greatest novels of the age' written by Christopher's friends—friends so famous once, so peacefully forgotten now. And he has left what he calls the 'Comedy of the Noctes Ambrosianæ,' i.e. 'that portion of the work which deals with or presents directly and dramatically to the reader, human life, and character, and passion, as distinguished from that portion of it which is critical, and devoted to the discussion of subjects of literary, artistic, or political interest only.' And, although Mr. Skelton uses thus the word 'comedy' in its older and wider meaning, it is evident that it is as an 'amazing humourist' that he would present to our generation the great Christopher North. And assuredly, at this the 'delighted spirit' of Christopher smiles delightedly in Hades. For, however the 'Comic Muse' may pout upon hearing from Mr. Skelton that 'the "Noctes Ambrosianæ" belong to her,' it is clear that the one great desire of Wilson's life was to cultivate her—was to be an 'amazing humourist,' in short. It is clear, besides, that there was one special kind of humour which he most of all affected, that which we call technically 'Rabelaisian.' To have gone down to posterity as the great English Rabelaisian of the nineteenth century, Christopher North would have freely given all his deserved fame as a prose poet, and all the thirty thousand pounds hard cash of which he was despoiled to boot. His personality was enormous. He had more of that demonic element—of which since Goethe's time we have heard so much—than any man in Scotland. Everybody seems to have been dominated

by him. De Quincey, with a finer intellect than even
his own—and that is using strong language—looked up
to him as a spaniel looks up to his master. It is positively ludicrous, while reading De Quincey's 'Auto-
biographic Sketches,' to come again and again upon
the naïve refrain : ' I think so, so does Professor Wilson.'
Gigantic as was the egotism of the Opium-eater, it was
overshadowed by the still more gigantic egotism of
Christopher North. In this, as in everything else, he
was the opposite of the finest Scottish humourist since
Burns, Sir Walter Scott. Scott's desire was to create
eccentric humourous characters, but to remain the
simple Scottish gentleman himself. Wilson's great
ambition was to be an eccentric humourous character
himself ; for your superlative egotist has scarcely even
the wish to create. He would like the universe to himself. If Wilson had created Falstaff, and if you had
expressed to him your admiration of the truthfulness of
that character, he would have taken you by the shoulder
and said, with a smile : ' Don't you see, you fool, that
Falstaff is I—John Wilson ? ' He always wished it to
be known that the Ettrick Shepherd and Tickler were
John Wilson—as much Wilson as Kit North himself, or,
rather, what he would have liked John Wilson to be considered. This determination to be a humourous character
it was—and no lack of literary ambition—that caused
him to squander his astonishing powers in the way that
Mr. Skelton, and all of us who admire the man, lament.
    Many articles in ' Blackwood '—notably the one
upon Shakspeare's four great tragedies and the one in
which he discusses Coleridge's poetry—show that his
insight into the principles of literary art was true and
deep—far too true and deep for him to be ignorant of
this inexorable law, that nothing can live in literature

without form, nothing but humour ; but that, let this flowery crown of literature show itself in the most formless kind of magazine-article or review-essay, and the writer is secure of his place according to his merits.

Has Wilson secured such a place ? We fear not ; and if Skelton were to ask us, on our oath, why Wilson's fourteen volumes of brilliant, eloquent, and picturesque writing are already in a sadly moribund state, while such slight and apparently fugitive essays as the ' Coverley ' papers, the essays of Elia, and the hurried review articles of Sydney Smith, seem to have more vitality than ever, we fear that our answer would have to be this bipartite one : first, that mere elaborated intellectual ' humour ' has the seeds of dissolution in it from the beginning, while temperamental humour alone can live ; and, secondly, that Wilson was probably not temperamentally a humourist at all, and certainly not temperamentally a Rabelaisian. But let us, by way of excuse for this rank blasphemy, say what precise meaning we attach to the word ' Rabelaisian '—though the subject is so wide that there is no knowing whither it may lead us. Without venturing upon a new definition of humour, this we will venture to say, that true humour, that is to say, the humour of temperament, is conveniently divisible into two kinds : Cervantic humour, i.e. the amused, philosophic mood of the dramatist—the comedian ; and Rabelaisian humour, i.e. the lawless abandonment of mirth, flowing mostly from exuberance of health and animal spirits, with a strong recognition of the absurdity of human life and the almighty joke of the Cosmos—a mood which in literature is rarer than in life—rarer, perhaps, because animal spirits are not the common and characteristic accompaniments of the literary temperament.

Of Cervantic humour Wilson has, of course, absolutely nothing. For this, the fairest flower in the garden, cannot often take root, save in the most unegotistic souls. It belongs to the Chaucers, the Shakspeares, the Molières, the Addisons, the Fieldings, the Steeles, the Scotts, the Miss Austens, the George Eliots—upon whom the rich tides of the outer life come breaking and drowning the egotism and yearning for self-expression which is the life of smaller souls. Among these—to whom to create is everything—Sterne would perhaps have been greatest of all had he never known Hall Stevenson, and never read Rabelais; while Dickens's growth was a development from Rabelaisianism to Cervantism. But surely so delicate a critic as Mr. Skelton has often proved himself to be, is not going to seriously tell us that there is one ray of dramatic humour to be found in Wilson. Why, the man had not even the mechanical skill of varying the locutions and changing the styles of his two or three characters. Even the humourless Plato could do that. Even the humourless Landor could do that. But, strip the ' Shepherd's ' talk of its Scottish accent and it is nothing but those same appalling mighty waters whose rush in the ' Recreations ' and the ' Essays ' we are so familiar with. While, as to his clumsy caricature of the sesquipedalian language of De Quincey, that is such obtrusive caricature that illusion seems to be purposely destroyed, and the ' Opium-Eater ' becomes a fantastic creature of Farce, and not of Comedy at all.

The ' amazing humour ' of Wilson, then, is not Cervantic. Is it Rabelaisian ? Again, we fear not. Very likely the genuine Rabelaisian does not commonly belong to the ' writing fellows ' at all. We have had the good luck to come across two Rabelaisians in our time.

One was a lawyer, who hated literature with a beautiful
and a pathetic hatred. The other was a drunken
cobbler, who loved it with a beautiful and a pathetic love.
And we have just heard from one of our finest critics
that a true Rabelaisian is, at this moment, to be found—
where he ought to be found—at Stratford-on-Avon.
This is interesting. Yet, as there were heroes before
Agamemnon, so there were Rabelaisians, even among the
'writing fellows,' before Rabelais; the greatest of
them, of course, being Aristophanes, though, from all
we hear, it may be reasonably feared that when
Alcibiades, instead of getting damages out of Eupolis
for libel, 'in a duck-pond drowned him,' he thereby
extinguished for ever a Rabelaisian of the very first rank.
But we can only judge from what we have; and, to
say nothing of the tabooed Lysistrata, the 'Birds' alone
puts Aristophanes at the top of all pre-Rabelaisian
Rabelaisians. But when those immortal words came
from that dying bed at Meudon : ' Let down the curtain ;
the farce is done,' they were prophetic as regards the
literary Rabelaisians—prophetic in this, that no writer
has since thoroughly caught the Rabelaisian mood—the
mood, that is, of the cosmic humourist, gasping with
merriment as he gobbles huge piles of meat and guzzles
from huge flagons of wine. Yet, if his mantle has fallen
upon no one pair of shoulders, a corner of it has dropped
upon several; for the great Curé divides his qualities
among his followers impartially, giving but one to each,
like the pine-apple in the 'Paradise of Fruits,' from
which every other fruit in the garden drew its own
peculiar flavour, and then charged its neighbour fruits
with stealing theirs. Among a few others, it may be
said that the cosmic humour has fallen to Swift (in
whom, however, earnestness half stifled it) Sterne, and

Richter; while the animal spirits—the love of life—
the fine passion for victuals and drink—has fallen to
several more, notably to Thomas Amory, the creator of
'John Bunele'; to Herrick, to old John Skelton, to
Burns (in the 'Jolly Beggars'), to John Skinner, the
author of 'Tullochgorum.' Shakspeare, having everything, has, of course, both sides of Rabelaisianism as well
as Cervantism. Some of the scenes in 'Henry the
Fourth' and 'Henry the Fifth' are rich with it. So is
'Twelfth Night,' to go no further. Dickens's
Rabelaisianism stopped with 'Pickwick.' If Hood's
gastric fluid had been a thousand times stronger, he
would have been the greatest Rabelaisian since Rabelais.
A good man, if his juices are right, may grow into Cervantism, but you cannot grow into Rabelaisianism.
Neither can you simulate it without coming to grief.
Yet, of simulated Rabelaisianism all literature is, alas!
full, and this is how the simulators come to grief;
simulated cosmic humour becomes the self-conscious
grimacing and sad posture-making of the harlequin
sage, such as we see in those who make life hideous by
imitating Mr. Carlyle. This is bad. But far worse is
simulated animal spirits, i.e. jolly-doggism. This is
insupportable. For we ask the reader—who may very
likely have been to an undergraduates' wine-party, or
to a medical students' revel, or who may have read the
'Noctes Ambrosianæ'—we seriously and earnestly ask
him whether, among all the dreary things of this sometimes dreary life, there is anything half so dreadful as
jolly-doggism.

And now we come reluctantly to the point. It
breaks our heart to say to Mr. Skelton—for we believed
in Professor Wilson once—it breaks our heart to say that
Wilson's Rabelaisianism is nothing but jolly-doggism of

the most prepense, affected, and piteous kind. In
reading the ' Noctes ' we feel, as Jefferson's Rip van
Winkle must have felt, surrounded by the ghosts on the
top of the Katskill mountains. We say to ourselves,
' How comparatively comfortable we should feel if those
bloodless, marrowless spectres wouldn't pretend to be
jolly—if they would not pretend to be enjoying their
phantom bowls and their ghostly liquor ! '

Though John Skinner and Thomas Amory have
but a small endowment of the great master's humour,
their animal spirits are genuine. They do not hop,
skip, and jump for effect. Their friskiness is the friskiness of the retriever puppy when let loose ; of the
urchin who runs shrieking against the shrieking wind in
the unsyllabled tongue that all creatures know, ' I live,
I live, I live ! ' But, whatever might have been the
physical health of Wilson, there is a hollow ring about
the literary cheerfulness of the ' Noctes ' that, notwithstanding all that has been said to the contrary,
makes us think that he was at heart almost a melancholy
man ; that makes us think that the real Wilson is the
Wilson of the ' Isle of Palms,' ' The City of the Plague,'
of the ' Trials of Margaret Lyndsay,' of the ' Lights
and Shadows of Scottish Life,' Wilson, the Words-
worthian, the lover of Nature, whom Jeffrey describes
when he says that ' almost the only passions with which
his poetry is conversant are the gentler sympathies of our
nature—tender compassion—confiding affection, and
gentleness and sorrow.'

He wished to be thought a rollicking, devil-me-care
protagonist, a good-tempered giant ready to swallow
with a guffaw the whole cockney army if necessary.
This kind of man he may have been—Mr. Skelton
inferentially says he was ; all we know is that his writings

lead us to think he was playing a part.   A temperamental
humourist, we say decidedly, he was not.

Is there, then, no humour to be found in this book ?
In a certain sense no doubt humour may be found there.
Just as science tells us that all the stars in heaven are
composed of pretty much the same elements as the
familiar earth on which we live, or dream we live, so is
every one among us composed of the same elements as
all the rest, and one of the most important elements
common to all human kind is humour.   And, if a man
takes to expressing in literary forms the little humour
within him, it is but natural that the more vigorous, the
more agile is his intellect and the greater is his literary
skill, the more deceptive is his mere intellectual humour,
the more telling his wit.   Now, Wilson's intellect was
exceedingly and wonderfully fine.   As strong as it was
swift, it could fly over many a wide track of knowledge
and of speculation unkenned by not a few of those who
now-a-days would underrate him, dropping a rain of
diamonds from his wings like the fabulous bird of North
Cathay."

No sooner had the article appeared than Appleton
went to Danes Inn and saw the author of it.   Appleton
was in a state of great excitement, and indeed of great
rage, for at that time there was considerable rivalry
between the ' Athenaeum ' and the ' Academy.'

"You belong to us," said Appleton.   "The
' Academy ' is the proper place for you.   You and I
have been friends for a long time, and so have Rossetti
and the rest of us, and yet you go into the enemy's
camp."

"And shall I tell you why I have joined the
' Athenæum ' in place of the ' Academy ' ? " said

Watts ; " it is simply because MacColl invited me, and you did not."

" For months and months I have been urging you to write in the ' Academy,' " said Appleton.

" That is true, no doubt," said Watts, " but while MacColl offered me an important post on his paper, and in the literary department, too, you invited me to do the drudgery of melting down into two columns books upon metaphysics. It is too late, my dear boy, it is too late. If to join the ' Athenæum ' is to go into the camp of the Philistines, why, then, a Philistine am I."

I do not know whether at that time Shirley (as Sir John Skelton was then called) and Mr. Watts-Dunton were friends, but I know they were friends afterwards. Shirley, in his ' Reminiscences ' of Rossetti, like most of his friends, urged Mr. Watts-Dunton to write a memoir of the poet-painter. I do know, however, that Mr. Watts-Dunton, besides cherishing an affectionate memory of Sir John Skelton as a man, is a genuine admirer of the Shirley Essays. I have heard him say more than once that Skelton's style had a certain charm for him, and he could not understand why Skelton's position is not as great as it deserves to be. ' Scotsmen,' he said, ' often complain that English critics are slow to do them justice. This idea was the bane of my dear old friend John Nichol's life. He really seemed to think that he was languishing and withering under the ban of a great anti-Scottish conspiracy known as the Savile Club. As a matter of fact, however, there is nothing whatever in the idea that a Scotsman does not fight on equal terms with the Englishman in the great literary cockpit of London. To say the truth, the Scottish cock is really longer in spur and beak than the English cock, and can more than take care of himself. For my part, with the exception of Swinburne, I really think that my most intimate friends are either Irish, Scottish, or Welsh. But I have sometimes thought that if Skelton had been an Englishman and moved in English sets, he would have taken an enormously higher position than he has secured, for he would have been more known among writers, and the more he was known the more he was liked.'

As will be seen further on, before the review of the 'Comedy of the Noctes Ambrosianæ' appeared, Mr. Watts-Dunton had contributed to the 'Athenæum' an article on 'The Art of Interviewing.' From this time forward he became the chief critic of the 'Athenæum,' and for nearly a quarter of a century —that is to say, until he published 'The Coming of Love,' when he practically, I think, ceased to write reviews of any kind—he enriched its pages with critical essays the peculiar features of which were their daring formulation of first principles, their profound generalizations, their application of modern scientific knowledge to the phenomena of literature, and, above all, their richly idiosyncratic style—a style so personal that, as Groome said in the remarks quoted in an earlier chapter, it signs all his work.

As I have more than once said, it is necessary to dwell with some fulness upon these criticisms, because the relation between his critical and his creative work is of the closest kind. Indeed, it has been said by Rossetti that 'the subtle and original generalizations upon the first principles of poetry which illumine his writings could only have come to him by a duplicate exercise of his brain when he was writing his own poetry.' The great critics of poetry have nearly all been great poets. Rossetti used humourously to call him 'The Symposiarch,' and no doubt the influence of his long practice of oral criticism in Cheyne Walk, at Kelmscott Manor, as well as in such opposite gatherings as those at Dr. Marston's, Madox Brown's, and Mrs. Procter's, may be traced in his writings. For his most effective criticism has always the personal magic of the living voice, producing on the reader the winsome effect of spontaneous conversation overheard. Its variety of manner, as well as of subject, differentiates it from all other contemporary criticism. In it are found racy erudition, powerful thought, philosophical speculation, irony silkier than the silken irony of M. Anatole France, airily mischievous humour, and a perpetual coruscation of the comic spirit. To the 'Athenæum' he contributed essays upon all sorts of themes such as 'The Poetic Interpretation of Nature,' 'The Troubadours and Trouvères,' 'The Children of the Open Air,' 'The Gypsies,' 'Cosmic Humour,' 'The Effect of Evolution upon Literature.' And although the most complete and most modern critical system in the English language lies buried in the vast ocean of the 'Examiner,' the 'Athenæum,' and the 'Encyclopædia Britannica,' there are still divers who are aware of its existence, as is proved by the latest appreciation of Mr. Watts-Dunton's work, that contributed by Madame Galimberti, the accomplished wife of the Italian minister, to the 'Rivista d' Italia.' In this article she makes frequent allusions to the 'Athenæum' articles, and quotes freely from them. Rossetti once said that 'the reason why Theodore Watts was so little known outside the inner circle of letters was that he sought obscurity as eagerly as other men sought fame'; but although his indifference to literary reputation is so

invincible that it has baffled all the efforts of all his friends
to persuade him to collect his critical essays, his influence
over contemporary criticism has been and is and will
be profound.

There is no province of pure literature which his criticism leaves untouched ; but it is in poetry that it cul-
minates.   His treatise in the ' Encyclopædia Britannica '
on ' Poetry ' is alone sufficient to show how deep has
been his study of poetic principles.   The essay on the
' Sonnet,' too, which appeared in ' Chambers's Encyclopædia,' is admitted by critics of the sonnet to be the
one indispensable treatise on the subject.   It has been
much discussed by foreign critics, especially by Dr. Karl
Leutzner in his treatise, ' Uber das Sonett in der
Englischen Dichtung.'   ,]

The principles upon which he carried on criticism in
the ' Athenæum ' are admirably expressed in the following dialogue between him and Mr. G. B. Burgin, who
approached him as the representative of the ' Idler.'
The allusion to the 'smart slaters' will be sufficient to
indicate the approximate date of the interview.

"Having read your treatise on poetry in the ' Encyclopædia Britannica,' which, it is said, has been an
influence in every European literature, I want to ask
whether a critic so deeply learned in all the secrets of
poetic art, and who has had the advantages of comparing his own opinions with those of all the great poets of
his time, takes a hopeful or despondent view of the condition of English poetry at the present moment.   There
are those who run down the present generation of poets,
but on this subject the men who are really entitled to
speak can be counted on the fingers of one hand.

It would be valuable to know whether our leading critic is in sympathy with the poetry of the present hour."

"I do not for a moment admit that I am the leading critic. To say the truth, I am often amused, and often vexed, at the grotesque misconception that seems to be afloat as to my relation to criticism. Years ago, Russell Lowell told me that all over the United States I was identified with every paragraph of a certain critical journal in which I sometimes write ; and, judging from the droll attacks that are so often made upon me by outside paragraph writers, the same misconception seems to be spreading in England—attacks which the smiling and knowing public well understands to spring from writing men who have not been happy in their relations with the reviewers."

"It has been remarked that you never answer any attack in the newspapers, howsoever unjust or absurd."

"I do not believe in answering attacks. The public, as I say, knows that there is a mysterious and inscrutable yearning in the slow-worm to bite with the fangs of the adder, and every attack upon a writer does him more good than praise would do. But, as a matter of fact, I have no connexion whatever with any journal save that of a student of letters who finds it convenient on occasion to throw his meditations upon literary art and the laws that govern it in the form of a review. It is a bad method, no doubt, of giving expression to one's excogitations, and although I do certainly contrive to put careful criticisms into my articles, I cannot imagine more unbusinesslike reviewing than mine. Yet it has one good quality, I think—it is never unkindly. I never will take a book for review unless I can say something in its favour, and a good deal in its favour."

"Then you never practise the smart 'slating' which certain would-be critics indulge in?"

"Never! In the first place, it would afford me no pleasure to give pain to a young writer. In the next place, this 'smart slating,' as you call it, is the very easiest thing of achievement in the world. Give me the aid of a good amanuensis, and I will engage to dictate as many miles of such smart 'slating' as could be achieved by any six of the smart slaters. A charming phrase of yours, 'smart slaters'! But I leave such work to them, as do all the really true critics of my time —men to whom the insolence which the smart slaters seem to mistake for wit would be as easy as to me, only that, like me, they hold such work in contempt. Take a critic like Mr. Traill, for instance. Unfortunately, Fate has decreed that many hours every day of his valuable life are wasted on 'leader' writing, but there is in any one of his literary essays more wit and humour than could be achieved by all the smart writers combined; and yet how kind is he! going out of his way to see merit in a rising poet, and to foster it. Or take Grant Allen, whose good things flow so naturally from him. While the typical smart writer is illustrating the primal curse by making his poor little spiteful jokes in the sweat of his poor little spiteful brow, Grant Allen's good-natured sayings have the very wit that the unlucky sweater and 'slater' is trying for. Read what he said about William Watson, and see how kind he is. Compare his geniality with the scurrility of the smart writers. Again, take Andrew Lang, perhaps the most variously accomplished man of letters in England or in Europe, and compare his geniality with the scurrility of the smart writers. But it was not, I suppose, of such as they that you came to talk about. You are asking me whether I am in sympathy with the

younger writers of my time.   My answer is that I cannot
imagine any one to be more in sympathy with them than
I am.   In spite of the disparity of years between me and
the youngest of them, I believe I number many of them
among my warmest and most loyal friends, and that is
because I am in true sympathy with their work and their
aims.   No doubt there are some points in which they
and I agree to differ."

"And what about our contemporary novelists?
Perhaps you do not give attention to fiction?"

"Give attention to novels!   Why, if I did not, I
should not give attention to literature at all.   In a true
and deep sense all pure literature is fiction—to use an
extremely inadequate and misleading word as a substitute for the right phrase, 'imaginative representation.'
'The Iliad,' 'The Odyssey,' 'The Æneid,' 'The
Divina Commedia,' are fundamentally novels, though
in verse, as certainly novels as is the latest story by the
most popular of our writers.   The greatest of all writers
of the novelette is the old Burmese parable writer,
who gave us the story of the girl-mother and the mus-
tard-seed.   A time which has given birth to such
novelists as many of ours of the present day is a great,
and a very great, time for the English novel.   Criticism
will have to recognize, and at once, that the novel, now-
a-days, stands plump in the front rank of the 'literature
of power,' and if criticism does not so recognize it, so
much the worse for criticism, I think.   That the novel
will grow in importance is, I say, quite certain.   In
such a time as ours (as I have said in print), poetry is
like the knickerbockers of a growing boy—it has become
too small somehow; it is not quite large enough for the
growing limbs of life.   The novel is more flexible; it
can be stretched to fit the muscles as they swell."

"I will conclude by asking you what I have asked another eminent critic : What is your opinion of anonymity in criticism ? "

" Well, there I am a ' galled jade ' that must needs ' wince ' a little. No doubt I write anonymously myself, but that is because I have not yet mastered that dislike of publicity which has kept me back, and my writing seems to lose its elasticity with its anonymity. The chief argument against anonymous criticism I take to be this : That any scribbler who can get upon an important journal is at once clothed with the journal's own authority—and the same applies, of course, to the dishonest critic; and this is surely very serious. With regard to dishonest criticism it is impossible for the most wary editor to be always on his guard against it. An editor cannot read all the books, nor can he know the innumerable ramifications of the literary world. When Jones asks him for Brown's book for review, the editor cannot know that Jones has determined to praise it or to cut it up irrespective of its merits; and then, when the puff or attack comes in, it is at once clothed with the authority, not of Jones's name, but that of the journal.

In the literary arena itself the truth of the case may be known, but not in the world outside, and it must not be supposed but that great injustice may flow from this. I myself have more than once heard a good book spoken of with contempt in London Society, and heard quoted the very words of some hostile review which I have known to be the work of a spiteful foe of the writer of the book, or of some paltry fellow who was quite incompetent to review anything."

Now that the day of the 'smart slaters' is over, it is interesting to read in connection with these obiter dicta

the following passage from the article in which Mr.
Watts-Dunton, on the seventieth birthday of the 'Athenæum,'spoke of its record and its triumphs :—

"The enormous responsibility of anonymous criticism
is seen in every line contributed by the Maurice and
Sterling group who spoke through its columns. Even
for those who are behind the scenes and know
that the critique expresses the opinion of only one
writer, it is difficult not to be impressed by the accent
of authority in the editorial 'we.' But with regard
to the general public, the reader of a review article
finds it impossible to escape from the authority of
the 'we,' and the power of a single writer to benefit or
to injure an author is so great that none but the most
deeply conscientious men ought to enter the ranks of
the anonymous reviewers. These were the views of
Maurice and Sterling ; and that they are shared by all
the best writers of our time there can be no doubt.
Some very illustrious men have given very emphatic
expression to them. On a certain memorable occasion,
at a little dinner-party at 16 Cheyne Walk, one of the
guests related an anecdote of his having accidentally met
an old acquaintance who had deeply disgraced himself,
and told how he had stood 'dividing the swift mind'
as to whether he could or could not offer the man his
hand. 'I think I should have offered him mine,' said
Rossetti, 'although no one detests his offence more than
I do.' And then the conversation ran upon the question
as to the various kinds of offenders with whom old
friends could not shake hands. 'There is one kind of
miscreant,' said Rossetti, 'whom you have forgotten
to name—a miscreant who in kind of meanness and
infamy cannot well be beaten, the man who in an anony-

mous journal tells the world that a poem or picture is bad when he knows it to be good. That is the man who should never defile my hand by his touch. By God, if I met such a man at a dinner-table I must not kick him, I suppose ; but I could not, and would not, taste bread and salt with him. I would quietly get up and go.' Tennyson, on afterwards being told this story, said, ' And who would not do the same ? Such a man has been guilty of sacrilege—sacrilege against art.' Maurice, Sterling, and the other writers in the first volume of the ' Athenæum ' worked on the great principle that the critic's primary duty is to seek and to bring to light those treasures of art and literature that the busy world is only too apt to pass by. Their pet abhorrence was the cheap smartness of Jeffrey and certain of his co-adjutors ; and from its commencement the ' Athenæum ' has striven to avoid slashing and smart writing. A difficult thing to avoid, no doubt, for nothing is so easy to achieve as that insolent and vulgar slashing which the half-educated amateur thinks so clever. Of all forms of writing, the founders of the ' Athenæum ' held the shallow, smart style to be the cheapest and also the most despicable. And here again the views of the ' Athenæum ' have remained unchanged. The critic who works ' without a conscience or an aim ' knows only too well that it pays to pander to the most lamentable of all the weaknesses of human nature—the love that people have of seeing each other attacked and vilified ; it pays for a time, until it defeats itself. For although man has a strong instinct for admiration—else had he never reached his present position in the conscious world—he has, running side by side with this instinct, another strong instinct—the instinct for contempt. A reviewer's ridicule poured upon a writer

titillates the reader with a sense of his own superiority.
It is by pandering to this lower instinct that the un-
principled journalist hopes to kill two birds with one
stone—to gratify his own malignity and low-bred love
of insolence, and to make profit while doing so. Although cynicism may certainly exist alongside great
talent, it is far more likely to be found where there is no
talent at all. Many brilliant writers have written in
this journal, but rarely, if ever, have truth and honesty
of criticism been sacrificed for a smart saying. One of
these writers—the greatest wit of the nineteenth century
—used to say, in honest disparagement of what were
considered his own prodigious powers of wit, ' I will
engage in six lessons to teach any man to do this kind of
thing as well as I do, if he thinks it worth his while to
learn.' And the ' Athenæum,' at the time when Hood
was reviewing Dickens in its columns, could have said
the same thing. The smart reviewer, however, mistakes
insolence for wit, and among the low-minded insolence
needs no teaching."

Of course, in the office of an important literary organ
there is always a kind of terror lest, in the necessary hurry
of the work, a contributor should ' come down a cropper '
over some matter of fact, and open the door to troublesome correspondence. As Mr. Watts-Dunton has said,
the mysterious ' we ' must claim to be Absolute Wisdom,
or where is the authority of the oracle ? When a contributor ' comes down a cropper,' although the matter
may be of infinitesimal importance, the editor cannot, it
seems, and never could (except during the imperial régime
of the ' Saturday Review ' under Cook) refuse to insert
a correction. Now, as Mr. Watts-Dunton has said, ' the
smaller the intelligence, the greater joy does it feel in

setting other intelligences right.' I have been told that it was a tradition in the office of the 'Examiner,' and also in the office of the 'Athenæum,' that Theodore Watts had not only never been known to 'come down a cropper,' but had never given the 'critical gnats' a chance of pretending that he had to. One day, however, in an article on Frederick Tennyson's poems, speaking of the position that the poet Alexander Smith occupied in the early fifties, and contrasting it with the position that he held at the time the article was written, Mr. Watts-Dunton affirmed that once on a time Smith—the same Smith whom 'Z' (the late William Allingham) had annihilated in the 'Athenæum '—had been admired by Alfred Tennyson, and also that once on a time Herbert Spencer had compared a metaphor of Alexander Smith's with the metaphors of Shakespeare. The touchiness of Spencer was proverbial, and on the next Monday morning the editor got the following curt note from the great man :—

'Will the writer of the review of Mr. Frederick Tennyson's poems, which was published in your last number, please say where I have compared the metaphors of Shakspeare and Alexander Smith ?

HERBERT SPENCER.'

The editor, taking for granted that the heretofore 'impeccable contributor had at last 'come down a cropper,' sent a proof of Spencer's note to Mr. Watts-Dunton, and intimated that it had better be printed without any editorial comment at all. Of course, if Mr. Watts-Dunton had at last 'come down a cropper,' this would have been the wisest plan. But he returned

the proof of the letter to the editor, with the following
footnote added to it :—

"It is many years since Mr. Herbert Spencer printed
in one of the magazines an essay dealing with the laws of
cause and effect in literary art—an essay so searching in
its analyses, and so original in its method and conclusions, that the workers in pure literature may well
be envious of science for enticing such a leader away
from their ranks—and it is many years since we had
the pleasure of reading it. Our memory is, therefore,
somewhat hazy as to the way in which he introduced
such metaphors by Alexander Smith as ' I speared him
with a jest,' etc.   Our only object, however, in alluding
to the subject was to show that a poet now ignored by
the criticism of the hour, a poet who could throw off such
Shakspearean sentences as this—

> —— My drooping sails
> Flap idly 'gainst the mast of my intent ;
> I rot upon the waters when my prow
> Should grate the golden isles—

had once the honour of being admired by Alfred Tennyson and favourably mentioned by Mr. Herbert Spencer."

Spencer told this to a friend, and with much laughter
said, ' Of course the article was Theodore Watts's.   I
had forgotten entirely what I had said about Shakspeare
and Alexander Smith.'

If I were asked to furnish a typical example of that
combination of critical insight, faultless memory, and
genial courtesy, which distinguishes Mr. Watts-Dunton's
writings, I think I should select this bland postscript
to Spencer's letter.

Another instance of the care and insight with which
Mr. Watts-Dunton always wrote his essays is connected
with Robert Louis Stevenson.   It occurred in connection
with 'Kidnapped.'   I will   quote   here   Mr. Watts-
Dunton's own version of the anecdote, which will be
found in the 'Athenæum' review of the Edinburgh
edition of Stevenson's works.   The playful allusion to
the 'Athenæum's' kindness is very characteristic :—

" Of Stevenson's sweetness of disposition and his good
sense we could quote many instances ; but let one suffice.
When 'Kidnapped' appeared, although in reviewing it
we enjoyed the great pleasure of giving high praise to
certain parts of that delightful narrative, we refused to
be scared from making certain strictures.   It occurred to
us that while some portions of the story were full of that
organic detail of which Scott was such a master, and without which no really vital story can be told, it was not so
with certain other parts.   From this we drew the conclusion that the book really consisted of two distinct parts,
two stories which Stevenson had tried in vain to weld
into one.   We surmised that the purely Jacobite adventures of Balfour and Alan Breck were written first, and
that then the writer, anxious to win the suffrages of the
general novel-reader (whose power is so great with Byles
the Butcher), looked about him for some story on the old
lines ; that he experienced great difficulty in finding one ;
and that he was at last driven upon the old situation of
the villain uncle plotting to make away with the nephew
by kidnapping him and sending him off to the plantations.
The 'Athenæum,' whose kindness towards all writers,
poets and prosemen, great and small, has won for it such
an infinity of gratitude, said this, but in its usual kind and
gentle way.   This aroused the wrath of the Steven-

sonians. Yet we were not at all surprised to get from the author of ' Kidnapped ' himself a charming letter.'

This letter appears in Stevenson's ' Letters,' and by the courtesy of Mr. Sidney Colvin and Mr. A. M. S. Methuen I am permitted to reprint it here :—

SKERRYVORE, BOURNEMOUTH.

DEAR MR. WATTS,—The sight of the last ' Athenæum ' reminds me of you, and of my debt now too long due. I wish to thank you for your notice of ' Kidnapped ' ; and that not because it was kind, though for that also I valued it ; but in the same sense as I have thanked you before now for a hundred articles on a hundred different writers. A critic like you is one who fights the good fight, contending with stupidity, and I would fain hope not all in vain ; in my own case, for instance, surely not in vain. What you say of the two parts in ' Kidnapped ' was felt by no one more painfully than by myself. I began it, partly as a lark, partly as a pot-boiler ; and suddenly it moved, David and Alan stepped out from the canvas, and I found I was in another world. But there was the cursed beginning, and a cursed end must be appended ; and our old friend Byles the Butcher was plainly audible tapping at the back door. So it had to go into the world, one part (as it does seem to me) alive, one part merely galvanised : no work, only an essay. For a man of tentative method, and weak health, and a scarcity of private means, and not too much of that frugality which is the artist's proper virtue, the days of sinecures and patrons look very golden : the days of professional literature very hard. Yet I do not so far deceive myself as to think I should change my character by changing my epoch ; the sum of virtue in our books is in a relation of equality to the sum of virtues in ourselves ; and my ' Kidnapped ' was doomed, while still in the womb and while I was yet in the cradle, to be the thing it is.

And now to the more genial business of defence. You attack my fight on board the ' Covenant,' I think it literal. David and Alan had every advantage on their side, position, arms, training, a good conscience ; a handful of merchant sailors, not well led in the first attack, not led at all in the second, could only by an accident have taken the roundhouse by attack ; and since the defenders had firearms and food, it is even doubtful if they could have been starved out. The only doubtful point with me is whether the seamen would have ever ventured on the second onslaught ; I half believe they would not ; still the illusion of numbers and the authority of Hoseason would perhaps stretch far enough to justify the extremity. —I am, dear Mr. Watts, your very sincere admirer,

ROBERT LOUIS STEVENSON.

Mr. Watts-Dunton has always been a warm admirer of Stevenson, of his personal character no less than his undoubted genius, and Stevenson, on his part, in conversation never failed to speak of himself, as in this letter he subscribes himself, as Mr. Watts-Dunton's sincere admirer. But Mr. Watts-Dunton's admiration of Stevenson's work was more tempered with judgment than was the admiration of some critics, who afterwards, when he became too successful, disparaged him. Greatly as he admired ' Kidnapped ' and ' Catriona,' there were certain of Stevenson's works for which his admiration was qualified, and certain others for which he had no admiration at all. His strictures upon the story which seems to have been at first the main source of Stevenson's popularity, ' Dr. Jekyll and Mr. Hyde,' were much resented at the time by those insincere and fickle worshippers to whom I have already alluded. Yet these strictures are surely full of wisdom, and they specially show that wide sweep over the entire field of literature which is characteristic of all his criticism. As they contain, besides, one of his many tributes to Scott, I will quote them here :—

" Take the little story ' Dr. Jekyll and Mr. Hyde,' the laudatory criticism upon which is in bulk, as regards the story itself, like the comet's tail in relation to the comet. On its appearance as a story, a ' shilling shocker ' for the railway bookstalls, the critic's attention was directed to its vividness of narrative and kindred qualities, and though perfectly conscious of its worthlessness in the world of literary art, he might well be justified in comparing it to its advantage with other stories of its class and literary standing. But when it is offered as a classic—and this is really how it is offered—it has to be judged by critical canons of a very different kind. It has then to be compared and contrasted with stories having a like motive— stories that deal with an idea as old as the oldest literature —as old, no doubt, as those primeval days when man awoke to the consciousness that he is a moral and a responsible being—stories whose temper has always been up to now of the loftiest kind.

It is many years since, in writing of the ' Parables of Buddhaghosha,' it was our business to treat at length of the grand idea of man's dual nature, and the many beautiful forms in which it has been embodied. We said then that, from the lovely modern story of Arsène Houssaye, where a young man, starting along life's road, sees on a lawn a beautiful girl and loves her, and afterwards—when sin has soiled him—finds that she was his own soul, stained now by his own sin ; and from the still more impressive, though less lovely modern story of Edgar Poe, 'William Wilson,' up to the earliest allegories upon the subject, no writer or story-teller had dared to degrade by gross treatment a motive of such universal appeal to the great heart of the 'Great Man, Mankind.' We traced the idea, as far as our knowledge went, through Calderon, back to Oriental sources, and found, as we then could truly affirm, that this motive—from the ethical point of view the most pathetic and solemn of all motives—had been always treated with a nobility and a greatness that did honour to literary art. Manu, after telling us that 'single is each man born into the world—single dies,' implores each one to 'collect virtue,' in order that after death he may be met by the virtuous part of his dual self, a beautiful companion and guide in traversing 'that gloom which is so hard to be traversed.' Fine as this is, it is surpassed by an Arabian story we then quoted (since versified by Sir Edwin Arnold)—the story of the wicked king who met after death a frightful hag for an eternal companion, and found her to be only a part of his own dual nature, the embodiment of his own evil deeds. And even this is surpassed by that lovely allegory in Arda Viraf, in which a virtuous soul in Paradise, walking amid pleasant trees whose fragrance was wafted from God, meets a part of his own dual nature, a beautiful maiden, who says to him, 'O youth, I am thine own actions.'

And we instanced other stories and allegories equally beautiful, in which this supreme thought has been treated as poetically as it deserves. It was left for Stevenson to degrade it into a hideous tale of murder and Whitechapel mystery—a story of astonishing brutality, in which the separation of the two natures of the man's soul is effected not by psychological development, and not by the 'awful

alchemy' of the spirit-world beyond the grave, as in all
the previous versions, but by the operation of a dose of
some supposed new drug.

If the whole thing is meant as a horrible joke, in imitation of De Quincey's ' Murder considered as One of the
Fine Arts,' it tells poorly for Stevenson's sense of humour.
If it is meant as a serious allegory, it is an outrage upon
the grand allegories of the same motive with which most
literatures have been enriched. That a story so coarse
should have met with the plaudits that ' Dr. Jekyll and
Mr. Hyde ' met with at the time of its publication—that
it should now be quoted in leading articles of important
papers every few days, while all the various and beautiful
renderings of the motive are ignored—what does it mean ?
Is it a sign that the ' shrinkage of the world,' the ' solid-
arity of civilisation,' making the record of each day's doings too big for the day, has worked a great change in our
public writers ? Is it that they not only have no time
to think, but no time to read anything beyond the publications of the hour ? Is it that good work is unknown
to them, and that bad work is forced upon them, and
that in their busy ignorance they must needs accept it
and turn to it for convenient illustration ? That Stevenson should have been impelled to write the story shows
what the ' Suicide Club ' had already shown, that underneath the apparent health which gives such a charm to
' Treasure Island ' and ' Kidnapped,' there was that
morbid strain which is so often associated with physical
disease.

Had it not been for the influence upon him of the
healthiest of all writers since Chaucer—Walter Scott—
Stevenson might have been in the ranks of those pompous
problem-mongers of fiction and the stage who do their
best to make life hideous. It must be remembered that

he was a critic first and a creator afterwards. He himself tells us how critically he studied the methods of other writers before he took to writing himself. No one really understood better than he Hesiod's fine saying that the muses were born in order that they might be a forgetfulness of evils and a truce from cares. No one understood better than he Joubert's saying, ' Fiction has no business to exist unless it is more beautiful than reality ; in literature the one aim is the beautiful ; once lose sight of that, and you have the mere frightful reality.' And for the most part he succeeded in keeping down the morbid impulses of a spirit imprisoned and fretted in a crazy body.

Save in such great mistakes as ' Dr. Jekyll and Mr. Hyde,' and a few other stories, Stevenson acted upon Joubert's excellent maxim. But Scott, and Scott alone, is always right in this matter—right by instinct. He alone is always a delight. If all art is dedicated to joy, as Schiller declares, and if there is no higher and more serious problem than how to make men happy, then the ' Waverley Novels ' are among the most precious things in the literature of the world."

Another writer of whose good-nature Mr. Watts-Dunton always speaks warmly is Browning. Among the many good anecdotes I have heard him relate in this connection, I will give one. I do not think that he would object to my doing so.

" It is one of my misfortunes," said he, " to be not fully worthy (to use the word of a very dear friend of mine), of Browning's poetry. Where I am delighted, stimulated, and exhilarated by the imaginative and intellectual substance of his work, I find his metrical movements in a general way not pleasing to my ear. When a

certain book of his came out—I forget which—it devolved
upon me to review it.   Certain eccentricities in it, for
some reason or another, irritated me, and I expressed my
irritation in something very like chaff.   A close friend of
mine, a greater admirer of Browning than I am myself—
in fact, Mr. Swinburne—chided me for it, and I feel that
he was right.   On the afternoon following the appearance
of the article I was at the Royal Academy private view,
when Lowell came up to me and at once began talking
about the review.   Lowell, I found, was delighted with
it—said it was the most original and brilliant thing
that had appeared for many years.   'But,' said he,
'You're a brave man to be here where Browning always
comes.'   Then, looking round the room, he said : ' Why
there he is, and his sister immediately on the side opposite to us.   Surely you will slip away and avoid a meeting ! '

'Slip away ! ' I said, ' to avoid Browning !   You
don't know him as well as I do, after all !   Now, let me
tell you exactly what will occur if we stand here for a
minute or two.   Miss Browning, whose eyes are looking
busily over the room for people that Browning ought to
speak to, in a moment will see you, and in another moment she will see me.   And then you will see her turn
her head to Browning's ear and tell him something.
And then Browning will come straight across to me and
be more charming and cordial than he is in a general
way, supposing that be possible.'

' No, I don't believe it.'

' If you were not such a Boston Puritan,' I said, ' I
would ask you what will you bet that I am wrong '

No sooner had I uttered these words than, as I had
prophesied, Miss Browning did spot, first Lowell and
then me, and did turn and whisper in Browning's ear,

and Browning did come straight across the room to us; and this is what he said, speaking to me before he spoke to the illustrious American—a thing which on any other occasion he would scarcely have done :

'Now,' said he, 'you're not going to put me off with generalities any longer. You promised to write and tell me when you could come to luncheon. You have never done so—you will never do so, unless I fix you with a distinct day. Will you come to-morrow ? '

'I shall be delighted,' I said. And he turned to Lowell and exchanged a few friendly words with him.

After these two adorable people left us, Lowell said : ' Well, this is wonderful.   You would have won the bet. How do you explain it ? '

'I explain it by Browning's greatness of soul and heart. His position is so great, and mine is so small, that an unappreciative review of a poem of his cannot in the least degree affect him. But he knows that I am an honest man, as he has frequently told Tennyson, Jowett, and others. He wishes to make it quite apparent that he feels no anger towards a man who says what he thinks about a poem.' ''

After hearing this interesting anecdote I had the curiosity to turn to the bound volume of my ' Athen æum ' and read the article on ' Ferishtah's Fancies,' which I imagine must have been the review in question. This is what I read ·—

' The poems in this volume can only be described as parable-poems—parable-poems, not in the sense that they are capable of being read as parables (as is said to be the case with the ' Ruba'iyát ' of Omar Khayyàm), but parable-poems in the sense that they must be read as parables, or they show no artistic raison d'être at all.

Now do our English poets know what it is to write a parable poem ? It is to set self-conscious philosophy singing and dancing, like the young Gretry, to the tune of a waterfall. Or rather, it is to imprison the soul of Dinah Morris in the lissome body of Esmeralda, and set the preacher strumming a gypsy's tambourine. Though in the pure parable the intellectual or ethical motive does not dominate so absolutely as in the case of the pure fable, the form that expresses it, yet it does, nevertheless, so far govern the form as to interfere with that entire abandon—that emotional freedom—which seems necessary to the very existence of song. Indeed, if poetry must, like Wordsworth's ideal John Bull, ' be free or die ' ; if she must know no law but that of her own being (as the doctrine of ' L'art pour l'art ' declares) ; if she must not even seem to know *that* (as the doctrine of bardic inspiration implies), but must bend to it apparently in tricksy sport alone—how can she—' the singing maid with pictures in her eyes '—mount the pulpit, read the text, and deliver the sermon ?

In European literature how many parable poems should we find where the ethical motive and the poetic form are not at deadly strife ? But we discussed all this in speaking of prose parables, comparing the stories of the Prodigal Son and Kiságotamí with even such perfect parable poetry as that of Jami. We said then what we reiterate now : that to sing a real parable and make it a real song requires a genius of a very special and peculiar, if somewhat narrow order—a genius rare, delicate, ethereal, such as can, according to a certain Oriental fancy, compete with the Angels of the Water Pot in floriculture. Mr. Browning, being so fond of Oriental fancies, and being, moreover, on terms of the closest intimacy with a certain fancy-weaving dervish, Ferishtah, must be quite familiar with the Persian story we allude to, the famous story of 'Poetry and Cabbages.' Still, we will record it here for a certain learned society.

The earth, says the wise dervish Feridun, was once without flowers, and men dreamed of nothing more beautiful then than cabbages. So the Angels of the Water Pot, watering the Tûba Tree (whose fruit becomes flavoured according to the wishes of the feeder), said one to another, 'The eyes of those poor cabbage growers down there may well be horny and dim, having none of our beautiful things to gaze upon ; for as to the earthly cabbage, though useful in earthly pot, it is in colour unlovely as ungrateful in perfume ; and as to the stars, they are too far off to be very clearly mirrored in the eyes of folk so very intent upon cabbages.' So the Angels of the Water Pot, who sit on the rainbow and brew the ambrosial rains, began fashioning flowers out of the paradisal gems, while Israfel sang to them ; and the words of his song were the mottoes that adorn the bowers of heaven. So bewitching, however, were the strains of the singer —for not only has Israfel a lute for viscera, but doth he not also, according to the poet—

> Breathe a stream of otto and balm,
> Which through a woof of living music blown
> Floats, fused, a warbling rose that makes all senses one ?

—so astonishing were the notes of a singer so furnished, that the angels at their jewel work could not help tracing his coloured and perfumed words upon the petals. And this was how the Angels of the Water Pot made flowers, and this is the story of 'Poetry and Cabbages.'

But the alphabet of the angels, Feridun goes on to declare, is nothing less than the celestial charactery of

heaven, and is consequently unreadable to all human
eyes save a very few—that is to say, the eyes of those
mortals who are ' of the race of Israfel.'   To common
eyes—the eyes of the ordinary human cabbage-grower—
what, indeed, is that angelic caligraphy with which the
petals of the flowers are ornamented ?   Nothing but a
meaningless maze of beautiful veins and scents and
colours.

But who are ' of the race of Israfel ' ?   Not the
prosemen, certainly, as any Western critic may see who
will refer to Kircher's idle nonsense about the ' Alphabet
of the Angels ' in his ' Ædipus Egyptiacus.'   Are they,
then, the poets ?   This is indeed a solemn query.   ' If,'
says Feridun, ' the mottoes that adorn the bowers of
Heaven have been correctly read by certain Persian
poets, who shall be nameless, what are those other
mottoes glowing above the caves of hell in that fiery
alphabet used by the fiends ? '

One kind of poet only is, it seems, of the race of
Israfel—the parable-poet—the poet to whom truth
comes, not in any way as reasoned conclusions, not even
as golden gnomes, but comes symbolized in concrete
shapes of vital beauty ; the poet in whose work the poetic
form is so part and parcel of the ethical lesson which
vitalizes it that this ethical lesson seems not to give birth
to the music and the colour of the poem, but to be itself
born of the sweet marriage of these, and to be as inseparable from them as the ' morning breath ' of the Sabæan
rose is inalienable from the innermost petals—' the subtle
odour of the rose's heart,' which no mere chemistry of
man, but only the morning breeze, can steal."

It was such writing as this which made it quite superfluous for Mr. Watts-Dunton to sign his articles, and

we have only to contrast it—or its richness and its rareness —with the naïve, simple, unadorned style of ' Aylwin ' to realize how wide is the range of Mr. Watts-Dunton as a master of the fine shades of literary expression.

Chapter XV

THE GREAT BOOK OF WONDER

A ND now begins the most difficult and the most responsible part of my task—the selection of one
typical essay from the vast number of essays expressing
more or less fully the great heart-thought which gives life
to all Mr. Watts-Dunton's work. I can, of course, give
only one, for already I see signs that this book will swell
to proportions far beyond those originally intended for it.
Naturally, I thought at first that I would select one of the
superb articles on Victor Hugo's works, such for instance
as 'La Légende des Siècles,' or that profound one on
'La Religion des Religion.' But, after a while, when I
had got the essay typed and ready for inclusion, I changed
my mind. I thought that one of those wonderful essays
upon Oriental subjects which had called forth writings
like those of Sir Edwin Arnold, would serve my purpose
better. Finally, I decided to choose an essay, which
when it appeared was so full of profound learning upon
the great book of the world, the Bible, that it was attributed to almost every great specialist upon the Bible in
Europe and in America. Mr. Watts-Dunton has often
been urged to reprint this essay as a brief text-book for
scholastic use, but he has never done so. It will be noted
by readers of 'Aylwin' that even so far back as the publication of this article in the 'Athenæum', in 1877, Mr.
Watts-Duntou—to judge from the allusion in it to 'Nin-

ki-gal, the Queen of Death '—seems to have begun to
draw upon Philip Aylwin's ' Veiled Queen ' :—

" There is not, in the whole of modern history, a more
suggestive subject than that of the persistent attempts
of every Western literature to versify the Psalms in its
own idiom, and the uniform failure of these attempts.
At the time that Sternhold was ' bringing ' the Psalms
into ' fine Englysh meter ' for Henry the Eighth and
Edward the Sixth, continental rhymers were busy at the
same kind of work for their own monarchs—notably
Clement Marot for Francis the First. And it has been
going on ever since, without a single protest of any importance having been entered against it. This is astonishing, for the Bible, even from the point of view of the
literary critic, is a sacred book. Perhaps the time for
entering such a protest is come, and a literary journal
may be its proper medium.

A great living savant has characterized the Bible as
' a collection of the rude imaginings of Syria,' ' the worn-
out old bottle of Judaism into which the generous new
wine of science is being poured.' The great savant was
angry when he said so. The ' new wine ' of science is a
generous vintage, undoubtedly, and deserves all the
respect it gets from us ; so do those who make it and
serve it out ; they have so much intelligence ; they are
so honest and so fearless. But whatever may become of
their wine in a few years, when the wine-dealers shall
have passed away, when the savant is forgotten as any
star-gazer of Chaldæa,—the ' old bottle ' is going to be
older yet,—the Bible is going to be eternal. For that
which decides the vitality of any book is precisely that
which decides the value of any human soul—not the
knowledge it contains, but simply the attitude it assumes

towards the universe, unseen as well as seen.   The attitude of the Bible is just that which every soul must, in
its highest and truest moods, always assume—that of a
wise wonder in front of such a universe as this—that of a
noble humility before a God such as He ' in whose great
Hand we stand.'   This is why—like Alexander's mirror
—like that most precious 'Cup of Jemshîd,' imagined
by the Persians—the Bible reflects to-day, and will reflect for ever, every wave of human emotion, every
passing event of human life—reflect them as faithfully
as it did to the great and simple people in whose great
and simple tongue it was written.   Coming from the
Vernunft of Man, it goes straight to the Vernunft.
This is the kind of literature that never does die : a fact
which the world has discovered long ago.   For the
Bible is Europe's one book.   And with regard to Asia,
as far back as the time of Chrysostom it could have been
read in languages Syrian, Indian, Persian, Armenian,
Ethiopic, Scythian, and Samaritan ; now it can be read
in every language, and in almost every dialect, under the
sun.

And the very quintessence of the Bible is the Book
of the Psalms.   Therefore the Scottish passion for
Psalm-singing is not wonderful ;   the wonder is that,
liking so much to sing, they can find it possible to sing so
badly.   It is not wonderful that the court of Francis I
should yearn to sing Psalms ; the wonderful thing is that
they should find it in their hearts to sing Marot's Psalms
when they might have sung David's—that Her Majesty
the Queen could sing to a fashionable jig, ' O Lord,
rebuke me not in Thine indignation ' ;   and that An-
thony, King of Navarre, could sing to the air of a dance
of Poitou, ' Stand up, O Lord, to revenge my quarrel.'
For, although it is given to the very frogs, says Pascal, to

find music in their own croaking, the ears that can find music in such frogs as these must be of a peculiar convolution.

In Psalmody, then, Scottish taste and French are both bad, from the English point of view ; but then the English, having Hopkins in various incarnations, are fastidious.

When Lord Macaulay's tiresome New Zealander has done contemplating the ruins of London Bridge, and turned in to the deserted British Museum to study us through our books—what volume can he take as the representative one—what book, above all others, can the ghostly librarian select to give him the truest, the pro foundest insight into the character of the strange people who had made such a great figure in the earth ? We, for our part, should not hesitate to give him the English Book of Common Prayer, with the authorized version of the Psalms at the end, as representing the British mind in its most exalted and its most abject phases. That in the same volume can be found side by side the beauty and pathos of the English Litany, the grandeur of the English version of the Psalms and the effusions of Brady and Tate—masters of the art of sinking compared with whom Rous is an inspired bard—would be adequate evidence that the Church using it must be a British Church —that British, most British, must be the public tolerating it.

> ' By thine agony and bloody Sweat ; by thy Cross and Passion ; by thy Precious Death and Burial ; by thy glorious Resurrection and Ascension ; and by the coming of the Holy Ghost,
> God Lord, deliver us.'

Among Western peoples there is but one that could have

uttered in such language this cry, where pathos and sublimity and subtlest music are so mysteriously blended—
blended so divinely that the man who can utter it,
familiar as it is, without an emotion deep enough to touch
close upon the fount of tears must be differently consti-
tuted from some of us.   Among Western peoples there
is, we say, but one that could have done this ; for as M.
Taine has well said :—' More than any race in Europe
they (the British) approach by the simplicity and energy
of their conceptions the old Hebraic spirit.   Enthusiasm
is their natural condition, and their Deity fills them with
admiration as their ancient deities inspired them with
fury.'   And now listen to this :—

> When we, our wearied limbs to rest,
>   Sat down by proud Euphrates' stream,
> We wept, with doleful thoughts opprest,
>   And Zion was our mournful theme.

Among all the peoples of the earth there is but one
that could have thus degraded the words : ' By the rivers
of Babylon, there we sat down, yea, we wept when we
remembered Zion.'   For, to achieve such platitude
there is necessary an element which can only be called
the ' Hopkins element,' an element which is quite an
insular birthright of ours, a characteristic which came
over with the ' White Horse,'—that ' dull and greasy
coarseness of taste ' which distinguishes the British mind
from all others ; that ' ächtbrittische Beschränktheit,'
which Heine speaks of in his tender way.   The Scottish
version is rough, but Brady and Tate's inanities are
worse than Rous's roughness.
   Such an anomaly as this in one and the same literature, in one and the same little book, is unnatural ; it
is monstrous : whence can it come ? It is, indeed,

singular that no one has ever dreamed of taking the story
of the English Prayer-book, with Brady and Tate at the
end, and using it as a key to unlock that puzzle of puzzles
which has set the Continental critics writing nonsense
about us for generations :—'What is it that makes the
enormous, the fundamental, difference between English
literature—and all other Western literatures—Teutonic
no less than Latin or Slavonic ? ' The simple truth of
the matter is, that the British mind has always been
bipartite as now—has always been, as now, half sublime
and half homely to very coarseness ; in other words, it
has been half inspired by David King of Israel, and half
by John Hopkins, Suffolk schoolmaster and archetype of
prosaic bards, who, in 1562, took such of the Psalms as
Sternhold had left unsullied and doggerellized them.
For, as we have said, Hopkins, in many and various incarnations, has been singing unctuously in these islands
ever since the introduction of Christianity, and before ;
for he is Anglo-Saxon tastelessness, he is Anglo-Saxon
deafness to music and blindness to beauty. When St.
Augustine landed here with David he found not only
Odin, but Hopkins, a heathen then, in possession of the
soil.

There is, therefore, half of a great truth in what M.
Taine says. The English have, besides the Hopkins element, which is indigenous, much of the Hebraic temper,
which is indigenous too ; but they have by nature none
of the Hebraic style. But, somehow, here is the difference between us and the Continentals ; that, though
style is born of taste—though le style c'est la race ; and
though the Anglo-Saxon started, as we have seen, with
Odin and Hopkins alone ; yet, just as instinct may be
sown and grown by ancestral habit of many years—
just as the pointer puppy, for instance, points, he knows

not why, because his ancestors were taught to point before him—so may the Hebraic style be sown and grown in a foreign soil if the soil be Anglo-Saxon, and if the seed-time last for a thousand years. The result of all this is, that the English, notwithstanding their deficiency of artistic instinct and coarseness of taste, have the Great Style, not only in poetry, sometimes, but in prose sometimes when they write emotively, as we see in the English Prayer-book, in parts of Raleigh's ' History of the World,' in Jeremy Taylor's sermons, in Hall's ' Contemplations,' and other such books of the seventeenth century.

The Great Style is far more easily recognized than defined. To define any kind of style, indeed, we must turn to real life. When we say of an individual in real life that he or she has style, we mean that the individual gives us an impression of unconscious power or unconscious grace, as distinguished from that conscious power or conscious grace which we call manner. The difference is fundamental. It is the same in literature ; style is unconscious power or grace—manner is conscious power or grace. But the Great Style, both in literature and in life, is unconscious power and unconscious grace in one.

And, whither must we turn in quest of this, as the natural expression of a national temper ? Not to the Celt, we think, as Mr. Arnold does. Not, indeed, to those whose languages, complex of syntax and alive with self-conscious inflections, bespeak the scientific knowingness of the Aryan mind—not, certainly, to those who, though producing Æschylus, turned into Aphrodite the great Astarte of the Syrians, but to the descendants of Shem,—the only gentleman among all the sons of Noah ; to those who, yearning always to look straight into the face of God and live, can see not much else. The Great

Style, in a word, is Semitic. It would be a mistake to call it Asiatic. For though two of its elements, unconsciousness and power, are, no doubt, plentiful enough in India, the element of grace is lacking, for the most part. The Vedic hymns are both nebulous and unemotive as compared with Semitic hymns, and, on the other hand, such a high reach of ethical writing as even that noble and well-known passage from Manu, beginning, ' Single is each man born into the world, single he dies,' etc., is quite logical and self-conscious when compared with the ethical parts of Scripture. The Persians have the grace always, the power often, but the unconsciousness almost never. We might perhaps say that there were those in Egypt once who came near to the great ideal. That description of the abode of ' Nin-ki-gal,' the Queen of Death, recently deciphered from a tablet in the British Museum, is nearly in the Great Style, yet not quite. Conscious power and conscious grace are Hellenic, of course. That there is a deal of unconsciousness in Homer is true ; but, put his elaborate comparisons by the side of the fiery metaphors of the sacred writers, and how artificial he seems. And note that, afterwards, when he who approached nearest to the Great Style wrote Prometheus and the Furies, Orientalism was overflowing Greece, like the waters of the Nile. It is to the Latin races—some of them—that has filtered Hellenic manner ; and whensoever, as in Dante, the Great Style has been occasionally caught, it comes not from the Hellenic fountain, but straight from the Hebrew.

What the Latin races lack, the Teutonic races have —unconsciousness ; often unconscious power ; mostly, however, unconscious brutalité. Sublime as is the Northern mythology, it is vulgar too. The Hopkins element,—the dull and stupid homeliness,—the coarse

grotesque, mingle with and mar its finest effects.   Over
it all the atmosphere is that of pantomime—singing
dragons, one-eyed gods, and Wagner's libretti.   Even
that great final conflict between gods and men and the
swarming brood of evil on the plain of Wigrid, foretold
by the Völu-seeress, when from Yötunland they come
and storm the very gates of Asgard ;—even this fine com-
bat ends in the grotesque and vulgar picture of the
Fenrir-wolf gulping Odin down like an oyster, and
digesting the universe to chaos.   But, out of the twenty-
three thousand and more verses into which the Bible has
been divided, no one can find a vulgar verse ; for the
Great Style allows the stylist to touch upon any subject
with no risk of defilement.   This is why style in literature is virtue.   Like royalty, the Great Style 'can do
no wrong.'

Of Teutonic graceless unconsciousness, the Anglo-
Saxons have by far the largest endowment.   They
wanted another element, in short, not the Hellenic element ; for there never was a greater mistake than that
of supposing that Hellenism can be engrafted on Teu-
tonism and live ; as Landor and Mr. Matthew Arnold—
two of the finest and most delicate minds of modern
times—can testify.

But, long before the memorable Hampton Court
Conference ; long before the Bishops' Bible or Cover-
dale's Bible ; long before even Aldhelm's time—Hebraism
had been flowing over and enriching the Anglo-Saxon
mind.   From the time when Cædmon, the forlorn
cow-herd, fell asleep beneath the stars by the stable-
door, and was bidden to sing the Biblical story, Anglo-
Saxon literature grew more and more Hebraic.   Yet, in
a certain sense, the Hebraism in which the English mind
was steeped had been Hebraism at second hand—that of

the Vulgate mainly—till Tyndale's time, or rather till the
present Authorized Version of the Bible appeared in 1611.
'There is no book,' says Selden, 'so translated as the
Bible for the purpose. If I translate a French book into
English, I turn it into English phrase, not into French-
English. "Il fait froid," I say, 'tis cold, not it makes
cold; but the Bible is rather translated into English
words than into English phrase, The Hebraisms are
kept, and the phrase of that language is kept.'

And in great measure this is true, no doubt; yet
literal accuracy—importation of Hebraisms—was not of
itself enough to produce a translation in the Great Style
—a translation such as this, which, as Coleridge says,
makes us think that 'the translators themselves were
inspired.' To reproduce the Great Style of the original
in a Western idiom, the happiest combination of circumstances was necessary. The temper of the people
receiving must, notwithstanding all differences of habitation and civilization, be elementally in harmony with
that of the people giving; that is, it must be poetic
rather than ratiocinative. Society must not be too
complex—its tone must not be too knowing and self-
glorifying. The accepted psychology of the time must
not be the psychology of the scalpel—the metaphysics
must not be the metaphysics of newspaper cynicism;
above all, enthusiasm and vulgarity must not be considered synonymous terms. Briefly, the tone of the
time must be free of the faintest suspicion of nineteenth
'century flavour. That this is the kind of national temper necessary to such a work might have been demon-
strated by an argument a priori. It was the temper of
the English nation when the Bible was translated. That
noble heroism—born of faith in God and belief in the
high duties of man—which we have lost for the hour—

was in the very atmosphere that hung over the island. And style in real life, which now, as a consequence of our loss, does not exist at all among Englishmen, and only among a very few Englishwomen—having given place in all classes to manner—flourished then in all its charm. And in literature it was the same : not even the euphuism imported from Spain could really destroy or even seriously damage the then national sense of style.

Then, as to the form of literature adopted in the translation, what must that be ? Evidently it must be some kind of form which can do all the high work that is generally left to metrical language, and yet must be free from any soupçon of that ' artifice,' in the ' abandonment ' of which, says an Arabian historian, ' true art alone lies.' For, this is most noteworthy, that of literature as an art, the Semites show but small conception, even in Job. It was too sacred for that—drama and epic in the Aryan sense were alike unknown.

But if the translation must not be metrical in the common acceptation of that word, neither must it be prose ; we will not say logical prose ; for all prose, however high may be its flights, however poetic and emotive, must always be logical underneath, must always be chained by a logical chain, and earth-bound like a captive ¡balloon ; just as poetry, on the other hand, however didactic and even ratiocinative it may become, must always be steeped in emotion. It must be neither verse nor prose, it seems. It must be a new movement altogether. The musical movement of the English Bible is a new movement ; let us call it ' Bible Rhythm.' And the movement was devised thus : Difficulty is the worker of modern miracles. Thanks to Difficulty—thanks to the conflict between what Selden calls ' Hebrew phrase and English phrase,' the translators fashioned, or rather,

Difficulty fashioned for them, a movement which was neither one nor wholly the other—a movement which, for music, for variety, splendour, sublimity, and pathos, is above all the effects of English poetic art, above all the rhythms and all the rhymes of the modern world—a movement, indeed, which is a form of art of itself—but a form in which ' artifice ' is really ' abandoned ' at last. This rhythm it is to which we referred as running through the English Prayer-book, and which governs every verse of the Bible, its highest reaches perhaps being in the Psalms—this rhythm it is which the Hopkinses and Rouses have—improved! It would not be well to be too technical here, yet the matter is of the greatest literary importance just now, and it is necessary to explain clearly what we mean.

Among the many delights which we get from the mere form of what is technically called Poetry, the chief, perhaps, is expectation and the fulfilment of expectation. In rhymed verse this is obvious : having familiarized ourselves with the arrangement of the poet's rhymes, we take pleasure in expecting a recurrence of these rhymes according to this arrangement. In blank verse the law of expectation is less apparent. Yet it is none the less operative. Having familiarized ourselves with the poet's rhythm, having found that iambic foot succeeds iambic foot, and that whenever the iambic waves have begun to grow monotonous, variations occur—trochaic, anapæstic, dactylic—according to the law which governs the ear of this individual poet ;—we, half consciously, expect at certain intervals these variations, and are delighted when our expectations are fulfilled. And our delight is augmented if also our expectations with regard to cæsuric effects are realized in the same proportions. Having, for instance, learned, half unconsciously, that the poet has

an ear for a particular kind of pause ; that he delights,
let us say, to throw his pause after the third foot of the
sequence,—we expect that, whatever may be the arrangement of the early pauses with regard to the initial foot of
any sequence,—there must be, not far ahead, that climac-
teric third-foot pause up to which all the other pauses
have been tending, and upon which the ear and the soul
of the reader shall be allowed to rest to take breath for
future flights. And when this expectation of cæsuric
effects is thus gratified, or gratified in a more subtle way,
by an arrangement of earlier semi-pauses, which obviates
the necessity of the too frequent recurrence of this final
third-foot pause, the full pleasure of poetic effects is the
result. In other words, a large proportion of the pleasure we derive from poetry is in the recognition of law.
The more obvious and formulated is the law,—nay, the
more arbitrary and Draconian,—the more pleasure it
gives to the uncultivated ear. This is why uneducated
people may delight in rhyme, and yet have no ear at all
for blank verse ; this is why the savage, who has not
even an ear for rhyme, takes pleasure in such unmistakable rhythm as that of his tom-tom. But, as the ear
becomes more cultivated, it demands that these indica-
tions of law should be more and more subtle, till at last
recognized law itself may become a tyranny and a burden.
He who will read Shakespeare's plays chronologically, as
far as that is practicable, from ' Love's Labour's Lost ' to
the ' Tempest,' will have no difficulty in seeing precisely
what we mean. In literature, as in social life, the progress is from lawless freedom, through tyranny, to freedom that is lawful. Now the great features of Bible
Rhythm are a recognized music apart from a recognized
law—' artifice ' so completely abandoned that we forget
we are in the realm of art—pauses so divinely set that

they seem to be 'wood-notes wild,' though all the while they are, and must be, governed by a mysterious law too subtly sweet to be formulated ; and all kind of beauties infinitely beyond the triumphs of the metricist, but beauties that are unexpected. There is a metre, to be sure, but it is that of the ' moving music which is life ' ; it is the living metre of the surging sea within the soul of him who speaks ; it is the free effluence of the emotions and the passions which are passing into the words. And if this is so in other parts of the Bible, what is it in the Psalms, where ' the flaming steeds of song,' though really kept strongly in hand, seem to run reinless as ' the wild horses of the wind ' ? "

Chapter XVI

A HUMOURIST UPON HUMOUR

THE reaching of a decision as to what article to select as typical of what I may call 'The Renascence of Wonder' essays gave me so much trouble that when I came to the still more difficult task of selecting an essay typical of Mr. Watts-Dunton's criticism dealing with what he calls 'the laws of cause and effect in literary art' it naturally occurred to me to write to him asking for a suggestive hint or two. In response to my letter I got a thoroughly characteristic reply, in which his affection for a friend took entire precedence of his own work ·—

" MY DEAR MR. DOUGLAS,—The selections from my critiques must really be left entirely to yourself. They are to illustrate your own critical judgment upon my work, and not mine. Overwhelmed as I am with avocations which I daresay you little dream of, for me to plunge into the countless columns of the 'Athenæum,' in quest of articles of mine which I have quite forgotten, would be an intolerable burden at the present moment. I can think of only one article which I should specially like reproduced, either in its entirety or in part—not on account of any merit in it which I can recall, but because it was the means of bringing me into contact with one of the most delightful men and one of the most splendidly

equipped writers of our time, whose sudden death
shocked and grieved me beyond measure. A few
days after the article appeared, the then editor of
the 'Athenaeum,' Mr. MacColl, the dear friend
with whom I was associated for more than twenty
years, showed me a letter that he had received from
Traill. It was an extremely kind letter. Among the
many generous things that Traill said was this—that
it was just the kind of review article which makes the
author regret that he had not seen it before his book
appeared. I wrote to Traill in acknowledgment of his
kind words ; but it was not until a good while after this
that we met at the Incorporated Authors' Society dinner.
At the table where I was sitting, and immediately
opposite me, sat a gentleman whose countenance,
especially when it was illuminated by conversation
with his friends, perfectly charmed me. Although
there was not the smallest regularity in his features,
the expression was so genial and so winsome that
I had some difficulty in persuading myself that it
was not a beautiful face after all, and his smile was really
quite irresistible. The contrast between his black eye-
brows and whiskers and the white hair upon his head
gave him a peculiarly picturesque appearance. Another
thing I noticed was a boyish kind of lisp, which somehow,
I could not say why, gave to the man an added charm.
I did not know it was Traill, but after the dinner was
over, when I was saying to myself, 'That is a man I
should like to know,' a friend who sat next him—I
forget who it was—brought him round to me and intro
duced him as 'Mr. Traill.' 'You and I ought to know
each other,' he said, 'for, besides having many tastes in
common, we live near each other.' And then I found
that he lived near the 'Northumberland Arms,' between

Putney and Barnes.   I think that he must have seen how
greatly I was drawn to him, for he called at The Pines
in a few days—I think, indeed, it was the very next day
—and then began a friendship the memory of which gives
me intense pleasure, and yet pleasure not unmixed with
pain, when I recall his comparatively early and sudden
death.   I used to go to his gatherings, and it was there
that I first met several interesting men that I had not
known before.   One of them, I remember, was Mr.
Sidney Low, then the editor of the 'St. James's Gazette.'
And I also used to meet there interesting men whom I
had known before, such as the late Sir Edwin Arnold,
whose 'Light of Asia,' and other such works, I had
reviewed in the 'Athenæum.'   I do not hesitate for a
moment to say that Traill was a man of genius.   Had he
lived fifty years earlier, such a writer as he who wrote
'The New Lucian,' 'Recaptured Rhymes,' 'Saturday
Songs,' 'The Canaanitish Press' and 'Israelitish Questions,' 'the Life of Sterne,' and the brilliant articles
in the 'Saturday Review' and the 'Pall Mall Gazette,'
would have made an unforgettable mark in literature.
But there is no room for anybody now—no room for
anybody but the very, very few.   When he was about
starting 'Literature,' he wrote to me, and a gratifying
letter it was.   He said that, although he had no desire
to wean me from the 'Athenæum,' he should be delighted to receive anything from me when I chanced to
be able to spare him something.   It was always an
aspiration of mine to send something to a paper edited
by so important a literary figure—a paper, let me say,
that had a finer, sweeter tone than any other paper of
my time—I mean, that tone of fine geniality upon
which I have often commented, that tone without
which, 'there can be no true criticism.'   A certain

statesman of our own period, who had pursued
literature with success, used to say (alluding to a
paper of a very different kind, now dead), that the
besetting sin of the literary class is that lack of
gentlemanlike feeling one towards another which is
to be seen in all the other educated classes. This
might have been so then, but, through the influence
mainly of 'Literature' and H. D. Traill, it is not so
now. Many people have speculated as to why a literary
journal, edited by such a man, and borne into the literary
arena on the doughty back of the 'Times,' did not succeed. I have a theory of my own upon that subject.
Although Traill's hands were so full of all kinds of
journalistic and magazine work in other quarters, it is
a mistake to suppose that his own journal was badly
edited. It was well edited, and it had a splendid staff,
but several things were against it. It confined itself to
literature, and did not, as far as I remember, give its
attention to much else. Its price was sixpence ; but
its chief cause of failure was what I may call its ' personal appearance.' If personal appearance is an enormously powerful factor at the beginning of the great
human struggle for life, it is at the first quite as important a factor in the life struggle of a newspaper or a
magazine. When the ' Saturday Review ' was started,
its personal appearance—something quite new then—
did almost as much for it as the brilliant writing. It
was the same with the ' Pall Mall Gazette ' when it
started. Carlyle was quite right in thinking that there
is a great deal in clothes. Now, as I told Traill when
we were talking about this, ' Literature ' in appearance
seemed an uninviting cross between the ' Law Times '
and 'The Lancet '—it seemed difficult to connect
the unbusiness-like genius of literature with such a

business-like looking sheet as that. Traill laughed, but ended by saying that he believed there was a great deal in that notion of mine. Some one was telling me the other day that Traill, who died only about four years ago, was beginning to be forgotten. I should be sorry indeed to think that. All that I can say is that for a book such as yours to be written about me, and no book to be written about Traill, presents itself to my mind as being as grotesque an idea as any that Traill's own delightful whimsical imagination could have pictured."

Of course I comply with Mr. Watts-Dunton's wishes, and I do this with the more alacrity because there is this connection between the essay on Sterne and the imaginative work—the theory of absolute humour exemplified in Mrs. Gudgeon is very brilliantly expounded in the article. It was a review of Traill's ' Sterne,' in the ' English Men of Letters,' and it appeared in the ' Athenæum ' of November 18, 1882. I will quote the greater part of it :—

" Contemporary humour, for the most part, even among cultivated writers, is in temper either cockney or Yankee, and both Sterne and Cervantes are necessarily more talked about than studied, while Addison as a humorist is not even talked about. In gauging the quality of poetry—in finding for any poet his proper place in the poetic heavens—there is always uncertainty and difficulty. With humour, however, this difficulty does not exist, if we bear steadily in mind that all humour is based upon a simple sense of incongruous relations, and that the quality of every man's humour depends upon the kind of incongruity which he recognizes and finds laughable. If, for instance, he shows himself to

have no sense of any incongruities deeper than those
disclosed by the parodist and the punster, his relation to
the real humourist and the real wit is that of a monkey
to a man ; for although the real humourist may descend
to parody, and the real wit may descend to punning, as
Aristophanes did, the pun and the parody are charged
with some deeper and richer intent. Again, if a man's
sense of humour, like that of the painter of society, is
confined to a sense of the incongruous relations existing
between individual eccentricity and the social conventions by which it is surrounded, he may be a humourist
no doubt—according, at least, to the general acceptation
of that word, though a caricaturist according to a definition of humour and caricature which we once ventured
upon in these columns ; but his humour is jejune, and
delightful to the Philistine only. If, like that of Cervantes and (in a lower degree) Fielding, Thackeray, and
Dickens, a writer's sense of the incongruous is deeper
than this, but is confined nevertheless to what Mr.
Traill calls 'the irony of human intercourse,' he is indeed
a humourist, and in the case of Cervantes a very great
humourist, yet not necessarily of the greatest ; for just
as the greatest poet must have a sense of the highest
and deepest harmonies possible for the soul of man to
apprehend, so the greatest humourist must have a sense
of the highest and deepest incongruities possible. And
it will be found that these harmonies and these incongruities lie between the very ' order of the universe '
itself and the mind of man. In certain temperaments
the eternal incongruities between man's mind and the
scheme of the universe produce, no doubt, the pessimism
of Schopenhauer and Novalis ; but to other temperaments—to a Rabelais or Sterne, for instance—the apprehension of them turns the cosmos into disorder, turns

it into something like that boisterous joke which to most
temperaments is only possible under the excitement of
some ' paradis artificiel.'   Great as may be the humourist
whose sense of irony is that of ' human intercourse,' if
he has no sense of this much deeper irony—the irony of
man's intercourse with the universal harmony itself—
he cannot be ranked with the very greatest.   Of this
irony in the order of things Aristophanes and Rabelais
had an instinctive, while Richter had an intellectual
enjoyment.   Of Swift and Carlyle it might be said that
they had not so much an enjoyment as a terrible apprehension of it.   And if we should find that this quality
exists in ' Tristram Shandy,' how high, then, must we
not place Sterne !   And if we should find that Cervantes
deals with the ' irony of human intercourse ' merely,
and that his humour is, with all its profundity, terrene,
what right have critics to set Cervantes above Sterne ?
Why is the sense of incongruity upon which the humour
of Cervantes is based so melancholy ? Because it only
sees the farce from the human point of view.   The sad
smile of Cervantes is the tearful humour of a soul deeply
conscious of man's ludicrous futility in his relations to
his fellow-man.   But while the futilities of ' Don Quixote '
are tragic because terrene, the futilities of ' Tristram
Shandy ' are comic because they are derived from the
order of things.   It is the great humourist Circumstance
who causes Mrs. Shandy to think of the clock at the
most inopportune moment, and who, stooping down
from above the constellations, interferes to flatten
Tristram's nose.   And if Circumstance proves to be so
fond of fun, he must be found in the end a benevolent
king ; and hence all is well.

While, however, it is, as we say, easy in a general
way to gauge a humourist and find his proper place, it

is not easy to bring Sterne under a classification. In Sterne's writings every kind of humour is to be found, from a style of farce which even at Crazy Castle must have been pronounced too wild, up to humour as chaste and urbane as Addison's, and as profound and dramatic as Shakespeare's. In loving sympathy with stupidity, for instance, even Shakespeare is outdone by Sterne in his ' fat, foolish scullion.' Lower than the Dogberry type there is a type of humanity made up of animal functions merely, to whom the mere fact of being alive is the one great triumph. While the news of Bobby's death, announced by Obadiah in the kitchen, suggests to Susannah the various acquisitions to herself that must follow such a sad calamity to the ' fat, foolish scullion,' scrubbing her pans on the floor, it merely recalls the great triumphant fact of her own life, and consequently to the wail that ' Bobby is certainly dead ' her soul merely answers as she scrubs, ' So am not I.' In four words that scullion lives for ever.

Sterne's humour, in short, is Shakespearean and Rabelaisian, Cervantic and Addisonian too ; how, then, shall we find a place for such a Proteus ? So great is the plasticity of genius, so readily at first does it answer to impressions from without, that in criticizing its work it is always necessary carefully to pierce through the method and seek the essential life by force of which methods can work. Sterne having, as a student of humourous literature, enjoyed the mirthful abandon of Rabelais no less than the pensive irony of Cervantes, it was inevitable that his methods should oscillate between that of Rabelais on the one hand, and that of Cervantes on the other, and that at first this would be so without Sterne's natural endowment of humour being necessarily either Rabelaisian or Cervantic, that is to say, either lyric or dramatic, either the humour of animal mirth or the humour of philosophic meditation. But the more deeply we pierce underneath his methods, the more certainly shall we find that he was by nature the very Proteus of humour which he pretended to be. And after all this is the important question as regards Sterne. Lamb's critical acuteness is nowhere more clearly seen than in that sentence where he speaks of his own ' self-pleasing quaintness.' When any form of art departs in any way from symmetrical and normal lines, the first question to ask concerning it is this : Is it self-pleasing or is it artificial and histrionic ? That which pleases the producer may perhaps not please us ; but if we feel that it does not really and truly please the artist himself, the artist becomes a mountebank, and we turn away in disgust. In the humourous portions of Sterne's work there is, probably, not a page, however nonsensical, which he did not write with gusto, and therefore, bad as some of it may be, it is not to the true critic an offence. . . .

' Yorickism ' is, there is scarcely need to say, the very opposite of the humour of Swift. One recognizes that the universe is rich in things to laugh at and to love ; the other recognizes that the universe is rich in things to laugh at and to hate. One recognizes that among these absurd things there is nothing else so absurd and (because so absurd) so lovable as a man ; the other recognizes that there is nothing else so absurd and (because so absurd) so hateful as a man. The intellectual process is the same ; the difference lies in the temperament—the temperament of Jaques and the temperament of Apemantus. And in regard to misanthropic ridicule it is difficult to say which fate is more terrible, Swift's or Carlyle's—that of the man whose heart must needs yearn towards a race which his piercing intellect bids him hate, or that of the man, religious, conscientious, and good, who would fain love his fellows and cannot. It is idle for men of this kind to try to work in the vein of Yorick. It needs the sweet temper of him who at the Mermaid kept the table in a roar, or of him who, in the words of the ' cadet of the house of Keppoch,' was ' sometimes called Tristram Shandy and sometimes Yorick, a very great favourite of the gentlemen.' . Sterne, like Jaques and Hamlet, deals with ' the irony of human intercourse,' but what he specially recognizes is a deeper irony still—the irony of man's intercourse with himself and with nature, the irony of the intercourse between man the spiritual being and man the physical being—the irony, in short, of man's position amid these natural conditions of life and death. It is in the apprehension of this anomaly—a spiritual nature enclosed in a physical nature—that Sterne's strength lies.

Man, the ' fool of nature,' prouder than Lucifer himself, yet ' bounded in a nutshell,' brother to the panniered donkey, and held of no more account by the winds and rains of heaven than the poor little ' beastie ' whose house is ruined by the ploughshare—here is, indeed, a creature for Swift and Carlyle and Sterne and Burns to marvel at and to laugh at, but with what different kinds of laughter ! There is nothing incongruous in the condition of the lower animals, because they are in entire harmony with their natural surroundings ; there is nothing more absurd in the existence and the natural functions of a horse or a cow than in the existence and the natural functions of the grass upon which they feed ; but imagine a spiritual being so placed, so surrounded, and so functioned, and you get an absurdity compared with which all other absurdities are non-existent, or, at least, are fit quarry for the satirist, but hardly for the humourist. That Sterne's donkey should owe his existence to the exercise of certain natural functions on the part of his unconscious progenitors, that he should continue to hold his place by the exercise on his own part of certain other natural functions, is in no way absurd, and contains in it no material for humoristic treatment. To render him absurd you must bring him into relation with man ; you must clap upon his back panniers of human devising or give him macaroons kneaded by a human cook. Then to the general observer he becomes absurd, for he is tried by human standards. But to Yorick it is not so much the donkey who is absurd as the fantastic creature who made the panniers and cooked the macaroons. All other humour is thin compared with this. Besides, it never grows old. It is difficult, no doubt, to think that the humour of Cervantes will ever lose its freshness ; but the kind of humour we have called Yorickism will be immortal, for no advance in human knowledge can dim its lustre. Certainly up to the present moment the anomaly of man's position upon the planet is not lessened by the revelations of science as to his origin and development. On the contrary, it is increased, as we hinted in speaking of Thoreau. If man was a strange and anomalous ' piece of work ' as Hamlet knew him under the old cosmogony, what a ' piece of work ' does he appear now ! He has the knack of advancing and leaving the woodchucks behind, but how has he done it ? By the fact of his being the only creature out of harmony with surrounding conditions. A contented conservatism is the primary instinct of the entire animal kingdom, and if any species should change, it is not (as Lamarck once supposed) from any ' inner yearning ' for progress, but because it was pushed on by overmastering circumstances. An ungulate becomes the giraffe, not because it is uncomfortable in its old condition and yearns for giraffehood, but because, being driven from grass to leaves by natural causes, it must elongate its neck or starve. But man really has this yearning for progress, and, because he is out of harmony with everything, he advances till at last he turns all the other creatures into food or else into weight-carriers, and outstrips them so completely that he forgets he is one of them. If Uncle Toby's progenitors were once as low down in the scale of life as the fly that buzzed about his nose, the fly had certainly more right to buzz than had that over-developed, incongruous creature, Captain Shandy, to be disturbed at its buzzing, and the patronizing speech of the captain as he opens the window gains an added humour, for it is the fly that should patronize and take pity upon the man.

And while Sterne's abiding sense of the struggle between man's spiritual nature and the conditions of his physical nature accounts for the metaphysical depth of some of his humour, it greatly accounts for his indecencies too. Sterne had that instinct for idealizing women, and the entire relations between the sexes which accompanies the poetic temperament. To such natures the spiritual side of sexual relations is ever present; and as a consequence of this the animal side never loses with them the atmosphere of wonder with which it was enveloped in their boyish days. Not that we are going to justify Sterne's indecencies. Coleridge's remark that the pleasure Sterne got from his double entendre was akin to ' that trembling daring with which a child touches a hot teapot because it has been forbidden,' partly explains, but it does not excuse, Sterne's transgressions herein.   The fact seems to be that if we divide love into the passion of love, the sentiment of love, and the appetite of love, and inquire which of these was really known to Sterne, we shall come to what will seem to most readers the paradoxical conclusion that it was the sentiment only.   There is abundant proof of this. In the ' Letter to the Earl of ——,' printed by his daughter, after dilating upon the manner in which the writing of the ' Sentimental Journey ' has worn out both his spirits and body, he says : ' I might indeed solace myself with my wife (who is come to France), but, in fact, I have long been a sentimental being, whatever your lordship may think to the contrary.   The world has imagined because I wrote " Tristram Shandy " that I was myself more Shandian than I really ever was.'   Upon this passage Mr. Traill has the pertinent remark :   ' The connubial affections are here, in all seriousness and good faith apparently, opposed to the sentimental emotions—as the lower to the higher. To indulge the former is to be " Shandian," that is to say, coarse and carnal ; to devote oneself to the latter, or, in other words, to spend one's days in semi-erotic languishings over the whole female sex indiscriminately, is to show spirituality and taste.'   Now, to men of this kind there is not uncommonly, per-haps, a charm in a licentious double entendre which is quite inscrutable to those of a more animal tempera-ment.   The incongruity between the ideal and the actual relations brings poignant distress at first, and afterwards a sense of irresistible absurdity.   Originally the fascina-tion of repulsion, it becomes the fascination of attraction, and it is not at all fanciful to say that in Uncle Toby and the Widow Wadman, Sterne (quite unconsciously to himself perhaps) realized to his own mind those two opposite sides of man's nature whose conflict in some form or another was ever present to Sterne's mind. And, as we say, it has a deep relation to the kind of humour with which Sterne was so richly endowed. After one of his most sentimental flights, wherein the spiritual side of man is absurdly exaggerated, there comes upon him a sudden revulsion (which at first was entirely natural, if even self-conscious afterwards). The incongruity of all this sentiment with man's actual condition as an animal strikes him with irresistible force, and he says to man, ' What right have you in that galley after all—you who came into the world in this extremely unspiritual fashion and keep in it by the agency of functions which are if possible more unspiritual and more absurd still ? '

No doubt the universal sense of shame in connection with sexual matters, which Hartley has discussed in his subtle but rather far-fetched fashion, arises from an acute apprehension of this great and eternal incongruity of man's existence—the conflict of a spiritual nature and such aspirations as man's with conditions entirely physical. And perhaps the only truly philosophical definition of the word ' indecency ' would be this : ' A painful and shocking contrast of man's spiritual with his physical nature.' When Hamlet, with his finger on Yorick's skull, declares that his ' gorge rises at it,' and asks if Alexander's skull ' smelt so,' he shocks us as deeply in a serious way as Sterne in his allusion to the winding up of the clock shocks us in a humourous way, and to express the sensation they each give there is, perhaps, no word but ' indecent.' "

I have now cited the opinions of Mr. Watts-Dunton upon the metaphysical meaning of humour. In order to show what are his opinions upon wit, I think I shall do well to turn from the ' Athenæum ' articles, and to quote from the ' Encyclopædia Britannica' a few sentences upon wit, and upon the distinction between comedy and farce. For the obvious reason that the 'Athenæum' articles are buried in oblivion, and the 'Encyclopædia Britannica' articles are certainly not so deeply buried, it is from the former that I have been mainly quoting; but some of the most important parts of Mr. Watts-Dunton's work are to be found in the ' Encyclopædia Britannica.'   Perhaps, however, I had better introduce my citations by saying a few words about Mr. Watts-Dunton's connection with that work.

The story of the way in which he came to write in the ' Encyclopædia' has been often told by Prof. Minto.   At the time when the ninth edition was started, he and Mr., Watts-Dunton were living in adjoining chambers and were seeing each other constantly.   When Minto was writing his articles upon Byron and Dickens, he told Mr. Watts-Dunton that Baynes would be delighted to get work from him. But at that time Mr. Watts-Dunton had got more critical work in hand than he wanted, and besides he had already a novel and a body of poetry ready for the press, and wished to confine his energies to creative work.   Besides this, he felt, as he declared, that he could not do the work fitted for the compact, business-like pedestrian style of an encyclopædia.   But when the most important treatise in the literary department of the work—the treatise on Poetry—was wanted, a peculiar difficulty in selecting the writer was felt.   The article in the previous edition had been written by David Macbeth Moir, famous under the name of ' Delta' as the author of ' The Autobiography of Mansie Wauch.'   Moir's article was intelligent enough, but quite inadequate to such a work as the publishers of the 'Encyclopædia' aspired to make. A history of Poetry was, of course, quite impossible ; it followed that the treatise must be an essay on the principles of poetic art in relation to all other arts, as exemplified by the poetry of the great literatures. It was decided, accord‑ing to Minto's account, that there were but three men, that is to say, Swinburne, Matthew Arnold, and Theodore Watts, who could produce this special kind of work, the other critics being entirely given up to the historic method of criticism. The choice fell upon Watts, and Baynes went to London for the purpose of inviting him to do the work, and explaining exactly what was wanted.

I think all will agree with me that there never was a happier choice. Mr. Arthur Symons, in an article on 'The Coming of Love' in the 'Saturday Review' has written very luminously upon this subject. He tells us that, wide as is the sweep of the treatise, it is but a brilliant fragment, owing to the treatise having vastly overflowed the space that could be given to it. The truth is that the essay is but the introduction to an exhaustive discussion of what the writer believes to be the most important event in the history of all poetry —the event discussed under the name of 'The Renascence of Wonder.' The introduction to the third volume of the new edition of Chambers's 'Cyclopædia of English Literature' is but a bare outline of Mr. Watts-Dunton's writings upon this subject. It has been said over and over again that since the best critical work of Coleridge there has been nothing in our literature to equal this treatise on Poetry. It has been ex‑haustively discussed in England, America, and on the Continent, especially in Germany, where it has been compared to the critical system of Goethe. Those who have not read it will be surprised to hear that it is not confined to the formulating of generalizations on poetic art; it is full of eloquent passages on human life and human conduct.

It was in an article upon a Restoration comic dramatist, Vanbrugh, that Mr. Watts-Dunton first formulated his famous distinction between comedy and farce :—

" In order to find and fix Vanbrugh's place among English comic dramatists, an examination of the very basis of the comedy of repartee inaugurated by Etheredge would be necessary, and, of course, such an examination would be impossible here. It is chiefly as a humourist, however, that he demands attention.

Given the humorous temperament — the temperament which impels a man to get his enjoyment by watching the harlequinade of life, and contrasting it with his own ideal standard of good sense, which the harlequinade seems to him to mock and challenge—given this temperament, then the quality of its humourous growth depends of course on the quality of the intellectual forces by means of which the temperament gains expression. Hence it is very likely that in original endowment of humour, as distinguished from wit, Vanbrugh was superior to Congreve. And this is saying a great deal : for, while Congreve's wit has always been made much of, it has, since Macaulay's time, been the fashion among critics to do less than justice to his humour —a humour which, in such scenes as that in ' Love for Love,' where Sir Sampson Legend discourses upon the human appetites and functions, moves beyond the humour of convention and passes into natural humour. It is, however, in spontaneity, in a kind of lawless merriment, almost Aristophanic in its verve, that Vanbrugh's humour seems so deep and so fine, seems indeed to spring from a fountain deeper and finer and rarer than Congreve's. A comedy of wit, like every other drama, is a story told by action and dialogue, but to tell a story lucidly and rapidly by means of repartee is exceedingly difficult, not but that it is easy enough to produce repartee. But in comic dialogue the difficulty is to move rapidly and yet keep up the brilliant ball-throwing demanded in this form ; and without lucidity and rapidity no drama, whether of repartee or of character, can live. Etheredge, the father of the comedy of repartee, has at length had justice done to him by Mr. Gosse. Not only could Etheredge tell a story by means of repartee alone : he could produce a tableau too ; so could Congreve, and so also could Vanbrugh ; but often—far too often—Vanbrugh's tableau is reached, not by fair means, as in the tableau of Congreve, but by a surrendering of probability, by a sacrifice of artistic fusion, by an inartistic mingling of comedy and farce, such as Congreve never indulges in. Jeremy Collier was perfectly right, therefore, in his strictures upon the farcical improbabilities of the 'Relapse.' So farcical indeed are the tableaux in that play that the broader portions of it were (as Mr. Swinburne discovered) adapted by Voltaire and acted at Sceaux as a farce. Had we space here to contrast the 'Relapse' with the 'Way of the World,' we should very likely come upon a distinction between comedy and farce such as has never yet been drawn. We should find that farce is not comedy with a broadened grin—Thalia with her girdle loose and run wild—as the critics seem to assume. We should find that the difference between the two is not one of degree at all, but rather one of kind, and that mere breadth of fun has nothing to do with the question. No doubt the fun of

comedy may be as broad as that of farce, as is shown
indeed by the celebrated Dogberry scenes in ' Much
Ado about Nothing ' and by the scene in ' Love for
Love ' between Sir Sampson Legend and his son, alluded
to above ; but here, as in every other department of art,
all depends upon the quality of the imaginative belief
that the artist seeks to arrest and secure. Of comedy
the breath of life is dramatic illusion. Of farce the
breath of life is mock illusion. Comedy, whether broad
or genteel, pretends that its mimicry is real. Farce,
whether broad or genteel, makes no such pretence, but,
by a thousand tricks, which it keeps up between itself
and the audience, says, ' My acting is all sham, and you
know it.' Now, while Vanbrugh was apt too often to
forget this the fundamental difference between comedy
and farce, Congreve never forgot it, Wycherly rarely.
Not that there should be in any literary form any arbitrary laws. There is no arbitrary law declaring that
comedy shall not be mingled with farce, and yet the fact
is that in vital drama they cannot be so mingled. The
very laws of their existence are in conflict with each
other, so much so that where one lives the other must
die, as we see in the drama of our own day. The fact
seems to be that probability of incident, logical sequence
of cause and effect, are as necessary to comedy as they
are to tragedy, while farce would stifle in such an air.
Rather, it would be poisoned by it, just as comedy is
poisoned by what farce flourishes on ; that is to say,
inconsequence of reasoning—topsy-turvy logic. Born in
the fairy country of topsy-turvy, the logic of farce would
be illogical if it were not upside-down. So with coincidence, with improbable accumulation of convenient
events—farce can no more exist without these than
comedy can exist with them. Hence we affirm that

Jeremy Collier's strictures on the farcical adulterations of the 'Relapse' pierce more deeply into Vanbrugh's art than do the criticisms of Leigh Hunt and Hazlitt. In other words, perhaps the same lack of fusion which mars Vanbrugh's architectural ideas mars also his comedy."

Without for a moment wishing to institute comparisons between the merit of Mr. Watts-Dunton's literary articles and the merit of other literary articles by other contemporary writers, I may at least say that between his articles and theirs the difference is not one of degree, it is one of kind. Theirs are compact, business-like compressions of facts admirably fitted for an Encyclopædia. No attempt is made to formulate generalizations upon the principles of literary art, and this must be said in their praise—they are faultless as articles in a book of reference. But no student of Mr. Watts-Dunton's work who turns over the pages of an article in the ' Encyclopædia Britannica ' can fail after reading a few sentences to recognize the author. Generalizations, hints of daring theories, novel and startling speculations, graze each other's heels ,until one is dazzled by the display of intellectual brilliance. That his essays are out of place in an Encyclopædia may be true, but they seem to lighten and alleviate it and to shed his fascinating idiosyncrasy upon their coldly impersonal environment.

Chapter XVII

'THE LIFE POETIC'

I HAVE been allowed to enrich this volume with photographs of 'The Pines' and of some of the exquisite works of art therein. But it is unfortunate for me that I am not allowed to touch upon what are the most important relations of Mr. Watts-Dunton's life—important though so many of them are. I mean his intimacy with the poet whose name is now beyond doubt far above any other name in the contemporary world of letters. I do not sympathize with the hyper-sensitiveness of eminent men with regard to privacy. The inner chamber of what Rossetti calls the 'House of Life' should be kept sacred. But Rossetti's own case shows how impossible it is in these days to keep those recesses inviolable. The fierce light that beats upon men of genius grows fiercer and fiercer every day, and it cannot be quenched. This was one of my arguments when I first answered Mr. Watts-Dunton's own objection to the appearance of this monograph. The times have changed since he was a young man. Then publicity was shunned like a plague by poets and by painters. If such men wish the light to be true as well as fierce, they must allow their friends to illuminate their 'House of Life' by the lamp of truth. If Rossetti during his lifetime had allowed one of his friends who knew the secrets of his 'House of Life' to write about him, we might have been spared those

THE PINES'
(From a Drawing by Mr. Herbert Railton)

Photo. Poole, Putney

canards about him and the wife he loved which were rife shortly after his death. Byron's reluctance to take payment for his poetry was not a more belated relic of an old quixotism than is this dying passion for privacy. Publicity may be an evil, but it is an inevitable evil, and great men must not let the wasps and the gadflies monopolize its uses. It may be a reminiscence of an older and a nobler social temper, the temper under the influence of which Rossetti in 1870 said that he felt abashed because a paragraph had appeared in the 'Athenæum' announcing the fact that a book from him was forthcoming. But that temper has gone by for ever. We live now in very different times. Scores upon scores of unauthorized and absolutely false paragraphs about eminent men are published, especially about these two friends who have lived their poetic life together for more than a quarter of a century. Only the other day I saw in a newspaper an offensive descriptive caricature of Mr. Swinburne, of his dress, etc. It is interesting to recall the fact that mendacious journalism was the cause of Mr. Watts-Dunton's very first contribution to the 'Athenæum,' before he wrote any reviews at all. At that time the offenders seem to have been chiefly Americans. The article was not a review, but a letter signed ' Z,' entitled ' The Art of Interviewing,' and it appeared in the ' Athenæum,' of March 11, 1876. As it shows the great Swinburne myth in the making, I will reproduce this merry little skit :—

    " ' Alas ! there is none of us without his skeleton-closet,' said a great writer to one who was congratulating him upon having reached the goal for which he had, from the first, set out. ' My skeleton bears the dreadful name of " American Interviewer." Pity me ! ' ' Is he

an American with a diary in his pocket ? ' was the terrified
question always put by another man of genius, whenever
you proposed introducing a stranger to him. But this
was in those ingenuous Parker-Willisian days when the
'Interviewer' merely invented the dialogue—not the
entire dramatic action—not the interview itself.
Primitive times ! since when the 'Interviewer' has
developed indeed ! His dramatic inspiration now is
trammelled by none of those foolish and arbitrary conditions which—whether his scene of action was at the
'Blue Posts' with Thackeray, or in the North with
Scottish lords—vexed and bounded the noble soul of
the great patriarch of the tribe. Uncribbed, uncabined,
unconfined, the 'Interviewer' now invents, not merely
the dialogue, but the 'situation,' the place, the time—
the interview itself. Every dramatist has his favourite
character—Sophocles had his ; Shakspeare had his ;
Schiller had his ; the 'Interviewer' has his. Mr.
Swinburne has, for the last two or three years, been—for
some reason which it might not be difficult to explain—
the 'Interviewer's' special favourite. Moreover, the
accounts of the interviews with him are always livelier
than any others, inasmuch as they are accompanied by
brilliant fancy-sketches of his personal appearance—
sketches which, if they should not gratify him exactly,
would at least astonish him ; and it is surely something
to be even astonished in these days. Some time ago,
for instance, an American lady journalist, connected
with a 'Western newspaper,' made her appearance in
London, and expressed many 'great desires,' the greatest
of all her 'desires' being to know the author of 'Atalanta,'
or, if she could not know him, at least to 'see him.'

The Fates, however, were not kind to the lady.
The author of 'Atalanta' had quitted London. She did

not see him, therefore—not with her bodily eyes could she see him. Yet this did not at all prevent her from ' interviewing ' him. Why should it ? The ' soul hath eyes and ears ' as well as the body — especially if the soul is an American soul, with a mission to ' interview.' There soon appeared in the lady's Western newspaper a graphic account of one of the most interesting interviews with this poet that has ever yet been recorded. Mr. Swinburne—though at the time in Scotland—' called ' upon the lady at her rooms in London ; but, notwithstanding this unexampled feat of courtesy, he seems to have found no favour in the lady's eyes. She ' misliked him for his complexion.' Evidently it was nothing but good-breeding that prevented her from telling the bard, on the spot, that he was physically an unlovely bard. His manners, too, were but so-so ; and the Western lady was shocked and disgusted, as well she might be. In the midst of his conversation, for example, he called out frantically for ' pen and ink.' He had become suddenly and painfully ' afflated.' When furnished with pen and ink he began furiously writing a poem, beating the table with his left hand and stamping the floor with both feet as he did so. Then, without saying a word, he put on his hat and rushed from the room like a madman ! This account was copied into other newspapers and into the magazines. It is, in fact, a piece of genuine history now, and will form valuable material for some future biographer of the poet. The stubborn shapelessness of facts has always distressed the artistically-minded historian. But let the American ' Interviewer ' go on developing thus, and we may look for History's becoming far more artistic and symmetrical in future. The above is but one out of many instances of the art of interviewing."

It is all very well to say that irresponsible statements of this kind are not in the true sense of the word believed by readers; they create an atmosphere of false mist which destroys altogether the picture of the poet's life which one would like to preserve. And I really think that it would have been better if I or some one else among the friends of the poets had been allowed to write more freely about the beautiful and intellectual life at 'The Pines.' But I am forbidden to do this, as the following passage in a letter which I have received from Mr. Watts-Dunton will show :

" I cannot have anything about our life at 'The Pines' put into print, but I will grant you permission to give a few reproductions of the interesting works of art here, for many of them may have a legitimate interest for the public ¡on account of their historic value, as having come to me from the magician of art, Rossetti. And I assure you that this is a concession which I have denied to very many applicants, both among friends and others."

Mr. Watts-Dunton's allusion to the Rossetti mementoes requires a word of explanation. Rossetti, it seems, was very fond of surprising his friends by unexpected tokens of generosity. I have heard Mr. Watts-Dunton say that during the week when he was moving into 'The Pines,' he spent as usual Wednesday night at 16 Cheyne Walk, and he and Rossetti sat talking into the small hours. Next morning after breakfast he strolled across to Whistler's house to have a talk with the ever-interesting painter, and this resulted in his getting home two hours later than usual. On reaching the new house he saw a waggon standing in

A CORNER IN 'THE PINES,' SHOWING ONE OF THE CHINESE CABINETS

front of it.   He did not understand this, for the furniture from the previous residence had been all removed.   He went up to the waggon, and was surprised to find it full of furniture of a choice kind.   But there was no need for him to give much time to an examination of the furniture, for he found he was familiar with every piece of it.   It had come straight from Rossetti's house, having been secretly packed and sent off by Dunn on the previous day. Some of the choicest things at 'The Pines' came in this way.   Not a word had Rossetti said about this generous little trick on the night before.   The superb Chinese cabinet, a photograph of which appears in this book, belonged to Rossetti.   It seems that on a certain occasion Frederick Sandys, or some one else, told Rossetti that the clever but ne'er-do-well artist, George Chapman, had bought of a sea-captain, trading in Chinese waters, a wonderful piece of lacquer work of the finest period—before the Manchu pig-tail time.   The captain had bought it of a Frenchman who had aided in looting the Imperial Palace.   Rossetti, of course, could not rest until he had seen it, and when he had seen it, he could not rest until he had bought it of Chapman ; and it was taken across to 16 Cheyne Walk, where it was greatly admired. The captain had barbarously mutilated it at the top in order to make it fit in his cabin, and it remained in that condition for some years.   Afterwards Rossetti gave it to Mr. Watts-Dunton, who got it restored and made up by the wonderful amateur carver, the late Mr. T. Keynes, who did the carving on the painted cabinet also photographed for this book.   There is a long and interesting story in connection with this piece of Chinese lacquer, but I have no room to tell it here.

All I am allowed to say about the relations between

Mr. Watts-Dunton and Mr. Swinburne is that the friendship began in 1872, that it soon developed into the closest intimacy, not only with the poet himself, but with all his family. In 1879 the two friends became house-mates at 'The Pines,' Putney Hill, and since then they have never been separated, for Mr. Watts-Dunton's visits to the Continent, notably those with the late Dr. Hake recorded in 'The New Day,' took place just before this time. The two poets thenceforth lived together, worked together, saw their common friends together, and travelled together. In 1882, after the death of Rossetti they went to the Channel Islands, staying at St. Peter's Port, Guernsey, for some little time, and then at Petit Bot Bay. Their swims in this beautiful bay Mr. Watts-Dunton commemorated in two of the opening sonnets of 'The Coming of Love ' —

NATURE'S FOUNTAIN OF YOUTH

(A MORNING SWIM OFF GUERNSEY WITH A FRIEND)

As if the Spring's fresh groves should change and shake
To dark green woods of Orient terebinth,
Then break to bloom of England's hyacinth,
So 'neath us change the waves, rising to take
Each kiss of colour from each cloud and flake
Round many a rocky hall and labyrinth,
Where sea-wrought column, arch, and granite plinth,
Show how the sea's fine rage dares make and break.
Young with the youth the sea's embrace can lend,
Our glowing limbs, with sun and brine empearled,
Seem born anew, and in your eyes, dear friend,
Rare pictures shine, like fairy flags unfurled,
Of child-land, where the roofs of rainbows bend
Over the magic wonders of the world.

SUMMER AT 'THE PINES.' I

Photo. Poole, Putney

THE LANGUAGE OF NATURE'S [FRAGRANCY

(THE TIRING-ROOM IN THE ROCKS)

These are the ' Coloured Caves' the sea-maid built;
Her walls are stained beyond that lonely fern,
For she must fly at every tide's return,
And all her sea-tints round the walls are spilt.
Outside behold the bay, each headland gilt
With morning's gold; far off the foam-wreaths burn
Like fiery snakes, while here the sweet waves yearn
Up sand more soft than Avon's sacred silt.
And smell the sea ! no breath of wood or field,
From lips of may or rose or eglantine,
Comes with the language of a breath benign,
Shuts the dark room where glimmers Fate revealed,
Calms the vext spirit, balms a sorrow unhealed,
Like scent of sea-weed rich of morn and brine.

The two friends afterwards went to Sark. A curious incident occurred during their stay in the island. The two poet-swimmers received a bravado challenge from ' Orion' Horne, who was also a famous swimmer, to swim with him round the whole island of Sark! I need hardly say that the absurd challenge was not accepted.

During the cruise Mr. Swinburne conceived and afterwards wrote some glorious poetry. In the same year the two friends went to Paris, as I have already mentioned, to assist at the Jubilee of ' Le Roi s'Amuse.' Since then their love of the English coasts and the waters which wash them, seems to have kept them in England. For two consecutive years they went to Sidestrand, on the Norfolk coast, for bathing. It was there that Mr. Swinburne wrote some of his East Anglian poems, and it was there that Mr. Watts-Dunton conceived the East coast parts of ' Aylwin.' It was during one of these visits that Mr. Swinburne first made the acquaintance of Grant Allen, who had long been an intimate friend of

Mr. Watts-Dunton's. The two, indeed, were drawn together by the fact that they both enjoyed science as much as they enjoyed literature. It was a very interesting meeting, as Grant Allen had long been one of Swinburne's most ardent admirers, and his social charm, his intellectual sweep and brilliance, made a great impression on the poet. Since then their visits to the sea have been confined to parts of the English Channel, such as Eastbourne, where they were near neighbours of Rossetti's friends, Lord and Lady Mount Temple, between whom and Mr. Watts-Dunton there had been an affectionate intimacy for many years—but more notably Lancing, whither they went for three consecutive years. For several years they stayed during their holiday with Lady Mary Gordon, an aunt of Mr. Swinburne's, at 'The Orchard,' Niton Bay, Isle of Wight. During the hot summer of 1904 they were lucky enough to escape to Cromer, where the temperature was something like twenty degrees lower than that of London. A curious incident occurred during this visit to Cromer. One day Mr. Watts-Dunton took a walk with another friend to 'Poppy-land,' where he and Mr. Swinburne had previously stayed, in order to see there again the landslips which he has so vividly described in 'Aylwin.' While they were walking from 'Poppyland' to the old ruined churchyard called 'The Garden of Sleep,' they sat down for some time in the shade of an empty hut near the cliff. Coming back Mr. Watts-Dunton said that the cliff there was very dangerous, and ought to be fenced off, as the fatal land-springs were beginning to show their work. Two or three weeks after this a portion of the cliff at that point, weighing many thousands of tons, fell into the sea, and the hut with it.

A friendship so affectionate and so long as the friend-

ship between these two poets is perhaps without a parallel
in literature. It has been frequently and beautifully
commemorated. When Mr. Swinburne's noble poem,
' By the North Sea,' was published, it was prefaced by
this sonnet :—

TO WALTER THEODORE WATTS

' WE ARE WHAT SUNS AND WINDS AND WATERS MAKE US.'

Landor.

Sea, wind, and sun, with light and sound and breath
   The spirit of man fulfilling—these create
   That joy wherewith man's life grown passionate
Gains heart to hear and sense to read and faith
To know the secret word our Mother saith
   In silence, and to see, though doubt wax great,
   Death as the shadow cast by life on fate,
Passing, whose shade we call the shadow of death.

Brother, to whom our Mother, as to me,
   Is dearer than all dreams of days undone,
This song I give you of the sovereign three
   That are, as life and sleep and death are, one :
A song the sea-wind gave me from the sea,
   Where nought of man's endures before the sun.

1882 was a memorable year in the life of Mr. Watts-
Dunton. The two most important volumes of poetry
published in that year were dedicated to him. Rossetti's
' Ballads and Sonnets,' the book which contains the
chief work of his life, bore the following inscription ·—

TO

THEODORE WATTS

THE FRIEND WHOM MY VERSE WON FOR ME,

THESE FEW MORE PAGES

ARE AFFECTIONATELY INSCRIBED.

A few weeks later Mr. Swinburne's 'Tristram of Lyonesse,' the volume which contains what I regard as his ripest and richest poetry, was thus inscribed :—

TO MY BEST FRIEND

THEODORE WATTS

I DEDICATE IN THIS BOOK

THE BEST I HAVE TO GIVE HIM.

Spring speaks again, and all our woods are stirred,
  And all our wide glad wastes aflower around,
  That twice have made keen April's clarion sound
Since here we first together saw and heard
Spring's light reverberate and reiterate word
  Shine forth and speak in season. Life stands crowned
  Here with the best one thing it ever found,
As of my soul's best birthdays dawns the third.

There is a friend that as the wise man saith
  Cleaves closer than a brother : nor to me
    Hath time not shown, through days like waves at strife
This truth more sure than all things else but death,
  This pearl most perfect found in all the sea
    That washes toward your feet these waifs of life.

THE PINES,
    April, 1882.

But the finest of all these words of affection are perhaps those opening the dedicatory epistle prefixed to the magnificent Collected Edition of Mr. Swinburne's poems issued by Messrs. Chatto and Windus in 1904 :—
'To my best and dearest friend I dedicate the first collected edition of my poems, and to him I address what I have to say on the occasion.'
Once also Mr. Watts-Dunton dedicated verses of his own to Mr. Swinburne, to wit, in 1897, when he pub-

lished that impassioned lyric in praise of a nobler and larger Imperialism, the 'Jubilee Greeting at Spithead to the Men of Greater Britain' :—

"TO OUR GREAT CONTEMPORARY WRITER OF
PATRIOTIC POETRY,
ALGERNON CHARLES SWINBURNE.

You and I are old enough to remember the time when, in the world of letters at least, patriotism was not so fashionable as it is now—when, indeed, love of England suggested Philistinism rather than 'sweetness and light.' Other people, such as Frenchmen, Italians, Irishmen, Hungarians, Poles, might give voice to a passionate love of the land of their birth, but not Englishmen. It was very curious, as I thought then, and as I think now. And at that period love of the Colonies was, if possible, even more out of fashion than was love of England; and this temper was not confined to the 'cultured' class. It pervaded society and had an immense influence upon politics. On one side the Manchester school, religiously hoping that if the Colonies could be insulted so effectually that they must needs (unless they abandoned all self-respect) 'set up for themselves,' the same enormous spurt would be given to British trade which occurred after the birth of the United States, bade the Colonies 'cut the painter.' On the other hand the old Tories and Whigs, with a few noble exceptions, having never really abandoned the old traditions respecting the unimportance of all matters outside the parochial circle of European diplomacy, scarcely knew where the Colonies were situated on the map.

There was, however, in these islands one person who saw as clearly then as all see now the infinite importance of the expansion of England to the true progress of mankind—the Great Lady whose praises in this regard I have presumed to sing in the opening stanza of these verses.

I may be wrong, but I, who am, as you know, no courtier, believe from the bottom of my heart that without the influence of the Queen this expansion would have been seriously delayed. Directly and indirectly her influence must needs be enormous, and, as regards this matter, it has always been exercised—energetically and even eagerly exercised—in one way. This being my view, I have for years been urging more than one friend clothed with an authority such as I do not possess to bring the subject prominently before the people of England at a time when England's expansion is a phrase in everybody's mouth. I have not succeeded. Let this be my apology for undertaking the task myself and for inscribing to you, as well as to the men of Greater Britain, these lines."

I feel that it is a great privilege to be able to present to my readers beautiful photogravures and photographs of interiors and pictures and works of art at 'The Pines.' Many of the pictures and other works of art at 'The Pines' are mementoes of a most interesting kind.

Among these is the superb portrait of Madox Brown, at this moment hanging in the Bradford Exhibition. Madox Brown painted it for the owner. An interesting story is connected with it. One day, not long after Mr. Watts-Dunton had become intimate with Madox Brown, the artist told him he specially wanted his boy Nolly to read to him a story that he had been writing, and asked him to meet the boy at dinner.

'Nolly been writing a story!' exclaimed Mr. Watts-Dunton.

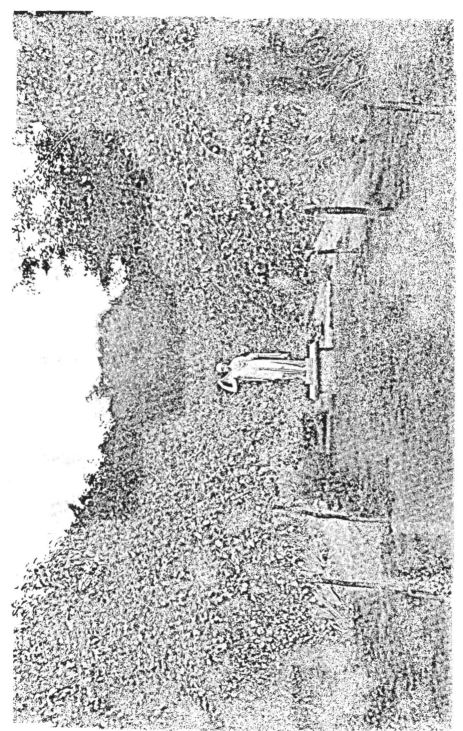

SUMMER AT 'THE PINES.' II

'I understand your smile,' said Madox Brown; 'but you will find it better than you think.'

At this time Oliver Madox Brown seemed a loose-limbed hobbledehoy, young enough to be at school. After dinner Oliver began to read the opening chapters of the story in a not very impressive way, and Mr. Watts-Dunton suggested that he should take it home and read it at his leisure. This was agreed to. Pressure of affairs prevented him from taking it up for some time. At last he did take it up, but he had scarcely read a dozen pages when he was called away, and he asked a member of his family to gather up the pages from the sofa and put them into an escritoire. On his return home at a very late hour he found the lady intently reading the manuscript, and she declared that she could not go to bed till she had finished it.

On the next day Mr. Watts-Dunton again took up the manuscript, and was held spellbound by it. It was a story of passion, of intense love, and intense hate, told with a crude power that was irresistible.

Mr. Watts-Dunton knew Smith Williams (the reader of Smith, Elder & Co.), whose name is associated with 'Jane Eyre.' He showed it to Williams, who was greatly struck by it, but pointed out that it terminated in a violent scene which the novel-reading public of that time would not like, and asked for a concluding scene less daring. The ending was modified, and the story, when it appeared, attracted very great attention. Madox Brown was so grateful to Mr. Watts-Dunton for his services in the matter that he insisted on expressing his gratitude in some tangible form. Miss Lucy Madox Brown (afterwards Mrs. W. M. Rossetti) was consulted, and at once suggested a portrait of the painter, painted by himself. This was done, and the result was the masterpiece which has been so often exhibited. From that moment Oliver Madox Brown took his place in the literary world of his time. The mention of Oliver Madox Brown will remind the older generation of his friendship with Philip Bourke Marston, the blind poet, one of the most pathetic chapters in literary annals.

Although Rossetti never fulfilled his intention of illustrating what he called 'Watts's magnificent star sonnet,' he began what would have been a superb picture illustrating Mr. Watts-Dunton's sonnet, 'The Spirit of the Rainbow.' He finished a large charcoal drawing of it, which is thus described by Mr. William Sharp in his book, 'Dante Gabriel Rossetti · a Record and a Study' :—

"It represents a female figure standing in a gauzy circle composed of a rainbow, and on the frame is written the following sonnet (the poem in question by Mr. Watts-Dunton) :

THE WOOD-HAUNTER'S DREAM

The wild things loved me, but a wood-sprite said :
    'Though meads are sweet when flowers at morn uncurl,
    And woods are sweet with nightingale and merle,
Where are the dreams that flush'd thy childish bed ?
The Spirit of the Rainbow thou would'st wed !'
    I rose, I found her—found a rain-drenched girl
    Whose eyes of azure and limbs like roseate pearl
Coloured the rain above her golden head.

But when I stood by that sweet vision's side
    I saw no more the Rainbow's lovely stains ;
To her by whom the glowing heavens were dyed
    The sun showed naught but dripping woods and plains :
'God gives the world the Rainbow, her the rains,'
The wood-sprite laugh'd, 'Our seeker finds a bride !'

'PICTURE FOR A STORY'
(Face and Instrument designed by D. G. Rossetti, background by Dunn)

Photo Poole, Putney

Rossetti meant to have completed the design with the 'woods and plains' seen in perspective through the arch ; and the composition has an additional and special interest because it is the artist's only successful attempt at the wholly nude—the 'Spirit' being extremely graceful in poise and outline.

I am able to give a reproduction of another of Rossetti's beautiful studies which has never been published, but which has been very much talked about. Many who have seen it at 'The Pines' agree with the late Lord de Tabley that Rossetti in this crayon created the loveliest of all his female faces. It is thus described by Mr. William Sharp : " The drawing, which, for the sake of a name, I will call 'Forced Music,' represents a nude half-figure of a girl playing on a mediæval stringed instrument elaborately ornamented. The face is of a type unlike that of any other of the artist's subjects, and extraordinarily beautiful."

I should explain that the background and the ragged garb of the girl in the version of the picture here reproduced, are by Dunn. These two exquisite drawings were made from the same girl, who never sat for any other pictures. Her face has been described as being unlike that of any other of Rossetti's models and yet combining the charm of them all.

I am strictly prohibited by the subject of this study from giving any personal description of him. For my part I do not sympathize with this extreme sensitiveness and dislike to having one's personal characteristics described in print.   What is there so dreadful or so sacred in mere print ?   The feeling upon this subject is a reminiscence, I think, of archaic times, when between conversation and printed matter there was 'a great gulf fixed.' Both Mr. Watts-Dunton and his friend Mr. Swinburne must be aware that as soon as they have left any gathering of friends or strangers, remarks—delicate enough, no doubt —are made about them, as they are made about every other person who is talked about in ever so small a degree.   Not so very long ago I remained in a room after Mr. Watts-Dunton had left it.   Straightway there were the freest remarks about him, not in the least unkind, but free.   Some did not expect to see so dark a man ; some expected to see him much darker than they found him to be ; some recalled the fact that Miss Corkran, in her reminiscences, described his dark-brown eyes as 'green'— through a printer's error, no doubt.   Some then began to contrast his appearance with that of his absent friend, Mr. Swinburne—and so on, and so on.   Now, what is the difference between being thus discussed in print and in conversation ?   Merely that the printed report reaches a wider—a little wider—audience   That is all.   I do not think it is an unfair evasion of his prohibition to reproduce one of the verbal snap-shots of him that have appeared in the papers.   Some energetic gentleman—possibly some one living in the neighbourhood—took the following 'Kodak' of him.   It appeared in 'M.A.P.' and it is really as good a thumb-nail portrait of him as could be painted.   In years to come, when he and I and the 'Kodaker' are dead, it may be found more interesting, perhaps, than anything I have written about him :—

" Every, or nearly every, morning, as the first glimmer

of dawn lightens the sky, there appears on Wimbledon Common a man, whose skin has been tanned by sun and wind to the rich brown of the gypsies he loves so well ; his forehead is round, and fairly high ; his brown eyes and the brow above them give his expression a piercing appearance. For the rest, his voice is firm and resonant, and his brown hair and thick moustache are partially shot with grey. But he looks not a day over forty-five. Generally he carries a book. Often, however, he turns from it to watch the birds and the rabbits. For—it will be news to lie-abeds of the district—Wimbledon Common is lively with rabbits, revelling in the freshness of the dawn, rabbits which ere the rush for the morning train begins, will all have vanished until the moon rises again. To him, morning, although he has seen more sunrises than most men, still makes an ever fresh and glorious pageant. This usually solitary figure is that of Mr. Theodore Watts-Dunton, and to his habit of early rising the famous poet, novelist, and critic ascribes his remarkable health and vigour."

The holidays of the two poets have not been confined to their visits to the sea-side. One place of retreat used to be the residence of the late Benjamin Jowett, at Balliol, when the men were down, or one of his country places, such as Boar's Hill.

I have frequently heard Mr. Swinburne and Mr. Watts-Dunton talk about the famous Master of Balliol. I have heard Mr. Swinburne recall the great admiration which Jowett used to express for Mr. Watts-Dunton's intellectual powers and various accomplishments. There was no one, I have heard Mr. Swinburne say, whom Jowett held in greater esteem. That air of the college don, which has been described by certain of Jowett's friends, left the Master entirely when he was talking to Mr. Watts-Dunton.

Among the pleasant incidents in Mr. Watts-Dunton's life were these visits with Mr. Swinburne to Jowett's house, where he had the opportunity of meeting some of the most prominent men of the time. He has described the Balliol dinner parties, but I have no room here to do more than allude to them. I must, however, quote his famous pen portrait of Jowett which appeared in the 'Athenæum' of December 22, 1894.

"It may seem difficult to imagine many points of sympathy between the poet of 'Atalanta' and the student of Plato and translator of Thucydides; and yet the two were bound to each other by ties of no common strength. They took expeditions into the country together, and Mr. Swinburne was a not infrequent guest at Balliol and also at Jowett's quiet autumnal retreat at Boar's Hill. The Master of Balliol, indeed, had a quite remarkable faculty of drawing to himself the admiration of men of poetic genius. To say which poet admired and loved him most deeply—Tennyson, Browning, Matthew Arnold, or Mr. Swinburne—would be difficult. He seemed to join their hands all round him, and these intimacies with the poets were not the result of the smallest sacrifice of independence on the part of Jowett. He was always quite as frank in telling a poet what he disliked in his verses as in telling him what he liked. And although the poets of our own epoch are, perhaps, as irritable a race as they were in times past, and are as little impervious as ever to flattery, it is, after all, in virtue partly of a superior intelligence that poets are poets, and in the long run their friendship is permanently given to straightforward men like Jowett. That Jowett's judgment in artistic matters, and especially in poetry, was borné no one knew better than himself, and he had a way of letting the poets see that upon poetical subjects he must be taken as only a partially qualified judge, and this alone gained for him a greater freedom in criticism than would otherwise have been allowed to him. For, notwithstanding the Oxford epigram upon him as a pretender to absolute wisdom, no man could be more modest than he upon subjects of which he had only the ordinary knowledge. He was fond of quoting Hallam's words that without an exhaustive knowledge of details there can be no accurate induction ; and where he saw that his interlocutor really had special knowledge, he was singularly diffident about expressing his opinion. They are not so far wrong who take it for granted that one who was able to secure the loving admiration of four of the greatest poets of the Victorian epoch, all extremely unlike each other, was not only a great and a rare intelligence, but a man of a nature most truly noble and most truly lovable. The kind of restraint in social intercourse resulting from what has been called his taciturnity passed so soon as his interlocutor realized (which he very quickly did) that Jowett's taciturnity, or rather his lack of volubility, arose from the peculiarly honest nature of one who had no idea of talking for talking's sake. If a proper and right response to a friend's remark chanced to come to his lips spontaneously, he was quite willing to deliver it ; but if the response was neither spontaneous nor likely to be adequate, he refused to manufacture one for the mere sake of keeping the ball rolling, as is so often the case with the shallow or uneducated man. It is, however, extremely difficult to write reminiscences of men so taciturn as Jowett. In order to bring out one of Jowett's pithy sayings, the interlocutor who would record it has also to record the words of his own which awoke the saying, and then it is almost impossible to avoid an appearance of egotism."

Still more pleasurable than these relaxations at Oxford were the visits that the two friends used to pay to Jowett's rural retreat at Boar's Hill, about three miles from Oxford, for the purpose of revelling in the riches of the dramatic room in the Bodleian. The two poets used to spend the entire day in that enchanted room, and then walk back with the Master to Boar's Hill. Every reader of Mr. Watts-Dunton's poetry will remember the following sonnets :—

THE LAST WALK FROM BOAR'S HILL

To A. C. S.

I

One after one they go ; and glade and heath,
   Where once we walked with them, and garden bowers
   They made so dear, are haunted by the hours
Once musical of those who sleep beneath ;
One after one does Sorrow's every wreath
   Bind closer you and me with funeral flowers,
   And Love and Memory from each loss of ours
Forge conquering glaives to quell the conqueror Death.

Since Love and Memory now refuse to yield
The friend with whom we walk through mead and field
   To-day as on that day when last we parted,
Can he be dead, indeed, whatever seem ?
Love shapes a presence out of Memory's dream,
   A living presence, Jowett golden-hearted.

II

Can he be dead ? We walk through flowery ways
   From Boar's Hill down to Oxford, fain to know

What nugget-gold, in drift of Time's long flow,
The Bodleian mine hath stored from richer days;
He, fresh as on that morn, with sparkling gaze,
   Hair bright as sunshine, white as moonlit snow,
   Still talks of Plato while the scene below
Breaks gleaming through the veil of sunlit haze.

Can he be dead? He shares our homeward walk,
And by the river you arrest the talk
   To see the sun transfigure ere he sets
The boatmen's children shining in the wherry
   And on the floating bridge the ply-rope wets,
Making the clumsy craft an angel's ferry.

III

The river crossed, we walk 'neath glowing skies
   Through grass where cattle feed or stand and stare
   With burnished coats, glassing the coloured air—
Fading as colour after colour dies:
We pass the copse; we round the leafy rise—
   Start many a coney and partridge, hern and hare;
   We win the scholar's nest—his simple fare
Made royal-rich by welcome in his eyes.

Can he be dead? His heart was drawn to you.
Ah! well that kindred heart within him knew
   The poet's heart of gold that gives the spell!
Can he be dead? Your heart being drawn to him,
How shall ev'n Death make that dear presence dim
   For you who loved him—us who loved him well?

Another and much lovelier retreat, whither Mr. Watts-Dunton has always loved to go, is the cottage at Box-hill. Not the least interesting among the beautiful friend ships between Mr. Watts-Dunton and his illustrious contemporaries is that between himself and Mr. George Meredith. Mr. William Sharp can speak with authority on this subject, being himself the intimate friend of Mr. Meredith, Mr. Swinburne, and Mr. Watts-Dunton.

Speaking of Swinburne's championship, in the 'Spectator,' of Meredith's first book of poems, Mr. Sharp, in an article in the 'Pall Mall Magazine,' of December 1901, says :—

"Among those who read and considered" [Meredith's work] " was another young poet, who had, indeed, already heard of Swinburne as one of the most promising of the younger men, but had not yet met him. . . . If the letter signed 'A. C. Swinburne' had not appeared, another signed 'Theodore Watts' would have been published, to the like effect. It was not long before the logic of events was to bring George Meredith, A. C. Swinburne, and Theodore Watts into personal communion."

The first important recognition of George Meredith as a poet was the article by Mr. Watts-Dunton in the 'Athenæum' on 'Poems and Lyrics of the Joy of Earth.' After this appeared articles appreciative of Meredith's prose fiction by W. E. Henley and others. But it was Mr. Watts-Dunton who led the way. The most touching of all the testimonies of love and admiration which Mr. Meredith has received from Mr. Watts-Dunton, or indeed, from anybody else, is the beautiful sonnet addressed to him on his seventy-fourth birthday. It appeared in the 'Saturday Review' of February 15, 1902 :—

TO GEORGE MEREDITH
(ON HIS SEVENTY-FOURTH BIRTHDAY)

This time, dear friend—this time my birthday greeting
Comes heavy of funeral tears—I think of you,
And say, ''Tis evening with him—that is true—
But evening bright as noon, if faster fleeting ;
Still he is spared—while Spring and Winter, meeting,
Clasp hands around the roots 'neath frozen dew—
To see the 'Joy of Earth' break forth anew,
And hear it on the hillside warbling, bleating.'

Love's remnant melts and melts ; but, if our days
    Are swifter than a weaver's shuttle, still,
Still Winter has a sun—a sun whose rays
    Can set the young lamb dancing on the hill.
And set the daisy, in the woodland ways,
    Dreaming of her who brings the daffodil.

The allusion to ' funeral tears ' was caused by one of the greatest bereavements which Mr. Watts-Dunton has sustained in recent years, namely, that of Frank Groome, whose obituary he wrote for the ' Athenæum.' I have not the honour of knowing Meredith, but I have often heard Mr. Watts-Dunton describe with a glow of affectionate admiration the fine charm of his character and the amazing pregnancy in thought and style of his conversation.

But the most memorable friendship that during their joint occupancy of 'The Pines' Mr. Watts-Dunton formed, was that with Tennyson.

I have had many conversations with Mr. Watts-Dunton on the subject of Tennyson, and I am persuaded that, owing to certain incongruities between the external facets of Tennyson's character and the ' abysmal deeps ' of his personality, Mr. Watts-Dunton, after the poet's son, is the only man living who is fully competent to speak with authority of the great poet. Not only is he himself a poet who must be placed among his contemporaries nearest to his more illustrious friend, but between Mr. Watts-Dunton and Tennyson from their first meeting there was an especial sympathy. So long ago as 1881 was published his sonnet to Tennyson on his seventy-first birthday. It attracted much attention, and although it was not sent to the Laureate, he read it and was much touched by it, as well he might be, for it is as noble a tribute as one poet could pay to another :—

Beyond the peaks of Kaf a rivulet springs
  Whose magic waters to a flood expand,
  Distilling, for all drinkers on each hand,
The immortal sweets enveiled in mortal things.
From honeyed flowers,—from balm of zephyr-wings,—
  From fiery blood of gems,[1] through all the land,
  The river draws ;—then, in one rainbow-band,
Ten leagues of nectar o'er the ocean flings.

Rich with the riches of a poet's years,
  Stained in all colours of Man's destiny,
So, Tennyson, thy widening river nears
  The misty main, and, taking now the sea,
Makes rich and warm with human smiles and tears
  The ashen billows of Eternity.

Some two or three years after this Mr. Watts-Dunton met the Laureate at a garden party, and they fraternized at once. Mr. Watts-Dunton had an open invitation to Aldworth and Farringford whenever he could go, and this invitation came after his very first stay at Aldworth. One point in which he does not agree with Coleridge (in the 'Table Talk') or with Mr. Swinburne, is the theory that Tennyson's ear was defective at the very first. He contends that if Tennyson in his earlier poems seemed to show a defective ear, it was always when in the great struggle between the demands of mere metrical music and those of the other great requisites of poetry, thought, emotion, colour and outline, he found it best occasionally to make metrical music in some measure yield. As an illustration of Tennyson's sensibility to the most

[1] According to a Mohammedan tradition, the mountains of Kaf are entirely composed of gems, whose reflected splendours colour the sky.

delicate nuances of metrical music, I remember at one of those charming 'symposia' at 'The Pines,' hearing Mr. Watts-Dunton say that Tennyson was the only English poet who gave the attention to the sibilant demanded by Dionysius of Halicarnassus; and I remember one delightful instance that he gave of this. It referred to the two sonnets upon 'The Omnipotence of Love' in the universe which I have always considered to be the keynote of 'Aylwin' and 'The Coming of Love.' These sonnets appeared in an article called 'The New Hero' in the 'English Illustrated Magazine' in 1883. Mr. Watts-Dunton was staying at Aldworth when the proof of the article reached him. The present Lord Tennyson (who, as Mr. Watts-Dunton has often averred, has so much literary insight that if he had not been the son of the greatest poet of his time, he would himself have taken a high position in literature) read out in one of the little Aldworth bowers to his father and to Miss Mary Boyle the article and the sonnets. Tennyson, who was a severe critic of his own work, but extremely lenient in criticising the work of other men, said there was one feature in one of the lines of one of the sonnets which he must challenge. The line was this :—

And scents of flowers and shadow of wavering trees.

Now it so chanced that this very line had been especially praised by two other fine critics, D. G. Rossetti and William Morris, to whom the sonnet had been read in manuscript. Tennyson's criticism was that there were too many sibilants in the line, and that although, other things being equal, 'scents' might be more accurate than 'scent,' this was a case where the claims of music ought to be dominant over other claims. The present Lord Tennyson took the same view, and I am sure they were right, and that Mr. Watts-Dunton was right, in finally adopting 'scent' in place of 'scents.'

Mr. Watts-Dunton has always contended that Tennyson's sensibility to criticism was the result, not of imperious egotism, but of a kind of morbid modesty. Tennyson used to say that "to whatsoever exalted position a poet might reach, he was not 'born to the purple,' and that if the poet's mind was especially plastic he could never shake off the reminiscence of the time when he was nobody."

On a certain occasion Tennyson took Mr. Watts-Dunton into the summer-house at Aldworth to read to him 'Becket,' then in manuscript. Although another visitor, whom he esteemed very highly, both as a poet and an old friend, was staying there, Tennyson said that he should prefer to read the play to Mr. Watts-Dunton alone. And this no doubt was because he desired an absolute freedom of criticism. Freedom of criticism we may be sure he got, for of all men Mr. Watts-Dunton is the most outspoken on the subject of the poet's art. The entire morning was absorbed in the reading ; and, says Mr. Watts-Dunton, ' the remarks upon poetic and dramatic art that fell from Tennyson would have made the fortune of any critic.'

On the subject of what has been called Tennyson's gaucherie and rudeness to women I have seen Mr. Watts-Dunton wax very indignant. 'There was to me,' he said, ' the greatest charm in what is called Tennyson's bluntness. I would there were a leaven of Tennyson's single-mindedness in the society of the present day.'

One anecdote concerning what is stigmatized as Tennyson's rudeness to women shows how entirely the man was misunderstood. Mrs. Oliphant has stated that Tennyson, in his own house, after listening in silence to an interchange of amiable compliments between herself and Mrs. Tennyson, said abruptly, 'What liars you women are!' 'I seem to hear,' said Mr. Watts-Dunton, 'Tennyson utter the exclamation—utter it in that tone of humourous playfulness, followed by that loud guffaw, which neutralized the rudeness as entirely as Douglas Jerrold's laugh neutralized the sting of his satire. For such an incident to be cited as as instance of Tennyson's rudeness to women is ludicrous. When I knew him I was, if possible, a more obscure literary man than I now am, and he treated me with exactly the same manly respect that he treated the most illustrious people. I did not feel that I had any claim to such treatment, for he was, beyond doubt, the greatest literary figure in the world of that time. There seems unfortunately to be an impulse of detraction, which springs up after a period of laudation.'

The only thing I have heard Mr. Watts-Dunton say in the way of stricture upon Tennyson's work was that, considering his enormous powers as a poet, he seemed deficient in the gift of inventing a story:—"The stanzas beginning, 'O, that 'twere possible'—the nucleus of 'Maud'—appeared originally in 'The Tribute.' They were the finest lines that Tennyson ever wrote—right away the finest. They suggested some superb story of passion and mystery; and every reader was compelled to make his own guess as to what the story could possibly be. In an evil moment some friend suggested that Tennyson should amplify this glorious lyric into a story. A person with more of the endowment of the inventor than Tennyson might perhaps have invented an adequate story—might perhaps have invented a dozen adequate stories; but he could not have invented a worse story than the one used by Tennyson in the writing of his monodrama. But think of the poetic riches poured into it !"

I remember a peculiarly subtle criticism that Mr. Watts-Dunton once made in regard to 'The Princess.' "Shakspeare," he said, " is the only poet who has been able to put sincere writing into a story the plot of which is fanciful. The extremely insincere story of 'The Princess' is filled with such noble passages of sincere poetry as ' Tears, idle tears,' ' Home they brought her warrior dead,' etc., passages which unfortunately lose two-thirds of their power through the insincere setting."

Not very long before Tennyson died, the editor of the ' Magazine of Art ' invited Mr. Watts-Dunton to write an article upon the portraits of Tennyson. Mr. Watts-Dunton consulted the poet upon this project, and he agreed, promising to aid in the selection of the portraits. The result was two of the most interesting essays upon Tennyson that have ever been written—in fact, it is no exaggeration to say that without a knowledge of these articles no student of Tennyson can be properly equipped. It is tantalizing that they have never been reprinted. Tennyson died before their appearance, and this, of course, added to the general interest felt in them.

After Tennyson's death Mr. Watts-Dunton wrote two penetrating essays upon Tennyson in the 'Nineteenth Century,' one of them being his reminiscences of Tennyson as the poet and the man, and the other a study of him as a nature-poet in reference to evolution. It will be a great pity if these essays too are not reprinted. Mr. Knowles, the editor, also included Mr. Watts-Dunton among the friends of Tennyson who were invited to write memorial verses on his death for the

'Nineteenth Century.' To this series Mr. Watts-Dunton contributed the following sonnet, which is one of the several poems upon Tennyson not published in 'The Coming of Love' volume, which, I may note in passing, contains 'What the Silent Voices Said,' the fine 'sonnet sequence' commemorating the burial of Tennyson :—

IN WESTMINSTER ABBEY

'THE CROWD IN THE ABBEY WAS VERY GREAT.'

Morning Newspaper.

I saw no crowd : yet did these eyes behold
   What others saw not—his lov'd face sublime
   Beneath that pall of death in deathless prime
Of Tennyson's long day that grows not old ;
And, as I gazed, my grief seemed over-bold ;
   And, 'Who art thou,' the music seemed to chime,
   'To mourn that King of song whose throne is Time ?'
Who loves a god should be of godlike mould.

Then spake my heart, rebuking Sorrow's shame :
   'So great he was, striving in simple strife
   With Art alone to lend all beauty life—
So true to Truth he was, whatever came—
   So fierce against the false when lies were rife—
That love o'erleapt the golden fence of Fame.'

By the invitation of the present Lord Tennyson, Mr. Watts-Dunton was one of the few friends of the poet, including Jowett, F. W. H. Myers, F. T. Palgrave, the late Duke of Argyll, and others, who contributed reminiscences of him to the 'Life.' In a few sentences he paints this masterly little miniature of Tennyson, entitled, 'Impressions : 1883–1892'[1] :—

" All are agreed that D. G. Rossetti's was a peculiarly winning personality, but no one has been in the least able

'Tennyson : A Memoir,' by his son (1897), vol. ii. p. 479.

to say why. Nothing is easier, however, than to find the charm of Tennyson. It lay in a great veracity of soul : it lay in a simple single-mindedness, so childlike that, unless you had known him to be the undoubted author of poems as marvellous for exquisite art as for inspiration, you could not have supposed but that all subtleties—even those of poetic art—must be foreign to a nature so simple.

Working in a language like ours—a language which has to be moulded into harmony by a myriad subtleties of art—how can this great, inspired, simple nature be the delicate-fingered artist of 'The Princess,' 'The Palace of Art,' 'The Day-Dream,' and 'The Dream of Fair Women' ?

Tennyson knew of but one justification for the thing he said—viz. that it was the thing he thought. Behind his uncompromising directness was apparent a noble and a splendid courtesy of the grand old type. As he stood at the porch of Aldworth meeting a guest or bidding him good-bye—as he stood there, tall far beyond the height of average men, his skin showing dark and tanned by the sun and wind—as he stood there, no one could mistake him for anything but a great forthright English gentleman. Always a man of an extraordinary beauty of presence, he showed up to the last the beauty of old age to a degree rarely seen. He was the most hospitable of men. It was very rare indeed for him to part from a guest without urging him to return, and generally with the words, 'Come whenever you like.'

Tennyson's knowledge of nature—nature in every aspect—was simply astonishing. His passion for 'stargazing' has often been commented upon by readers of his poetry. Since Dante, no poet in any land has so loved the stars. He had an equal delight in watching the lightning; and I remember being at Aldworth once during a thunderstorm, when I was alarmed at the temerity with which he persisted, in spite of all remonstrances, in gazing at the blinding lightning. For moonlight effects he had a passion equally strong, and it is especially pathetic to those who know this to remember that he passed away in the light he so much loved—in a room where there was no artificial light—nothing to quicken the darkness but the light of the full moon, which somehow seems to shine more brightly at Aldworth than anywhere else in England.

In a country having a composite language such as ours it may be affirmed with special emphasis that there are two kinds of poetry : one appealing to the uncultivated masses, the other appealing to the few who are sensitive to the felicitous expression of deep thought and to the true beauties of poetic art.

Of all poets Shakespeare is the most popular, and yet in his use of what Dante calls the ' sieve for noble words ' his skill transcends that of even Milton, Coleridge, Shelley, and Keats. His felicities of thought and of diction in the great passages seem little short of miraculous, and there are so many that it is easy to understand why he is so often spoken of as being a kind of inspired improvisatore. That he was not an improvisatore, however, any one can see who will take the trouble to compare the first edition of ' Romeo and Juliet ' with the received text, the first sketch of ' The Merry Wives of Windsor ' with the play as we now have it, and the ' Hamlet ' of 1603 with the ' Hamlet ' of 1604, and with the still further varied version of the play given by Heminge and Condell in the Folio of 1623. Next to Shakespeare in this great power of combining the forces of the two great classes of English poets, appealing both to the commonplace public and to the artistic sense of the few, stands, perhaps, Chaucer ; but since Shakespeare's time no one has met with anything like Tennyson's success in effecting a reconciliation between popular and artistic sympathy with poetry in England."

Chapter XVIII

AMERICAN FRIENDS : LOWELL, BRET HARTE, AND OTHERS

I FEEL that my hasty notes about Mr. Watts-Dunton's literary friendships would be incomplete without a word or two upon his American friends. There is a great deal of interest in the story of the first meeting between him and James Russell Lowell. Shortly after Lowell had accepted the post of American Minister in England, Mr. Watts-Dunton met him at dinner. During the dinner Mr. Watts-Dunton was somewhat attracted by the conversation of a gentleman who sat next to him but one. He observed that the gentleman seemed to talk as if he wished to entice him into the conversation. The gentleman was passing severe strictures upon English writers—Dickens, Thackeray, and others. As the dinner wore on, his conversation left literary names and took up political ones, and he was equally severe upon the prominent political figures of the time, and also upon the prominent political men of the previous generation—Palmerston, Lord John Russell, and the like. Then the name of the Alabama came up ; the gentleman (whom Mr. Watts-Dunton now discovered to be an American), dwelt with much emphasis upon the iniquity of England in letting the Alabama escape. This diatribe he concluded thus : 'You know we owe England nothing.' In saying this he again looked at Mr. Watts-Dunton, manifestly addressing his remarks to him.

These attacks upon England and Englishmen and everything English had at last irritated Mr. Watts-Dunton, and addressing the gentleman for the first time, he said : " Pardon me, sir, but there you are wrong. You owe England a very great deal, for I see you are an American."

" What do we owe England ? " said the gentleman, whom Mr. Watts-Dunton now began to realize was no other than the newly appointed American Minister.

" You owe England," he said, " for an infinity of good feeling which you are trying to show is quite unreciprocated by Americans. So kind is the feeling of English people towards Americans that socially, so far as the middle classes are concerned, they have an immense advantage over English people themselves. They are petted and made much of, until at last it has come to this, that the very fact of a person's being American is a letter of introduction."

Mr. Watts-Dunton spoke with such emphasis, and his voice is so penetrating, that those on the opposite side of the table began to pause in their conversation to listen to it, and this stopped the little duel between the two. After the ladies had retired, Mr. Lowell drew up his chair to Mr. Watts-Dunton and said :

" You were very sharp upon me just now, sir."

" Not in the least," said Mr. Watts-Dunton. " You were making an onslaught on my poor little island, and you really seemed as though you were addressing your conversation to me."

" Well," replied Mr. Lowell, " I will confess that I did address my conversation partially to you ; you are, I think, Mr. Theodore Watts."

" That is my little name," said Mr. Watts-Dunton. " But I really don't see why that should induce you to address your conversation to me.   I suppose it is because absurd paragraphs have often appeared in the American newspapers stating that I am strongly anti-American in my sympathies.   An entire mistake!   I have several charming American friends, and I am a great admirer of many of your most eminent writers.   But I notice that whensoever an American book is severely handled in the 'Athenæum,' the article is attributed to me."

"I do not think," said Mr. Lowell, "that you are a lover of my country, but I am not one of those who attribute to you articles that you never wrote."

And he then drew his chair nearer to his interlocutor, and became more confidential.

"Well," he said, "I will tell you something that, I think, will not be altogether unpleasant to you.   When I came to take up my permanent residence in London a short time ago, I was talking to a friend of mine about London and Londoners, and I said to him: 'There is one man whom I very much want to meet.' 'You!' said he, 'why, you can meet anybody from the royal family downwards.   Who is the man you want to meet?' 'It is a man in the literary world,' said I, 'and I have no doubt you can introduce me to him.   It is the writer of the chief poetical criticism in the "Athenæum."' My friend laughed. 'Well, it is curious,' he replied: 'that is one of the few men in the literary world I cannot introduce you to.   I scarcely know him, and, besides, not long ago he passed strictures on my writing which I don't much approve of.'   Does that interest you?" added Mr. Lowell.

"Very much," said Mr. Watts-Dunton.

"Would it interest you to know that ever since your first article in the 'Athenæum' I have read every article you have written?"

" Very much," said Mr. Watts-Dunton.

" Would it interest you to know that on reading your first article I said to a friend of mine : ' At last there is a new voice in English criticism ? ' "

" Very much," said Mr. Watts-Dunton. " But you must first tell me what that article was, for I don't be lieve there is one of my countrymen who could do so."

" That article," said Lowell, " was an essay upon the ' Comedy of the Noctes Ambrosianæ,' and it opened with an Oriental anecdote."

" Well," said Mr. Watts-Dunton, " that does interest me very much."

" And I will go further," said Lowell : " every line you have written in the ' Athenæum ' has been read by me, and often re-read."

" Well," said Mr. Watts-Dunton, " I confess to being amazed, for I assure you that in my own country, except within a narrow circle of friends, my name is absolutely unknown. And I must add that I feel honoured, for it is not a week since I told a friend that I have a great admiration for some of your critical essays. But still, I don't quite forgive you for your onslaught upon my poor little island ! My sympathies are not strongly John Bullish, and they tell me that my verses are more Celtic than Anglo-Saxon in temper. But I am some-what of a patriot, in my way, and I don't quite forgive you."

The meeting ended in the two men fraternizing with each other.

" Won't you come to see me," said Lowell, " at the Embassy ? "

" I don't know where it is."

" Then you ought to know ! " said Lowell. "Another proof of the stout sufficiency of the English temper—

not to know where the American Embassy is ! It is in Lowndes Square." Then he named the number.

"Why," said Mr. Watts-Dunton, " that is next door to Miss Swinburne, aunt of the poet, a perfectly marvellous lady, possessing the vitality of the Swinburne family—a lady who makes watercolour landscape drawings in the open air at I don't know what age of life—something like eighty. She was a friend of Turner's, and is the possessor of some of Turner's finest works."

" So you actually go next door, and don't know where the American Embassy is ! A crowning proof of the insolent self-sufficiency of the English temper ! However, as you come next door, won't you come and see me ? "

" I shall be delighted," said Mr. Watts-Dunton ; " but I am perfectly sure you can spare no time to see an obscure literary man."

" On the contrary," said Lowell, " I always reserve to myself an hour, from five to six, when I see nobody but a friend over a cigarette."

Some time after this Mr. Watts-Dunton did call on Lowell, and spent an hour with him over a cigarette ; and at last it became an institution, this hour over a cigarette once a week.

This went on for a long time, and Mr. Watts-Dunton is fond of recalling the way in which Lowell's Anglophobia became milder and milder, 'fine by degrees and beautifully less,' until at last it entirely vanished. Then it was followed by something like Anglo-mania. Lowell began to talk with the greatest appreciation of a thousand English institutions and ways which he would formerly have deprecated. The climax of this revolution was reached when Mr. Watts-Dunton said to him :

" Lowell, you are now so much more of a John Bull

than I am that I have ceased to be able to follow you.
The English ladies are—let us say, charming; English
gentlemen are—let us say, charming, or at least some of
them.   Everything is charming ! But there is one thing
you cannot say a word for, and that is our detestable
climate."

"And you can really speak thus of the finest climate
in the world!" said Lowell. "I positively cannot live
out of it."

"Well," said Mr. Watts-Dunton, "you and I will
cease to talk about England and John Bull, if you please.
I cannot follow you."

In relating this anecdote Mr. Watts-Dunton, however, insisted that with all his love of England, Lowell
never bated one jot of his loyalty to his own country.
There never was a stauncher American than James
Russell Lowell. Let one unjust word be said about
America, and he was a changed man.   Mr. Watts-
Dunton has always contended that the present good
feeling between the two great branches of the Anglo
Saxon race was due mainly to Lowell.   Indeed, he expressed this conviction in one of his finest sonnets.   It
appeared in the 'Athenæum' after Lowell's death, and
it has been frequently reprinted in the United States.
It now appears in 'The Coming of Love.' It was ad-
dressed 'To Britain and America : On the Death of
James Russell Lowell,'

Ye twain who long forgot your brotherhood
   And those far fountains whence, through glorious years,
   Your fathers drew, for Freedom's pioneers,
Your English speech, your dower of English blood—
Ye ask to-day, in sorrow's holiest mood,
   When all save love seems film—ye ask in tears—
   'How shall we honour him whose name endears
The footprints where beloved Lowell stood ? '

Your hands he joined—those fratricidal hands,
  Once trembling, each, to seize a brother's throat:
How shall ye honour him whose spirit stands
  Between you still?—Keep Love's bright sails afloat
  For Lowell's sake, where once ye strove and smote
On waves that must unite, not part, your strands.

This perhaps is the place to say a word about Mr.
Watts-Dunton's feelings towards America, which were
once supposed to be hostile. Apart from his intimacy with Lowell, he numbered among his American
friends Clarence Stedman, Mrs. Moulton (between
whom and himself there has been the most cordial
intimacy during twenty-five years), Bret Harte, Edwin
Abbey, Joaquin Miller, Colonel Higginson, and, indeed,
many prominent Americans. Between Whistler and himself there was an intimacy so close that during several
years they saw each other nearly every day. That was
before Whistler's genius had received full recognition.
I may recall that during a certain controversy concerning Whistler's animosity against the Royal Academy the
following letter from Mr. Watts-Dunton appeared in
the 'Times' of August 12, 1903:—

"In the 'Times' of to-day Mr. G. D. Leslie, R.A.,
says: 'I was on friendly terms with Whistler for nearly
forty years, and I never heard him at any time testify
animosity against the Academy or its members.'
My own acquaintance with Whistler did not extend
over forty years, but for about ten years I was very
intimate with him, so intimate that during part of this
period we met almost every day. Indeed, at one time
we were jointly engaged on a weekly periodical called
'Piccadilly,' for which Du Maurier designed the cover,
and for which Whistler furnished his very first litho-

graphs, by the valuable aid of Mr. T. Way.   During that time there were not many days when he failed to ' testify animosity ' against the Academy and its members.   To say the truth, the testifications on this subject by ' Jimmy,' as he was then called, were a little afflictive to his friends. Whether he was right or wrong in the matter is a point on which I feel unqualified to express an opinion.

May I be allowed to conclude this note by expressing my admiration of your New York Correspondent's amazingly vivid portrait of one of the most vivid personalities of our time ?   It is a masterpiece. . . . "

When Bret Harte died, in May 1902, one of the best and most appreciative estimates of him was written by Mr. Watts-Dunton for the ' Athenæum.'   I am tempted to quote it nearly in full, as it shows deep sympathy with American literature, and it will prove more conclusively than any words of mine how warm are Mr. Watts-Dunton's feelings towards Americans :—

" As a personality Bret Harte seems to have exercised a great charm over his intimate friends, and I am not in the least surprised at his being a favourite.   It is many years since I last saw him.   I think it must have been at a club dinner given by William Black ; but I have a very vivid remembrance of my first meeting him, which must have been more than twenty-six years ago, and on that occasion it occurred to me that he had great latent histrionic gifts, and, like Charles Dickens, might have been an admirable actor.   On that account the following incident is worth recording.   A friend of mine, an American poet, who at that time was living in London, brought him to my chambers, and did me the honour of introducing me to him.   Bret Harte had read something about the London music-halls, and proposed that we should all three take a drive round the town and see something of them. At that time these places took a very different position in public estimation from what they appear to be doing now. People then considered them to be very cockney, very vulgar, and very inane, as, indeed, they were, and were shy about going to them. I hope they have improved now, for they seem to have become quite fashionable. Our first visit was to the Holborn Music Hall, and there we heard one or two songs that gave the audience immense delight—some comic, some more comic from being sentimental-maudlin. And we saw one or two shapeless women in tights. Then we went to the 'Oxford,' and saw something on exactly the same lines. In fact, the performers seemed to be the same as those we had just been seeing. Then we went to other places of the same kind, and Bret Harte agreed with me as to the distressing emptiness of what my fellow-countrymen and women seemed to be finding so amusing. At that time, indeed, the almost only interesting entertainment outside the opera and the theatres was that at Evans's supper-rooms, where, under the auspices of the famous Paddy Green, one could enjoy a Welsh rarebit while listening to the 'Chough and Crow' and 'The Men of Harlech,' given admirably by choir-boys. Years passed before I saw Bret Harte again. I met him at a little breakfast party, and he amused those who sat near him by giving an account of what he had seen at the music-halls—an account so graphic that I think a fine actor was lost in him. He not only vivified every incident, but gave verbal descriptions of every performer in a peculiarly quiet way that added immensely to the humour of it. His style of acting would have been that of Jefferson of 'Rip Van Winkle' fame. This proved to me what a genius he had for accurate observation, and also what a remarkable memory for the details of a scene. His death has touched English people very deeply.

It is easy to be unjust to Bret Harte—easy to say that he was a disciple of Dickens—easy to say that in richness, massiveness, and variety he fell far short of his great and beloved master. No one was so ready to say all this and more about Bret Harte as Bret Harte himself. For of all the writers of his time he was perhaps the most modest, the most unobtrusive, the most anxious to give honour where he believed honour to be due.

But the comparison between the English and American story-tellers must not be pushed too far to the disadvantage of the latter. If Dickens showed great superiority to Bret Harte on one side of the imaginative writer's equipment, there were, I must think, other sides of that equipment on which the superiority was Bret Harte's.

Therefore I am not one of those who think that in a court of universal criticism Bret Harte's reputation will be found to be of the usual ephemeral kind. It is, of course, impossible to speak on such matters with anything like confidence. But it does seem to me that Bret Harte's reputation is more likely than is generally supposed to ripen into what we call fame. For in his short stories—in the best of them, at least—there is a certain note quite indescribable by any adjective—a note which is, I believe, always to be felt in the literature that survives. The charge of not being original is far too frequently brought against the imaginative writers of America. What do we mean by 'originality'? Scott did not invent the historic method. Dickens simply carried the method of Smollett further, and with wider range.

Thackeray is admittedly the nineteenth century Fielding. Perhaps, indeed, there is but one absolutely original writer of prose fiction of the nineteenth century—
Nathaniel Hawthorne. By original I mean simply
original. I do not mean that he was the greatest imaginative writer of his epoch. But he invented a new kind
of fiction altogether, a fiction in which the material world
and the spiritual world were not merely brought into
touch, but were positively intermingled one with the
other.

Bret Harte had the great good fortune to light upon
material for literary treatment of a peculiarly fresh and a
peculiarly fascinating kind, and he had the artistic instinct to treat it adequately. This is what I mean : in
the wonderful history of the nineteenth century there are
no more picturesque figures than those goldseekers—
those 'Argonauts' of the Pacific slope—who in 1848
and 1849 showed the world what grit lies latent in the
racial amalgam we agree to call ' the Anglo-Saxon race.'
The Australian gold-diggers of 1851 who followed them,
although they were picturesque and sturdy too, were not
exactly of the strain of the original Argonauts. The
romance of the thing had been in some degree worn away.
The land of the Golden Fleece had degenerated into a
Tom Tiddler's Ground. Moreover, the Tom Tiddler's
Grounds of Ballarat and Bendigo were at a comparatively
easy distance from the Antipodean centre of civilization.
' Canvas Town ' could easily be reached from Sydney.
But to reach the Golden Fleece sought by the original
Californian Argonauts the adventurer had before him a
journey of an almost unparalleled kind. Every Argo-
naut, indeed, was a kind of explorer as well as seeker of
gold. He must either trek overland—that is to say, over
those vast prairies and then over those vast mountain

chains which to men of the time of Fenimore Cooper and Dr. Bird made up the limitless ' far West ' regions which only a few pioneers had dared to cross—or else he must take a journey, equally perilous, round Cape Horn in the first crazy vessel in which he could get a passage. It follows that for an adventurer to succeed in reaching the land of the Golden Fleece at all implied in itself that grit which adventurers of the Anglo-Saxon type are generally supposed to show in a special degree. What kind of men these Argonauts were, and what kind of life they led, the people of the Eastern states of America and the people of England had for years been trying to gather from newspaper reports and other sources ; but had it not been for the genius of Bret Harte this most pictur-esque chapter of nineteenth-century history would have been obliterated and forgotten. Thanks to the admir-able American writer whom England had the honour and privilege of entertaining for so many years, those wonder-ful regions and those wonderful doings in the Sierra Nevada are as familiar to us as is Dickens's London. Surely those who talk of Bret Harte as being ' Dickens among the Californian pines ' do not consider what their words imply. It is true, no doubt, that there was a kind of kinship between the temperament of Dickens and the temperament of Bret Harte. They both held the same principles of imaginative art, they both felt that the function of the artist is to aid in the emancipation of man by holding before him beautiful ideals ; both felt that to give him any kind of so-called realism which lowers man in his aspirations—which calls before man's imagination degrading pictures of his ' animal origin '—is to do him a disservice. For man has still a long journey before he reaches the goal. Yet though they were both by in-stinct idealists as regards character-drawing, they bot sought to give their ideals a local habitation and a name by surrounding those ideals with vividly painted real accessories, as real as those of the ugliest realist.

With regard to Bret Harte's Argonauts and the romantic scenery in which they lived and worked, it would, no doubt, be a bold thing to say whether Dickens could or could not have painted them, and whether, if he had painted them, the pictures would or would not have been as good as Bret Harte's pictures. But Dickens never did paint these Argonauts; he never had the chance of painting them. Bret Harte did paint them, and succeeded as wonderfully as Dickens succeeded in painting certain classes of London life. Now, assuredly, I should have never dreamt of instituting a comparison of this kind between two of the most delightful writers and the most delightful men that have lived in my time had not critics been doing so to the disparagement of one of them. But if one of these writers must be set up against another, I feel that something should be said upon the other side of the question—I feel that something should be said on those points where the American had the advantage. Take the question of atmosphere, for instance. Let us not forget how enormously important is atmosphere in any imaginative picture of life. Without going so far as to say that atmosphere is as important, or nearly as important, as character, let me ask, What was it that captured the readers of 'Robinson Crusoe'? Was it the character of Defoe's hero, or was it the scenery and the atmosphere in which he placed him? Again, see what an important part scenery and atmosphere played in 'The Lay of the Last Minstrel,' in 'The Lady of the Lake,' in 'Marmion,' and in 'Waverley.' And surely it was the atmosphere of Byron's 'Giaour,' 'The Bride of Abydos,' and 'The Corsair,' that mainly gave

these poems their vogue.   And, in a certain sense, it may
be said that Dickens gave to his readers a new atmosphere, for he was the first to explore what was something
new to the reading world—the great surging low-life of
London and the life of the lower stratum of its middle
class.   It seems that the pure novelist of manners only
can dispense with a new and picturesque atmosphere.
It was natural for England to look to American writers
to enrich English literature with a new imaginative
atmosphere, and she did not look in vain.   But, notwithstanding all that had been done by writers like Brockden
Brown, Fenimore Cooper, Dr. Bird, and others to bring
American atmosphere into literature, Bret Harte gave
us an atmosphere that was American and yet as new as
though the above-mentioned writers had never written.
He had the advantage of depicting a scenery that was as
unlike the backwoods of his predecessors as it was unlike
everything else in the world.   It is doubtful whether there
is any scenery in the world so fascinating as the mountain
ranges of the Pacific side of the United States and Canada.

Every one is born with an instinct for loving some
particular kind of scenery, and this bias has not so much
to do with the birth-environment as is generally supposed.   It would have been of no avail for Bret Harte
to be familiar with the mighty canons, peaks, and cata-
racts of the Nevada regions unless he had had a natural
genius for loving and depicting them ; and this, undoubtedly, he had, as we see by the effect upon us of his
descriptions.   Once read, his pictures are never forgotten.
But it was not merely that the scenery and atmosphere
of Bret Harte's stories are new—the point is that the
social mechanism in which his characters move is also
new.   And if it cannot be denied that in temperament
his characters are allied to the characters of Dickens, we

must not make too much of this. Notwithstanding all the freshness and newness of Dickens's characters they were entirely the slaves of English sanctions. Those incongruities which gave them their humourous side arose from their contradicting the English social sanctions around them. But in Bret Harte's Argonauts we get characters that move entirely outside those sanctions of civilization with which the reader is familiar. And this is why the violent contrasts in his stories seem, somehow, to be better authenticated than do the equally violent contrasts in Dickens's stories. Bret Harte's characters are amenable to no laws except the improvised laws of the camp; and the final arbiter is either the six-shooter or the rope of Judge Lynch. And yet underlying this apparent lawlessness there is that deep 'law-abidingness' which the late Grant Allen despised as being ' the Anglo-Saxon characteristic.' To my mind, indeed, there is nothing so new, fresh, and piquant in the fiction of my time as Bret Harte's pictures of the mixed race we call Anglo-Saxon finding itself right outside all the old sanctions, exercising nevertheless its own peculiar instinct for law-abidingness of a kind.

We get the Anglo-Saxon beginning life anew far removed from the old sanctions of civilization, retaining of necessity a good deal of that natural liberty which, according to Blackstone, was surrendered by the first human compact in order to secure its substitute, civil liberty. We get vivid pictures of the racial qualities which enable the Anglo-Saxon to plant his roots and flourish in almost every square mile of the New World that lies in the temperate zone. Let a group of this great race of universal squatters be the dwellers in Roaring Camp, or a party of whalers in New Zealand when it is a ' no man's land,' or even a gang of mutineers from the Bounty, it is all one as regards their methods as squatters. The moment that the mutineers set foot on Pitcairn Island they improvise a code of laws something like the camp laws of Bret Harte's Argonauts, and the code on the whole works well.

Therefore I think that, apart altogether from the literary excellence of the presentation, Bret Harte's pictures of the Anglo-Saxon in these conditions will, even as documents, pass into literature. And again, year by year, as nature is being more and more studied, are what I may call the open-air qualities of literature being more sought after. This accounts in a large measure for the growing interest in a writer once strangely neglected, George Borrow ; and if there should be any diminution in the great and deserved vogue of Dickens, it will be because he is not strong in open-air qualities.

Bret Harte's stories give the reader a sense of the open air second only to Borrow's own pictures. And if I am right in thinking that the love of nature and the love of open-air life are growing, this also will secure a place in the future for Bret Harte.

And now what about his power of creating new characters—not characters of the soil merely, but dramatic characters ? Well, here one cannot speak with quite so much confidence on behalf of Bret Harte ; and here he showed his great inferiority to Dickens. Dickens, of course, used a larger canvas—gave himself more room to depict his subjects.

If Bret Harte's scenes and characters seem somewhat artificial, may it not be often accounted for by the fact that he wrote short stories and not long novels ? For it is very difficult in a short story to secure the freedom and flexibility of movement which belong to nature— the last perfection of imaginative art.

All artistic imitations of nature, of course, consist of selection. In actual life we form our own picture of a character not by having the traits selected for us and presented to us in a salient way, as in art, but by selecting in a semi-conscious way for ourselves from the great mass of characteristics presented to us by nature. The shorter the story, the more economic must be its methods, and hence the more rigid must its selection of characteristics be ; and this, of course, is apt to give an air of artificiality to a short story from which a long novel may be free."

Chapter XIX

WALES

IT is impossible within the space at my command to follow Mr. Watts-Dunton into Wales, or through those Continental journeys described by Dr. Hake in 'The New Day.' I can best show the impression that Alpine scenery made upon him by quoting further on the end of 'The Coming of Love.' But with regard to Wales, it seems necessary that a word or two should be said, for it is a fact that the Welsh nation has accepted 'Aylwin' as the representative Welsh novel. And this is not surprising, because, as many Welsh writers have averred, Mr. Watts-Dunton's passionate sympathy for Wales is as sincere as though he had been born upon her soil. The 'Arvon' edition is thus dedicated :—

"To Ernest Rhys, poet and romancist, and my very dear friend, this edition of 'Aylwin' is affectionately inscribed.

It was as far back as those summer days when you used to read the proofs of 'Aylwin'—used to read them in the beautiful land the story endeavours to depict— that the wish came to me to inscribe it to you, whose paraphrases of 'The Lament of Llywarch Hën,' 'The Lament of Urien,' and 'The Song of the Graves' have so entirely caught the old music of Kymric romance.

When I described my Welsh heroine as showing that 'love of the wind' which is such a fascinating char-

Ogwen and the Glyders from Carnedd Dafydd

acteristic of the Snowdonian girls I had only to recall
that poetic triumph, your paraphrase of Taliesin's ' Song
of the Wind '—

> Oh, most beautiful One!
> In the wood and in the mead,
> How he fares in his speed!
> And over the land,
> Without foot, without hand,
> Without fear of old age,
> Or Destiny's rage.
>
> *
>
> His banner he flings
> O'er the earth as he springs
> On his way, but unseen
> Are its folds; and his mien,
> Rough or fair, is not shown,
> And his face is unknown.

Had I anticipated that ' Aylwin ' would achieve a
great success among the very people for whom I wrote
it, I should without hesitation have asked you to accept
the dedication at that time. But I felt that it would
seem like endeavouring to take a worldly advantage of
your friendship to ask your permission to do this—to
ask you to stand literary sponsor, as it were, to a story
depicting Wales and the great Kymric race with which
the name of Rhys is so memorably and so grandly associated. For although my heart had the true ' Kymric
beat '—if love of Wales may be taken as an indication of
that ' beat '—the privilege of having been born on the
sacred soil of the Druids could not be claimed by me,
and I feared that in the vital presentation of that organic
detail, which is the first requisite in all true imaginative
art, I might in some degree be found wanting. You
yourself always prophesied, I remember, that ' Aylwin '

would win the hearts of your countrymen and country-
women ; but I knew your generous nature ; I knew also
if I may say it, your affection for me.   How could I then
help feeling that the kind wish was father to the kind
thought ?

But now that your prophecies have come true, now
that there is, if I am to accept the words of another
Welsh writer, ' scarcely any home in Wales where a well-
thumbed copy of " Aylwin " is not to be found,' and now
that thousands of Welsh women and Welsh girls have
read, and, as I know by letters from strangers, have smiled
and wept over the story of their countrywoman, Winifred
Wynne, I feel that the time has come when I may look
for the pleasure of associating your name with the
book.

Sometimes I have been asked whether Winifred
Wynne is not an idealised Welsh girl ; but never by you,
who know the characteristics of the race to which you
belong—know it far too well to dream of asking that
question.   There are not many people, I think, who know
the Kymric race so intimately as I do ; and I have said
on a previous occasion what I fully meant and mean,
that, although I have seen a good deal of the races of
Europe, I put the Kymric race in many ways at the top
of them all.   They combine, as I think, the poetry, the
music, the instinctive love of the fine arts, and the humour
of the other Celtic peoples with the practicalness and
bright-eyed sagacity of the very different race to which
they are so closely linked by circumstance—the race
whom it is the fashion to call the Anglo-Saxon.   And
as to the charm of the Welsh girls, no one who knows
them as you and I do can fail to be struck by it continually.   Winifred Wynne I meant to be the typical Welsh
girl as I have found her—affectionate, warm-hearted,

self-sacrificing, and brave. And I only wish that my power to do justice to her and to the country that gave her birth had been more adequate. There are, however, writers now among you whose pictures of Welsh scenery and Welsh life can hold their own with almost anything in contemporary fiction ; and to them I look for better work than mine in the same rich field. Although I am familiar with the Alps and the other mountain ranges of Europe, in their wildest and most beautiful recesses, no hill scenery has for me the peculiar witchery of that around Eryri. And what race in Europe has a history so poetic, so romantic, and so pathetic as yours ? That such a country, so beautiful in every aspect, and surrounded by such an atmosphere of poetry, will soon give birth to its Walter Scott is with me a matter of fervid faith."

As to the descriptions of North Wales in ' Aylwin,' they are now almost classic ; especially the descriptions of the Swallow Falls and the Fairy Glen. Long before ' Aylwin ' was published, Welsh readers had been delighted with the ' Athenæum ' article containing the description of Mr. Watts-Dunton and Sinfi Lovell walking up the Capel Curig side of Snowdon at break of day.

Fine as is that description of a morning on Snowdon, it is not finer than the description of a Snowdon sunset, which forms the nobly symbolic conclusion of ' Aylwin ' :—

"We were now at the famous spot where the triple echo is best heard, and we began to shout like two children in the direction of Llyn Ddu'r Arddu. And then our talk naturally fell on Knockers' Llyn and the echoes to be heard there. She then took me to another famous sight on this side of Snowdon, the enormous stone, said to be five thousand tons in weight, called the Knockers' Anvil. While we lingered here Winnie gave me as many anecdotes and legends of this stone as would fill a little volume. But suddenly she stopped.

'Look!' she said, pointing to the sunset. 'I have seen that sight only once before. I was with Sinfi. She called it "The Dukkeripen of the Trúshul."'

The sun was now on the point of sinking, and his radiance, falling on the cloud-pageantry of the zenith, fired the flakes and vapoury films floating and trailing above, turning them at first into a ruby-coloured mass, and then into an ocean of rosy fire. A horizontal bar of cloud which, until the radiance of the sunset fell upon it, had been dull and dark and grey, as though a long slip from the slate quarries had been laid across the west, became for a moment a deep lavender colour, and then purple, and then red-gold. But what Winnie was pointing at was a dazzling shaft of quivering fire where the sun had now sunk behind the horizon. Shooting up from the cliffs where the sun had disappeared, this shaft intersected the bar of clouds and seemed to make an irregular cross of deep rose."

It is no wonder, therefore, that the path Henry Aylwin and Sinfi Lovell took on the morning when the search for Winifred began was a source of speculation, notably in 'Notes and Queries.' Mr. Watts-Dunton deals with this point in the preface to the twenty-second edition :—

"Nothing," he says, "in regard to 'Aylwin' has given me so much pleasure as the way in which it has been received both by my Welsh friends and my Romany friends. I little thought, when I wrote it, that within three years of its publication the gypsy pictures in it would be discoursed upon to audiences of 4,000 people by a man so well equipped to express an opinion on such a subject as the eloquent and famous ' Gypsy Smith,' and described by him as ' the most trustworthy picture of Romany life in the English language, containing in Sinfi Lovell the truest representative of the Gypsy girl.'

Since the first appearance of the book there have been many interesting discussions by Welsh readers, in various periodicals, upon the path taken by Sinfi Lovell and Aylwin in their ascent of Snowdon.

A very picturesque letter appeared in ' Notes and Queries ' on May 3, 1902, signed C. C. B., in answer to a query by E. W., which I will give myself the pleasure of quoting because it describes the writer's ascent of Snowdon (accompanied by a son of my old friend, Harry Owen, late of Pen-y-Gwryd) along a path which was almost the same as that taken by Aylmin and Sinfi Lovell, when he saw the same magnificent spectacle that was seen by them :—

' The mist was then clearing (it was in July) and in a few moments was entirely gone. So marvellous a transformation scene, and so immense a prospect, I have never beheld since. For the first and only time in my life I saw from one spot almost the whole of North and Mid Wales, a good part of Western England, and a glimpse of Scotland and Ireland. The vision faded all too quickly, but it was worth walking thirty-three or thiry-four miles, as I did that day, for even a briefer view than that.'

Referring to Llyn Coblynau, this interesting writer says :—

' Only from Glaslyn would the description in " Aylwin " of y Wyddfa standing out against the sky " as narrow and as steep as the sides of an acorn " be correct, but from the north and north-west sides of Glaslyn this answers with quite curious exactness to the appearance of the mountain. We must suppose the action of the story to have taken place before the revival of the copper-mining industry on Snowdon.'

With regard, however, to the question here raised, I can save myself all trouble by simply quoting the admirable remarks of Sion o Ddyli in the same number of ' Notes and Queries ' :—

' None of us are very likely to succeed in " placing " this llyn, because the author of " Aylwin," taking a privilege of romance often taken by Sir Walter Scott before him, probably changed the landmarks in idealising the scene and adapting it to his story. It may be, indeed, that the Welsh name given to the llyn in the book is merely a rough translation of the gipsies' name for it, the " Knockers " being gnomes or goblins of the mine ; hence " Coblynau "—goblins. If so, the name itself can give us no clue unless we are lucky enough to secure the last of the Welsh gipsies for a guide. In any case, the only point from which to explore Snowdon for the small llyn, or perhaps llyns (of which Llyn Coblynau is a kind of composite ideal picture), is no doubt, as E. W. has suggested, Capel Curig ; and I imagine the actual scene lies about a mile south from Glaslyn, while it owes something at least of its colouring in the book to that strange lake. The " Knockers," it must be remembered, usually depend upon the existence of a mine near by, with old partly fallen mine-workings where the dropping of water or other subterranean noises produce the curious phenomenon which is turned to such imaginative account in the Snowdon chapters of " Aylwin." ' "

SNOWDON AND GLASLYN

Pbo *G. P. Abrabam, Keswick*

In 'Aylwin' Mr. Watts-Dunton is fond of giving his readers little pictorial glimpses of Welsh life :—

"The peasants and farmers all knew me. 'Sut mae dy galon ? (How is thy heart ?)' they would say in the beautiful Welsh phrase as I met them. 'How is my heart, indeed!' I would sigh as I went on my way.

Before I went to Wales in search of Winifred I had never set foot in the Principality. Before I left it there was scarcely a Welshman who knew more familiarly than I every mile of the Snowdonian country. Never a trace of Winifred could I find.

At the end of the autumn I left the cottage and re-moved to Pen-y-Gwryd, as a comparatively easy point from which I could reach the mountain llyn where I had breakfasted with Winifred on that morning."

His intense affection for Welsh characteristics is seen in the following description of the little Welsh girl and her fascinating lisp :—

"'Would you like to come in our garden ? It's such a nice garden.'

I could resist her no longer. That voice would have drawn me had she spoken in the language of the Toltecs or the lost Zamzummin. To describe it would of course be impossible. The novelty of her accent, the way in which she gave the 'h' in 'which,' 'what,' and 'when,' the Welsh rhythm of her intonation, were as bewitching to me as the timbre of her voice. And let me say here, once for all, that when I sat down to write this narrative, I determined to give the English reader some idea of the way in which, whenever her emotions were deeply touched, her talk would run into soft Welsh diminutives; but I soon abandoned the attempt in despair. I found that to use colloquial Welsh with effect in an English context is impossible without wearying English readers and disappointing Welsh ones.

Here, indeed, is one of the great disadvantages under which this book will go out to the world. While a story-teller may reproduce, by means of orthographical devices, something of the effect of Scottish accent, Irish accent, or Manx accent, such devices are powerless to represent Welsh accent."

Chapter XX

IMAGINATIVE AND DIDACTIC PROSE

BUT the interesting subjects touched upon in the last four chapters have led me far from the subject of 'The Renascence of Wonder.' In its biographical sketch of Mr. Watts-Dunton the 'Encyclopædia Britannica' says: " Imaginative glamour and mysticism are prominent characteristics both of 'The Coming of Love' and 'Aylwin,' and the novel in particular has had its share in restoring the charms of pure romance to the favour of the general public." This is high praise, but I hope to show that it is deserved. When it was announced that a work of prose fiction was about to be published by the critic of the 'Athenæum,' what did Mr. Watts-Dunton's readers expect ? I think they expected something as unlike what the story turned out to be as it is possible to imagine. They expected a story built up of a discursive sequence of new and profound generalizations upon life and literature expressed in brilliant picturesque prose such as had been the delight of my boyhood in Ireland ; they expected to be fascinated more than ever by that ' easy authoritative greatness and comprehensiveness of style' with which they had been familiar for long ; they expected also that subtle irony after the fashion of Fielding, which suggests so much between the lines, that humour which had been an especial joy to me in scores of articles signed by the writer's style as indubitably as if they had been signed by his name. I think everybody cherished this expectation : everybody took it for granted that heaps of those 'intellectual nuggets' about which Minto talked would smother the writer as a story-teller, that the book as literature would be admirable—but as a novel a failure. Great as was Mr. Watts-Dunton's esoteric reputation, I believe that many of the booksellers declined (as the author had prophesied that they would decline) to subscribe for the book. They expected it to fail as a marketable novel—to fail in that 'artistic convincement' of which Mr. Watts-Dunton has himself so often written. What neither I nor any one else save those who, like Mr. Swinburne, had read the story in manuscript, did expect, was a story so poetic, so unworldly, and so romantic that it might have been written by a young Celt—a love story of intense passion, which yet by some magic art was as convincingly realistic as any one of those 'flat-footed' sermon-stories which the late W. E. Henley was wont to deride.

In fact, from this point of view 'Aylwin' is a curiosity of literature. The truth seems to be, however, that, as one of Mr. Watts-Dunton's most intimate friends has said, its style represents one facet only of Watts-Dunton's character. Like most of us, he has a dual existence—one half of him is the romantic youth, Henry Aylwin, the other half is the world-wise philosopher of the 'Athenæum.' This other half of him lives in the style of another story altogether, where the creator of Henry Aylwin takes up the very different rôle of a man of the world. Now I have views of my own upon this duality. I think that if the brilliant worldly writing of the mass of his work be examined, it will be found to be a 'shot' texture scintillating with various hues where sometimes repressed passion and sometimes mysticism and dreams are constantly shining through the glossy silk of the style. Sometimes from the smooth, even flow of the criticisms gleams of a passion far more intense than anything in 'Aylwin' will flash out. I will cite a passage in his critical writings wherein he discusses the inadequacy of language to express the deepest passion :—

" As compared with sculpture and painting the great infirmity of poetry, as an 'imitation' of nature, is of course that the medium is always and of necessity words —even when no words could, in the dramatic situation, have been spoken. It is not only Homer who is obliged sometimes to forget that passion when at white heat is never voluble, is scarcely even articulate ; the dramatists also are obliged to forget that in love and in hate, at their tensest, words seem weak and foolish when compared with the silent and satisfying triumph and glory of deeds, such as the plastic arts can render. This becomes manifest enough when we compare the Niobe group or the Laocoon group, or the great dramatic paintings of the modern world, with even the finest efforts of dramatic poetry, such as the speech of Andromache to Hector, or the speech of Priam to Achilles ; nay, such as even the cries of Cassandra in the 'Agamemnon,' or the wailings of Lear over the dead Cordelia. Even when writing the words uttered by Œdipus, as the terrible truth breaks in upon his soul, Sophocles must have felt that, in the holiést chambers of sorrow and in the highest agonies of suffering reigns that awful silence which not poetry, but painting sometimes, and sculpture always, can render. What human sounds could render the agony of Niobe, or the agony of Laocoon, as we see them in the sculptor's rendering ? Not articulate speech at all ; not words, but wails. It is the same with hate ; it is the same with love. We are not speaking merely of the unpacking of the heart in which the angry warriors of the 'Ilaid' indulge. Even such subtle writing as that of Æschylus and Sophocles falls below the work of the painter. Hate, though voluble perhaps as Clytæmnestra's when hate is at that red-heat glow which the poet can render, changes in a moment whenever that redness has been fanned into hatred's own last complexion—whiteness as of iron at the melting-point—when the heart has grown far too big to be 'unpacked' at all, and even the bitter epigrams of hate's own rhetoric, though brief as the terrier's snap before he fleshes his teeth, or as the short snarl of the tigress as she springs before her cubs in danger, are all too slow and sluggish for a soul to which language at its tensest has become idle play. But this is just what cannot be rendered by an art whose medium consists solely of words."

Could any one reading this passage doubt that the real work of the writer was to write poetry and not criticism ?

But this makes it necessary for me to say a word upon the question of the style of ' Aylwin '—a question that has often been discussed. The fascination of the story is largely due to the magnetism of its style. And yet how undecorated, not to say how plain, the style in the more level passages often is ! When the story was first written the style glittered with literary ornament. But the author deliberately struck out many of the poetic passages. Coleridge tells us that an imaginative work should be written in a simple style, and that the more imaginative the work the simpler the style should be. I often think of these words when I labour in the sweat of my brow to read the word-twisting of precious writers! It is then that I think of 'Aylwin,' for 'Aylwin' stands alone in its power of carrying the reader away to climes of new and rare beauty peopled by characters as new and as rare. It was clearly Mr. Watts-Dunton's idea that what such a story needed was mastery over 'artistic convincement.' He has more than once commented on the acuteness of Edgar Poe's remark that in the expression of true passion there is always something of the 'homely.' 'Aylwin' is one long unbroken cry of passion, mostly in a 'homely key,' but this 'homely key' is left for loftier keys whenever the proper time for the change comes. In beginning to write, the author seems to have felt that 'The Renascence of Wonder' and the quest of beauty, although adequately expressed in the poetry of the newest romantic school—that of Rossetti, Morris, and Swinburne—had only found its way into imaginative prose through the highly elaborate technique of his friend, George Meredith. He seems to have felt that the great imaginative prose writers of the time, Thackeray, Dickens, and Charles Reade, were in a certain sense Philistines of genius who had done but little to bring beauty, romance and culture into prose fiction. And as to Meredith, though a true child of romanticism who never did and never could breathe the air of Philistia, he had adopted a style too self-conscious and rich in literary qualities to touch that great English pulse that beats outside the walls of the Palace of Art.

Mrs. Craigie has lately declared that at the present moment all the most worthy English novelists, with the exception of Mr. Thomas Hardy, are distinguished disciples of Mr. George Meredith. But to belong to 'the mock Meredithians' is not a matter of very great glory. No one adores the work of Mr. Meredith more than I do, though my admiration is not without a certain leaven of distress at his literary self-consciousness. I say this with all reverence.   Great as Meredith is, he would be greater still if, when he is delivering his priceless gifts to us, he would bear in mind that immortal injunction in 'King Henry the Fourth'—'I prithee now, deliver them like a man of this world.'   I can imagine how the great humourist must smile when the dolt, who once found 'obscurity' in his most lucid passages, praises him for the defects of his qualities, and calls upon all other writers to write Meredithese.

To be a classic—to be immortal—it is necessary for an imaginative writer to deliver his message like 'a man of this world.'   Shakespeare himself, occasionally, will seem to forget this, but only occasionally, and we never think of it when falling down in worship before the shrine of the greatest imaginative writer that has ever lived.   Dr. Johnson said that all work which lives is without eccentricity.   Now, entranced as I have been, ever since I was a boy, by Meredith's incomparable romances, I long to set my imagination free of Meredith and fly away with his characters, as I can fly away with the characters of the classic imaginative writers from Homer down to Sir Walter Scott.   But I seldom succeed. Now and then I escape from the obsession of the picture of the great writer seated in his chalet with the summer sunshine gleaming round his picturesque head, but illuminating also all too vividly his inkstand, and his paper and his pens ; but only now and then, and not for long. If it had pleased Nature to give him less intellectual activity, less humour and wit and literary brilliance, I feel sure that he would have lived more securely as an English classic.   I adore him, I say, and although I do not know him personally, I love him.   We all love him : and when

I am in a very charitable mood, I can even forgive him for having begotten the 'mock Meredithians.' As to those who, without a spark of his humourous imagination and supple intellect can manage to mimic his style, if they only knew what a torture their word-twisting is to the galled reviewer who wants to get on, and to know what on earth they have got to tell him, I think they would display a little more mercy, and even for pity's sake deliver their gifts like ' men of this world.'

In ' Aylwin ' Mr. Watts-Dunton seems to have determined to be as romantic and as beautiful as the romanticists in poetry had ever dared to be, and yet by aid of a simplicity and a naïveté of diction of which his critical writings had shown no sign, to carry his beautiful dreams into Philistia itself. Never was there a bolder enterprise, and never was there a greater success. That ' Aylwin ' would appeal strongly to imaginative minds was certain, for it was written by ' the most widely cultivated writer in the English belles lettres of our time.' But the strange thing is that a story so full of romance, poetry, and beauty, should also appeal to other minds.

I am no believer in mere popularity, and I confess that when books come before me for review I cannot help casting a suspicious eye upon any story by any of the very popular novelists of the day. But it is necessary to explain why the most poetical romance written within the last century is also one of the most popular. It was in part owing to its simplicity of diction, its naïveté of utterance, and its freedom from superfluous literary ornamentation. I do not as a rule like using a foreign word when an English word will do the same work, but neither ' artlessness,' ' candour ' nor ' simplicity ' seem to express the unique charm of the style of ' Aylwin,' so completely as does the word 'naïveté.' It was by naïveté, I believe, that he carried the Renascence of Wonder into quarters which his great brothers in the Romantic movement could never reach.

For such a writer as he, the critic steeped in all the latest subtleties of the style of to-day, and indeed the originator of many of these subtleties, the intimate friend of such superb and elaborate literary artists as Tennyson, Browning, George Meredith, Rossetti and Swinburne, it must have been inconceivably difficult to write the 'working portions' of his narrative in a style as unbookish at times as if he had written in the pre-Meredithian epoch. Having set out to convince his readers of the truth of what he was telling them, he determined to sacrifice all literary 'self-indulgence' to that end. I do not recollect that any critic, when the book came out, noted this. But if 'Aylwin' had been a French book published in France, the naïve style adopted by the autobiographer would have been recognized by the critics as the crowning proof of the author's dramatic genius. Whenever the style seems most to suggest the pre-Meredithian writers, it is because the story is an autobiography and because the hero lived in pre-Meredithian times. Difficult as was Thackeray's tour de force in 'Esmond,' it was nothing to the tour de force of 'Aylwin.' The tale is told 'as though inspired by the very spirit of youth' because the hero was a youth when he told it. It is hard to imagine a writer past the meridian of life being able to write a story 'more flushed with the glory and the passion and the wonder of youth than any other in English fiction.'

It should be noted that whenever the incidents become especially tragic or romantic or weird or poetic, the 'homeliness' of the style goes—the style at once rises to the occasion, it becomes not only rich, but too rich for prose.   I have now and then heard certain word-twisters of second-hand Meredithese speak of the 'baldness' of the style of 'Aylwin.'   Roll fifty of these word-twisters into one, and let that one write a sentence or two of such prose as this, published at the time that 'Aylwin' was written.   It occurs in a passage on the greatest of all rich writers, Shakespeare :—

"In the quality of richness Shakespeare stood quite alone till the publication of 'Endymion.'   Till then it was 'Eclipse first—the rest nowhere.'   When we think of Shakespeare, it is his richness more than even his higher qualities that we think of first.   In reading him, we feel at every turn that we have come upon a mind as rich as Marlowe's Moor, who

> Without control can pick his riches up,
> And in his house heap pearls, like pebble-stones.

Nay, he is richer still ; he can, by merely looking at the 'pebble-stones,' turn them into pearls for himself, like the changeling child recovered from the gnomes in the Rosicrucian story.   His riches burden him.   And no wonder : it is stiff flying with the ruby hills of Badakhshân on your back.   Nevertheless, so strong are the wings of his imagination, so lordly is his intellect, that he can carry them all ; he could carry, it would seem, every gem in Golconda—every gem in every planet from here to Neptune—and yet win his goal.   Now, in the matter of richness this is the great difference between him and Keats, the wings of whose imagination, aërial at starting, and only iridescent like the sails of a dragon-fly, seem to change as he goes—become overcharged with beauty, in fact—abloom 'with splendid dyes, as are the tiger-moth's deep-damasked wings.'   Or, rather, it may be said that he seems to start sometimes with Shakespeare's own eagle-pinions, which, as he mounts, catch and retain colour after colour from the earth below, till, heavy with beauty as the drooping wings of a golden pheasant, they fly low and level at last over the earth they cannot leave for its loveliness, not even for the holiness of the skies."

I will give a few instances of passages in 'Aylwin' quite as rich as this. One shall be from that scene in which Winifred unconsciously reveals to her lover that her father has stolen the jewelled cross and brought his own father's curse upon her beloved head :—

"Winifred picked up the sea weed and made a necklace of it, in the old childish way, knowing how much it would please me.

'Isn't it a lovely colour ?' she said, as it glistened in the moonlight. 'Isn't it just as beautiful and just as precious as if it were really made of the jewels it seems to rival ?'

'It is as red as the reddest ruby,' I replied, putting out my hand and grasping the slippery substance.

'Would you believe,' said Winnie, 'that I never saw a ruby in my life ? And now I particularly want to know all about rubies.'

'Why do you want particularly to know ?'

'Because,' said Winifred, 'my father, when he wished me to come out for a walk, had been talking a great deal about rubies.'

'Your father had been talking about rubies, Winifred—how very odd !'

'Yes,' said Winifred, 'and he talked about diamonds too.'

'THE CURSE !' I murmured, and clasped her to my breast. 'Kiss me, Winifred !'

There had come a bite of sudden fire at my heart, and I shuddered with a dreadful knowledge, like the captain of an unarmed ship, who, while the unconscious landsmen on board are gaily scrutinizing a sail that like a speck has appeared on the horizon, shudders with the knowledge of what the speck is, and hears in imagination the yells, and sees the knives, of the Lascar pirates just starting in pursuit. As I took in the import of those innocent words, falling from Winifred's bright lips, falling as unconsciously as water-drops over a coral reef in tropical seas alive with the eyes of a thousand sharks, my skin seemed to roughen with dread, and my hair began to stir."

Another instance occurs in Wilderspin's ornate description of his great picture. ' Faith and Love ' :—

" 'Imagine yourself standing in an Egyptian city, where innumerable lamps of every hue are shining. It is one of the great lamp-fêtes of Sais, which all Egypt has come to see. There, in honour of the feast, sits a tall woman, covered by a veil. But the painting is so wonderful, Mr. Aylwin, that, though you see a woman's face expressed behind the veil—though you see the warm flesh-tints and the light of the eyes through the aërial film—you cannot judge of the character of the face—you cannot see whether it is that of woman in her noblest, or woman in her basest, type. The eyes sparkle, but you cannot say whether they sparkle with malignity or benevolence—whether they are fired with what Philip Aylwin calls " the love-light of the seventh heaven," or are threatening with " the hungry flames of the seventh hell !" There she sits in front of a portico, while, asleep, with folded wings, is crouched on one side of her the figure of Love, with rosy feathers, and on the other the figure of Faith, with plumage of a deep azure. Over her head, on the portico, are written the words :—" I am all that hath been, is, and shall be, and no mortal hath uncovered my veil." The tinted lights falling on the group are shed, you see, from the rainbow-coloured lamps of Sais, which are countless. But in spite of all these lamps, Mr. Aylwin, no mortal can see the face behind that veil. And why ? Those who alone could uplift it, the figures folded with wings—Faith and Love—are fast asleep, at the great Queen's feet. When Faith and Love are sleeping there, what are the many-coloured lamps of science !—of what use are they to the famished soul of man ? '

' A striking idea ! ' I exclaimed.

' Your father's,' replied Wilderspin, in a tone of such reverence that one might have imagined my father's spectre stood before him. ' It symbolises that base Darwinian cosmogony which Carlyle spits at, and the great and good John Ruskin scorns. But this design is only the predella beneath the picture " Faith and Love." Now look at the picture itself, Mr. Aylwin,' he continued, as though it were upon an easel before me. ' You are at Sais no longer : you are now, as the architecture around you shows, in a Greek city by the sea. In the light of innumerable lamps, torches, and wax tapers, a procession is moving through the streets. You see Isis, as Pelagia, advancing between two ranks, one of joyous maidens in snow white garments, adorned with wreaths, and scattering from their bosoms all kinds of dewy flowers ; the other of youths, playing upon pipes and flutes mixed with men with shaven shining crowns, playing upon sistra of brass, silver, and gold. Isis wears a Dorian tunic, fastened on her breast by a tasselled knot,

—an azure-coloured tunic bordered with silver stars,—
and an upper garment of the colour of the moon at moonrise.   Her head is crowned with a chaplet of sea-flowers,
and round her throat is a necklace of seaweeds, wet still
with sea-water, and shimmering with all the shifting hues
of the sea.   On either side of her stand the awakened
angels, uplifting from her face a veil whose folds flow soft
as water over her shoulders and over the wings of Faith
and Love.   A symbol of the true cosmogony which
Philip Aylwin gave to the world ! ' "

Another instance I take from that scene in the crypt
whither Aylwin had been drawn against his will by the
ancestral impulses in his blood to replace the jewelled
cross upon the breast of his father :—

" Having, with much difficulty, opened the door, I
entered the crypt.   The atmosphere, though not noi-
some, was heavy, and charged with an influence that
worked an extraordinary effect upon my brain and
nerves.   It was as though my personality were becoming dissipated, until at last it was partly the reflex of
ancestral experiences.   Scarcely had this mood passed
before a sensation came upon me of being fanned as if
by clammy bat-like wings ; and then the idea seized me
that the crypt scintillated with the eyes of a malignant
foe.   It was as if the curse which, until I heard Winnie
a beggar singing in the street, had been to me but a
collocation of maledictory words, harmless save in their
effect upon her superstitious mind, had here assumed an
actual corporeal shape.   In the uncertain light shed by
thé lantern, I seemed to see the face of this embodied
curse with an ever-changing mockery of expression ; at
one moment wearing the features of my father ; at an-

other, those of Tom Wynne ; at another the leer of the old woman I had seen in Cyril's studio.

" ' It is an illusion,' I said, as I closed my eyes to shut it out ; ' it is an illusion, born of opiate fumes or else of an over-taxed brain and an exhausted stomach.' Yet it disturbed me as much as if my reason had accepted it as real. Against this foe I seemed to be fighting towards my father's coffin as a dreamer fights against a nightmare, and at last I fell over one of the heaps of old Danish bones in a corner of the crypt. The candle fell from my lantern, and I was in darkness. As I sat there I passed into a semi-conscious state. I saw sitting at the apex of a towering pyramid, built of phosphorescent human bones that reached far, far above the stars, the ' Queen of Death, Nin-ki-gal,' scattering seeds over the earth below. At the pyramid's base knelt the suppliant figure of a Sibyl pleading with the Queen of Death :

> What answer, O Nin-ki-gal ?
> Have pity, O Queen of Queens !

I sprang up, struck a light and relit the candle, and soon reached the coffin resting on a stone table. I found, on examining it, that although it had been screwed down after the discovery of the violation, the work had been so loosely done that a few turns of the screwdriver were sufficient to set the lid free. Then I paused ; for to raise the loosened lid (knowing as I did that it was only the blood's inherited follies that had conquered my rationalism and induced me to disturb the tomb) seemed to require the strength of a giant. Moreover, the fantastic terror of old Lantoff's story, which at another time would have made me smile, also took bodily shape, and the picture of a dreadful struggle at the edge of the cliff between

Winnie's father and mine seemed to hang in the air—a fascinating mirage of ghastly horror . . .

" At last, by an immense effort of will, I closed my eyes and pushed the lid violently on one side

The ' sweet odours and divers kinds of spices ' of the Jewish embalmer rose like a gust of incense—rose and spread through the crypt like the sweet breath of a new-born blessing, till the air of the charnel-house seemed laden with a mingled odour of indescribable sweetness. Never had any odour so delighted my senses ; never had any sensuous influence so soothed my soul.

While I stood inhaling the scents of opobalsam, and cinnamon and myrrh, and wine of palm and oil of cedar, and all the other spices of the Pharaohs, mingled in one strange aromatic cloud, my, personality seemed again to become, in part, the reflex of ancestral experiences.

I opened my eyes. I looked into the coffin. The face (which had been left by the embalmer exposed) confronted mine. ' Fenella Stanley ! ' I cried, for the great transfigurer Death had written upon my father's brow that self-same message which the passions of a thousand Romany ancestors had set upon the face of her whose portrait hung in the picture-gallery. And the rubies and diamonds and beryls of the cross as it now hung upon my breast, catching the light of the opened lantern in my left hand, shed over the features an indescribable reflex hue of quivering rose.

Beneath his head I placed the silver casket : I hung the hair-chain round his neck : I laid upon his breast the long-loved memento of his love and the parchment scroll.

Then I sank down by the coffin, and prayed. I knew not what or why. But never since the first human prayer was breathed did there rise to heaven a supplication so incoherent and so wild as mine. Then I rose, and lay-

ing my hand upon my father's cold brow, I said : ' You
have forgiven me for all the wild words that I uttered
in my long agony. They were but the voice of intolerable misery rebelling against itself. You, who suffered
so much—who know so well those flames burning at
the heart's core—those flames before which all the forces
of the man go down like prairie-grass before the fire
and wind—you have forgiven me. You who knew the
meaning of the wild word Love—you have forgiven your
suffering son, stricken like yourself. You have forgiven
me, father, and forgiven him, the despoiler of your tomb :
you have removed the curse, and his child—his innocent
child—is free '

I replaced the coffin-lid, and screwing it down left
the crypt, so buoyant and exhilarated that I stopped in
the churchyard and asked myself : ' Do I, then, really
believe that she was under a curse ? Do I really believe
that my restoring the amulet has removed it ? Have I
really come to this ? '

Throughout all these proceedings—yes, even amidst
that prayer to Heaven, amidst that impassioned appeal
to my dead father—had my reason been keeping up that
scoffing at my heart which I have before described."

My last instance shall be from D'Arcy's letter, in which
he records the marvellous events that led to his meeting
with Winifred :—

" And now, my dear Aylwin, having acted as a somewhat prosaic reporter of these wonderful events, I should
like to conclude my letter with a word or two about what
took place when I parted from you in the streets of London. I saw then that your sufferings had been very great,
and since that time they must have been tenfold greater.

And now I rejoice to think that, of all the men in this world who have ever loved, you, through this very suffering, have been the most fortunate. As Job's faith was tried by Heaven, so has your love been tried by the power which you call 'circumstance' and which Wilderspin calls 'the spiritual world.' All that death has to teach the mind and the heart of man you have learnt to the very full, and yet she you love is restored to you, and will soon be in your arms. I, alas ! have long known that the tragedy of tragedies is the death of a beloved mistress, or a beloved wife. I have long known that it is as the King of Terrors that Death must needs come to any man who knows what the word 'love' really means. I have never been a reader of philosophy, but I understand that the philosophers of all countries have been preaching for ages upon ages about resignation to Death—about the final beneficence of Death—that 'reasonable moderator and equipoise of justice,' as Sir Thomas Browne calls him. Equipoise of justice indeed ! He who can read with tolerance such words as these must have known nothing of the true passion of love for a woman as you and I understand it. The Elizabethans are full of this nonsense ; but where does Shakespeare, with all his immense philosophical power, ever show this temper of acquiescence ? All his impeachments of Death have the deep ring of personal feeling—dramatist though he was. But, what I am going to ask you is, How shall the modern materialist, who you think is to dominate the Twentieth Century and all the centuries to follow—how shall he confront Death when a beloved mistress is struck down ? When Moschus lamented that the mallow, the anise, and the parsley had a fresh birth every year, whilst we men sleep in the hollow earth a long, unbounded, never-waking sleep, he told us what your modern materialist tells us,

and he re-echoed the lamentation which, long before
Greece had a literature at all, had been heard beneath
Chaldean stars and along the mud-banks of the Nile.
Your bitter experience made you ask materialism, What
comfort is there in being told that death is the very
nursery of new life, and that our heirs are our very selves,
if when you take leave of her who was and is your world
it is ' Vale, vale, in æternum vale ' ? ''

These quotations may be taken as specimens of the
passages of decorated writing which the author, in order
to get closer to the imagination of the reader, mercilessly
struck out in proof.   Whether he did wisely or unwisely
in striking them out is an interesting question for
criticism.

But certainly the reader has only to go through the
book with this criticism in his mind, and he will see that
when the story passes into such lofty speculation as that
of the opening sentences of the book, or into some equally
lofty mood of the love passion, the style becomes not
only full of literary qualities, but almost over-full; it
becomes a style which can best be described in his own
words about richness of style which I have quoted from
the ' Athenæum.'   I do not doubt that Mr. Watts-
Dunton was quite right in acting upon Coleridge's
theory ; for, notwithstanding the ' fairy-like beauty ' of
the story it is as convincing as a story told upon a
prosaic subject by Defoe.   In fact, it would be hard to
name any novel wherein those laws of means and ends
in art which Mr. Watts-Dunton has formulated in the
' Athenæum ' are more fully observed than in ' Aylwin.'

Madame Galimberti says in the ' Rivista d'Italia ' :—
" ' Aylwin ' was begun in verse, and was written in prose
only when the plot, taking, so to say, the poet by the

hand, showed the necessity of a form more in keeping with the nature of the work; and in 'The Coming of Love,' in which the facts are condensed so as to give full relief to the philosophical motive, the result is, in my opinion, more perfect." [1] My remarks upon 'The Coming of Love' will show that I agree with the accomplished wife of the Italian Minister in placing it above 'Aylwin' as a satisfactory work of art, but that is because I consider 'The Coming of Love' the most important as well as the most original poem that has been published for many years.

Madame Galimberti touches here upon a very important subject for the literary student. I may say for myself that I have invariably spoken of 'Aylwin' as a poem, and I have done so deliberately. Indeed, I think the fact that it is a poem is at once its strength and its weakness. It does not come under the critical canons that are applied to a prose novel or romance. As a prose novel its one defect is that the quest for mere beauty is pushed too far; lovely picture follows lovely picture until the novel reader is inclined at last to cry, 'Hold, enough!'

In one of his essays on Morris, Mr. Watts-Dunton asks, 'What is poetic prose?' And then follows a passage which must always be borne in mind when criticizing 'Aylwin.'

"On no subject in literary criticism," says he, "has

---

[1] "Tanto è vero, che 'Aylwin' fu cominciato a scrivere in versi, e mutato di forma soltanto quando l'intreccio, in certo modo prendendo la mano al poeta, rese necessario un genere di sua natura meno astretto alla rappresentazione di scorcio; e che l'Avvento d'amore, ove le circostanze di fatto sono condensate in modo da dar pieno risalto al motivo filosofico, riesce una cosa, a mio credere, più perfetta."

there been a more persistent misconception than upon this. What is called poetic prose is generally rhetorical prose, and between rhetoric and poetry there is a great difference. Poetical prose, we take it, is that kind of prose which above all other kinds holds in suspense the essential qualities of poetry. If ' eloquence is heard and poetry overheard,' where shall be placed the tremendous perorations of De Quincey, or the sonorous and highly-coloured descriptions of Ruskin ? Grand and beautiful are such periods as these, no doubt, but prose to be truly poetical must move far away from them. It must, in a word, have all the qualities of what we technically call poetry except metre. We have, indeed, said before that while the poet's object is to arouse in the listener an expectancy of cæsuric effects, the great goal before the writer of poetic prose is in the very opposite direction ; it is to make use of the concrete figures and impassioned diction that are the poet's vehicle, but at the same time to avoid the expectancy of metrical bars. The moment that the regular bars assert themselves and lead the reader's ears to expect other bars of the like kind, sincerity ends."

Mr. Watts-Dunton himself has given us the best of all canons for answering the question, ' What is a poem as distinguished from other forms of imaginative literature ? " In his essay on Poetry he says :—

" Owing to the fact that the word ποιητής (first used to designate the poetic artist by Herodotus) means maker, Aristotle seems to have assumed that the indispensable basis of poetry is invention. He appears to have thought that a poet is a poet more on account of the composition of the action than on account of the composition of his verses. Indeed, he said as much as this. Of epic poetry he declared emphatically that it produces its imitations either by mere articulate words or by metre superadded. This is to widen the definition of poetry so as to include all imaginative literature, and Plato seems to have given an equally wide meaning to the word ποίησις. Only, while Aristotle considered ποίησις to be an imitation of the facts of nature, Plato considered it to be an imitation of the dreams of man. Aristotle ignored, and Plato slighted, the importance of versification (though Plato on one occasion admitted that he who did not know rhythm could be called neither musician nor poet). It is impossible to discuss here the question whether an imaginative work in which the method is entirely concrete and the expression entirely emotional, while the form is unmetrical, is or is not entitled to be called a poem. That there may be a kind of unmetrical narrative so poetic in motive, so concrete in diction, so emotional in treatment, as to escape altogether from those critical canons usually applied to prose, we shall see when, in discussing the epic, we come to touch upon the Northern sagas.

" Perhaps the first critic who tacitly revolted against the dictum that substance, and not form, is the indispensable basis of poetry was Dionysius of Halicarnassus, whose treatise upon the arrangement of words is really a very fine piece of literary criticism. In his acute remarks upon the arrangement of the words in the sixteenth book of the Odyssey, as compared with that in the story of Gyges by Herodotus, was perhaps first enunciated clearly the doctrine that poetry is fundamentally a matter of style. The Aristotelian theory as to invention, however, dominated all criticism after as well as before Dionysius. When Bacon came to discuss the subject (and afterwards), the only division between the poetical critics was perhaps between the followers of Aristotle and those of Plato as to what poetry should, and what it should not, imitate. It is curious to speculate as to what would have been the result had the poets followed the critics in this matter. Perhaps there are critics of a very high rank who would class as poems romances so concrete in method and diction, and so full of poetic energy, as ' Wuthering Heights ' and ' Jane Eyre,' where we get absolutely all that Aristotle requires for a poem."

Now, if this be so in regard to those great romances, it must be still more so with regard to ' Aylwin,' where beauty and nothing but beauty seems to be the be-all and the end-all of the work.

As ' Aylwin ' was begun in metre, it would be very interesting to know on what lines the metre was constructed. Readers of ' Aylwin ' have been struck with the music of the opening sentences, which are given as an extract from Philip Aylwin's book, ' The Veiled Queen ' :—

" Those who in childhood have had solitary communings with the sea know the sea's prophecy. They know that there is a deeper sympathy between the sea and the soul of man than other people dream of. They know that the water seems nearer akin than the land to the spiritual world, inasmuch as it is one and indivisible, and has motion, and answers to the mysterious call of the winds, and is the writing tablet of the moon and stars. When a child who, born beside the sea, and beloved by the sea, feels suddenly, as he gazes upon it, a dim sense of pity and warning ; when there comes, or seems to come, a shadow across the waves, with never a cloud in the sky to cast it ; when there comes a shudder-

Henry Aylwin and Winifred under the Cliff

ing as of wings that move in dread or ire, then such a child feels as if the bloodhounds of calamity are let loose upon him or upon those he loves ; he feels that the sea has told him all it dares tell or can.   And, in other moods of fate, when beneath a cloudy sky the myriad dimples of the sea begin to sparkle as though the sun were shining bright upon them, such a child feels, as he gazes at it, that the sea is telling him of some great joy near at hand, or, at least, not far off."

Many a reader will echo the words of a writer in ' Notes and Queries,' who says that this passage has haunted him since first he read it : I know it haunted me after I read it.   But I wonder how many critics have read this passage in connection with Mr. Watts-Dunton's metrical studies which have been carried on in the 'Athenæum' during more than a quarter of a century.   They are closely connected with what he has said upon Bible rhythm in his article upon the Psalms, which I have already quoted, and in many other essays.   Mr. Watts-Dunton, acknowledged to be a great authority on metrical subjects, has for years been declaring that we are on the verge of a new kind of metrical art altogether—a metrical art in which the emotions govern the metrical undulations.   And I take the above passage and the following to be examples of what the movement in ' Aylwin ' would have been if he had not abandoned the project of writing the story in metre :—

" Then quoth the Ka'dee, laughing until his grinders appeared : ' Rather, by Allah, would I take all the punishment thou dreadest, thou most false donkey-driver of the Ruby Hills, than believe this story of thine

—this mad, mad story, that she with whom thou wast seen was not the living wife of Hasan here (as these four legal witnesses have sworn), but thine own dead spouse, Alawiyah, refashioned for thee by the Angel of Memory out of thine own sorrow and unquenchable fountain of tears.'

Quoth Ja'afar, bowing low his head : ' Bold is the donkey-driver, O Ka'dee ! and bold the Ka'dee who dares say what he will believe, what disbelieve—not knowing in any wise the mind of Allah—not knowing in any wise his own heart and what it shall some day suffer.' "

Break these passages up into irregular lines, and you get a new metre of a very emotional kind, governed as to length by the sense pause. Mr. Watts-Dunton has been arguing for many years that English verse is, as Coleridge long ago pointed out, properly governed by the number of accents and not by the number of syllables in a line, and that this accentual system is governed, or should be governed, by emotion. It is a singular thing, by the bye, that writer after writer of late has been arguing over and over again Mr. Watts-Dunton's arguments, and seems to be saying a new thing by using the word ' stress' for ' accent.' ' Stress ' may or may not be a better word than ' accent,' the word used by Coleridge, and after him by Mr. Watts-Dunton, but the idea conveyed is one and the same. I, for my part, believe that rare as new ideas may be in creative work, they are still rarer in criticism.

Chapter XXI

THE METHODS OF PROSE FICTION

A ND now a word upon the imaginative power of
'Aylwin.' Very much has been written both in
England and on the Continent concerning the source of
the peculiar kind of 'imaginative vividness' shown in
the story. The rushing narrative, as has been said,
' is so fused in its molten stream that it seems one
sentence, and it carries the reader irresistibly along
through pictures of beauty and mystery till he becomes
breathless.' The truth is, however, that the mere
method of the evolution of the story has a great
deal more to do with this than is at first apparent.
Upon this artistic method very little has been
written save what I myself said when it first
appeared. If the unequalled grip of the story upon
the reader had been secured by methods as primitive,
as unconscious as those of ' Jane Eyre ' and ' Wuthering
Heights,' I should estimate the pure, unadulterated
imaginative force at work even more highly than I
now do. But, as a critic, I must always inquire
whether or not a writer's imaginative vision is strengthened by constructive power. I must take into account
the aid that the imagination of the writer has received
from his mere self-conscious artistic skill. Now it
is not to praise ' Aylwin,' but, I fear, to disparage it
in a certain sense to say that the power of the scenes
owes much to the mere artistic method, amounting at

times to subtlety.   I have heard the greatest of living poets mention 'Tom Jones,' 'Waverley,' and 'Aylwin' as three great novels whose reception by the outside public has been endorsed by criticism.   One of the signs of Scott's unique genius was the way in which he invented and carried to perfection the method of moving towards the dénouement by dialogue as much as by narrative.   This gave a source of new brilliance to prose fiction, and it was certainly one of the most effective causes of the enormous success of 'Waverley.'   This masterpiece opens, it will be remembered, in distinct imitation of the method of Fielding, but soon broke into the new dramatic method with which Scott's name is associated.   But in 'Waverley' Scott had not yet begun to use the dramatic method so freely as to sacrifice the very different qualities imported into the novel by Fielding, whose method was epic rather than dramatic.   I think Mr. Watts-Dunton has himself somewhere commented upon this, and said that Scott carried the dramatic method quite as far as it could go without making the story suffer from that kind of stageyness and artificial brightness which is fatal to the novel. Scott's disciple, Dumas, a more brilliant writer of dialogue than Scott himself, but not so true a one, carried the dramatic method too far and opened the way to mimics, who carried it further still.   In 'Aylwin,' the blending of the two methods, the epic and the dramatic, is so skilfully done as to draw all the advantages that can be drawn from both ; and this skill must be an enormous aid to the imaginative vision—an aid which Charlotte and Emily Brontë had to dispense with : but it is in the arrangement of the material on self-conscious constructive principles that I am chiefly thinking when I compare the imaginative vision in 'Aylwin' with that in ' Jane Eyre ' and 'Wuthering Heights.'   On   the whole, no one seems to have studied 'Aylwin' from all points of view with so much insight as Madame Galimberti, unless it be M. Jacottet in 'La Semaine Littéraire.'   Mr. Watts-Dunton in one of his essays has himself remarked that nine-tenths of the interest of any dramatic situation are lost if before approaching it the reader has not been made to feel an interest in the characters, as Fielding makes us feel an interest in Tom and Sophia long before they utter a word—indeed, long before they are introduced at all.   This is true, no doubt, and the contemporary method of beginning a story like the opening of a play with long dialogues between characters that are strangers to the reader, is one among the many signs that, so far as securing illusion goes, there is a real retrogression in fictive art.   A play, of course, must open in this way, but in an acted play the characters come bodily before the audience as real flesh and blood. They come surrounded by real accessories.   They win our sympathy or else our dislike as soon as we see them and hear them speak.   The dramatic scenes between Jane Eyre and Rochester would miss half their effect were it not for the picture of Jane as a child.   In 'Aylwin,' by the time that there is any introduction of dramatic dialogue the atmosphere of the story has enveloped us : we have become so deeply in love with the two children that the most commonplace words from their lips would have seemed charged with beauty.   This kind of perfection of the novelist's art, in these days when stories are written to pass through magazines and newspapers, seemed impossible till 'Aylwin' appeared.   It is curious to speculate as to what would have been the success of the opening chapters of 'Aylwin' if an instalment of the story had first made its appearance in a magazine.

One of the most remarkable features of 'Aylwin' is

that in spite of the strength and originality of the mere story and in spite of the fact that the book is fundamentally the expression of a creed, the character painting does not in the least suffer from these facts. Striking and new as the story is, there is nothing mechanical about the structure. The characters are not, to use a well known phrase of the author's, ' plot-ridden ' in the least degree, as are the characters of the great masters of the plot-novel, Lytton, Charles Reade, and Wilkie Collins, to mention only those who are no longer with us. Perhaps in order to show what I mean I ought to go a little into detail here. In ' Man and Wife,' for instance, Collins, with his eye only upon his plot, makes the heroine, a lady whose delicacy of mind and nobility of character are continually dwelt upon, not only by the author but by a sagacious man of the world like Sir Peter, who afterwards marries her, succumb to the animal advances of a brute like Geoffrey. Many instances of the same sacrifice of everything to plot occur in most of Collins's other stories, and as to the ' long arm of coincidence ' he not only avails himself of that arm whenever it is convenient to do so, but he positively revels in his slavery to it. In ' Armadale,' for instance, besides scores of monstrous improbabilities, such as the ship ' La Grace de Dieu ' coming to Scotland expressly that Allan Armadale should board her and have a dream upon her, and such as Midwinter's being by accident brought into touch with Allan in a remote village in Devonshire when he was upon the eve of death, we find coincidences which are not of the smallest use, introduced simply because the author loves coincidences—such as that of making a family connection of Armadale's rescue Miss Gwilt from drowning and get drowned himself, and thus bring about the devolution of the property upon Allan

Armadale—an entirely superfluous coincidence, for the
working power of this incident could have been secured
in countless other ways. 'No Name' bristles with
coincidences, such as that most impudent one where the
heroine is at the point of death by destitution, and the
one man who loves her and who had just returned to
England passes down the obscure and squalid street he
had never seen before at the very moment when she is
sinking. It is the same with Bulwer Lytton's novels.
In 'Night and Morning,' for instance, people are tossed
against each other in London, the country, or Paris at
every moment whensoever the story demands it. As to
Gawtry, one of the few really original villains in modern
fiction, as soon as the story opens we expect him to turn
up every moment like a jack in-the-box ; we expect him
to meet the hero in the most unlikely places, and to meet
every other character in the same way. Let his presence
be required, and we know that he will certainly turn
up to put things right. But in 'Aylwin,' which has
been well called by a French critic, 'a novel without a
villain,' where sinister circumstance takes the place of
the villain, there is not a single improbable coincidence ;
everything flows from a few simple causes, such as
the effect upon an English patrician of love baffled by
all kinds of fantastic antagonisms, the influence of the
doctrines of the dead father upon the minds of several
individuals, and the influence of the impact of the
characters upon each other. Another thing to note
is that in spite of the strange, new scenes in which the
characters move, they all display that 'softness of
touch' upon which the author has himself written so
eloquently in one of his articles in the 'Athenæum.' I
must find room to quote his words on this interesting
subject :—

" The secret of the character-drawing of the great masters seems to be this : while moulding the character from broad general elements, from universal types of humanity, they are able to delude the reader's imagination into mistaking the picture for real portraiture, and this they achieve by making the portrait seem to be drawn from particular and peculiar traits instead of from generalities, and especially by hiding away all purposes— æsthetic, ethic, or political.

One great virtue of the great masters is their winsome softness of touch in character drawing. We are not fond of comparing literary work with pictorial art, but between the work of the novelist and the work of the portrait painter there does seem a true analogy as regards the hardness and softness of touch in the drawing of characters. In landscape painting that hardness which the general public love is a fault ; but in portrait painting so important is it to avoid hardness that unless the picture seems to have been blown upon the canvas, as in the best work of Gainsborough, rather than to have been laid upon it by the brush, the painter has not achieved a perfect success. In the imaginative literature of England the two great masters of this softness of touch in portraiture are Addison and Sterne. Three or four hardly-drawn lines in Sir Roger or the two Shandys, or Corporal Trim, would have ruined the portraits so completely that they would never have come down to us. Close upon Addison comes Scott, in whose vast gallery almost every portrait is painted with a Gainsborough softness. Scarcely one is limned with those hard lines which are too often apt to mar the glorious work of Dickens. After Scott comes Thackeray or Fielding, unless it be Mrs. Gaskell. We are not in this article dealing with, or even alluding to, contemporary writers, or we might easily say what novelists follow Mrs. Gaskell."

Read in the light of these remarks the characters in 'Aylwin' become still more interesting to the critic. Observe how soft is the touch of the writer compared with that of a novelist of real though eccentric genius, Charles Reade. Now and again in Reade's portraits we get softness, as in the painting of the delightful Mrs. Dodd and her daughter, but it is very rare. The contrast between him and Mr. Watts-Dunton in this regard is most conspicuously seen in their treatment of members of what are called the upper classes. No doubt Reade does occasionally catch (what Charles Dickens never catches) that unconscious accent of high breeding which Thackeray, with all his yearning to catch it, scarcely ever could catch, save perhaps, in such a character as Lord Kew, but which Disraeli catches perfectly in St. Aldegonde.

On the appearance of 'Aylwin' it was amusing to see how puzzled many of the critics were when they came to talk about the various classes in which the various figures moved. How could a man give pictures of gypsies in their tents, East Enders in their slums, Bohemian painters in their studios, aristocrats in their country houses, and all of them with equal vividness? But vividness is not always truth. Some wondered whether the gypsies were true, when 'up and spake' the famous Tarno Rye himself, Groome, the greatest authority on gypsies in the world, and said they were true to the life. Following him, 'up and spake' Gypsy Smith, and proclaimed them to be 'the only pictures of the gypsies that were true.' Some wondered whether the painters and Bohemians were rightly painted, when 'up and spake' Mr. Hake—more intimately acquainted with them than any living man left save W. M. Rossetti and Mr. Sharp— and said the pictures were as true as photographs. But before I pass on I must devote a few parenthetical words to the most curious thing connected with this matter. Not even the most captious critic, as far as I remember, ventured to challenge the manners of the patricians who play such an important part in the story. The Aylwin family, as Madame Galimberti has hinted, belonged to the only patriciate which either Landor or Disraeli recognized : the old landed untitled gentry. The best delineator of this class is, of course, Whyte Melville. But those who have read Mr. Watts-Dunton's remarks upon Byron in Chambers's 'Cyclopædia of English Literature' will understand how thoroughly he too has studied this most interesting class. The hero himself, in spite of all his eccentricity and in spite of all his Bohemianism, is a patrician—a patrician to the very marrow. 'There is not throughout Aylwin's narrative—a narrative running to something under 200,000 words—a single wrong note.' This opinion I heard expressed by a very eminent writer, who from his own birth and environment can speak with authority. The way in which Henry Aylwin as a child is made to feel that his hob-a-nobbing on equal terms with the ragamuffin of the sands cannot really degrade an English gentleman ; the way in which Henry Aylwin, the hobbledehoy, is made to feel that he cannot be lowered by living with gypsies, or by marrying the daughter of 'the drunken organist who violated my father's tomb' ; the way in which he says that 'if society rejects him and his wife, he shall reject society';—all this shows a mastery over 'softness of touch' in depicting this kind of character such as not even Whyte Melville has equalled. Henry Aylwin's mother, to whom the word trade and plebeianism were synonymous terms, is the very type of the grande dame, untouched by the vulgarities of the smart set of her time (for there were vulgar smart sets then as there were vulgar smart sets in the time of Beau Brummell, and as there are vulgar smart sets now). Then there is that wonderful aunt, of whom we see so little but whose influence is so great and so mischievous. What a type is she of the meaner and more withered branch of a patrician tree! But the picture of Lord Sleaford is by far the most vivid portrait of a nobleman that has appeared in any novel since 'Lothair.' Thackeray never 'knocked off' a nobleman so airily and so unconsciously as this delightful lordling, whose portrait Mr. Watts-Dunton has 'blown' upon his canvas in the true Gainsborough way. I wish I could have got permission to give more than a bird's-eye glance at Mr. Watts-Dunton's wide experience of all kinds of life, but I can only touch upon what the reading public is already familiar with. At one period of his life—the period during which he and Whistler were brought together—the period when 'Piccadilly,' upon which they were both engaged, was having its brief run, Mr. Watts-Dunton mixed very largely with what was then, as now, humourously called 'Society.' It has been said that 'for a few years not even "Dicky Doyle" or Jimmy Whistler went about quite so much as Theodore Watts.' I have seen Whistler's presentation copy of the first edition of 'The Gentle Art of Making Enemies' with this inscription:— 'To Theodore Watts, the Worldling.' Below this polite flash of persiflage the famous butterfly flaunts its elusive wings. But this was only Whistler's fun. Mr. Watts-Dunton was never, we may be sure, a worldling. Still one wonders that the most romantic of poets ever fell so low as to go into 'Society' with a big S. Perhaps it was because, having studied life among the gypsies, life among the artists, life among the literary men of the old Bohemia, life among the professional and scientific classes, he thought he would study the butterflies too. However, he seems soon to have got satiated, for he suddenly dropped out of the smart Paradise. I mention this episode because it alone, apart from the power of his dramatic imagination, is sufficient to show why in Henry Aylwin he has so successfully painted for us the finest picture that has ever been painted of a true English gentleman tossed about in scenes and among people of all sorts and retaining the pristine bloom of England's patriciate through it all.

In my essay upon Mr. Watts-Dunton in Chambers's 'Cyclopædia of English Literature,' I made this re-mark :—" Notwithstanding the vogue of ' Aylwin,' there is no doubt that it is on his poems, such as ' The Com-ing of Love,' 'Christmas at the Mermaid,' ' Prophetic Pictures at Venice,' ' John the Pilgrim,' ' The Omni-potence of Love,' ' The Three Fausts,' ' What the Silent Voices Said,' ' Apollo in Paris,' ' The Wood-haunters' Dream,' ' The Octopus of the Golden Isles,' ' The Last Walk with Jowett from Boar's Hill,' and ' Omar Khay-yàm,' that Mr. Watts-Dunton's future position will mainly rest."

I did not say this rashly. But in order to justify my opinion I must quote somewhat copiously from Mr. Watts-Dunton's remarks upon absolute and relative vision, in the 'Encyclopædia Britannica.' It has been well said that 'in judging of the seeing power of any work of imagination, either in prose or in verse, it is now necessary always to try the work by the critical canons upon absolute and relative vision laid down in this treatise.' If we turn to it, we shall find that absolute vision is defined to be that vision which in its highest dramatic exercise is unconditioned by the personal tem-perament of the writer, while relative vision is defined to be that vision which is more or less conditioned by the personal temperament of the writer. And then follows a long discussion of various great imaginative works in which the two kinds of vision are seen :—

" For the achievement of most imaginative work relative vision will suffice. If we consider the matter thoroughly, in many forms—which at first sight might seem to require absolute vision—we shall find nothing but relative vision at work. Between relative and absolute vision the difference is this, that the former only enables the imaginative writer even in its very highest exercise, to make his own individuality, or else humanity as represented by his own individuality, live in the imagined situation ; the latter enables him in its highest exercise to make special individual characters other than the poet's own live in the imagined situation. In the very highest reaches of imaginative writing art seems to become art no longer—it seems to become the very voice of Nature herself. The cry of Priam when he puts to his lips the hand that slew his son, is not merely the cry of a bereaved and aged parent ; it is the cry of the individual king of Troy, and expresses above everything else that most naïve, pathetic, and winsome character. Put the cry into the mouth of the irascible and passionate Lear, and it would be entirely out of keeping. While the poet of relative vision, even in its very highest exercise, can only, when depicting the external world, deal with the general, the poet of absolute vision can compete with Nature herself and deal with both general and particular."

Now, the difference between ' The Coming of Love ' and ' Aylwin ' is this, that in ' Aylwin ' the impulse is,

or seems to be, lyrical, and therefore too egoistic for absolute vision to be achieved.   Of course, if we are to take
Henry Aylwin in the novel to be an entirely dramatic character, then that character is so full of vitality that it is
one of the most remarkable instances of purely dramatic
imagination that we have had in modern times.   For
there is nothing that he says or does that is not inevitable
from the nature of the character placed in the dramatic
situation.   Those who are as familiar as I am with Mr.
Watts-Dunton's prose writings outside 'Aylwin' find
it extremely difficult to identify the brilliant critic of
the 'Athenæum,' full of ripe wisdom and sagacity,
with the impassioned boy of the story.   Indeed, I should
never have dreamed of identifying the character with
the author any more than I should have thought of
identifying Philip Aylwin with the author had it not
been for the fact that Mr. Watts-Dunton, in his preface
to one of the constantly renewed editions of his book, seems
to suggest that identification himself.   I have already
quoted the striking passage in the introduction to the
later editions of the book in which this identification
seems to be suggested.   But, matters being as they
are with regard to the identification of the hero of
the prose story with the author, it is to 'The Coming
of Love' that we must for the most part turn for
proof that the writer is possessed of absolute vision.
Percy Aylwin and Rhona are there presented in the
purely dramatic way, and they give utterance to their
emotions, not only untrammelled by the lyricism of
the dramatist, but untrammelled also, as I have before
remarked, by the exigencies of a conscious dramatic
structure.   In no poetry of our time can there be
seen more of that absolute vision so lucidly discoursed
upon in the foregoing extract.   From her first love-

letter Rhona leaps into life, and she seems to be more elaborately painted not only than any woman in recent poetry, but any woman in recent literature. Percy Aylwin lives also with almost equal vitality. I need not give examples of this here, for later I shall quote freely from the poem in order that the reader may form his own judgment, unbiassed by the views of myself or any other critic.

With regard to 'Aylwin,' however, apart from the character of the hero, who is drawn lyrically or dramati cally, according, as I have said, to the evidence that he is or is not the author himself, there are still many instances of a vision that may be called absolute. Among the many letters from strangers that reached the author when 'Aylwin' first appeared was one from a person who, like Henry Aylwin, had been made lame by accident. This gentleman said that he felt sure that the author of 'Aylwin' had also been lame, and gave several instances from the story which had made him come to this conclusion. One was the following :—

" ' Shall we go and get some strawberries ? ' she said, as we passed to the back of the house. ' They are quite ripe.'

But my countenance fell at this. I was obliged to tell her that I could not stoop.

' Ah ! but I can, and I will pluck them and give them to you. I should like to do it. Do let me, there's a good boy.'

I consented, and hobbled by her side to the verge of the strawberry-beds. But when I foolishly tried to follow her, I stuck ignominiously, with my crutches sunk deep in the soft mould of rotten leaves. Here was a trial for the conquering hero of the coast. I

looked into her face to see if there was not, at last, a
laugh upon it. That cruel human laugh was my only
dread. To everything but ridicule I had hardened
myself ; but against that I felt helpless.

I looked into her face to see if she was laughing at
my lameness. No : her brows were merely knit with
anxiety as to how she might best relieve me. This
surpassingly beautiful child, then, had evidently accepted
me—lameness and all—crutches and all—as a subject of
peculiar interest.

As I slowly approached the child, I could see by her
forehead (which in the sunshine gleamed like a globe of
pearl), and especially by her complexion, that she was
uncommonly lovely, and I was afraid lest she should
look down before I got close to her, and so see my
crutches before her eyes encountered my face."

As a matter of fact, however, the author never
had been lame.

The following passages have often been quoted as
instances of the way in which a wonderful situation is
realized as thoroughly as if it had been of the most
commonplace kind ·—

" And what was the effect upon me of these communings with the ancestors whose superstitions I have,
perhaps, been throughout this narrative treating in a
spirit that hardly becomes their descendant ?

The best and briefest way of answering this question
is to confess not what I thought, as I went on studying
my father's book, its strange theories and revelations,
but what I did. I read the book all day long : I read
it all the next day. I cannot say what days passed.
One night I resumed my wanderings in the streets for

an hour or two, and then returned home and went to bed—but not to sleep. For me there was no more sleep till those ancestral voices could be quelled—till the sound of Winnie's song in the street could be stopped in my ears. For very relief from them I again leapt out of bed, lit a candle, unlocked the cabinet, and, taking out the amulet, proceeded to examine the facets as I did once before when I heard in the Swiss cottage these words of my stricken father—

'Should you ever come to love as I have loved, you will find that materialism is intolerable—is hell itself—to the heart that has known a passion like mine. You will find that it is madness, Hal, madness, to believe in the word " never " ! You will find that you dare not leave untried any creed, howsoever wild, that offers the heart a ray of hope.'

And then while the candle burnt out dead in the socket I sat in a waking dream.

The bright light of morning was pouring through the window. I gave a start of horror, and cried, 'Whose face ?' Opposite to me there seemed to be sitting on a bed the figure of a man with a fiery cross upon his breast. That strange wild light upon the face, as if the pains at the heart were flickering up through the flesh—where had I seen it ? For a moment when, in Switzerland, my father bared his bosom to me, that ancestral flame had flashed up into his dull lineaments. But upon the picture of 'The Sibyl' in the portrait-gallery that illumination was perpetual !

'It is merely my own reflex in a looking-glass,' I exclaimed.

Without knowing it I had slung the cross round my neck.

And then Sinfi Lovell's voice seemed murmuring in

my ears, 'Fenella Stanley's dead and dust, and that's why she can make you put that cross in your feyther's tomb, and she will, she will.'

I turned the cross round : the front of it was now next to my skin. Sharp as needles were those diamond and ruby points as I sat and gazed in the glass. Slowly a sensation arose on my breast, of pain that was a pleasure wild and new. I was feeling the facets. But the tears trickling down, salt, through my moustache were tears of laughter ; for Sinfi Lovell seemed again murmuring, 'For good or for ill, you must dig deep to bury your daddy.' . . .

What thoughts and what sensations were mine as I sat there, pressing the sharp stones into my breast, thinking of her to whom the sacred symbol had come, not as a blessing, but as a curse—what agonies were mine as I sat there sobbing the one word 'Winnie '— could be understood by myself alone, the latest blossom of the passionate blood that for generations had brought bliss and bale to the Aylwins. . . .

I cannot tell what I felt and thought, but only what I did. And while I did it my reason was all the time scoffing at my heart (for whose imperious behoof the wild, mad things I am about to record were done)— scoffing, as an Asiatic malefactor will sometimes scoff at the executioner whose pitiless and conquering saw is severing his bleeding body in twain. I arose and murmured ironically to Fenella Stanley as I wrapped the cross in a handkerchief and placed it in a hand-valise : 'Secrecy is the first thing for us sacrilegists to consider, dear Sibyl, in placing a valuable jewel in a tomb in a deserted church. To take any one into our confidence would be impossible ; we must go alone. But to open the tomb and close it again, and leave no trace of what has been done, will require all our skill. And as burglars' jemmies are not on open sale we must buy, on our way to the railway-station, screw-drivers, chisels, a hammer, and a lantern; for who should know better than you, dear Sibyl, that the palace of Nin-ki-gal is dark.'"

But after all I am unable to express any opinion worth expressing upon the chief point which would decide the question as to whether the imagination at work in 'Aylwin' and 'The Coming of Love' is lyrical or dramatic, because I do not know whether, like Henry Aylwin and Percy Aylwin, the author has a dash of Romany blood in his veins. If he has not that dash, and I certainly never heard that he has, and neither Groome's words in the 'Bookman' nor 'Gypsy Smith's' words can be construed into an expression of opinion on the subject, then I will say with confidence that his delineation of two English gentleman with an ancestral Romany strain so like and yet so unlike as Henry Aylwin and Percy Aylwin could only have been achieved by a wonderful exercise of absolute vision. It was this that struck the late Grant Allen so forcibly. On the other hand, if he has that strain, then, as I have said before, it is not in the story but in the poem that we must look for the best dramatic character drawing. On this most interesting subject no one can speak but himself, and he has not spoken. But here is what he has said upon the similarity and the contrast between Percy and Henry Aylwin :—

"Certain parts of 'The Coming of Love' were written about the same time as 'Aylwin.' The two Aylwins, Henry and Percy, were then very distinct in my own mind; they are very distinct now. And I confess that the possibility of their being confounded with each other had never occurred to me. A certain similarity between the two there must needs be, seeing that the blood of the same Romany ancestress, Fenella Stanley, flows in the veins of both. I say there must needs be this similarity, because the ancestress was Romany. For, without starting the inquiry here as to whether or not the Romanies as a race are superior or inferior to all or any of the great European races among which they move, I will venture to affirm that in the Romanies the mysterious energy which the evolutionists call 'the prepotency of transmission' in races is specially strong—so strong, indeed, that evidences of Romany blood in a family may be traced down for several generations. It is inevitable, therefore, that in each of the descendants of Fenella Stanley the form taken by the love-passion should show itself in kindred ways. But the reader who will give a careful study to the characters of Henry and Percy Aylwin will come to the conclusion, I think, that the similarity between the two is observable in one aspect of their characters only. The intensity of the love-passion in each assumes a spiritualizing and mystical form."

Chapter XXII

A STORY WITH TWO HEROINES

ONE thing seems clear to me : having fully intended to make Winifred the heroine of 'Alwyn' round whom the main current of interest should revolve, the author failed to do so. And the reason of his failure is that Winifred has to succumb to the superior vitality of Sinfi's commanding figure. For the purpose of telling the story of Winifred and bringing out her character he conceived and introduced this splendid descendant of Fenella Stanley, and then found her, against his will, growing under his hand until, at last, she pushed his own beloved heroine off her pedestal, and stood herself for all time. Never did author love his heroine 'as Mr. Watts-Dunton loves Winifred, and there is nothing so curious in all fiction as the way in which he seems at times to resent Sinfi's dominance over the Welsh heroine ; and this explains what readers have sometimes said about his 'unkindness to Sinfi.'

It is quite certain that on the whole Sinfi is the reader's heroine. When Madox Brown read the story in manuscript, he became greatly enamoured of Sinfi, and talked about her constantly. It was the same with Mr. Swinburne, who says that 'Aylwin' is the only novel he ever read in manuscript, and found it as absorbing as if he were reading it in type. Mr. George Meredith in a letter said :—" I am in love with Sinfi. Nowhere can fiction give us one to match her, not even the 'Kriegspiel' heroine, who touched me to the deeps. Winifred's infancy has infancy's charm. The young woman is taking. But all my heart has gone to Sinfi. Of course it is part of her character that her destiny should point to the glooms. The sun comes to me again in her conquering presence. I could talk of her for hours. The book has this defect,—it leaves in the mind a cry for a successor." And the author of 'Kriegspiel' himself, F. H. Groome, accepts Sinfi as the true heroine of the story. "In Sinfi Lovell," says he, "Mr. Watts-Dunton would have scored a magnificent success had he achieved nothing more than this most splendid figure—supremely clever but utterly illiterate, eloquent but ungrammatical, heroic but altogether womanly. Winifred is good, and so too is Henry Aylwin himself, and so are many of the minor characters (the mother, for instance, the aunt, and Mrs. Gudgeon), but it is as the tragedy of Sinfi's sacrifice that 'Aylwin' should take its place in literature." Yes, it seems cruel to tell the author this, but Sinfi, and not Winifred, with all her charm, is evidently the favourite of his English public. That admirable novelist, Mr. Richard Whiteing, said in the 'Daily News' that 'Sinfi Lovell is one of the most finished studies of its type and kind in all romantic literature.'

I have somewhere seen Sinfi compared with Isopel Berners. In the first place, while Sinfi is the crowning type of the Romany chi, Isopel is, as the author has pointed out, the type of the 'Anglo-Saxon road girl' with a special antagonism to Romany girls. Grand as is the character of Borrow's Isopel Berners, she is not in the least like Sinfi Lovell. And I may add that she is not really like any other of the heroic women who figure in Mr. Watts-Dunton's gallery of noble women.

SINFI LOVELL AND PHARAOH.

give us one to match her, not even the 'Kriegspiel' heroine, who terrified us to the deeps. Winifred's in fancy has ...... The young woman is taking. But all my ..... to Sinfi. Of course it is part of her ...... that her destiny should point to the gloom. ...... to me again in her conquering presence. I could talk of her for hours. The book has ...... in the mind a cry for a successor." And the author of 'Kriegspiel' himself, F. H. Groome, accepts Sinfi as the true heroine of the story. "In Sinfi Lovell, says he, Mr. Watts-Dunton would have scored a significant success had he achieved nothing more than this most splendid figure—supremely clever but utterly illiterate, eloquent but ungrammatical, heroic but altogether womanly. Winifred is good, and so too is Henry Aylwin himself, and so are many of the minor characters (the mother, for instance, the aunt, and Mrs. Gudgeon), but it is as the tragedy of Sinfi's sacrifice that 'Aylwin' should take its place in literature." Yes, it seems cruel to tell the author this, but Sinfi, and not Winifred, with all her charm, is evidently the favourite of the English public. That admirable novelist, Mr. Richard Whiteing, said in the 'Daily News' that 'Sinfi Lovell is one of the most finished studies of its type and kind in all romantic literature.'

I have somewhere seen Sinfi compared with Isopel Berners. In the first place, while Sinfi is the crowning type of the Romany chi, Isopel is, as the author has pointed out, the type of the 'Anglo-Saxon road girl' with a special antagonism to Romany girls. Grand as is the character of Borrow's Isopel Berners, she is not in the least like Sinfi Lovell. And I may add that she is not really like any other of the heroic women who figure in Mr. Watts-Dunton's gallery of noble women.

SINFI LOVELL AND PHARAOH.

It is, however, interesting here to note that Mr. Watts-Dunton has a special sympathy with women of this heroic type and a special strength of hand in delineating them. There is nothing in them of Isopel's hysterical tears. Once only does Sinfi, in the nobility of her affection for Aylwin, yield to weakness. Mr. Watts-Dunton's sympathy with this kind of woman is apparent in his eulogy of ' Shirley ' :—

"Note that it is not enough for the ideal English girl to be beautiful and healthy, brilliant and cultivated, generous and loving : she must be brave, there must be in her a strain of Valkyrie ; she must be of the high blood of Brynhild, who would have taken Odin himself by the throat for the man she loved. That is to say, that, having all the various charms of English women, the ideal English girl must top them all with that quality which is specially the English man's, just as the English hero, the Nelson, the Sydney, having all the various glories of other heroes, must top them all with that quality which is specially the English woman's—tenderness. What we mean is, that there is a symmetry and a harmony in these matters ; that just as it was an English sailor who said, ' Kiss me, Hardy,' when dying on board the ' Victory '—just as it was an English gentleman who on the burning ' Amazon,' stood up one windy night, naked and blistered, to make of himself a living screen between the flames and his young wife ; so it was an Englishwoman who threw her arms round that fire-screen, and plunged into the sea ; and an Englishwoman who, when bitten by a dog, burnt out the bite from her beautiful arm with a red-hot poker, and gave special instructions how she was to be smothered when hydrophobia should set in."

But Mr. Watts-Dunton himself, in his sonnet, 'Brynhild on Sigurd's Funeral Pyre,' so powerfully illustrated by Mr. Byam Shaw, has given us in fourteen lines a picture of feminine courage and stoicism that puts even Charlotte Brontë's picture of Shirley in the shade :—

> With blue eyes fixed on joy and sorrow past,
>   Tall Brynhild stands on Sigurd's funeral pyre ;
>   She stoops to kiss his mouth, though forks of fire
> Rise fighting with the reek and wintry blast ;
> She smiles, though earth and sky are overcast
>   With shadow of wings that shudder of Asgard's ire ;
>   She weeps, but not because the gods conspire
> To quell her soul and break her heart at last.
>
> "Odin," she cries, "it is for gods to droop !—
>   Heroes ! we still have man's all-sheltering tomb,
>   Where cometh peace at last, whate'er may come :
> Fate falters, yea, the very Norns shall stoop
> Before man's courage, naked, bare of hope,
>   Standing against all Hell and Death and Doom.

Rhona Boswell, too, under all her playful humour, is of this strain, as we see in that sonnet on 'Kissing the Maybuds' in 'The Coming of Love' (given on page 406 of this book).

As Groome's remarks upon 'Aylwin' are in many ways of special interest, I will for a moment digress from the main current of my argument, and say a few words about it. Of course as the gypsies figure so largely in this story, there were very few writers competent to review it from the Romany point of view. Leland was living when it appeared, but he was residing on the Continent ; moreover, at his age, and engrossed as he was, it was not likely that he would undertake to review it. There was another Romany scholar, spoken of with enthusiasm by Groome—I allude to

Mr. Sampson, of Liverpool, who has since edited Borrow's 'Romany Rye' for Messrs. Methuen, and who is said to know more of Welsh Romany than any Englishman ever knew before. At that time, however, he was almost unknown. Finally, there was Groome himself, whose articles in the 'Encyclopædia Britannica' and 'Chambers's Encyclopædia,' had proclaimed him to be the greatest living gypsologist. The editor of the 'Bookman,' being anxious to get a review of the book from the most competent writer he could find, secured Groome himself. I can give only a few sentences from the review. Groome, it will be seen, does not miss the opportunity of flicking in his usual satirical manner the omniscience of some popular novelists :—

"Novelty and truth," he says, "are 'Aylwin's' chief characteristics, a rare combination nowadays. Our older novelists—those at least still held in remembrance—wrote only of what they knew, or of what they had painfully mastered. Defoe, Richardson, Fielding, Smollett, Sterne, Jane Austen, Scott, Dickens, Thackeray, the Brontës, and George Eliot belong to the foremost rank of these ; for types of the second or the third may stand Marryat, Lever, Charles Reade, James Grant, Surtees, Whyte Melville, and Wilkie Collins. But now we have changed all that ; the maximum of achievement seldom rises above school board nescience. With a few exceptions (one could count them on the ten fingers) our present-day novelists seem to write only about things of which they clearly know nothing. One of the most popular lays the scene of a story in Paris : the Seine there is tidal, it rolls a murdered corpse upwards. In another work by her a gambler shoots himself in a cab. 'I trust,' cries a friend who has heard the shot, 'he has missed.'

'No,' says a second friend, 'he was a dead shot'   Mr. X. writes a realistic novel about betting.   It is crammed with weights, acceptances, and all the rest of it; but, alas! on an early page a servant girl wins 12s. 6d. at 7 to 1. Mrs. Y. takes her heroine to a Scottish deer-forest : it is full of primeval oaks.   Mrs. Z. sends her hero out deer-stalking.   Following a hill-range, he sights a stag upon the opposite height, fires at it, and kills his benefactor, who is strolling below in the glen.   And Mr. Ampersand in his masterpiece shows up the littleness of the Establishment : his ritualistic church presents the inconceivable conjunction of the Ten Commandments and a gorgeous rood-screen.   I have drawn upon memory for these six examples, but subscribers to Mudie's should readily recognize the books I mean ; they have sold by thousands on thousands.   'Aylwin' is not such as these   There is much in it of the country, of open-air life, of mountain scenery, of artistic fellowship, of Gypsydom ; it might be called the novel of the two Bohemias.

Many readers have expressed the desire to know something about the prototypes of Sinfi Lovell and Rhona Boswell.   The following words from the Introduction to the 20th edition (called the 'Snowdon Edition') may therefore be read with interest :—

" Although Borrow belonged to a different generation from mine, I enjoyed his intimate friendship in his later years—during the time when he lived in Hereford Square. When, some seven or eight years ago, I brought out an edition of 'Lavengro,' I prefaced that delightful book by a few desultory remarks upon Borrow's gypsy characters. On that occasion I gave a slight sketch of the most remarkable 'Romany Chi' that had ever been met with in the part of East Anglia known to Borrow and myself—Sinfi

Lovell. I described her playing on the crwth. I discussed her exploits as a boxer, and I contrasted her in many ways with the glorious Anglo-Saxon road-girl Isopel Berners.

Since the publication of 'Aylwin' and 'The Coming of Love' I have received very many letters from English and American readers inquiring whether 'the Gypsy girl described in the introduction to "Lavengro" is the same as the Sinfi Lovell of "Aylwin," and also whether 'the Rhona Boswell that figures in the prose story is the same as the Rhona of "The Coming of Love?"'' The evidence of the reality of Rhona so impressed itself upon the reader that on the appearance of Rhona's first letter in the 'Athenæum,' where the poem was printed in fragments, I got among other letters one from the sweet poet and adorable woman Jean Ingelow, who was then very ill,—near her death indeed,—urging me to tell her whether Rhona's love-letter was not a versification of a real letter from a real gypsy to her lover. As it was obviously impossible for me to answer the queries individually, I take this opportunity of saying that the Sinfi of 'Aylwin' and the Sinfi described in my introduction to 'Lavengro' are one and the same character—except that the story of the child Sinfi's weeping for the 'poor dead Gorgios' in the churchyard, given in the Introduction, is really told by the gypsies, not of Sinfi, but of Rhona Boswell. Sinfi is the character alluded to in the now famous sonnet describing 'the walking lord of gypsy lore,' Borrow, by his most intimate friend, Dr. Gordon Hake.

Now that so many of the gryengroes (horse-dealers), who form the aristocracy of the Romany race, have left England for America, it is natural enough that to some readers of 'Aylwin' and 'The Coming of Love,' my pictures of Romany life seem a little idealized. The 'Times,' in a kindly notice of 'The Coming of Love,' said that the kind of gypsies there depicted are a very interesting people, ' unless the author has flattered them unduly.' Those who best knew the gypsy women of that period will be the first to aver that I have not flattered them unduly."

It is Winifred who shares, not only with Henry Aylwin, but also with the author himself, that love of the wind which he revealed in the 'Athenæum' many years before 'Aylwin' was published. I may quote this passage in praise of the wind as an example of the way in which his imaginative work and his critical work are often interwoven :—

"There is no surer test of genuine nature instinct than this. Anybody can love sunshine. No people had less of the nature instinct than the Romans, but they could enjoy the sun ; they even took their solaria or sun-baths, and gave them to their children. And, if it may be said that no Roman loved the wind, how much more may this be said of the French ! None but a born child of the tent could ever have written about the winds of heaven as Victor Hugo has written in ' Les Travailleurs de la Mer,' as though they were the ministers of Ahriman. ' From Ormuzd, not from Ahriman, ye come.' And here, indeed, is the difference between the two nationalities. Love of the wind has made England what she is ; dread of the wind has greatly contributed to make France what she is. The winds are the breathings of the Great Mother. Under the ' olden spell ' of dumbness, nature can yet speak to us by her winds. It is they that express her every mood, and, if her mood is rough at times, her heart is kind. This is why the true child of the open-air—never mind how much he may suffer from the wind—loves it, loves it as much when it comes and ' takes the ruffian billows by the top ' to the peril of his life, as when it comes from the sweet South. In the wind's most boisterous moods, such as those so splendidly depicted by Dana in the doubling of Cape Horn, there is an ex-hilaration, a fierce delight, in struggling with it. It is delightful to read Thoreau when he writes about the wind, and that which the wind so loves—the snow."

Chapter XXIII

THE RENASCENCE OF WONDER IN RELIGION

AND now as to the real inner meaning of 'Alwyin,' about which so much has been written. "'Aylwin,'" says Groome, "is a passionate love-story, with a mystical idée mère. For the entire dramatic action revolves around a thought that is coming more and more to the front—the difference, namely, between a materialistic and a spiritualistic cosmogony." And Dr. Nicoll, in his essay on "The Significance of 'Aylwin,'" in the 'Contemporary Review,' says :—

" Every serious student will see at a glance that 'Aylwin' is a concrete expression of the author's criticism of life and literature, and even—though this must be said with more reserve—a concrete expression of his theory of the universe. This theory I will venture to define as an optimistic confronting of the new cosmogony of growth on which the author has for long descanted. Throughout all his writings there is evidence of a mental struggle as severe as George Eliot's with that materialistic reading of the universe which seemed forced upon thinkers when the doctrine of evolution passed from hypothesis to an accepted theory. Those who have followed Mr. Watts-Dunton's writings in the 'Examiner' and in the 'Athenæum' must have observed with what passionate eagerness he insisted that Darwinism, if properly understood, would carry us no nearer to materialism than did the spiritualistic cosmogonies of old, unless it could establish abiogenesis against biogenesis. As every experiment of every biologist has failed to do so, a new spiritualist cosmogony must be taught."

And yet the student of 'Aylwin' must bear in mind that some critics, taking the very opposite view, have said that its final teaching is not meant to be mystical at all, but anti-mystical—that what to Philip Aylwin and his disciples seems so mystical is all explained by the operation of natural laws. This theory reminds me of a saying of Goethe's about the enigmatic nature of all true and great works of art. I forget the exact words, but they set me thinking about the chameleon-like iridescence of great poems and dramas.

With regard to the fountain-head of all the mysticism of the story, Philip Aylwin, much has been said. Philip is the real protagonist of the story—he governs, as I have said, the entire dramatic action from his grave, and illustrates at every point Sinfi Lovell's saying, 'You must dig deep to bury your daddy.' Everything that occurs seems to be the result of the father's speculations, and the effect of them upon other minds like that of his son and that of Wilderspin.

The appearance of this new epic of spiritual love came at exactly the right moment—came when a new century was about to dawn which will throw off the trammels of old modes of thought. While I am writing these lines Mr. Balfour at the British Association has been expounding what must be called 'Aylwinism,' and (as I shall show in the last chapter of this book saying in other words what Henry Aylwin's father said in 'The Veiled Queen.' In the preface to the edition of 'Aylwin' in the 'World's Classics' the author says :—

"The heart-thought of this book being the peculiar doctrine in Philip Aylwin's 'Veiled Queen,' and the effect of it upon the fortunes of the hero and the other characters, the name 'The Renascence of Wonder' was the first that came to my mind when confronting the difficult question of finding a name for a book that is at once a love-story and an expression of a creed. But eventually I decided, and I think from the worldly point of view wisely, to give it simply the name of the hero.

The important place in the story, however, taken by this creed, did not escape the most acute and painstaking of the critics. Madame Galimberti, for instance, in the elaborate study of the book which she made in the 'Rivista d'Italia,' gave great attention to its central idea; so did M. Maurice Muret, in the 'Journal des Débats'; so did M. Henri Jacottet in 'La Semaine Littéraire.' Mr. Baker, again, in his recently published 'Guide to Fiction,' described 'Aylwin' as "an imaginative romance of modern days, the moral idea of which is man's attitude in face of the unknown, or, as the writer puts it, 'the renascence of wonder.'"" With regard to the phrase itself, in the introduction to the latest edition of 'Aylwin'—the twenty-second edition—I made the following brief reply to certain questions that I have been raised by critics both in England and on the Continent concerning it. The phrase, I said, 'The Renascence of Wonder,' 'is used to express that great revived movement of the soul of man which is generally said to have begun with the poetry of Wordsworth, Scott, Coleridge, and others, and after many varieties of expression reached its culmination in the poems and pictures of Rossetti.'

The painter Wilderspin says to Henry Aylwin, 'The one great event of my life has been the reading of "The Veiled Queen," your father's book of inspired wisdom upon the modern Renascence of Wonder in the mind of man.' And further on he says that his own great picture symbolical of this renascence was suggested by Philip Aylwin's vignette. Since the original writing of 'Aylwin,' many years ago, I have enlarged upon its central idea in the 'Encyclopædia Britannica,' in the introductory essay to the third volume of 'Chambers's Cyclopædia of English Literature,' and in other places. Naturally, therefore, the phrase has been a good deal discussed. Quite lately Dr. Robertson Nicoll has directed attention to the phrase, and he has taken it as a text of a remarkable discourse upon the 'Renascence of Wonder in Religion.'

Mr. Watts-Dunton then quotes Dr. Nicoll's remarks upon the Logia recently discovered by the explorers of the Egypt Fund. He shows how men came to see 'once more the marvel of the universe and the romance of man's destiny. They became aware of the spiritual world, of the supernatural, of the lifelong struggle of soul, of the power of the unseen.'

"The words quoted by Dr. Nicoll might very appropriately be used as a motto for 'Aylwin' and also for its sequel 'The Coming of Love : Rhona Boswell's Story.'"

When 'Aylwin' first appeared, the editor of a well-known journal sent it to me for review. I read it : never shall I forget that reading. I was in Ireland at the time —an Irish Wedding Guest at an Irish Wedding. Now an Irish Wedding is more joyous than any novel, and Irish girls are lovelier than any romance. A duel between Life and Literature ! Picture it ! Behold the Irish Wedding Guest spell-bound by a story-teller as cunning as 'The Ancient Mariner' himself ! He heareth the bridal music, but Aylwin continueth his tale : he cannot choose but hear, until 'The Curse' of the 'The Moonlight Cross' of the Gnostics is finally expiated, and Aylwin and Winnie see in the soul of the sunset 'The Dukkeripen of the Trushùl," the blessed Cross of Rose and Gold. Amid the 'merry din' of the Irish Wedding Feast the Irish Wedding Guest read and wrote. And among other lyrical things, he said that 'since Shakespeare created Ophelia there has been nothing in literature so moving, so pathetic, so unimaginably sorrowful as the madness of Winnie Wynne.' And he also said that " the majority of readers will delight in 'Aylwin' as the most wonderful of love stories, but as the years go by an ever increasing number will find in it the germ of a new religion, a clarified spiritualism, free from charlatanry, a solace and a consolation for the soul amid the bludgeonings of circumstance and the cruelties of fate."

Mr. Watts-Dunton, when I told him that I was going to write this book, urged me to moderate my praise and to call into action the critical power that he was good enough to say that I possessed. He especially asked me not to repeat the above words, the warmth of which, he said, might be misconstrued ; but the courage of my opinions I will exercise ‿so long as I write at all. The 'newspaper cynics' that once were and perhaps still are strong, I have always defied and always will defy. I am glad to see that there is one point of likeness between us of the younger generation and the great one to which Mr. Watts-Dunton and his illustrious friends belong.

We are not afraid and we are not ashamed of being enthusiastic. This, also, I hope, will be a note of the twentieth century.

No doubt mine was a bold prophecy to utter in a rapid review of a romance, but time has shown that it was not a rash one. The truth is that the real vogue of 'Aylwin' as a message to the soul is only beginning. Five years have elapsed since the publication of 'Aylwin,' and during that time it has, I think, passed into twenty-four editions in England alone, the latest of all these editions being the beautiful 'Arvon Edition,' not to speak of the vast issue in sixpenny form.

I, will now quote the words of a very accomplished scholar and critic upon the inner meaning of 'Aylwin' generally. They appeared in the 'Saturday Review' of October 1904, and they show that the interest in the book, so far from waning, is increasing :—

"Public taste has for once made a lucky shot, and we are only too pleased to be able to put an item to the credit of an account in taste, where the balance is so heavily on the wrong side. How 'Aylwin' ever came to be a popular success is hard indeed to understand. We cannot wonder at the doubts of a popular reception confessed to by Mr. Watts-Dunton in his dedication of the latest edition to Mr. Ernest Rhys. How did a book, notable for its poetry and subtlety of thought, come to appeal to an English public ? That it should have a vogue in Wales was natural ; Welsh patriotism would assure a certain success, though by itself it could not indeed have made the book the household word it has now become throughout all Wales. And undoubtedly its Welsh reception has been the more intelligent ; it has been welcomed there for the qualities that most deserved a welcome; while in England we fear that in many quarters it has rather been welcomed in spite of them. The average English man and woman do not like mystery and distrust poetry. They have little sympathy with the ' renascence of wonder,' which some new passages unfold to us in the Arvon edition, passages originally omitted for fear of excessive length and now restored from the MS. We are glad to have them, for they illustrate further the intellectual motive of the book. We are of those who do not care to take ' Aylwin ' merely as a novel."

These words remind me of two reviews of ' Aylwin,' one by Mr. W. P. Ryan, a fellow-countryman of mine, which was published when ' Aylwin' first appeared, the other by an eminent French writer.

" The salient impression on the reader is that he is looking full into deep reaches of life and spirituality rather than temporary pursuits and mundane ambitions. In this regard, in its freedom from littleness, its breadth of life, its exaltation of mood, its sense of serene issues that do not pass with the changing fashions of a generation, the book is almost epic.

But ' Aylwin ' has yet other sides. It is a vital and seizing story. The girl-heroine is a beautiful present-ment, and the struggle with destiny, when, believing in the efficacy of a mystic's curse she loses her reason, and flies from poignantly idyllic life to harrowing life, her stricken lover in her wake, is nearly Greek in its intensity and pathos. The long, long quest through the mountain magic of Wales, the wandering spheres of Romany-land, and the art-reaches of London, could only be made real and convincing by triumphant art. A less expert pioneer would enlarge his effects in details that would dissipate their magic ; Mr. Watts-Dunton knows that one inspired touch is worth many uninspired chapters, as Shakespeare knew that ' she should have died hereafter.'

> Death came on her like an untimely frost,
> Upon the fairest flower of all the field.

or

> Childe Rowland to the dark tower came,

is worth an afternoon of emphasis, a night of mystical elaboration.

Incidentally, the Celtic and Romany types of character reveal their essence. Here, too, the author preserves the artistic unities. Delightful as one realizes these characters to be, full-blooded personalities though they are, it is still their spirit, and through it the larger spirit of their race, that shines clearest. Their story is all realistic, and yet it leaves the flavour of a fairy tale of Regeneration. At first sight one is inclined to speak of their beautiful kinship with Nature ; but the truth is that Nature and they together are seen with spiritual eyes ; that they and Nature are different but kindred embodiments of the underlying, all-extending, universal soul ; that Henry's love, and Winnie's rapture, and Snowdon's magic, and Sinfi's crwth, and the little song of y Wydffa, and the glorious mountain dawn are but drops and notes in a melodic mystic ocean, of which the farthest stars and the deepest loves are kindred and inevitable parts—parts of a whole, of whose ministry we hardly know the elements, yet are cognisant that our highest joy is to feel in radiant moments that we, too, are part of the harmony. In idyll, despair or tragedy, the beauty of ' Aylwin ' is that always the song of the divine in humanity is beneath it. Everything merges into one consistent, artistically suggested, spiritual conception of life ; love tried, tortured, finally rewarded as the supreme force utilized to drive home the intolerable negation and atrophy of materialism ; in Henry's gnostic father, in the scientific Henry himself, the Romany Sinfi, Winnie whose nature is a song, Wilderspin who believes that his model is a heavenly visitant with an immaterial body, D'Arcy who stands for Rossetti, the end is the same ; and the striking trait is the felicity with which so many dissimilar personalities, while playing the drama of divergent actuality to the full, yet realize and illustrate, without apparent manipulation by the author, the one abiding spiritual unity.

In execution, ' Aylwin ' is far above the accomplished English novel-work of latter years ; as a conception of life it surely transcends all. The ' schools ' we have known : the realistic, the romantic, the quasi-historical, the local, seem but parts of the whole when their motives are measured with the idea that permeates this novel. They take drear or gallant roads through limited lands ; it rises like a stately hill from which a world is clearer, above and beyond whose limits there are visions, Voices, and the verities."

With equal eloquence M. Jacottet on the same day wrote about " Aylwin " in ' La Semaine Littéraire ' :—

" The central idea of this poetic book is that of love stronger than death, love elevating the soul to a mys tical conception of the universe. It is a singular fact that at the moment when England, intoxicated with her successes, seems to have no room for thought except with regard to her fleet and her commerce, and allows herself to be dazzled by dreams of universal empire, the book in vogue should be Mr. Watts-Dunton's romance—the most idealistic, the farthest removed from the modern Anglo-Saxon conception of life that ne could possibly conceive. But this fact has often been observable in literary history. Is not the true charm of letters that of giving to the soul respite from the brutalities of contemporary events ? "

Chapter XXIV

THE RENASCENCE OF WONDER IN HUMOUR

THE character of Mrs. Gudgeon in ' Aylwin ' stands as entirely alone among homourous characters as does Sancho Panza, Falstaff, Mrs. Quickly or Mrs. Partridge. In my own review of ' Aylwin ' I thus noted the entirely new kind of humour which characterizes it :—" To one aspect of this book we have not yet alluded, namely, its humour. Whimsical Mrs. Gudgeon, the drunken virago who pretends that Winnie is her daughter, is inimitable, with her quaint saying : ' I shall die a-larfin', they say in Primrose Court, and so I shall—unless I die a-crying.' " Few critics have done justice to Mrs. Gudgeon, although the ' Times said : ' In Mrs. Gudgeon, one of his characters, the author has accomplished the feat of creating what seems to be a new comic figure,' and the ' Saturday Review ' singled her out as being the triumph of the book. Could she really have been a real character ? Could there ever have existed in the London of the mid-Victorian period a real flesh and blood costermonger so rich in humour that her very name sheds a glow of laughter over every page in which it appears ? According to Mr. Hake, she was suggested by a real woman, and this makes me almost lament my arrival in London too late to make her acquaintance. " With regard to the most original character of the story," says Mr. Hake, " those who knew Clement's Inn, where I myself once resided, and Lincoln's Inn Fields, will be able at once to identify Mrs.

Gudgeon, who lived in one of the streets running into Clare Market. Her business was that of night coffee-stall keeper. At one time, I believe—but I am not certain about this—she kept a stall on the Surrey side of Waterloo Bridge, and it might have been there that, as I have been told, her portrait was drawn for a specified number of early breakfasts by an unfortunate artist who sank very low, but had real ability. Her constant phrase was ' I shall die o'-laughin'—I know I shall ! ' On account of her extraordinary gift of repartee, and her inexhaustible fund of wit and humour, she was generally supposed to be an Irishwoman. But she was not ; she was cockney to the marrow. Recluse as Rossetti was in his later years, he had at one time been very different, and could bring himself in touch with the lower orders of London in a way such as was only known to his most intimate friends. With all her impudence, and I may say insolence, Mrs. Gudgeon was a great favourite with the police, who were the constant butts of her chaff." [1] But, of course, this interesting costermonger could have only suggested our unique Mrs. Gudgeon.

She shows that it is possible to paint a low-class humourist as rich in the new cosmic humour as any one of Dickens's is rich in the old terrene humour, and yet without one Dickensian touch. The difficulty of achieving this feat is manifested every day, both in novels and on the stage. Until Mrs. Gudgeon appeared I thought that Dickens had made it as impossible for another writer to paint humourous pictures of low-class London women as Swinburne has made it impossible for another poet to write in anapæsts. But there is in all that Mrs. Gudgeon says or does a profundity of humour so much deeper than

[1] ' Notes and Queries,' June 7, 1902.

the humour of Mrs. Gamp, that it wins her a separate niche in our gallery of humourous women. The chief cause of the delight which Mrs. Gudgeon gives me is that she illustrates Mr. Watts-Dunton's theory of absolute humour as distinguished from relative humour—a theory which delighted me in those boyish days in Ireland, to which I have already alluded . I have read his words on this theme so often that I think I could repeat them as fluently as a nursery rhyme. In their original form I remember that the word ' caricature ' took the place of the phrase ' relative humour.' I do not think there is anything in Mr. Watts-Dunton's writings so suggestive and so profound, and to find in reading ' Aylwin ' that they were suggested to him by a real living character was exhilarating indeed.

Mr. Watts-Dunton's theory of humour is one of his most original generalizations, and it is vitally related both to his theory of poetry and to his generalization of generalizations, ' The Renascence of Wonder.' I think Mrs. Gudgeon is a cockney Anacharsis in petticoats. The Scythian philosopher, it will be remembered, when jesters were taken to him, could not be made to smile, but afterwards, when a monkey was brought to him, broke out into a fit of laughter and said, ' Now this is laughable by nature, the other by art.' I will now quote the essay on absolute and relative humour :—

" Anarcharsis, who found the humour of Nature alone laughable, was the absolute humourist as distinguished from the relative humourist, who only finds food for laughter in the distortions of so-called humourous art. The quality which I have called absolute humour is popularly supposed to be the characteristic and special temper of the English. The bustling, money-

grubbing, rank-worshipping British slave of convention claims to be the absolute humourist ! It is very
amusing. The temper of absolute humour, on the contrary, is the temper of Hotei, the fat Japanese god of
'contentment with things as they be,' who, when the
children wake him up from his sleep in the sunshine, and
tickle and tease him, and climb over his 'thick rotundity
of belly,' good-naturedly bribes them to leave him in
peace by telling them fairy stories and preaching humourous homilies upon the blessings of contentment, the
richness of Nature's largess, the exceeding cheapness of
good things, such as sunshine and sweet rains and the
beautiful white cherry blossoms on the mountain side.
Between this and relative humour how wide is the gulf !

That an apprehension of incongruity is the basis of
both relative and absolute humour is no doubt true
enough ; but while in the case of relative humour it is
the incongruity of some departure from the normal, in
the case of absolute humour it is the sweet incongruity
of the normal itself. Relative humour laughs at the
breach of the accustomed laws of nature and the conventional laws of man, which laws it accepts as final.
Absolute humour (comparing them unconsciously with
some ideal standard of its own, or with that ideal or
noumenal or spiritual world behind the cosmic show)
sees the incongruity of those very laws themselves—laws
which are the relative humourist's standard. Absolute
humour, in a word, is based on metaphysics—relative
humour on experience. A child can become a relative
humourist by adding a line or two to the nose of Wellington, or by reversing the nose of the Venus de Medici.
The absolute humourist has so long been saying to himself, 'What a whimsical idea is the human nose !' that
he smiles the smile of Anacharsis at the child's laughter

on seeing it turned upside down. So with convention
and its codes of etiquette—from the pompous harlequinade of royalty—the ineffable gingerbread of an
aristocracy of names without office or culture, down to
the Draconian laws of Philistia and bourgeois respect-
ability; whatever is a breach of the local laws of the game
of social life, whether the laws be those of a village
pothouse or of Mayfair; whether it displays an ignorance
of matters of familiar knowledge, these are the quarry of
the relative humourist. The absolute humourist, on
the other hand, as we see in the greatest masters of absolute humour, is so perpetually overwhelmed with the
irony of the entire game, cosmic and human, from the
droll little conventions of the village pothouse to those
of London, of Paris, of New York, of Pekin—up to the
apparently meaningless dance of the planets round the
sun—up again to that greater and more meaningless
waltz of suns round the centre—he is so delighted with
the delicious foolishness of wisdom, the conceited ignorance of knowledge, the grotesqueness even of the standard
of beauty itself; above all, with the whim of the absolute
humourist Nature, amusing herself, not merely with her
monkeys, her flamingoes, her penguins, her dromedaries,
but with these more whimsical creatures still—these
' bipeds ' which, though ' featherless ' are proved to be
not ' plucked fowls '; these proud, high-thinking organ-
isms—stomachs with heads, arms, and legs as useful
appendages—these countless little ' me's,' so all alike and
yet so unlike, each one feeling, knowing itself to be *the*
me, the only true original me, round whom all other *me's*
revolve—so overwhelmed is the absolute humourist with
the whim of all this—with the incongruity, that is, of
the normal itself—with the ' almighty joke ' of the Cosmos as it is—that he sees nothing ' funny ' in departures

from laws which to him are in themselves the very quintessence of fun.   And he laughs the laugh of Rabelais and of Sterne ; for he feels that behind this rich incongruous show there must be a beneficent Showman.   He knows that although at the top of the constellation sits Circumstance, Harlequin and King, bowelless and blind, shaking his starry cap and bells, there sits far above even Harlequin himself another Being greater than he—a Being who because he has given us the delight of laughter must be good, and who in the end will somewhere set all these incongruities right—who will, some day, show us the meaning of that which now seems so meaningless. With Charles Lamb he feels, in short, that humour ' does not go out with life ' ; and in answer to Elia's question, ' Can a ghost laugh ? ' he says, ' Assuredly, if there be ghosts at all,' for he is as unable as Soame Jenyns himself to imagine that even the seraphim can be perfectly happy without a perception of the ludicrous.

If this, then, is the absolute humourist as distinguished from the relative humourist, his type is not Dickens or Cruikshank, but Anacharsis, or, better still, that old Greek who died of laughter from seeing a donkey eat, and who, perhaps, is the only man who could have told us what the superlative feeling of absolute humour really is, though he died of a sharp and sudden recognition of the humour of the bodily functions merely.   And naturally what is such a perennial source of amusement to the absolute humourist he gets to love.   Mere representation, therefore, is with him the be-all and the end-all of art.   Exaggeration offends him.   Nothing to him is so rich as the real.   He pronounces Tennyson's ' Northern Farmer ' or the public-house scene in ' Silas Marner ' to be more humourous than the trial scene in ' Pickwick.'   Wilkie's realism he finds more humourous

than the funniest cartoon in the funniest comic journal.
And this mood is as much opposed to satire as to relative
humour. Of all moods the rarest and the finest—re-
quiring, indeed, such a ' blessed mixing of the juices ' as
nature cannot every day achieve—it is the mood of each
one of those fatal ' Paradis Artificiels,' the seeking of
which has devastated the human race : the mood of
Christopher Sly, of Villon ; of Walter Mapes in the following verse :—

> Meum est propositum in taberna mori,
> Vinum sit appositum morientis ori,
> Ut dicant cum venerint angelorum chori,
> Deus sit propitius huic potatori."

Now it is because Mrs. Gudgeon is the very type of
the absolute humourist as defined in this magnificent
fugue of prose, and the only example of absolute humour
which has appeared in prose fiction, that she is to me a
fount of esoteric and fastidious joy. If I were asked
what character in ' Aylwin ' shows the most unmistakable
genius, I should reply, ' Mrs. Gudgeon ! and again, Mrs.
Gudgeon ! '

Chapter XXV

GORGIOS AND ROMANIES

THE publication of ' The Coming of Love ' in book form preceded that of ' Aylwin ' by about a year, but it had been appearing piecemeal in the ' Athenæum ' since 1882.

"So far as regards Rhona Boswell's story," says Mr. Watts-Dunton, "' The Coming of Love ' is a sequel to ' Aylwin.' If the allusions to Rhona's lover, Percy Aylwin, in the prose story have been, in some degree, misunderstood by some readers—if there is any danger of Henry Aylwin, the hero of the novel, being confounded with Percy Aylwin, the hero of this poem—it only shows how difficult it is for the poet or the novelist (who must needs see his characters from the concave side only) to realize that it is the convex side only which he can present to his reader.

The fact is that the motive of ' Aylwin '—dealing only as it does with that which is elemental and unchangeable in man—is of so entirely poetic a nature that I began to write it in verse. After a while, however, I found that a story of so many incidents and complications as the one that was growing under my hand could only be told in prose. This was before I had written any prose at all—yes, it is so long ago as that. And when, afterwards, I began to write criticism, I had (for certain reasons—important then, but of no importance now) abandoned the idea of offering the novel to the outside public at all. Among my friends it had been widely read, both in manuscript and in type.

But with regard to Romany women, Henry Aylwin's feeling towards them was the very opposite of Percy's. When, in speaking of George Borrow some years ago, I made the remark that between Englishmen of a certain type and gypsy women there is an extraordinary physical attraction—an attraction which did not exist between Borrow and the gypsy women with whom he was brought into contact—I was thinking specially of the character depicted here under the name of Percy Aylwin. And I asked then the question—Supposing Borrow to have been physically drawn with much power towards any woman, could she possibly have been Romany ? Would she not rather have been of the Scandinavian type ?—would she not have been what he used to call a ' Brynhild ' ? From many conversations with him on this subject, I think she must necessarily have been a tall blonde of the type of Isopel Berners— who, by-the-by, was much more a portrait of a splendid East-Anglian road-girl than is generally imagined. And I think, besides, that Borrow's sympathy with the Anglo-Saxon type may account for the fact that, notwithstanding his love of the free and easy economies of life among the better class of Gryengroes, his gypsy women are all what have been called ' scenic characters.'

When he comes to delineate a heroine, she is the superb Isopel Berners—that is to say, she is physically (and indeed mentally, too), the very opposite of the Romany chi. It was here, as I happen to know, that Borrow's sympathies were with Henry Aylwin far more than with Percy Aylwin.

The type of the Romany chi, though very delightful to Henry Aylwin as regards companionship, had no phy-

sical attractions for him, otherwise the witchery of the
girl here called Rhona Boswell, whom he knew as a child
long before Percy Aylwin knew her, must surely have
eclipsed such charms as Winifred Wynne or any other
winsome 'Gorgie' could possess. On the other hand,
it would, I believe, have been impossible for Percy Ayl
win to be brought closely and long in contact with a
Romany girl like Sinfi Lovell and remain untouched by
those unique physical attractions of hers—attractions
that made her universally admired by the best judges of
female beauty as being the most splendid 'face-model'
of her time, and as being in form the grandest woman
ever seen in the studios—attractions that upon Henry
Aylwin seem to have made almost no impression.

There is no accounting for this, as there is no accounting for anything connected with the mysterious witchery
of sex. And again, the strong inscrutable way in which
some gypsy girls are drawn towards a 'Tarno Rye' (as
a young English gentleman is called), is quite inexplicable. Some have thought—and Borrow was one of
them—that it may arise from that infirmity of the Romany Chal which causes the girls to 'take their own part'
without appealing to their men-companions for aid—
that lack of masculine chivalry among the men of their
own race.

And now for a word or two upon a matter in connection with 'Aylwin' and 'The Coming of Love'
which interests me more deeply. Some of those who
have been specially attracted towards Sinfi Lovell have
had misgivings, I find, as to whether she is not an ideal-
ization, an impossible Romany chi, and some of those who
have been specially attracted towards Rhona Boswell
have had the same misgivings as to her.

One of the great racial specialities of the Romany

is the superiority of the women to the men. For it is not merely in intelligence, in imagination, in command over language, in comparative breadth of view regarding the Gorgio world that the Romany women (in Great Britain, at least) leave the men far behind. In everything that goes to make nobility of character this superiority is equally noticeable. To imagine a gypsy hero is, I will confess, rather difficult. Not that the average male gypsy is without a certain amount of courage, but it soon gives way, and, in a conflict between a gypsy and an Englishman, it always seems as though ages of oppression have damped the virility of Romany stamina.

Although some of our most notable prize-fighters have been gypsies, it used to be well known, in times when the ring was fashionable, that a gypsy could not always be relied upon to ' take punishment ' with the stolid indifference of an Englishman or a negro, partly, perhaps, because his more highly-strung nervous system makes him more sensitive to pain.

The courage of, a gypsy woman, on the other hand, has passed into a proverb ; nothing seems to daunt it. This superiority of the women to the men extends to everything, unless, perhaps, we except that gift of music for which the gypsies as a race are noticeable. With regard to music, however, even in Eastern Europe (Russia alone excepted), where gypsy music is so universal that, according to some writers, every Hungarian musician is of Romany extraction, it is the men, and not, in general, the women, who excel. Those, however, who knew Sinfi Lovell may think with me that this state of things may simply be the result of opportunity and training."

Chapter XXVI

'THE COMING OF LOVE'

IN my article on Mr. Watts-Dunton in Chambers's
'Cyclopædia of English Literature' I devoted most
of my space to 'The Coming of Love.' I put the two
great romantic poems 'The Coming of Love' and
'Christmas at the "Mermaid"' far above everything he
has done. I think I see both in the conception and in
the execution of these poems the promise of immortality—
if immortality can be predicted of any poems of our time.
In reading them one remembers in a flash Mr. Watts-
Dunton's own noble words about the poetic impulse :—

" In order to produce poetry the soul must for the
time being have reached that state of exaltation, that
state of freedom from self-consciousness, depicted in the
lines—

> I started once, or seemed to start, in pain
> Resolved on noble things, and strove to speak,
> As when a great thought strikes along the brain
> And flushes all the cheek.

Whatsoever may be the poet's 'knowledge of his
art,' into this mood he must always pass before he can
write a truly poetic line. For, notwithstanding all that
we have said and are going to say upon poetry as a fine
art, it is in the deepest sense of the word an ' inspiration '
indeed. No man can write a line of genuine poetry

without having been 'born again' (or, as the true rendering of the text says, 'born from above'); and then
the mastery over those highest reaches of form which are
beyond the ken of the mere versifier comes to him as a
result of the change.   Hence, with all Mrs. Browning's
metrical blemishes, the splendour of her metrical triumphs at her best.

For what is the deep distinction between poet and
proseman ?   A writer may be many things besides a
poet ; he may be a warrior like Æschylus, a man of business like Shakespeare, a courtier like Chaucer, or a cos-
mopolitan philosopher like Goethe ; but the moment
the poetic mood is upon him all the trappings of the
world with which for years he may perhaps have been
clothing his soul—the world's knowingness, its cynicism,
its self-seeking, its ambition—fall away, and the man
becomes an inspired child again, with ears attuned to
nothing but the whispers of those spirits from the Golden Age, who, according to Hesiod, haunt and bless the
degenerate earth.   What such a man produces may
greatly delight and astonish his readers, yet not so
greatly as it delights and astonishes himself.   His
passages of pathos draw no tears so deep or so sweet as
those that fall from his own eyes while he writes ; his
sublime passages overawe no soul so imperiously as his
own ; his humour draws no laughter so rich or so deep
as that stirred within his own breast.

It might almost be said, indeed, that Sincerity and
Conscience, the two angels that bring to the poet the
wonders of the poetic dream, bring him also the deepest,
truest delight of form.   It might almost be said that by
aid of sincerity and conscience the poet is enabled to see
more clearly than other men the eternal limits of his own
art—to see with Sophocles that nothing, not even poetry

itself, is of any worth to man, invested as he is by the whole army of evil, unless it is in the deepest and highest sense good, unless it comes linking us all together by closer bonds of sympathy and pity, strengthening us to fight the foes with whom fate and even nature, the mother who bore us, sometimes seem in league—to see with Milton that the high quality of man's soul which in English is expressed by the word virtue is greater than even the great poem he prized, greater than all the rhythms of all the tongues that have been spoken since Babel—and to see with Shakespeare and with Shelley that the high passion which in England is called love is lovelier than all art, lovelier than all the marble Mercuries that 'await the chisel of the sculptor' in all the marble hills."

The reason why the criticism of the hour does not always give Mr. Watts-Dunton the place accorded to him by his great contemporaries is not any lack of generosity : it arises from the unprecedented, not to say eccentric, way in which his poetry has reached the public. In this respect alone, apart from its great originality, 'The Coming of Love' is a curiosity of literature. I know nothing in the least like the history of this poem. It was written, circulated in manuscript among the very élite of English letters, and indeed partly published in the 'Athenæum,' very nearly a quarter of a century ago. I have before alluded to Mrs. Chandler Moulton's introduction to Philip Bourke Marston's poems, where she says that it was Mr. Watts-Dunton's poetry which won for him the friendship of Tennyson, Rossetti, Morris, and Swinburne. Yet for lustre after lustre it was persistently withheld from the public ; cenacle after poetic cenacle rose, prospered and faded away, and still this poet, who was talked of by all the poets and called 'the friend of all the poets,' kept his work back until he had passed middle age. Then, at last, owing I believe to the energetic efforts of Mr. John Lane, who had been urging the matter for something like five years, he launched a volume which seized upon the public taste and won a very great success so far as sales go. It is now in its sixth edition. There can be no doubt whatever that if the book had appeared, as it ought to have appeared, at the time it was written, critics would have classed the poet among his compeers and he would have come down to the present generation, as Swinburne has come down, as a classic. But, as I have said, it is not in the least surprising that, notwithstanding Rossetti's intense admiration of the poem, notwithstanding the fact that Morris intended to print it at the Kelmscott Press, and notwithstanding the fact that Swinburne, in dedicating the collected edition of his works to Mr. Watts-Dunton, addresses him as a poet of the greatest authority—it is only the true critics who see in the right perspective a poet who has so perversely neglected his chances. If his time of recognition has not yet fully come, this generation is not to blame. The poet can blame only himself, although to judge by Rossetti's words, and by the following lines from Dr. Hake's 'New Day,' he is indifferent to that :—

> You tell me life is all too rich and brief,
>   Too various, too delectable a game,
> To give to art, entirely or in chief ;
>   And love of Nature quells the thirst for fame.

The 'parable poet'. then goes on to give voice to the opinion, not only of himself, but of most of the great poets of the mid-Victorian epoch :—

You who in youth the cone-paved forest sought,
  Musing until the pines to musing fell;
You who by river-path the witchery caught
  Of waters moving under stress of spell;
You who the seas of metaphysics crossed,
  And yet returned to art's consoling haven—
Returned from whence so many souls are lost,
  With wisdom's seal upon your forehead graven—
Well may you now abandon learning's seat,
  And work the ore all seek, not many find;
No sign-post need you to direct your feet,
  You draw no riches from another's mind.
Hail Nature's coming; bygone be the past;
Hail her New Day; it breaks for man at last.

Fulfil the new-born dream of Poesy!
  Give her your life in full, she turns from less—
Your life in full—like those who did not die,
  Though death holds all they sang in dark duress.
You, knowing Nature to the throbbing core,
  You can her wordless prophecies rehearse.
The murmers others heard her heart outpour
  Swell to an anthem in your richer verse.
If wider vision brings a wider scope
  For art, and depths profounder for emotion,
Yours be the song whose master-tones shall ope
  A new poetic heaven o'er earth and ocean.
The New Day comes apace; its virgin fame
Be yours, to fan the fiery soul to flame.

Indeed, he has often said to me: 'There is a tide in the affairs of men, and I did not throw myself upon my little tide until it was too late, and I am not going to repine now.'   For my part, I have been a student of English poetry all my life—it is my chief subject of study —and I predict that when poetic imagination is again perceived to be the supreme poetic gift, Mr. Watts-Dunton's genius will be acclaimed. In respect of

imaginative power, apart from the other poetic qualities
—' the power of seeing a dramatic situation and flashing
it upon the physical senses of the listener,' none of his
contemporaries have surpassed him.

I have said in print more than once that I, a Celt
myself, can see more Celtic glamour in his poetry than
in many of the Celtic poets of our time.   And, if we are
to judge by the vogue of 'The Coming of Love' and
'Aylwin' in Wales, the Welsh people seem to see it
very clearly.   Take, for instance, the sonnet called 'The
Mirrored Stars' again, given on page 29.   It is impos
sible for Celtic glamour to go further than this; and yet
it is rarely noted by critics in discussing the Celtic note
in poetry.

In order fully to understand 'The Coming of Love'
it is necessary to bear in mind a distinction between the
two kinds of poetry upon which Mr. Watts-Dunton has
often dwelt.   "There are," he tells us, "but two kinds
of poetry, but two kinds of art—that which interprets,
and that which represents.   'Poetry is apparent pictures of unapparent realities,' says the Eastern mind
through Zoroaster; ' the highest, the only operation of
art is representation (Gestaltung),' says the Western
mind through Goethe. Both are right." Madame
Galimberti has called Mr. Watts-Dunton ' the poet of
the sunrise': There are richer descriptions of sunrise in 'Aylwin' and 'The Coming of Love' than in
any other writer I know. "Few poets," Mr. Watts-
Dunton says, "have been successful in painting a sunrise, for the simple reason that, save through the bed-
curtains, they do not often see one.   They think
that all they have to do is to paint a sunset, which they
sometimes do see, and call it a sunrise.   They are entirely mistaken, however ; the two phenomena are both

like and unlike. Between the cloud-pageantry of sunrise and of sunset the difference to the student of Nature is as apparent as is the difference to the poet between the various forms of his art."

'The Coming of Love' shows that independence of contemporary vogues and influences which characterizes all Mr. Watts-Dunton's work, whether in verse or prose, whether in romance or criticism, or in that analysis and exposition of the natural history of minds about which Sainte Beuve speaks. It was as a poet that his energies were first exercised, but this for a long time was known only to his poetical friends. His criticism came many years afterwards, and, as Rossetti used to say, 'his critical work consists of generalizations of his own experience in the poet's workshop.' For many years he was known only in his capacity as a critic. James Russell Lowell is reported to have said: 'Our ablest critics hitherto have been 18-carat; Theodore Watts goes nearer the pure article.' Mr. William Sharp, in his study of Rossetti, says: 'In every sense of the word the friendship thus begun resulted in the greatest benefit to the elder writer, the latter having greater faith in Mr. Watts-Dunton's literary judgment than seems characteristic with so dominant and individual an intellect as that of Rossetti. Although the latter knew well the sonnet-literature of Italy and England, and was a much-practised master of the heart's key himself, I have heard him on many occasions refer to Theodore Watts as having still more thorough knowledge on the subject, and as being the most original sonnet-writer living.'

'Aylwin' and 'The Coming of Love' are vitally connected with the poet's peculiar critical message. Henry Aylwin and Percy Aylwin may be regarded as the embodiment of his philosophy of life. The very popu-

larity of 'Aylwin' and 'The Coming of Love' is apt
to make readers forget the profundity of the philosophical thought upon which they are based, although this
profundity has been indicated by such competent critics
as Dr. Robertson Nicoll in the 'Contemporary Review,' M. Maurice Muret in the 'Journal des Débats,'
and other thoughtful writers.   Upon the inner meaning
of the romance and the poem I have, however, ideas of
my own to express, which are not in full accordance with
any previous criticisms.   To me it seems that the two
cousins, Henry Aylwin of the romance, and Percy Aylwin
of the poem, are phases of a modern Hamlet, a Hamlet
who has travelled past the pathetic superstitions of the
old cosmogonies to the last milestone of doubting hope and
questioning fear, a Hamlet who stands at the portals of
the outer darkness, gazing with eyes made wistful by the
loss of a beloved woman.   In both the romance and the
poem the theme is love at war with death.   Mr. Watts-
Dunton, in his preface to the illustrated edition of
'Aylwin' says :—

"It is a story written as a comment on Love's war-
fare with death—written to show that, confronted as man
is every moment by signs of the fragility and brevity of
human life, the great marvel connected with him is not
that his thoughts dwell frequently upon the unknown
country beyond Orion, where the beloved dead are loving
us still, but that he can find time and patience to think
upon anything else : a story written further to show how
terribly despair becomes intensified when a man has lost
—or thinks he has lost—a woman whose love was the
only light of his world—when his soul is torn from his
body, as it were, and whisked off on the wings of the
'viewless winds' right away beyond the farthest star, till

the universe hangs beneath his feet a trembling point of twinkling light, and at last even this dies away and his soul cries out for help in that utter darkness and loneliness. It was to depict this phase of human emotion that both 'Aylwin' and 'The Coming of Love' were written. They were missives from the lonely watch-tower of the writer's soul, sent out into the strange and busy battle of the world—sent out to find, if possible, another soul or two to whom the watcher was, without knowing it, akin. In 'Aylwin' the problem is symbolized by the victory of love over sinister circumstance, whereas in the poem it is symbolized by a mystical dream of 'Natura Benigna.'

In 'The Coming of Love' Percy Aylwin is a poet and a sailor, with such an absorbing love for the sea that he has no room for any other passion; to him an imprisoned seabird is a sufferer almost more pitiable than any imprisoned man, as will be seen by the opening section of the poem, 'Mother Carey's Chicken.' On seeing a storm-petrel in a cage on a cottage wall near Gypsy Dell, he takes down the cage in order to release the bird; then, carrying the bird in the cage, he turns to cross a rustic wooden bridge leading past Gypsy Dell, when he suddenly comes upon a landsman friend of his, a Romany Rye, who is just parting from a young gypsy-girl. Gazing at her beauty, Percy stands dazzled and forgets the petrel. It is symbolical of the inner meaning of the story that the bird now flies away through the half-open door. From that moment, through the magic of love, the land to Percy is richer than the sea: this ends the first phase of the story. The first kiss between the two lovers is thus described :—

If only in dreams may Man be fully blest,
Is heaven a dream ?   Is she I claspt a dream ?
Or stood she here even now where dew-drops gleam
And miles of furze shine yellow down the West ?
I seem to clasp her still—still on my breast
Her bosom beats : I see the bright eyes beam.
I think she kissed these lips, for now they seem
Scarce mine : so hallowed of the lips they pressed.
Yon thicket's breath—can that be eglantine ?
Those birds—can they be Morning's choristers ?
Can this be Earth ?   Can these be banks of furze ?
Like burning bushes fired of God they shine !
I seem to know them, though this body of mine
Passed into spirit at the touch of hers !

Percy stays with the gypsies, and the gypsy-girl,
Rhona, teaches him Romany.   This arouses the jealousy
of a gypsy rival—Herne the ' Scollard.'   Percy Aylwin's
family afterwards succeeds in separating him from her,
and he is again sent to sea.   While cruising among the
coral islands he receives the letter from Rhona which
paints her character with unequalled vividness ·—

RHONA'S LETTER

On Christmas Eve I seed in dreams the day
When Herne the Scollard come and said to me,
gentleman   He s off, that rye o yourn, gone clean away
Till swallow-time ; hes left this letter : see.
In dreams I heerd the bee and grasshopper,
Like on that mornin, buz in Rington Hollow,
die   Shell live till swallow-time and then shell mer,
gentleman   For never will a rye come back to her
Wot leaves her till the comin o the swallow.

All night I heerd them bees and grasshoppers ;
All night I smelt the breath o grass and may,
Mixed sweet wi' smells o honey from the furze
Like on that mornin when you went away ; ·

All night I heerd in dreams my daddy sal,   laugh
Sayin, De blessed chi ud give de chollo   girl-whole
O Bozzles breed—tans, vardey, greis, and all   tents : waggons :
                                                             horses
To see dat tarno rye o hern palall   back
Wots left her till the comin o the swallow.

I woke and went a-walkin on the ice
All white with snow-dust, just like sparklin loon,   salt
And soon beneath the stars I heerd a vice,
A vice I knowed and often, often shoon ;   hear
An then I seed a shape as thin as tuv ;   smoke
I knowed it wur my blessed mammy s mollo.[1]   spirit
Rhona, she sez, that tarno rye you love,
He s thinkin on you ; don t you go and rove ;   weep
You ll see him at the comin o the swallow.

Sez she, For you it seemed to kill the grass
When he wur gone, and freeze the brooklets gillies ;   songs
There wornt no smell, dear, in the sweetest cas,   hay
And when the summer brought the water-lilies,
And when the sweet winds waved the golden giv,   wheat
The skies above em seemed as bleak and kollo [2]   black
As now, when all the world seems frozen yiv.   snow
The months are long, but mammy says you ll live
By thinkin o the comin o the swallow.

She sez, The whinchat soon wi silver throat
Will meet the stonechat in the buddin whin,
And soon the blackcaps airliest gillie ull float   song
From light-green boughs through leaves a-peepin thin ;
The wheat-ear soon ull bring the willow-wren,
And then the fust fond nightingale ull follow,
A-callin Come, dear, to his laggin hen
Still out at sea, the spring is in our glen ;
Come, darlin, wi the comin o the swallow.

[1] Mostly pronounced ' mullo,' but sometimes in the East Midlands
' mollo.'
[2] Mostly pronounced ' kaulo,' but sometimes in the East Midlands
' kollo.'

And she wur gone! And then I read the words
In mornin twilight wot you rote to me;
They made the Christmas sing with summer birds,
And spring-leaves shine on every frozen tree;
And when the dawnin kindled Rington spire,
<small>red</small> And curdlin winter-clouds burnt gold and lollo
Round the dear sun, wot seemed a yolk o fire,
Another night, I sez, has brought him nigher;
He s comin wi the comin o the swallow.

And soon the bull-pups found me on the Pool
You know the way they barks to see me slide—
But when the skatin bors o Rington scool
Comed on, it turned my head to see em glide.
I seemed to see you twirlin on your skates,
And somethin made me clap my hans and hollo;
<small>cutting</small> It s him, I sez, achinnin o them 8s.
But when I woke-like—Im the gal wot waits
Alone, I sez, the comin o the swallow.

Comin seemed ringin in the Christmas-chime;
Comin seemed rit on everything I seed,
In beads o frost along the nets o rime,
Sparklin on every frozen rush and reed;
And when the pups began to bark and play,
And frisk and scrabble and bite my frock and wallow
Among the snow and fling it up like spray,
I says to them, You know who rote to say
He s comin wi the comin o the swallow.

The thought on t makes the snow-drifts o December
Shine gold, I sez, like daffodils o spring
Wot wait beneath: hes comin, pups, remember;
If not—for me no singin birds ull sing:
<small>cuckoo</small> No choring chiriklo ull hold the gale
Wi Cuckoo, cuckoo,[1] over hill and hollow:
Therell be no crakin o the meadow-rail,

---

[1] The gypsies are great observers of the cuckoo, and call certain spring winds 'cuckoo storms,' because they bring over the cuckoo earlier than usual.

Therell be no Jug-jug o the nightingale,
For her wot waits the comin o the swallow.

Come back, minaw, and you may kiss your han   mine own
To that fine rawni rowin on the river ;   lady
I ll never call that lady a chovihan   witch
Nor yit a mumply gorgie—I'll forgive her.   miserable Gentile
Come back, minaw : I wur to be your wife.
Come back—or, say the word, and I will follow
Your footfalls round the world : Ill leave this life
(Ive flung away a-ready that ere knife)
I m dyin for the comin o the swallow.

Percy returns to England and reaches Gypsy Dell at the very moment when ' the Schollard,' maddened by the discovery that Rhona is to meet Percy that night, has drawn his knife upon the girl under the starlight by the river-bank. Percy on one side of the river witnesses the death-struggle on the other side without being able to go to Rhona's assistance. But the girl hurls her antagonist into the water, and he is drowned. There are other witnesses—the stars, whose reflected light, according to a gypsy superstition, writes in the water, just above where the drowned man sank, mysterious runes, telling the story of the deed. For a Romany woman who marries a Gorgio the penalty is death. Nevertheless, Rhona marries Percy. I will quote the sonnets describing Rhona as she wakes in the tent at dawn :—

The young light peeps through yonder trembling chink
The tent's mouth makes in answer to a breeze ;
The rooks outside are stirring in the trees
Through which I see the deepening bars of pink.
I hear the earliest anvil's tingling clink
From Jasper's forge ; the cattle on the leas
Begin to low. She's waking by degrees :

Sleep's rosy fetters melt, but link by link.
What dream is hers ?   Her eyelids shake with tears ;
The fond eyes open now like flowers in dew :
She sobs I know not what of passionate fears :
" You'll never leave me now ?   There is but you ;
I dreamt a voice was whispering in my ears,
' The Dukkeripen o' stars comes ever true.' "

She rises, startled by a wandering bee
Buzzing around her brow to greet the girl :
She draws the tent wide open with a swirl,
And, as she stands to breathe the fragrancy
Beneath the branches of the hawthorn tree—
Whose dews fall on her head like beads of pearl,
Or drops of sunshine firing tress and curl
The Spirit of the Sunrise speaks to me,
And says, ' This bride of yours, I know her well,
And so do all the birds in all the bowers
Who mix their music with the breath of flowers
When greetings rise from river, heath and dell.
See, on the curtain of the morning haze
The Future's finger writes of happy days.'

Rhona, half-hidden by ' the branches of the hawthorn
tree,' stretches up to kiss the white and green May buds
overhanging the bridal tent, while Percy Aylwin stands
at the tent's mouth and looks at her :—

Can this be she, who, on that fateful day
    When Romany knives leapt out at me like stings
    Hurled back the men, who shrank like stricken things
From Rhona's eyes, whose lightnings seemed to slay ?
Can this be she, half-hidden in the may,
    Kissing the buds for ' luck o' love ' it brings,
    While from the dingle grass the skylark springs
And merle and mavis answer finch and jay ?

                    [He goes up to the hawthorn, pulls the branches
                      apart, and clasps her in his arms.

Can she here, covering with her childish kisses
   These pearly buds—can she so soft, so tender,
So shaped for clasping—dowered of all love-blisses
   Be my fierce girl whose love for me would send her,
An angel storming hell, through death's abysses,
   Where never a sight could fright or power could bend her ?

But Rhona is haunted by forebodings, and one night when the lovers are on the river she reads the scripture of the stars. I must give here the sonnet quoted on page 29 :—

The mirrored stars lit all the bulrush-spears,
   And all the flags and broad-leaved lily-isles ;
The ripples shook the stars to golden smiles,
   Then smoothed them back to happy golden spheres.
We rowed—we sang ; her voice seemed in mine ears
   An angel's, yet with woman's dearer wiles ;
But shadows fell from gathering cloudy piles
   And ripples shook the stars to fiery tears.

What shaped those shadows like another boat
   Where Rhona sat and he Love made a liar ?
There, where the Scollard sank, I saw it float,
   While ripples shook the stars to symbols dire ;
We wept—we kissed—while starry fingers wrote,
   And ripples shook the stars to a snake of fire.

The most tragically dramatic scene in the poem is that in which Percy confronts the cosmic mystery, defying its menace. The stars write in the river :—

Falsehold can never shield her : Truth is strong.

Percy reads the rune and answers ·—

I read your rune : is there no pity, then,
In Heav'n that wove this net of life for men ?
Have only Hell and Falsehood heart for ruth ?
Show me, ye mirrored stars, this tyrant Truth—
   King that can do no wrong !
Ah ! Night seems opening ! There, above the skies,

Who sits upon that central sun for throne
Round which a golden sand of worlds is strown,
Stretching right onward to an endless ocean,
Far, far away, of living, dazzling motion?
Hearken, King Truth, with pictures in thine eyes
Mirrored from gates beyond the furthest portal
Of infinite light, 'tis Love that stands immortal,
The King of Kings.

The gypsies read the starry rune, and, discovering
Rhona's secret, secretly slay her. Percy, having returned
to Gypsy Dell, vainly tries to find her grave. Then he
flies from the dingle, lest the memory of Rhona should
drive him mad, and lives alone in the Alps, where he passes
into the strange ecstasy, described in the sonnet called
'Natura Maligna,' which has been much discussed by
the critics :—

The Lady of the Hills with crimes untold
Followed my feet with azure eyes of prey;
By glacier-brink she stood—by cataract-spray—
When mists were dire, or avalanche-echoes rolled.
At night she glimmered in the death-wind cold,
And if a footprint shone at break of day,
My flesh would quail, but straight my soul would say:
''Tis hers whose hand God's mightier hand doth hold.'
I trod her snow-bridge, for the moon was bright,
Her icicle-arch across the sheer crevasse,
When lo, she stood! . . . God made her let me pass,
Then felled the bridge! . . . Oh, there in sallow light,
There down the chasm, I saw her cruel, white,
And all my wondrous days as in a glass.

This awful vision, quick with supernatural seership, is
unique in poetry. Sir George Birdwood, the orientalist,
wrote in the 'Athenæum' of February 5, 1881: "Even
in its very epithets it is just such a hymn as a Hindu
Puritan (Saivite) would address to Kali ('the malignant')

or Parvati ('the mountaineer'). It is to be delivered from her that Hindus shriek to God in the delirium of their fear."

Then we are shown Percy standing at midnight in front of his hut, while New Year's morning is breaking :—

Through Fate's mysterious warp another weft
   Of days is cast ; and see ! Time's star-built throne,
   From which he greets a new-born year, is shown
Between yon curtains where the clouds are cleft !
Old Year, while here I stand, with heart bereft
   Of all that was its music—stand alone,
   Remembering happy hours for ever flown,
Impatient of the leaden minutes left—

The plaudits of mankind that once gave pleasure,
   The chidings of mankind that once gave pain,
Seem in this hermit hut beyond all measure
   Barren and foolish, and I cry, ' No grain,
No grain, but winnowings in the harvest sieve ! '
And yet I cannot join the dead—and live.

Old Year, what bells are ringing in the New
   In England, heedless of the knells they ring
   To you and those whose sorrow makes you cling
Each to the other ere you say adieu !—
I seem to hear their chimes—the chimes we knew
   In those dear days when Rhona used to sing,
   Greeting a New Year's Day as bright of wing
As this whose pinions soon will rise to view.

If these dream-bells which come and mock mine ears
   Could bring the past and make it live again,
   Yea, live with every hour of grief and pain,
And hopes deferred and all the grievous fears—
   And with the past bring her I weep in vain—
Then would I bless them, though I blessed in tears.

             [The clouds move away and show the
               stars in dazzling brightness.

Those stars ! they set my rebel-pulses beating
   Against the tyrant Sorrow, him who drove

My footsteps from the Dell and haunted Grove—
They bring the mighty Mother's new-year greeting :
'All save great Nature is a vision fleeting'—
So says the scripture of those orbs above.
'All, all,' I cry, 'except man's dower of love !—
Love is no child of Nature's mystic cheating !'

And yet it comes again, the old desire
   To read what yonder constellations write
   On river and ocean—secrets of the night—
To feel again the spirit's wondering fire
   Which, ere this passion came, absorbed me quite,
To catch the master-note of Nature's lyre.

New Year, the stars do not forget the Old !
   And yet they say to me, most sorely stung
   By Fate and Death, 'Nature is ever young,
Clad in new riches, as each morning's gold
Blooms o'er a blasted land : be thou consoled :
   The Past was great, his harp was greatly strung ;
   The Past was great, his songs were greatly sung ;
The Past was great, his tales were greatly told ;

The Past has given to man a wondrous world,
But curtains of old Night were being upcurled
   Whilst thou wast mourning Rhona ; things sublime
In worlds of worlds were breaking on the sight
   Of Youth's fresh runners in the lists of Time.
Arise, and drink the wine of Nature's light !'

Finally, a dream prepares the sorrowing lover for the true reading of 'The Promise of the Sunrise' and the revelation of 'Natura Benigna' :—

Beneath the loveliest dream there coils a fear :
Last night came she whose eyes are memories now ;
Her far-off gaze seemed all forgetful how
Love dimmed them once, so calm they shone and clear.
'Sorrow,' I said, 'has made me old, my dear ;
'Tis I, indeed, but grief can change the brow
Beneath my load a seraph's neck might bow,

Vigils like mine would blanch an angel's hair.'
Oh, then I saw, I saw the sweet lips move!
I saw the love-mists thickening in her eyes
I heard a sound as if a murmuring dove
Felt lonely in the dells of Paradise;
But when upon my neck she fell, my love,
Her hair smelt sweet of whin and woodland spice.

And now 'Natura Benigna' reveals to him her mystic consolation :—

What power is this? What witchery wins my feet
To peaks so sheer they scorn the cloaking snow,
All silent as the emerald gulfs below,
Down whose ice-walls the wings of twilight beat?
What thrill of earth and heaven—most wild, most sweet—
What answering pulse that all the senses know,
Comes leaping from the ruddy eastern glow
Where, far away, the skies and mountains meet?
Mother, 'tis I, reborn: I know thee well:
That throb I know and all it prophesies,
O Mother and Queen, beneath the olden spell
Of silence, gazing from thy hills and skies!
Dumb Mother, struggling with the years to tell
The secret at thy heart through helpless eyes.

This is not the pathetic fallacy. It is the poetic interpretation of the latest discovery of science, to wit, that dead matter is alive, and that the universe is an infinite stammering and whispering, that may be heard only by the poet's finer ear.

The extracts I have given are sufficient to show the originality of Mr. Watts-Dunton's poetry, both in subject and in form. The originality of any poet is seen, not in fantastic metrical experiments, but rather in new and original treatment of the metres natural to the genius of the language. In 'The Coming of Love' the poet has invented a new poetic form. Its object is to combine

the advantages and to avoid the disadvantages of lyrical
narrative, of poetic drama, of the prose novel, and of
the prose play.   In Tennyson's 'Maud' and in Mr.
Watts-Dunton's other lyrical drama, " Christmas at the
' Mermaid,' " the special functions of all the above mentioned forms are knit together in a new form.   The
story is told by brief pictures.   In 'The Coming of
Love' this method reaches its perfection.   Lyrics, songs,
elegaic quatrains, and sonnets, are used according to an
inner law of the poet's mind.   The exaltation of these
moments is intensified by the business parts of the
narrative being summarized in bare prose.   The inter-
play of thought, mood, and passion is revealed wholly
by swift lyrical visions.   In Dante's ' Vita Nuova ' a
method something like this is adopted, but there the
links are in a kind of poetical prose akin to the verse,
and as Dante's poems are all sonnets, there is no har-
monic scheme of metrical music like that in ' The
Coming of Love.'   Here the very ' rhyme-colour '
and the subtle variety of vowel sounds from beginning
to end are evidently part of the metrical composition.
Wagner's music is the only modern art-form which is
comparable with the metrical architecture of 'The
Coming of Love,' and "Christmas at the 'Mermaid.'"   No
one can fully understand the rhythmic triumph of these
great poems who has not studied it by the light of Mr.
Watts-Dunton's theory of elaborate rhythmic effects in
music formulated in his treatise on Poetry in the ' Encyclopædia Britannica '—a theory which shows that
metrical and rhythmical art, as compared with the art
of music, is still developing.   Both these lyrical dramas
ought to be carefully studied by all students of English
metres.
   The novelty of these forms is not a fortuitous eccen-

tricity, but an extremely valuable experiment in a new kind of dramatic poetry. It is remarkable that in this new and difficult form the poet has achieved in Rhona Boswell a feat of characterization quite without parallel under such conditions. Rhona is so vivid that it is hardly fair to hang her portrait on the same wall as those of the ordinary heroines of poetry. But if, for the sake of comparison, Rhona be set beside Tennyson's Maud, the difference is startling. Maud does not tingle with personality. She is a type, an abstraction, a common denominator of 'creamy English girls.' Rhona, on the other hand, is nervously alive with personality. One makes pictures of her in one's brain—pictures that never become blurred, pictures that do not run into other pictures of other poetic heroines. How much of this is due to the poetic form ? Could Rhona have lived so intensely in a novel or a play ? I do not think so. At any rate, she lives with incomparable vitality in this lyrical drama-novel, and therefore the poetic vehicle in which she rushes upon our vision is well worth the study of critics and craftsmen. Mr. Kernahan has called attention to the baldness of the enlinking prose narrative. Perhaps this defect could be remedied by using a more poetic and more romantic prose like that of the opening of 'Aylwin,' which would lead the imagination insensibly from one situation or mood to another.

In connection with the opening sonnets of 'The Coming of Love,' a very interesting point of criticism presents itself. These sonnets, in which Mr. Watts-Dunton tells the story of the girl who lived in the Casket lighthouse, appeared in the 'Athenæum' a week after Mr. Swinburne and he returned from a visit to the Channel Islands. They record a real incident. Some time afterwards Mr. Swinburne published in the 'English Illustrated Magazine' his version of the story, a splendid specimen of his sonorous rhythms.

Mr. Watts-Dunton's version of the story may interest the reader :—

LOVE BRINGS WARNING OF NATURA MALIGNA

(THE POET SAILING WITH A FRIEND PAST THE CASKET LIGHTHOUSE)

Amid the Channel's wiles and deep decoys,
Where yonder Beacons watch the siren-sea,
A girl was reared who knew nor flower nor tree
Nor breath of grass at dawn, yet had high joys :
The moving lawns whose verdure never cloys
Were hers. At last she sailed to Alderney,
But there she pined. 'The bustling world,' said she,
'Is all too full of trouble, full of noise.'
The storm-child, fainting for her home, the storm,
Had winds for sponsor—one proud rock for nurse,
Whose granite arms, through countless years, disperse
All billowy squadrons tide and wind can form :
The cold bright sea was hers for universe
Till o'er the waves Love flew and fanned them warm.

But love brings Fear with eyes of augury :—
Her lover's boat was out ; her ears were dinned
With sea-sobs warning of the awakened wind
That shook the troubled sun's red canopy.
Even while she prayed the storm's high revelry
Woke petrel, gull—all revellers winged and finned
And clutched a sail brown-patched and weather-thinned,
And then a swimmer fought a white, wild sea.
'My songs are louder, child, than prayers of thine,'
The Mother sang. 'Thy sea-boy waged no strife
With Hatred's poison, gangrened Envy's knife—
With me he strove, in deadly sport divine,
Who lend to men, to gods, an hour of life,
Then give them sleep within these arms of mine ! '

Two poems more absolutely unlike could not be found in our literature than these poems on the same subject by two intimate friends. It seems impossible that the two writers could ever have read each other's work or ever have known each other well. The point which I wish to emphasize is that two poets or two literary men may be more intimate than brothers, they may live with each other constantly, they may meet each other every day, at luncheon, at dinner, they may spend a large portion of the evening in each other's society ; and yet when they sit down at their desks they may be as far asunder as the poles. From this we may perhaps infer that among the many imaginable divisions of writers there is this one : there are men who can collaborate and men who cannot.

Many well-known writers have expressed their ad-miration of this poem. I may mention that the other day I came across a little book called 'Authors that have Influenced me,' and found that Mr. Rider Haggard instanced the opening section of 'The Coming of Love,' 'Mother Carey's Chicken,' as being the piece of writing that had influenced him more than all others. I think this is a compliment, for the originality of invention displayed in 'King Solomon's Mines' and 'She' sets Rider Haggard apart among the story-tellers of our time, and I agree with Mr. Andrew Lang in thinking that the invention of a story that is new and also good is a rare achievement.

I can find no space to give as much attention as I should like to give to Mr. Watts-Dunton's miscellaneous sonnets. Some of them have had a great vogue : for instance, 'John the Pilgrim.' Like all Mr. Watts-Dunton's sonnets, it lends itself to illustration, and Mr. Arthur Hacker, A.R.A., as will be seen, has done

full justice to the imaginative strength of the subject.
It is no exaggeration to say that there is a simple grandeur in this design which Mr. Hacker has seldom
reached elsewhere, the sinister power of Natura Benigna
being symbolized by the desert waste and nature's
mockery by the mirage :—

> Beneath the sand-storm John the Pilgrim prays ;
>   But when he rises, lo ! an Eden smiles,
>   Green leafy slopes, meadows of chamomiles,
> Claspt in a silvery river's winding maze :
> ' Water, water !   Blessed be God ! ' he says,
>   And totters gasping toward those happy isles.
>   Then all is fled !   Over the sandy piles
> The bald-eyed vultures come and stand at gaze.
>
> ' God heard me not,' says he, ' blessed be God ! '
>   And dies.   But as he nears the pearly strand,
>   Heav'n's outer coast where waiting angels stand,
> He looks below : ' Farewell, thou hooded clod,
>   Brown corpse the vultures tear on bloody sand :
> God heard my prayer for life—blessed be God ! '

This sonnet is a miracle of verbal parsimony : it has
been called an epic in fourteen lines, yet its brevity does
not make it obscure, or gnarled, or affected ; and the
motive adumbrates the whole history of religious faith
from Job to Jesus Christ, from Moses to Mahomet.
The rhymes in this sonnet illustrate my own theory
as to the rhymer's luck, good and ill.   To have
written this little epic upon four rhymes would not
have been possible, even for Mr. Watts-Dunton, had
it not been for the luck of ' chamomiles ' and ' isles,'
' chamomiles ' giving the picture of the flowers, and
' isles ' giving the false vision of the mirage.   The same
thing is notable in the case of another amazing tour
de force, ' The Bedouin Child ' (see p. 448), where the

'John the Pilgrim': the Mirage in Egypt

same verbal parsimony is exemplified. Without the fortunate rhyme-words 'pashas,' 'camel-maws,' and 'claws' in the octave, the picture could not have been given in less than a dozen lines.

The kinship between Mr. Watts-Dunton's poetry and that of Coleridge has been frequently discussed. It has the same romantic glamour and often the same music, as far as the music of decasyllabic lines can call up the music of the ravishing octosyllabics of 'Christabel.' This at least I know, from his critical remarks on Coleridge,—he owns the true wizard of romance as master. I do not think that any one of his sonnets affords me quite the unmixed delight which I find in the sonnet on Coleridge, and his friend George Meredith is here in accord with me, for he wrote to the author as follows · 'The sonnet is pure amber for a piece of descriptive analogy that fits the poet wonderfully, and one might beat about through volumes of essays and not so paint him. There is Coleridge! But whence the source of your story—if anything of such aptness could have been other than dreamed after a draught of Xanadu —I cannot tell. It is new to me.'

After that flash of critical divination, it is fitting to present the reader with the 'pure amber' itself :—

> I see thee pine like her in golden story
> Who, in her prison, woke and saw, one day,
> The gates thrown open—saw the sunbeams play,
> With only a web 'tween her and summer's glory;
> Who, when that web—so frail, so transitory,
> It broke before her breath—had fallen away,
> Saw other webs and others rise for aye
> Which kept her prisoned till her hair was hoary.
>
> Those songs half-sung that yet were all divine—
> That woke Romance, the queen, to reign afresh—

Had been but preludes from that lyre of thine,
  Could thy rare spirit's wings have pierced the mesh
  Spun by the wizard who compels the flesh,
But lets the poet see how heav'n can shine.

Here again the verbal parsimony is notable. I defy any one to find anything like it except in Dante, the great master of verbal parsimony. There are only six adjectives in the whole sonnet. Every word is cunningly chosen, not for ornament, but solely for clarity of meaning. The metrical structure is subtly moulded so as to suspend the rising imagery until the last word of the octave, and then to let it glide, as a sunbeam glides down the air, to its lovely dying fall. Metrical students will delight in the double rhymes of the octave, which play so great a part in the suspensive music.

I have frequently thought that one of the most daring things, as well as one of the wisest, done by the editor of the 'Athenæum,' was that of printing Rhona's letters, bristling with Romany words, with a glossary at the foot of the page, and printing them without any of the context of the poem to shed light upon it and upon Rhona. It certainly showed immense confidence in his contributor to do that; and yet the poems were a great success. The best thing said about Rhona has been said by Mr. George Meredith · " I am in love with Rhona, not the only one in that. When I read her love-letter in the 'Athenæum,' I had the regret that the dialect might cause its banishment from literature. Reading the whole poem through, I see that it is as good as salt to a palate. We are the richer for it, and that is a rare thing to say of any poem now printed." And, discussing 'The Coming of Love,' Meredith wrote: 'I will not speak of the tours de force except to express a bit of astonishment at the dexterity which can perform them without immolating the tender spirit of the work.' Indeed, the technical mastery of Mr. Watts-Dunton's poetry is so consummate that it is concealed from the reader. There is no sense of difficulty overcome, no parade of artifice. Yet the metrical structure of the very poem which seems the simplest is actually the subtlest. 'Rhona's Love Letter' is written in an extremely complex rhyme-pattern, each stanza of eight lines being built on two rhymes, like the octave of a sonnet. But so cunningly are the Romany words woven into a naïve, unconscious charm that the reader forgets the rhyme-scheme altogether, and does not realize that this spontaneous sweetness and bubbling humour are produced by the most elaborate art.

I have emphasized the originality of Mr. Watts-Dunton's poetry. There can be no doubt that he is the most original poet since Coleridge, not merely in verbal, metrical, and rhythmical idiosyncrasy, but in the deeper quality of imaginative energy. By 'the most original poet' I do not mean the greatest poet : the student of poetry will know at once what I mean. Poe's 'Raven' is more 'original' than Shelley's 'Epipsychidion,' but it is not so great. In my article on Blake in Chambers's 'Cyclopædia of English Literature,' I pointed out that there are greater poets than Blake (or Donne) but none more original. There are many poets who possess that ordinary kind of imagination which is mainly a perpetual matching of common ideas with common metaphors. But few poets have the rarer kind of imagination which creates not only the metaphor but also the idea, and then fuses both into one piece of beauty. Now Mr. Watts-Dunton has this supreme gift. He uses the symbol to suggest ideas which cannot be suggested otherwise. His theory of the universe is optimistic, but his optimism is interwoven with sombre threads. He sees the dualism of Nature, and he shows her alternately as malignant and as benignant. Indeed, he has concentrated his spiritual cosmogony into the two great sonnets, 'Natura Maligna' and 'Natura Benigna,' which I have already quoted.

All the critics were delighted with the humour of Rhona Boswell. Upon this subject Mr. Watts-Dunton makes some pregnant remarks in the introduction to the later editions of the poem :—

" But it is with regard to the humour of gypsy women that Gorgio readers seem to be most sceptical. The humourous endowment of most races is found to be more abundant and richer in quality among the men than among the women. But among the Romanies the women seem to have taken humour with the rest of the higher qualities.

A question that has been most frequently asked me in connection with my two gypsy heroines has been : Have gypsy girls really the esprit and the humourous charm that you attribute to them ? My answer to this question shall be a quotation from Mr. Groome's delightful book, 'Gypsy Folk-Tales.' Speaking of the Romany chi's incomparable piquancy, he says :—

'I have known a gypsy girl dash off what was almost a folk-tale impromptu. She had been to a pic-nic in a four-in-hand with " a lot o' real tip-top gentry "; and " Reia," she said to me afterwards, " I'll tell you the comicalest thing as ever was. We'd pulled up to put the brake on, and there was a púro hotchiwitchi (old hedgehog) come and looked at us through the hedge ; looked at me hard. I could see he'd his eye upon me. And home he'd go, that old hedgehog, to his wife, and 'Missus,' he'd say, ' what d'ye think ? I seen a little gypsy gal just now in a coach and four horses ' ; and ' Dabla,' she'd say, ' sawkumni 'as varde kenaw ' " [' Bless us ! every one now keeps a carriage '].'

Now, without saying that this impromptu folk-lorist was Rhona' Boswell, I will at least aver, without fear of contradiction from Mr. Groome, that it might well have been she. Although there is as great a difference between one Romany chi and another as between one English girl and another, there is a strange and fascinating kinship between the humour of all gypsy girls. No three girls could possibly be more unlike than Sinfi Lovell, Rhona Boswell, and the girl of whom Mr. Groome gives his anecdote ; and yet there is a similarity between the fanciful humour of them all. The humour of Rhona Boswell must speak for itself in these pages—where, however, the passionate and tragic side of her character and her story dominates everything."

Chapter XXVII

" CHRISTMAS AT THE ' MERMAID ' "

SECOND in importance to ' The Coming of Love ' among Mr. Watts-Dunton's poems is the poem I have already mentioned — the poem which Mr. Swinburne has described as ' a great lyrical epic '—" Christmas at the ' Mermaid.' " The originality of this wonderful poem is quite as striking as that of ' The Coming of Love.' No other writer would have dreamed of depicting the doomed Armada as being led to destruction by a golden skeleton in the form of one of the burnt Incas, called up by ' the righteous sea,' and squatting grimly at the prow of Medina's flag-ship. Here we get ' The Renascence of Wonder ' indeed. Some Aylwinians put it at the head of all his writings. The exploit of David Gwynn is accepted by Motley and others as historic, but it needed the co-operation of the Golden Skeleton to lift his narrative into the highest heaven of poetry. Extremely unlike ' The Coming of Love ' as it is in construction, it is built on the same metrical scheme ; and it illustrates equally well with ' The Coming of Love ' the remarks I have made upon a desideratum in poetic art—that is to say, it is cast in a form which gives as much scope to the dramatic instinct at work as is given by a play, and yet it is a form free from the restrictions by which a play must necessarily be cramped. The poem was written, or mainly written, during one of those visits which, as I have already said, Mr. Watts-Dunton used to pay to Stratford-on-Avon. The scene is laid, however, in London, at that famous 'Mermaid' tavern which haunts the dreams of all English poets :—

"With the exception of Shakespeare, who has quitted London for good, in order to reside at New Place, Stratford-on-Avon, which he has lately rebuilt, all the members of the 'Mermaid' Club are assembled at the 'Mermaid' Tavern. At the head of the table sits Ben Jonson dealing out wassail from a large bowl. At the other end sits Raleigh, and at Raleigh's right hand, the guest he had brought with him, a stranger, David Gwynn, the Welsh seaman, now an elderly man, whose story of his exploits as a galley-slave in crippling the Armada before it reached the Channel had, years before, whether true or false, given him in the low countries a great reputation, the echo of which had reached England. Raleigh's desire was to excite the public enthusiasm for continuing the struggle with Spain on the sea, and generally to revive the fine Elizabethan temper, which had already become almost a thing of the past, save, perhaps, among such choice spirits as those associated with the 'Mermaid' club."

It opens with a chorus ·—

> Christmas knows a merry, merry place,
> Where he goes with fondest face,
>   Brightest eye, brightest hair ·
> Tell the Mermaid where is that one place :
>   Where ?

Then Ben Jonson rises, fills the cup with wassail and drinks to Shakespeare, and thus comments upon his absence :—

That he, the star of revel, bright-eyed Will,
With life at golden summit, fled the town
And took from Thames that light to dwindle down
O'er Stratford farms, doth make me marvel still.

Then he calls upon Shakespeare's most intimate friend
—the mysterious Mr. W. H. of the sonnets—to give
them reminiscences of Shakespeare with a special reference to the memorable evening when he arrived at Stratford on quitting London for good and all.

To the sixth edition of the poem Mr. Watts-Dunton
prefixed the following remarks, and I give them here
because they throw light upon his view of Shakespeare's
friend :—

" Since the appearance of this volume, there has been
a great deal of acute and learned discussion as to the
identity of that mysterious 'friend' of Shakespeare, to
whom so many of the sonnets are addressed.   But everything that has been said upon the subject seems to fortify
me in the opinion that ' no critic has been able to identify ' that friend.   Southampton seems at first to fit
into the sacred place ; so does Pembroke at first.   But,
after a while, true and unbiassed criticism rejects them
both.   I therefore feel more than ever justified in ' ima-
gining the friend for myself.'   And this, at least, I know,
that to have been the friend of Shakespeare, a man must
needs have been a lover of nature ;—he must have been
a lover of England, too.   And upon these two points, and
upon another—the movement of a soul dominated by
friendship as a passion—I have tried to show Shakespeare's probable influence upon his ' friend of friends.'
It would have been a mistake, however, to cast the sonnets
in the same metrical mould as Shakespeare's."

Shakspeare's friend thus records what Shakespeare had told him about his return to Stratford :—

As down the bank he strolled through evening dew,
Pictures (he told me) of remembered eves
Mixt with that dream the Avon ever weaves,
And all his happy childhood came to view;
He saw a child watching the birds that flew
Above a willow, through whose musky leaves
A green musk-beetle shone with mail and greaves
That shifted in the light to bronze and blue.
These dreams, said he, were born of fragrance falling
From trees he loved, the scent of musk recalling,
With power beyond all power of things beholden
Or things reheard, those days when elves of dusk
Came, veiled the wings of evening feathered golden,
And closed him in from all but willow musk.

And then a child beneath a silver sallow—
A child who loved the swans, the moorhen's 'cheep'
Angled for bream where river holes were deep—
For gudgeon where the water glittered shallow,
Or ate the 'fairy cheeses' of the mallow,
And wild fruits gathered where the wavelets creep
Round that loved church whose shadow seems to sleep
In love upon the stream and bless and hallow;
And then a child to whom the water-fairies
Sent fish to 'bite' from Avon's holes and shelves,
A child to whom, from richest honey-dairies,
The flower-sprites sent the bees and 'sunshine elves';
Then, in the shifting vision's sweet vagaries,
He saw two lovers walking by themselves—

Walking beneath the trees, where drops of rain
Wove crowns of sunlit opal to decoy
Young love from home; and one, the happy boy,
Knew all the thoughts of birds in every strain
Knew why the cushat breaks his fond refrain
By sudden silence, 'lest his plaint should cloy'—
Knew when the skylark's changing note of joy

Saith, ' Now will I return to earth again '—
Knew every warning of the blackbird's shriek,
And every promise of his joyful song—
Knew what the magpie's chuckle fain would speak ;
And, when a silent cuckoo flew along,
Bearing an egg in her felonious beak,
Knew every nest threatened with grievous wrong.
He heard her say, ' The birds attest our troth ! '
Hark to the mavis, Will, in yonder may
Fringing the sward, where many a hawthorn spray
Round summer's royal field of golden cloth
Shines o'er the buttercups like snowy froth,
And that sweet skylark on his azure way,
And that wise cuckoo, hark to what they say :
' We birds of Avon heard and bless you both.'
And, Will, the sunrise, flushing with its glory,
River and church, grows rosier with our story !
This breeze of morn, sweetheart, which moves caressing,
Hath told the flowers ; they wake to lovelier growth !
They breathe—o'er mead and stream they breathe—the blessing.
' We flowers of Avon heard and bless you both ! '

When Mr. ' W. H.' sits down, the friend and brother
of another great poet, Christopher Marlowe, who had
been sitting moody and silent, oppressed by thoughts
of the dead man, many of whose unfriends were at the
gathering, recites these lines ' On Seeing Kit Marlowe
Slain at Deptford ' ·—

'Tis Marlowe falls !   That last lunge rent asunder
Our lyre of spirit and flesh, Kit Marlowe's life,
Whose chords seemed strung by earth and heaven at strife,
Yet ever strung to beauty above or under !
Heav'n kens of Man, but oh ! the stars can blunder,
If Fate's hand guided yonder villain's knife
Through that rare brain, so teeming, daring, rife
With dower of poets—song and love and wonder.
Or was it Chance ?   Shakspeare, who art supreme
O'er man and men, yet sharest Marlowe's sight

To pierce the clouds that hide the inhuman height
Where man and men and gods and all that seem
Are Nature's mutterings in her changeful dream—
Come, spell the runes these bloody rivulets write!

After they have all drunk in silence to the memory of
Marlowe, Marlowe's friend speaks :—

Where'er thou art, ' dead Shepherd,' look on me ;
  The boy who loved thee loves more dearly now,
  He sees thine eyes in yonder holly-bough ;
Oh, Kit, my Kit, the Mermaid drinks to thee !

Then Raleigh rises, and the great business of the evening begins with the following splendid chorus :—

RALEIGH

(Turning to David Gwynn)

Wherever billows foam
The Briton fights at home :
His hearth is built of water—

CHORUS

Water blue and green ;

RALEIGH

There's never a wave of ocean
The wind can set in motion
That shall not own our England

CHORUS

Own our England queen.[1]

RALEIGH

The guest I bring to-night
Had many a goodly fight
On seas the Don hath found

[1] 'England is a country that can never be conquered while the
Sovereign thereof has the command of the sea.'—RALEIGH.

CHORUS

Hath found for English sails ;

RALEIGH

And once he dealt a blow
Against the Don to show
What mighty hearts can move—

CHORUS

Can move in leafy Wales.

RALEIGH

Stand up, bold Master Gwynn,
Who hast a heart akin
To England's own brave hearts—

CHORUS

Brave hearts where'er they beat ;

RALEIGH

Stand up, brave Welshman, thou,
And tell the Mermaid how
A galley-slave struck hard—

CHORUS

Struck hard the Spanish fleet.

Christmas knows a merry, merry place,
Where he goes with fondest face,
Brightest eye, brightest hair :
Tell the Mermaid where is that one place :
Where ?

Upon being thus called forth the old sea-dog rises, and
tells a wonderful story indeed, the ' story of how he and
the Golden Skeleton crippled the Great Armada sailing
out ' ·—

' A galley lie ' they called my tale ; but he
Whose talk is with the deep kens mighty tales :
The man, I say, who helped to keep you free

Stands here, a truthful son of truthful Wales.
Slandered by England as a loose-lipped liar,
  Banished from Ireland, branded rogue and thief,
Here stands that Gwynn whose life of torments dire
Heaven sealed for England, sealed in blood and fire—
  Stands asking here Truth's one reward, belief!

And Spain shall tell, with pallid lips of dread,
  This tale of mine—shall tell, in future days,
How Gwynn, the galley-slave, once fought and bled
  For England when she moved in perilous ways;
But say, ye gentlemen of England, sprung
  From loins of men whose ghosts have still the sea
Doth England—she who loves the loudest tongue—
Remember mariners whose deeds are sung
  By waves where flowed their blood to keep her free ?

I see—I see ev'n now—those ships of Spain
  Gathered in Tagus' mouth to make the spring;
I feel the cursed oar, I toil again,
  And trumpets blare, and priests and choir-boys sing;
And morning strikes with many a crimson shaft,
  Through ruddy haze, four galleys rowing out—
Four galleys built to pierce the English craft,
Each swivel-gunned for raking fore and aft,
  Snouted like sword-fish, but with iron snout.

And one we call the ' Princess,' one the ' Royal,'
  ' Diana ' one ; but 'tis the fell ' Basana '
Where I am toiling, Gwynn, the true, the loyal,
  Thinking of mighty Drake and Gloriana ;
For by their help Hope whispers me that I—
  Whom ten hours' daily travail at a stretch
Has taught how sweet a thing it is to die—
May strike once more where flags of England fly,
  Strike for myself and many a haggard wretch.

True sorrow knows a tale it may not tell :
  Again I feel the lash that tears my back ;
Again I hear mine own blaspheming yell,
  Answered by boatswain's laugh and scourge's crack ;
Again I feel the pang when trying to choke

Rather than drink the wine, or chew the bread
Wherewith, when rest for meals would break the stroke,
They cram our mouths while still we sit at yoke;
Again is Life, not Death, the shape of dread.

By Finisterre there comes a sudden gale,
And mighty waves assault our trembling galley
With blows that strike her waist as strikes a flail,
And soldiers cry, ' What saint shall bid her rally ? '
Some slaves refuse to row, and some implore
The Dons to free them from the metal tether
By which their limbs are locked upon the oar;
Some shout, in answer to the billows' roar,
' The Dons and we will drink brine-wine together.'

' Bring up the slave,' I hear the captain cry,
' Who sank the golden galleon " El Dorado,"
The dog can steer.'
                    ' Here sits the dog,' quoth I,
' Who sank the ship of Commodore Medrado ! '
With hell-lit eyes, blistered by spray and rain,
Standing upon the bridge, saith he to me:
' Hearken, thou pirate—bold Medrado's bane !—
Freedom and gold are thine, and thanks of Spain,
If thou canst take the galley through this sea.'

' Ay ! ay ! ' quoth I. The fools unlock me straight !
And then 'tis I give orders to the Don,
Laughing within to hear the laugh of Fate,
Whose winning game I know hath just begun.
I mount the bridge when dies the last red streak
Of evening, and the moon seems fain for night
Oh then I see beneath the galley's beak
A glow like Spanish *auto's* ruddy reek—
Oh then these eyes behold a wondrous sight !

A skeleton, but yet with living eyes—
A skeleton, but yet with bones like gold—
Squats on the galley-beak, in wondrous wise,
And round his brow, of high imperial mould,
A burning circle seems to shake and shine,

Bright, fiery bright, with many a living gem,
Throwing a radiance o'er the foam-lit brine:
  'Tis God's Revenge,' methinks. 'Heaven sends for sign
  That bony shape—that Inca's diadem.'

At first the sign is only seen of me,
  But well I know that God's Revenge hath come
To strike the Armada, set old ocean free,
  And cleanse from stain of Spain the beauteous foam.
Quoth I, ' How fierce soever be the levin
  Spain's hand can hurl—made mightier still for wrong
By that great Scarlet One whose hills are seven
Yea, howsoever Hell may scoff at Heaven—
  Stronger than Hell is God, though Hell is strong.'

' The dog can steer,' I laugh ; ' yea, Drake's men know
  How sea-dogs hold a ship to Biscay waves.'
Ah ! when I bid the soldiers go below,
  Some 'neath the hatches, some beside the slaves,
And bid them stack their muskets all in piles
  Beside the foremast, covered by a sail,
The captives guess my plan—I see their smiles ı
As down the waist the cozened troop defiles,
  Staggering and stumbling landsmen, faint and pale.

I say, they guess my plan—to send beneath
  The soldiers to the benches where the slaves
Sit, armed with eager nails and eager teeth—
  Hate's nails and teeth more keen than Spanish glaives,
Then wait until the tempest's waxing might
  Shall reach its fiercest, mingling sea and sky,
Then seize the key, unlock the slaves, and smite
The sea-sick soldiers in their helpless plight,
  Then bid the Spaniards pull at oar or die.

Past Ferrol Bay each galley 'gins to stoop,
  Shuddering before the Biscay demon's breath.
Down goes a prow—down goes a gaudy poop:
  ' The Don's " Diana " bears the Don to death,'
Quoth I, ' and see the " Princess " plunge and wallow
  Down purple trough, o'er snowy crest of foam :

See ! see ! the " Royal," how she tries to follow
By many a glimmering crest and shimmering hollow,
   Where gull and petrel scarcely dare to roam.'

Now, three queen-galleys pass Cape Finisterre ;
   The Armada, dreaming but of ocean-storms,
Thinks not of mutineers with shoulders bare,
   Chained, bloody-wealed and pale, on galley-forms,
Each rower murmuring o'er my whispered plan,
   Deep-burnt within his brain in words of fire,
' Rise, every man, to tear to death his man—
Yea, tear as only galley-captives can,
   When God's Revenge sings loud to ocean's lyre.'

Taller the spectre grows 'mid ocean's din ;
   The captain sees the Skeleton and pales :
I give the sign : the slaves cry, ' Ho for Gwynn ! '
   ' Teach them,' quoth I, ' the way we grip in Wales.'
And, leaping down where hateful boatswains shake,
   I win the key—let loose a storm of slaves :
' When captives hold the whip, let drivers quake,'
They cry ; ' sit down, ye Dons, and row for Drake,
   Or drink to England's Queen in foaming waves.'

We leap adown the hatches ; in the dark
   We stab the Dons at random, till I see
A spark that trembles like a tinder-spark,
   Waxing and brightening, till it seems to be
A fleshless skull, with eyes of joyful fire :
   Then, lo : a bony shape with lifted hands—
A bony mouth that chants an anthem dire,
O'ertopping groans, o'ertopping Ocean's quire—
   A skeleton with Inca's diadem stands !

It sings the song I heard an Indian sing,
   Chained by the ruthless Dons to burn at stake,
When priests of Tophet chanted in a ring,
   Sniffing man's flesh at roast for Christ His sake.
The Spaniards hear : they see : they fight no more ;
   They cross their foreheads, but they dare not speak.
Anon the spectre, when the strife is o'er,

Melts from the dark, then glimmers as before,
　Burning upon the conquered galley's beak.

And now the moon breaks through the night, and shows
　The 'Royal' bearing down upon our craft—
Then comes a broadside close at hand, which strows
　Our deck with bleeding bodies fore and aft.
I take the helm; I put the galley near:
　We grapple in silver sheen of moonlit surge.
Amid the 'Royal's' din I laugh to hear
The curse of many a British mutineer,
　The crack, crack, crack of boatswain's biting scourge.

' Ye scourge in vain,' quoth I, ' scourging for life
　Slaves who shall row no more to save the Don ' ;
For from the 'Royal's' poop, above the strife,
　Their captain gazes at our Skeleton !
' What ! is it thou, Pirate of " El Dorado " ? '
　He shouts in English tongue.　And there, behold !
Stands he, the devil's commodore, Medrado.
' Ay ! ay ! ' quoth I, ' Spain owes me one strappado
　For scuttling Philip's ship of stolen gold.'

' I come for that strappado now,' quoth I.
　' What means yon thing of burning bones ? ' he saith.
' 'Tis God's Revenge cries, " Bloody Spain shall die ! "
　The king of El Dorado's name is Death.
Strike home, ye slaves ; your hour is coming swift,'
　I cry ; ' strong hands are stretched to save you now ;
Show yonder spectre you are worth the gift.'
But when the ' Royal,' captured, rides adrift,
　I look : the skeleton hath left our prow.

When all are slain, the tempest's wings have fled,
　But still the sea is dreaming of the storm :
Far down the offing glows a spot of red,
　My soul knows well it hath that Inca's form.
' It lights,' quoth I, ' the red cross banner of Spain
　There on the flagship where Medina sleeps—
Hell's banner, wet with sweat of Indian's pain,
And tears of women yoked to treasure train,
　Scarlet of blood for which the New World weeps.'

There on the dark the flagship of the Don
 To me seems luminous of the spectre's glow ;
But soon an arc of gold, and then the sun,
 Rise o'er the reddening billows, proud and slow ;
Then, through the curtains of the morning mist,
 That take all shifting colours as they shake,
I see the great Armada coil and twist
Miles, miles along the ocean's amethyst,
 Like hell's old snake of hate—the winged snake.

And, when the hazy veils of Morn are thinned,
 That snake accursed, with wings which swell and puff
Before the slackening horses of the wind,
 Turns into shining ships that tack and luff.
' Behold,' quoth I, ' their floating citadels,
 The same the priests have vouched for musket-proof,
Caracks and hulks and nimble caravels,
That sailed with us to sound of Lisbon bells—
 Yea, sailed from Tagus' mouth, for Christ's behoof.

For Christ's behoof they sailed : see how they go
 With that red skeleton to show the way
There sitting on Medina's stem aglow—
 A hundred sail and forty-nine, men say ;
Behold them, brothers, galleon and galeasse—
 Their dizened turrets bright of many a plume,
Their gilded poops, their shining guns of brass,
Their trucks, their flags—behold them, how they pass—
 With God's Revenge for figurehead—to Doom ! '

Then Ben Jonson, the symposiarch, rises and calls
upon Raleigh to tell the story of the defeat of the Great
Armada. I can give only a stanza or two and the
chorus ·—

RALEIGH

 The choirboys sing the matin song,
  When down falls Seymour on the Spaniard's right.
 He drives the wing—a huddled throng—
  Back on the centre ships, that steer for flight.

While galleon hurtles galeasse,
And oars that fight each other kill the slaves,
   As scythes cut down the summer grass,
   Drake closes on the writhing mass,
Through which the balls at closest ranges pass,
         Skimming the waves.

Fiercely do galley and galeasse fight,
Running from ship to ship like living things.
   With oars like legs, with beaks that smite,
Winged centipedes they seem with tattered wings.
   Through smoke we see their chiefs encased
In shining mail of gold where blood congeals ;
   And once I see within a waist
   Wild English captives ashen-faced,
Their bending backs by Spanish scourges laced
         In purple weals.

> [DAVID GWYNN here leaps up, pale and panting, and
> bares a scarred arm, but at a sign from RALEIGH
> sits down again.

. The Don fights well, but fights not now
The cozened Indian whom he kissed for friend,
   To pluck the gold from off the brow,
Then fling the flesh to priests to burn and rend.
   He hunts not now the Indian maid
With bloodhound's bay—Peru's confiding daughter,
   Who saw in flowery bower or glade
   The stranger's god-like cavalcade,
And worshipped, while he planned Pizarro's trade
         Of rape and slaughter.

His fight is now with Drake and Wynter,
Hawkins, and Frobisher, and English fire,
   Bullet and cannon ball and splinter,
Till every deck gleams, greased with bloody mire :
   Heaven smiles to see that battle wage,
Close battle of musket, carabine, and gun :
   Oh, vainly doth the Spaniard rage
   Like any wolf that tears his cage !
'Tis English sails shall win the weather gauge
         Till set of sun !

Their troops, superfluous as their gold,
Out-numbering all their seamen two to one,
    Are packed away in every hold—
Targets of flesh for every English gun—
    Till, like Pizarro's halls of blood,
Or slaughter-pens where swine or beeves are pinned,
    Lee-scuppers pour a crimson flood,
    Reddening the waves for many a rood,
As eastward, eastward still the galleons scud
        Before the wind.

The chief leit-motiv of the poem is the metrical idea
that whenever a stanza ends with the word ' sea,' Ben
Jonson and the rest of the jolly companions break into this superb chorus :—

        The sea !
    Thus did England fight ;
    And shall not England smite
With Drake's strong stroke in battles yet to be ?
    And while the winds have power
    Shall England lose the dower
    She won in that great hour—
        The sea ?

Raleigh leaves off his narrative at the point when the
Armada is driven out to the open sea.   He sits down, and
Gwynn, worked into a frenzy of excitement, now starts
up and finishes the story in the same metre, but in quite
a different spirit.   In Gwynn's fevered imagination
the skeleton which he describes in his own narrative now
leads the doomed Armada to its destruction ·—

        GWYNN
    With towering sterns, with golden stems
    That totter in the smoke before their foe,
        I see them pass the mouth of Thames,
    With death above the billows, death below !
    Who leads them down the tempest's path,

From Thames to Yare, from Yare to Tweedmouth blown,
    Past many a Scottish hill and strath,
    All helpless in the wild wind's wrath,
Each mainmast stooping, creaking like a lath ?
        The Skeleton !

At length with toil the cape is passed,
And faster and faster still the billows come
    To coil and boil till every mast
Is flecked with clinging flakes of snowy foam.
    I see, I see, where galleons pitch,
That Inca's bony shape burn on the waves,
    Flushing each emerald scarp and ditch,
    While Mother Carey, Orkney's witch,
Waves to the Spectre's song her lantern-switch
        O'er ocean-graves.

    The glimmering crown of Scotland's head
They pass. No foe dares follow but the storm.
    The Spectre, like a sunset red,
Illumines mighty Wrath's defiant form,
    And makes the dreadful granite peak
Burn o'er the ships with brows of prophecy ;
    Yea, makes that silent countenance speak
    Above the tempest's foam and reek,
More loud than all the loudest winds that shriek,
        ' Tyrants, ye die ! '

    The Spectre, by the Orkney Isles,
Writes ' God's Revenge ' on waves that climb and dash,
    Foaming right up the sand-built piles,
Where ships are hurled. It sings amid the crash ;
    Yea, sings amid the tempest's roar,
Snapping of ropes, crackling of spars set free,
    And yells of captives chained to oar,
    And cries of those who strike for shore,
' Spain's murderous breath of blood shall foul no more
        The righteous sea ! '

The poem ends with the famous wassail chorus which
has been often quoted in anthologies :—

WASSAIL CHORUS

CHORUS

Christmas knows a merry, merry place,
Where he goes with fondest face,
  Brightest eye, brightest hair ·
Tell the Mermaid where is that one place :
  Where ?

RALEIGH

'Tis by Devon's glorious halls,
  Whence, dear Ben, I come again :
Bright with golden roofs and walls—
  El Dorado's rare domain—
Seem those halls when sunlight launches
Shafts of gold through leafless branches,
Where the winter's feathery mantle blanches
  Field and farm and lane.

CHORUS

Christmas knows a merry, merry place,
Where he goes with fondest face,
  Brightest eye, brightest hair :
Tell the Mermaid where is that one place :
  Where ?

DRAYTON

'Tis where Avon's wood-sprites weave
  Through the boughs a lace of rime,
While the bells of Christmas Eve
  Fling for Will the Stratford-chime
O'er the river-flags embossed
Rich with flowery runes of frost—
O'er the meads where snowy tufts are tossed
  Strains of olden time.

CHORUS

Christmas knows a merry, merry place,
Where he goes with fondest face,
  Brightest eye, brightest hair :
Tell the Mermaid where is that one place :
  Where ?

SHAKSPEARE'S FRIEND

'Tis, methinks, on any ground
   Where our Shakspeare's feet are set.
There smiles Christmas, holly-crowned
   With his blithest coronet:
Friendship's face he loveth well ·
'Tis a countenance whose spell
Sheds a balm o'er every mead and dell
   Where we used to fret.

CHORUS

Christmas knows a merry, merry place,
   Where he goes with fondest face,
   Brightest eye, brightest hair ·
Tell the Mermaid where is that one place
   Where ?

HEYWOOD

More than all the pictures, Ben,
   Winter weaves by wood or stream,
Christmas loves our London, when
   Rise thy clouds of wassail-steam—
Clouds like these, that, curling, take
Forms of faces gone, and wake
Many a lay from lips we loved, and make
   London like a dream.

CHORUS

Christmas knows a merry, merry place,
   Where he goes with fondest face,
   Brightest eye, brightest hair ·
Tell the Mermaid where is that one place:
   Where ?

BEN JONSON

Love's old songs shall never die,
   Yet the new shall suffer proof;
Love's old drink of Yule brew I,
   Wassail for new love's behoof:
Drink the drink I brew, and sing

Till the berried branches swing,
Till our song make all the Mermaid ring—
Yea, from rush to roof.

FINALE

Christmas loves this merry, merry place :—
Christmas saith with fondest face
Brightest eye, brightest hair ·
Ben ! the drink tastes rare of sack and mace :
Rare ! '

This poem, when it first appeared in the volume of
' The Coming of Love,' fine as it is, was overshadowed
by the wild and romantic poem which lends its name to
the volume. But in 1902, Mr. John Lane included it
in his beautiful series, ' Flowers of Parnassus,' where it
was charmingly illustrated by Mr. Herbert Cole, and this
widened its vogue considerably. There is no doubt
that for originality, for power, and for music, " Christmas at the ' Mermaid ' " is enough to form the base
of any poet's reputation.   It has been enthusiastically
praised by some of the foremost writers of our time. I
have permission to print only one of the letters in its
praise which the author received, but that is an important one, as it comes from Thomas Hardy, who wrote :—

" I have been beginning Christmas, in a way, by reading
over the fire your delightful little ' Christmas at the
" Mermaid " ' which it was most kind of you to send. I
was carried back right into Armada times by David
Gwynn's vivid story : it seems remarkable that you should
have had the conjuring power to raise up those old years
so brightly in your own mind first, as to be able to
exhibit them to readers in such high relief of three
dimensions, as one may say.

The absence of Shakespeare strikes me as being one of the finest touches of the poem it throws one into a ' humourous melancholy '—and we feel him, in some curious way, more than if he had been there."

Chapter XXVIII

CONCLUSION

' ASSUREDLY,' says] Mr. Watts-Dunton, in his essay on Thoreau, ' there is no profession so courageons as that of the pen.' Well, in coming to the end of my task—a task which has been a labour of love—I wish I could feel confident that I have not been too courageous —that I have satisfactorily done what I set out to do. But I have passed my four-hundred and fortieth page, and yet I seem to have let down only a child's bucket into a sea of ideas that has no limit. Out of scores upon scores of articles buried in many periodicals I have been able to give three or four from the ' Athenæum,' none from the ' Examiner,' and none out of the ' Nineteenth Century,' 'The Fortnightly Review,' ' Harper's Magazine,' etc. Still, I have been able to show that a large proportion of Mr. Watts-Dunton's scattered writings preaches the same peculiar doctrine in a ratiocinative form which in ' Aylwin ' and ' The Coming of Love ' is artistically enunciated ; that this doctrine is of the greatest importance at the present time, when science seems to be revealing a system of the universe so deeply opposed to the system which in the middle of the last century seemed to be revealed ; and that this doctrine of Mr. Watts-Dunton's is making a very deep impression upon the generation to which I belong. If it should be said that in speaking for the younger generation I am speaking for a pigmy race (and I sometimes fear that we are pigmies when I remember the stature of our fathers), I am content to appeal to one of the older generation, who has spoken words in praise of Mr. Watts-Dunton as a poet, which would demand even my courage to echo. I mean Dr. Gordon Hake, whose volume of sonnets, entitled, 'The New Day,' was published in 1890. It was these remarkable sonnets which moved Frank Groome to dub Mr. Watts-Dunton 'homo ne quidem unius libri,' a literary celebrity who had not published a single book. I have already referred to 'The New Day,' but I have not given an adequate account of this sonnet-sequence. In their nobility of spirit, their exalted passion of friendship, their single-souled purity of loyal-hearted love, I do not think they have ever been surpassed. It is a fine proof of Mr. Watts-Dunton's genius for friendship that he should be able unconsciously to enlink himself to the souls of his seniors, his coevals and his juniors, and that there should be between him and the men of three generations, equal links of equal affection. But I must not lay stress on the whimsies of chronology and the humours of the calendar, for all Mr. Watts-Dunton's friends are young, and the youngest of them, Mr. George Meredith, is the oldest. The youthfulness of 'The New Day' makes it hard to believe that it was written by a septuagenarian. The dedication is full of the fine candour of a romantic boy :—

"To 'W. T. W.,' the friend who has gone with me through the study of Nature, accompanied me to her loveliest places at home and in other lands, and shared with me the reward she reserves for her ministers and interpreters, I dedicate this book."

The following sonnet on 'Friendship' expresses a very rare mood and a very high ideal :—

Friendship is love's full beauty unalloyed
  With passion that may waste in selfishness,
Fed only at the heart and never cloyed :
  Such is our friendship ripened but to bless.
It draws the arrow from the bleeding wound
  With cheery look that makes a winter bright ;
It saves the hope from falling to the ground,
  And turns the restless pillow towards the light.
To be another's in his dearest want,
  At struggle with a thousand racking throes,
When all the balm that Heaven itself can grant
  Is that which friendship's soothing hand bestows :
How joyful to be joined in such a love,—
We two,—may it portend the days above !

The volume consists of ninety-three sonnets of the same fine order. Many English and American critics have highly praised them, but not too highly. This venerable 'parable poet' did not belong to my generation. Nor did he belong to Mr. Watts-Dunton's generation. His day was the day before yesterday, and yet he wrote these sonnets when he was past seventy, not to glorify himself, but to glorify his friend. They are one long impassioned appeal to that friend to come forward and take his place among his peers. The indifference to fame of Theodore Watts is one of the most bewildering enigmas of literature. I have already quoted what Gordon Hake says about the man who when the 'New Day' was written had not published a single book.

With regard to the unity binding together all Mr. Watts-Dunton's writings, I can, at least, as I have shown in the Introduction, speak with the authority of a careful student of them. With the exception of the late Professor Strong, who when 'The Coming of Love' appeared, spoke out so boldly upon this subject in 'Literature,' I doubt if anyone has studied those writings more carefully than I have; and yet the difficulty of discovering the one or two quotable essays which more than the others expound and amplify their central doctrine has been so great that I am dubious as to whether, in the press of my other work, I have achieved my aim as satisfactorily as it would have been achieved by another—especially by Professor Strong, had he not died be fore he could write his promised essay upon the inner thought of 'Aylwinism' in the 'Cyclopædia of English Literature.'   But, even if I have failed adequately to expound the gospel of 'Aylwinism,' it is undeniable that, since the publication of 'Aylwin' (whether as a result of that publication or not), there has been an amazing growth of what may be called the transcendental cosmogony of 'Aylwinism.'

Dr. Robertson Nicoll, discussing the latest edition of 'Aylwin'—the 'Arvon' illustrated edition—says :—

"When 'Aylwin' was in type, the author, getting alarmed at its great length, somewhat mercilessly slashed into it to shorten it, and the more didactic parts of the book went first.   Now Mr. Watts-Dunton has restored one or two of these excised passages, notably one in which he summarizes his well-known views of the 'great Renascence of Wonder, which set in in Europe at the close of the eighteenth century and the beginning of the nineteenth.'   In one of these passages he has anticipated and bettered Mr. Balfour's speculations at the recent meeting of the British Association."

Something like the same remark was made in the 'Athenæum' of September 3, 1904 :—

"The writer has restored certain didactic passages of

the story which were eliminated before the publication of the book, owing to its great length. Though the teaching of the book is complete without the restorations, it seems a pity that they were ever struck out, because they appear to have anticipated the striking remarks of Mr. Balfour at the British Association the other day, to say nothing of the utterances of certain scientific writers who have been discussing the transcendental side of Nature."

The restorations to which Dr. Nicoll and 'The Athenæum' refer are excerpts from 'The Veiled Queen,' by Aylwin's father. The first of these comes in at the conclusion of the chapter called 'The Revolving Cage of Circumstance' and runs thus ·—

"'The one important fact of the twentieth century will be the growth and development of that great Renascence of Wonder which set in in Europe at the close of the eighteenth century and the beginning of the nineteenth.

The warring of the two impulses governing man—the impulse of wonder and the impulse of acceptance—will occupy all the energies of the next century.

The old impulse of wonder which came to the human race in its infancy has to come back—has to triumph—before the morning of the final emancipation of man can dawn.

But the wonder will be exercised in very different fields from those in which it was exercised in the past. The materialism, which at this moment seems to most thinkers inseparable from the idea of evolution, will go. Against their own intentions certain scientists are showing that the spiritual force called life is the maker and not the creature of organism—is a something outside the material world, a something which uses the material world as a means of phenomenal expression.

The materialist, with his primitive and confiding belief in the testimony of the senses, is beginning to be left out in the cold, when men like Sir W. R. Groves turn round on him and tell him that " the principle of all certitude " is not and cannot be the testimony of his own senses ; that these senses, indeed, are no absolute tests of phenomena at all ; that probably man is surrounded by beings he can neither see, feel, hear, nor smell; and that, notwithstanding the excellence of his own eyes, ears, and nose, the universe the materialist is mapping out so deftly is, and must be, monophysical, lightless, colourless, soundless—a phantasmagoric show—a deceptive series of undulations, which become colour, or sound, or what not, according to the organism upon which they fall.'

These words were followed by a sequence of mystical sonnets about ' the Omnipotence of Love,' which showed, beyond doubt, that if my father was not a scientific thinker, he was, at least, a very original poet."

The second restored excerpt from ' The Veiled Queen ' comes in at the end of the chapter called ' The Magic of Snowdon,' and runs thus :—

" I think, indeed, that I had passed into that sufistic ecstasy expressed by a writer often quoted by my father, an Oriental writer, Ferridoddin :—

> With love I burn : the centre is within me ;
> While in a circle everywhere around me
> Its Wonder lies—

that exalted mood, I mean, described in the great chapter on the Renascence of Wonder which forms the very core and heart-thought of the strange book so strangely destined to govern the entire drama of my life, 'The Veiled Queen.'

The very words of the opening of that chapter came to me :

'The omnipotence of love—its power of knitting together the entire universe—is, of course, best understood by the Oriental mind. Just after the loss of my dear wife I wrote the following poem called " The Bedouin Child," dealing with the strange feeling among the Bedouins about girl children, and I translated it into Arabic. Among these Bedouins a father in enumerating his children never counts his daughters, because a daughter is considered a disgrace.

> Ilyàs the prophet, lingering 'neath the moon,
>   Heard from a tent a child's heart-withering wail,
>   Mixt with the message of the nightingale,
> And, entering, found, sunk in mysterious swoon,
> A little maiden dreaming there alone.
>   She babbled of her father sitting pale
> 'Neath wings of Death—'mid sights of sorrow and bale,
> And pleaded for his life in piteous tone.
>
> " Poor child, plead on," the succouring prophet saith,
>   While she, with eager lips, like one who tries
>   To kiss a dream, stretches her arms and cries
> To Heaven for help—" Plead on ; such pure love-breath,
> Reaching the throne, might stay the wings of Death
>   That, in the Desert, fan thy father's eyes."
>
> The drouth-slain camels lie on every hand ;
>   Seven sons await the morning vultures' claws ;
>   'Mid empty water-skins and camel maws
> The father sits, the last of all the band.
> He mutters, drowsing o'er the moonlit sand,
>   " Sleep fans my brow ; sleep makes us all pashas ;
>   Or, if the wings are Death's, why Azraeel draws
> A childless father from an empty land."

" Nay," saith a Voice, " the wind of Azraeel's wings
　　A child's sweet breath has stilled : so God decrees : "
　A camel's bell comes tinkling on the breeze,
　Filling the Bedouin's brain with bubble of springs
　　And scent of flowers and shadow of wavering trees,
　Where, from a tent, a little maiden sings.

'Between this reading of Nature, which makes her
but " the superficial film " of the immensity of God, and
that which finds a mystic heart of love and beauty beating
within the bosom of Nature herself, I know no real difference.　Sufism, in some form or another, could not possibly be confined to Asia.　The Greeks, though strangers
to the mystic element of that Beauty-worship which in
Asia became afterwards Sufism, could not have exhibited
a passion for concrete beauty such as theirs without feeling that, deeper than Tartarus, stronger than Destiny
and Death, the great heart of Nature is beating to the
tune of universal love and beauty.' "

With regard to the two sonnets quoted above, a great
poet has said that the method of depicting the power of
love in them is sublime.　' The Slave girl's Progress to
Paradise,' however, is equally powerful and equally original.　The feeling in the ' Bedouin Child ' and in ' The
Slave Girl's Progress to Paradise ' is exactly like that
which inspires ' The Coming of Love.'　When Percy
sees Rhona's message in the sunrise he exclaims : —

But now—not all the starry Virtues seven
　Seem strong as she, nor Time, nor Death, nor Night.
　And morning says, ' Love hath such godlike might
That if the sun, the moon, and all the stars,
Nay, all the spheral spirits who guide their cars,
Were quelled by doom, Love's high-creative leaven
　Could light new worlds.'　If, then, this Lord of Fate,

When death calls in the stars, can re-create,
Is it a madman's dream that Love can show
Rhona, my Rhona, in yon ruby glow,
    And build again my heaven?

The same mystical faith in the power of love is passionately affirmed in the words of 'The Spirit of the Sunrise,' addressed to the bereaved poet :—

Though Love be mocked by Death's obscene derision,
    Love still is Nature's truth and Death her lie;
    Yet hard it is to see the dear flesh die,
To taste the fell destroyer's crowning spite
That blasts the soul with life's most cruel sight,
Corruption's hand at work in Life's transition:
    This sight was spared thee : thou shalt still retain
    Her body's image pictured in thy brain ;
The flowers above her weave the only shroud
Thine eye shall see : no stain of Death shall cloud
    Rhona !   Behold the vision !

Some may call this too mystical—some may dislike it on other accounts—but few will dream of questioning its absolute originality.

Let me now turn to those words of Mr. Balfour's to which the passages quoted from 'The Veiled Queen' have been compared. In his presidential address to the British Association, entitled, 'Reflections suggested by the New Theory of Matter,' he said :—

" We claim to found all our scientific opinions on experience : and the experience on which we found our theories of the physical universe is our sense of perception of that universe.   That is experience ; and in this region of belief there is no other.   Yet the conclusions which thus profess to be entirely founded upon experience are to all appearance fundamentally opposed to it ; our knowledge of reality is based upon illusion, and the very conceptions we use in describing it to others, or in thinking of it ourselves, are abstracted from anthropomorphic fancies, which science forbids us to believe and nature compels us to employ.

Observe, then, that in order of logic sense perceptions supply the premisses from which we draw all our knowledge of the physical world. It is they which tell us there is a physical world ; it is on their authority that we learn its character. But in order of causation they are effects due (in part) to the constitution of our orders of sense. What we see depends, not merely on what there is to be seen, but on our eyes. What we hear depends, not merely on what there is to hear, but on our ears."

I may mention here a curious instance of the way in which any idea that is new is ridiculed, and of the way in which it is afterwards accepted as a simple truth. One of the reviewers of ‘ Aylwin ’ was much amused by the description of the hero’s emotions when he stood in the lower room of Mrs. Gudgeon’s cottage waiting to be confronted upstairs by Winifred’s corpse, stretched upon a squalid mattress :—

“ At the sight of the squalid house in which Winifred had lived and died I passed into a new world of horror. Dead matter had become conscious, and for a second or two it was not the human being before me, but the rusty iron, the broken furniture, the great patches of brick and dirty mortar where the plaster had fallen from the walls, —it was these which seemed to have life—a terrible life— and to be talking to me, telling me what I dared not listen to about the triumph of evil over good. I knew that the woman was still speaking, but for a time I heard no sound—my senses could receive no impressions save from the sinister eloquence of the dead and yet living matter around me. Not an object there that did not seem charged with the wicked message of the heartless Fates."

' Fancy,' said the reviewer, ' any man out of Bedlam feeling as if dead matter were alive!'

Well, apart from the psychological subtlety of this passage, our critic must have been startled by the declaration lately made by a sane man of science, that there is no such thing as dead matter—and that every particle of what is called dead matter is alive and shedding an aura around it !

Had the mass of Mr. Watts-Dunton's scattered writings been collected into volumes, or had a representative selection from them been made, their unity as to central idea with his imaginative work, and also the importance of that central idea, would have been brought prominently forward, and then there would have been no danger of his contribution to the latest movement—the anti-materialistic movement—of English thought and English feeling being left unrecognized. Lost such teachings as his never could have been, for, as Minto said years ago, their colour tinges a great deal of the literature of our time. The influence of the ' Athenæum,' not only in England, but also in America and on the Continent, was always very great—and very great of course must have been the influence of the writer who for a quarter of a century spoke in it with such emphasis. Therefore, if Mr. Watts-Dunton had himself collected or selected his essays, or if he had allowed any of his friends to collect or select them, this book of mine would not have been written, for more competent hands would have undertaken the task. But a study of work which, originally issued in fragments, now lies buried ' full fathom five ' in the columns of various journals, could, I felt, be undertaken only by a cadet of letters like myself. There are many of us younger men who express views about Mr. Watts-Dunton's work which startle at times those who are unfamiliar with it. And I, coming forward for the moment as their spokesman, have long had the desire to justify the faith that is in us, and in the wide and still widening audience his imaginative work has won. But I doubt if I should have undertaken it had I realized the magnitude of the task. For it must be remembered that the articles, called ' reviews,' are for the most part as unlike reviews as they can well be. No matter what may have been the book placed at the head of the article, it was used merely as an opportunity for the writer to pour forth generalizations upon literature and life, or upon the latest scientific speculations, or upon the latest reverie of philosophy, in a stream, often a torrent, coruscating with brilliancies, and alive with interwoven colours like that of the river in the mountains of Kaf described in his birthday sonnet to Tennyson. Take, for instance, that great essay on the Psalms which I have used as the key-note of this study. The book at the head of the review was not, as might have been supposed, a discourse learned, or philosophical, or emotional, upon the Psalms—but a little unpretentious metrical version of the Psalms by Lord Lorne. Only a clear-sighted and daring editor would have printed such an article as a review. But I doubt if there ever was a more prescient journalist than he who sat in the editorial chair at that time. A man of scholarly accomplishments and literary taste, he knew that an article such as this would be a huge success; would resound through the world of letters. The article, I believe, was more talked about in literary circles than any book that had come out during that month.

Again, take that definition of humour which I seized upon (page 384) to illustrate my exposition of that wonderful character in 'Aylwin'—Mrs. Gudgeon, a definition that seems, as one writer has said, to make all other talk about humour cheap and jejune. It is in a review of an extremely futile history of humour. Now let the reader consider the difficult task before a writer in my position—the task of searching for a few among the innumerable half-remembered points of interest that turn up in the most unexpected places. Of course, if the space allotted to me by my publishers had been unlimited, and if my time had been unlimited, I should have been able to give so large a number of excerpts from the articles as to make my selection really representative of what has been called the " modern Sufism of 'Aylwin.' " But in this regard my publishers have already been as liberal and as patient as possible. After all, the best, as well as the easiest way, to show that 'Aylwin,' and 'The Coming of Love,' are but the imaginative expression of a poetic religion familiar to the readers of Mr. Watts-Dunton's criticism for twenty-five years, is to quote an illuminating passage upon the subject from one of the articles in the 'Athenæum.' Moreover, I shall thus escape what I confess I dread—the sight of my own prose at the end of my book in juxtaposition to the prose of a past master of English style :—

" The time has not yet arrived for poetry to utilize even the results of science ; such results as are offered to her are dust and ashes. Happily, however, nothing in science is permanent save mathematics. As a great man of science has said, 'everything is provisional.' Dr. Erasmus Darwin, following the science of his day, wrote a long poem on the 'Loves of the Plants,' by no means a foolish poem, though it gave rise to the 'Loves of the Triangles,' and though his grandson afterwards discovered that the plants do not love each other at all, but, on the contrary, hate each other furiously—'struggle for life' with each other, 'survive' against each other—just as though they were good men and 'Christians.' But if a poet were to set about writing a poem on the 'Hates of the Plants,' nothing is more likely than that, before he could finish it, Mr. Darwin will have discovered that the plants do love after all ; just as—after it was a settled thing that the red tooth and claw did all the business of progression —he delighted us by discovering that there was another factor which had done half the work—the enormous and very proper admiration which the females have had for the males from the very earliest forms upwards. In such a case, the 'Hates of the Plants' would have become 'inadequate.' Already, indeed, there are faint signs of the physicists beginning to find out that neither we nor the plants hate each other quite so much as they thought, and that Nature is not quite so bad as she seems. 'She is an Æolian harp,' says Novalis, 'a musical instrument whose tones are the re-echo of higher strings within us.' And after all there are higher strings within us just as real as those which have caused us to 'survive,' and poetry is right in ignoring 'interpretations,' and giving us 'Earthly Paradises' instead. She must wait, it seems ; or rather, if this aspiring 'century' will keep thrusting these unlovely results of science before her eyes, she must treat them as the beautiful girl Kisāgotamī treated the ugly pile of charcoal. A certain rich man woke up one morning and found that all his enormous wealth was turned to a huge heap of charcoal. A friend who called upon him in his misery, suspecting how the case really stood, gave him certain advice, which he thus acted upon. 'The Thuthe, following his friend's instructions, spread some mats in the bazaar, and, piling them upon a large heap of his property which was turned into charcoal, pretended to be selling it. Some people, seeing it, said, "Why does he sell charcoal?" Just at this time a young girl, named Kisāgotamī, who was worthy to be owner of the property, and who, having lost both her parents, was in a wretched condition, happened to come to the bazaar on some business. When she saw the heap, she said, "My lord Thuthe, all the people sell clothes, tobacco, oil, honey, and treacle; how is it that you pile up gold and silver for sale?" The Thuthe said, "Madam, give me that gold and silver." Kisāgotamī, taking up a handful of it, brought it to him. What the young girl had in her hand no sooner touched the Thuthe's hand than it became gold and silver.'"

I cannot find a clearer note for the close of this book than that which sounds in one of the latest and one of the finest of Mr. Watts-Dunton's sonnets. It was composed on the last night of the Nineteenth Century, a century which will be associated with many of the dear friends Mr. Watts-Dunton has lost, and, as I must think, associated also with himself. The lines have a very special charm for me, because they show the turn which the poet's noble optimism has taken; they show that faith in my own generation which for so many years has illumined his work, and which has endeared him to us all. I wish I could be as hopeful as this nineteenth century poet with regard to the poets who will carry the torch of imagination and romance through the twentieth century; but whether or not there are any poets among us who are destined to bring in the Golden Fleece, it is good to see 'the Poet of the Sunrise' setting the trumpet of optimism to his lips, and heralding so cheerily the coming of the new argonauts :—

THE ARGONAUTS OF THE NEW AGE

THE POET

[In starlight, listening to the chimes in the distance, which sound clear through the leafless trees.

Say, will new heroes win the ' Fleece,' ye spheres
Who—whether around some King of Suns ye roll
Or move right onward to some destined goal
In Night's vast heart—know what Great Morning nears ?

THE STARS

Since Love's Star rose have nineteen hundred years
Written such runes on Time's remorseless scroll,
Impeaching Earth's proud birth, the human soul,
That we, the bright-browed stars, grow dim with tears.

Did those dear poets you loved win Light's release ?
What ' ship of Hope ' shall sail to such a world ?

[The night passes, and morning breaks gorgeously over the tree top.

THE POET

Ye fade, ye stars, ye fade with night's decease !
Above yon ruby rim of clouds empearled—
There, through the rosy flags of morn unfurled
I see young heroes bring Light's ' Golden Fleece.'

THE END

Index

Index

477

Sufism, 449 ; in 'Aylwin,' 454
'Suicide Club, The,' 220
Sully, Professor, contributor to 'Examiner,' 184
Sunrise, Poet of the, 398
Sunsets, in the Fens, 62
Surtees, 367
Swallow Falls, 315
Swift, his humour the opposite of Sterne's, 250
Swinburne, Algernon Charles, acquaintance with J. O. Watts, 58 ; intercourse and friendship with Watts-Dunton, 89, 268–74 ; 'Jubilee Greeting' dedicated to, 273 ; partly identified with Percy Aylwin, see description of his swimming, 268 ; 279–84 ; at Théâtre Française, 124 ; dedications to Watts-Dunton, 271, 272 ; offensive newspaper caricatures of, 263 ; championship of Meredith, 284 ; on 'Tom Jones,' 'Waverley,' 'Aylwin,' 346 ; on 'Aylwin,' 363 ; references to, 1, 12, 27, 117, 123, 139, 147, 157, 170, 180, 181, 184, 328, 413

ANECDOTES OF :—
chambers in Great James St., 89 ; never a playgoer, 117 ; life at 'The Pines,' 262 et seq. ; the great Swinburne myth, 263 ; the American lady journalist, 264 ; an imaginary interview, 265 ; an unlovely bard ; painfully 'afflated' ; method of composition ; 'stamping with both feet,' 265 ; friendship with Watts began in 1872, 268 ; inseparable since ; housemates at 'The Pines' ; visit to Channel Islands ; swimming in Petit Bot Bay, 268 ; Sark ; 'Orion'

Horne's bravado challenge, 269 ; visits Paris for Jubilee of 'Le Roi s'Amuse,' 269 ; swimming at Sidestrand; meets Grant Allen, 269 ; visits Eastbourne, Lancing, Isle of Wight, Cromer, 270 ; visits to Jowett ; Jowett's admiration of Watts, 279 ; Balliol dinner parties, 280 ; at the Bodleian, 282 ; great novels which are popular, 273
Swinburne, Miss, 299
Symons, Arthur, 'Coming of Love,' article on, 257

Table-Talk, Watts-Dunton's, Rossetti on, 183
Tabley, Lord de, 277
Taine, 232
'Tale of Beowulf,' 173
Taliesin, 'Song of the Wind,' 313
Talk on Waterloo Bridge,' 'A, 116
Tarno Rye, 351, 391
Tate and Brady, 232
Telepathy, dogs and, 82–6   [270
Temple, Lord and Lady Mount,
Tenderness, in English hero, 365
'Tennyson, Alfred, Birthday Address,' 32
'Tennyson, Alfred,' sonnet to, 286
Tennyson, Lord, 4, 32, 144 ; dishonest criticism, opinion of, 211 ; Watts-Dunton's friendship with, 285 ; Watts-Dunton's criticism of and essays on, 289, 290 ; 'Memoir,' Watts-Dunton's contribution, 291 ; anecdotes concerning, 287–89 ; 'The Princess,' defects of, 290 ; portraits of, Watts-Dunton's articles on, 290 ; 'Maud,' compared with Rhona Boswell, 413

lithographs, 301–2; engaged with Watts on ' Piccadilly,' 301, 353; ' To Theodore Watts, the Worldling,' 353

Watts-Dunton, Theodore, Swinburne's sonnets to, 271, 272
' Waverley,' Swinburne on; its new dramatic method; cause of its success; imitated by Dumas, 346
Way, T., Whistler's first lithographs, 301, 302
Webster, ' Spirit of Wonder' in, 16
' Well at the World's End,' 173
Wells, Charles, 53–55
' Westminster Abbey, In ' (Burial of Tennyson), 291
' W. H. Mr.,' 424–26
' What the Silent Voices said,' 291
Whewell, intimacy with J. K. Watts, 52
Whistler, J. McNeill :—
      Cyril Aylwin not a portrait of, 88 ; anecdotes of De Castro, 142; neighbour of Rossetti, 156; close friendship with Watts, 301; his first lithographs, 301–2; hostility to Royal Academy, 301–2; engaged with Watts on ' Piccadilly,' 301, 353; ' To Theodore Watts, the Worldling,' 353
White, Gilbert, 50
Whiteing, Richard, 364
' White Ship, The,' 153, 154
Whittlesea Mere, 104
Whyte-Melville, 352, 367
Wilderspin, 331 : see Smetham, James

Wilkie, his realism, humour of, 387
Williams, ' Scholar,' contributor to ' Examiner,' 184
Williams, Smith, 275
' William Wilson,' 219
Willis, Parker, 264
Wilson, Professor, Watts-Dunton's essay on his ' Noctes Ambrosianæ,' 190–201
Wimbledon Common, Borrow and, 101 ; Watts-Dunton and, 279
Wind, love of the, Thoreau's, 370, 371
Women, as actresses, 131 ; heroic type of, 365
Wonder : see Renascence of Wonder ; old and new, 15 ; Bible as great book of, 228 ; place in race development, 14
' Wood-Haunter's Dream, The,' 276
Wordsworth, William, definition of language, 39 ; his ideal John Bull, 224
Word-twisting, 325, 327
Work, heresy of, 68
' World,' The, Rossetti's letter to, 155
' World's Classics,' edition of ' Aylwin' in, 374
' Wuthering Heights,' 342, 345
Wynne, Winifred, character of, 314, 315, 363 ; love of the wind, 371

Yarmouth, 106
Yorickism, 250

Zoroaster, heresy of work, 68 ; definition of poetry, 398

Butler & Tanner, The Selwood Printing Works, Frome, and London.

Lightning Source UK Ltd.
Milton Keynes UK
UKOW06f1832250116

267111UK00008B/206/P